By

WILFRED E. BINKLEY

American Political Parties
Their Natural History

WITH MALCOLM C. MOOS
A Grammar of American Politics

*These are Borzoi Books
published by* ALFRED A. KNOPF *in New York*

American Political Parties

AAK Fellowship
HISTORY
W·E·B

American Political Parties

Their Natural History

BY

WILFRED E. BINKLEY

PROFESSOR OF
HISTORY AND POLITICAL SCIENCE
OHIO NORTHERN UNIVERSITY

Fourth Edition, Enlarged

NEW YORK *Alfred A. Knopf* 1964

THIS IS A BORZOI BOOK,
PUBLISHED BY ALFRED A. KNOPF, INC.

PUBLISHED SEPTEMBER 20, 1943. SECOND EDITION,
SEPTEMBER 1945. THIRD EDITION, REVISED AND ENLAR-
GED, MAY 1958. FOURTH EDITION, ENLARGED, AUGUST 1962.
SECOND PRINTING, SEPTEMBER 1963
THIRD PRINTING, AUGUST 1964

TO

DORA STOTTS BINKLEY

PREFACE TO THE FIRST EDITION

T HIS book is an essay at a natural history of American political parties. In it I have attempted to do two things in particular. First I have sought to ascertain and account for the social or group composition of each of our major political parties. In the second place I have endeavored to discover the part played by national political leaders in building these great group combinations and how they learned and practiced the art of "group diplomacy."

The paramount question of every one of these leaders has had to be: "What motivates the voter in making his decision how to vote?" The answer is perhaps as complex and varied as human nature itself. By and large the decision is reached by non-logical processes. If there is any one determining factor it is probably the climate of opinion in which the voter has lived, and this was originally provided for him by his family. Hence no one need be astonished to learn that three out of every four voters have the same political affiliations as their fathers, according to an estimate of Charles E. Merriam.

Economic motivation may then be only indirect, when it is a factor at all. That is to say, the voter does not seem deliberately to put to himself the question: "What do I get out of this?" and simply on the basis of the answer to the question vote one way or another. Economic interests seem rather to create the ideological atmosphere in which the voter lives and moves and develops his patterns of political thought and behavior. This is as true of a luncheon club as of a labor union or a rural grange. A striking historical example is that of the Negroes of New York City more than a century ago. As house slaves they had readily imbibed the ideas of their Federalist masters before their emancipation, and later as grateful freedmen they talked Federalist politics and proudly cast Federalist ballots in support of the candidates and policies of "the rich, the well born and the good" — that is to say, the old ruling class of the land. Nor need anyone serenely assume that such naïveté is peculiar to any one group, ethnic or otherwise.

It has now become common knowledge that the men who made the Constitution did not expect the development of political parties. They believed, instead, that public policies would be determined by transitory majorities consisting of combinations of interests that would agree on a particular solution of a current issue presumably formulated in a statute. Those who assume that Madison and the fathers of the Constitution generally hoped to prevent the formation of majorities disregard important passages in Madison's writings. As will be shown, he believed that within the narrow confines of a state a majority might be formed bent upon a radical and socially destructive policy. In a continent-wide union of states, however, this would not be so likely to happen. "In the extended republic of the United States," as Madison expressed it in the fifteenth number of the *Federalist*, "and among the great variety of interests, parties and sects which it embraces, a coalition of a majority of the whole society could seldom take place on any other principles than those of justice and the general good." That is to say, the group coherence of a majority could be obtained only on a moderate policy since any attempt at a radical one would prove disintegrating in its effect on the combination. The fathers evidently expected such an *ad hoc* combination to dissolve as soon as its purpose had been consummated. As they conceived it, a succession of such group combinations would take form from time to time as new major issues emerged and then dissolve as policies were agreed upon and executed. Something very like this does indeed still take place on non-partisan issues, with majority votes in Congress cutting across party lines in a manner disconcerting to the uninitiated who have been indoctrinated with the conventional mythology of party politics.

Scarcely had the new government under the Constitution got under way when an utterly unexpected development began to take place. The combination of groups that had concurred in making the Constitution and had managed its ratification were in charge of the Federal government established according to its prescriptions. Under Hamilton's leadership the combination presently put into effect a set of policies so biased in favor of the commercial and financial interests as to arouse the opposition of the agrarians of the hinterland. This very opposition constituted a sharp challenge to the dominant majority and tended to cement its elements into a permanent political party; that is to say, it unexpectedly institutionalized that particular combination. In the face of the militant though unorganized opposition the dominant combination dared not dissolve but persisted in sheer self-defense and thus by a quite natural social process there emerged the Federalist Party.

The fact that almost from the beginning of the national period two major interests, the mercantile-financial on the one hand and independent farming on the other, have contended for supremacy has undoubtedly provided the basis of our two-party alignments. A peculiar feature of our Federal system, however, the popular election of the President, facilitated if it did not practically compel the regimentation of the major interest combinations into nation-wide party organizations. For example, the scattered and unorganized agrarian opposition to the Federalists presently perceived that they must capture the "stakes of power" inherent in the presidential office if they were to make the Federal government serve their interests as it was already serving those of the Federalists. This required organization and permanency, and under the leadership of Thomas Jefferson, as we shall see, focal points of agreement among the diverse elements of the opposition were discovered for integrating the nation-wide combination that, as the first Republican Party, captured complete control of the political branches of the Federal government in 1801.

Jefferson as a veritable pioneer in American politics set the pattern of party leadership. No less than Jackson, Lincoln, or the two Roosevelts, he could lead the people only where they were willing to go. The hard facts of the history of party leadership in the United States play havoc with the Carlylean conception of heroes. More pertinent is the old story of the French Revolutionary leader who, hearing a tumult outside in the street, exclaimed excitedly to the group in the house where he happened to be at the time: "There goes the mob. I am their leader. I must follow them."

The great American political chieftains without exception have had to be astute opportunists free from petrified ideas, and expediency has accordingly been the key to their party practices. The political career of Andrew Jackson is not at all an exception. There is something refreshing in finding "Old Hickory," when he had decided to check the internal improvement policy, turning to his adviser, Martin Van Buren, and asking him to select for veto a minor project that would alienate the fewest voters. The little twenty-mile Maysville Road Act answered the purpose perfectly. Jackson would have understood the remark of our professor-politician T. V. Smith, once Congressman at Large from Illinois, when he said: "The politician adjusts manually instead of ideologically. He does something and sees who hollers and then invents a remedy and sees who hollers over the remedy."

For many a decade party history was interpreted in terms of ideologies of "loose construction" and "strict construction," of "national sovereignty" and "state rights." Partisans prided themselves on their devotion to party "principles," oblivious of the fact that these were quite often stereotypes – that is, emotion-evoking, *ex post facto* rationalizations of group combinations that had in some way or other coalesced. The romantic interpretation of the politics of the post Civil War period so indoctrinated two generations of Americans that it became almost sacrilegious to regard the statesmen of an earlier generation as human beings. The magic spell of party mythology seems to have been broken largely by Beard's presentation of hitherto neglected data revealing a correlation between economics and politics in the making of the Constitution and the establishment of the Federal government. Against such revelations not even the academicians were shock-proof and the poignant distress of the laity was immediately epitomized in the curt remark of an ex-President of the United States on the *Economic Interpretation of the Constitution:* "The professor seems to have his facts all right but what did the d— fool mean by publishing them?"

It remained, as we shall see, for a politician-statesman turned biographer to give us the outstanding analysis and interpretation in American historical writing of the natural development of a great national political leader. There is more than a touch of tragedy in the torture of soul suffered by Albert J. Beveridge, already within the long shadows and with premonitions that he might, as he put it in a letter to his wife, "bump off" before he had finished, facing for the first time the raw facts he found in the unexplored source material concerning Lincoln. Claude Bowers has related the whole entrancing story of this painful intellectual adventure in his *Beveridge and the Progressive Era*. Here was an erudite man inured to party politics but reared in the grand Republican tradition of an apotheosized Lincoln. Now in his middle sixties he waded diligently through the sources, literally overwhelmed by the mass of disillusioning facts that blasted his most cherished convictions. It was distressing to find Lincoln, the Illinois legislator, shifting with every breeze of constituent opinion — "of all uncertain halting and hesitating conduct, his takes the prize," Beveridge confided to Worthington C. Ford; agonizing to discover Lincoln saying not a word against the Mexican War during his successful campaign for Congress, even making a pro-war speech just before starting for Washington to take his seat, where he somersaulted and joined the Whig leaders in their bitter attack on President Polk for provoking the "unjust" war. Strangely enough, however, Beveridge was to confess to the historian Channing: "I have seen the same thing myself and possibly have taken part in such performances." It was even more disconcerting not to find the "Emancipator" taking a public stand against slavery until in the fifties, after the anti-slavery sentiment in the North had begun to be pronounced. But out of the ordeal of Beveridge emerged that "noble fragment," the first practically scientific analysis of the development of a great American political leader. Carefully examined, Lincoln's method is by no means unique, but conforms to the practice of all the other national leaders, since each in his own day had to discover the points of agreement, the centripetal ideas, that would give cohesive force to a multi-group combination.

Scores of students working in my seminar courses in recent years have turned up stray bits of pertinent matter that would otherwise have escaped my attention. I am grateful indeed to the group of students who undertook to read the two thousand biographies of the more than ordinary Congressmen scattered through the twenty volumes of the *Dictionary of American Biography*, particularly with a view to ascertaining their methods in the art of "group diplomacy." Not so much of specific fact was discovered as of important generalization, such, for example, as that many Southern Congressmen after the Civil War were railroad promoters.

I am especially indebted to Charles A. Beard, who graciously consented to read this entire work in manuscript. His scrutinizing eye caught slips of phrasing, fact, and interpretation, and his penciled marginal questions, comments, and suggestions facilitated revision. Homer C. Hockett of the Ohio State University had already given the first nine chapters the benefit of his incomparable knowledge of the period of our history treated in that portion of the work and Charles A. Barrell of Bowling Green State University critically examined the last six chapters. Demass E. Barnes, assistant to the president of Ohio Northern University and a disciple of the late Frederick Jackson Turner, gave the benefit of his careful reading of the chapters leading to and dealing with the Jacksonian movement. Subsequent revisions, however, certainly absolve them from all accountability for remaining errors and I alone am responsible for matters of interpretation, with many of which they doubtless would not wholly agree.

I am indebted to my son, Robert G. Binkley, who typed the manuscript during the latter part of his senior year in college. Majoring in history, with some training in research, he proved to be no ordinary typist, but, after the manner of his generation, occasionally took liberties with his father's phrasing and other matters, to the distinct improvement of the work.

WILFRED E. BINKLEY

Ada, Ohio, June 1943

PREFACE TO THE FOURTH EDITION

W HEN I began making notes for this history of our political parties late in the thirties, the Republican Party had sunk to its nadir. In the presidential election of 1936 the Republicans had won only eight out of 531 electoral votes, and *The World Almanac* of 1938 reveals that the party had only 16 of the 96 Senators, 90 of the 425 Representatives, and, incredible though it may seem, only five of the 48 state Governors.

By the time the first edition of this book was published, Republican prospects were looking up somewhat. The present edition appears under far different party circumstances. The opinion polls continue to indicate that the Republicans are a minority party, but so nearly has a healthy balance been restored in our two-party system that the 1960 election revealed that neither party dares to rest on its oars.

The present edition brings the history of our political parties up to the present and consequently includes an account of the last four presidential campaigns. This requires that the rather striking changes in the electorate's habits with respect to political parties be given due attention. I found that only very few important changes in my judgments about our earlier party history were called for by recent historical research; such changes of outmoded interpretations as seem appropriate have been made for this edition.

I wish to take this opportunity to express my very great appreciation of the gracious reception that the earlier editions of this book have had, not only here at home, but also abroad — as indicated by publication in five foreign languages.

WILFRED E. BINKLEY

Ada, Ohio, April 1962

CONTENTS

CONTENTS

American Political Parties

CHAPTER I

THE FEDERALISTS — PROPONENTS OF THE CONSTITUTION

"By giving to every group its rightful claim to consideration the representative system provides the best means of determining the interests which are common to all by neutralizing of the interests peculiar to each. The national interest in actual practice is that which remains after mutual cancellation by opposing groups of interests too narrow and particular to be acceptable to a majority of representatives." H. W. STOKE: The Paradox of Representative Government.

EVEN to the earliest settlers America seemed to be preeminently a continent to be exploited. This opportunity more than all other factors combined motivated the migration that settled the land. Some of the indentured servants who had purchased passage hither by selling themselves into several years of servitude went mad when once they recognized the opportunity for a good living not at once within their grasp. Peasants fleeing from a Europe where vestigial forms of a feudal era still fastened land tenure securely in the hands of the privileged few flocked here to satisfy the ancient land hunger. Presently common folk were walking proudly across their very own acres as only lords and ladies had done in the homeland. Here was a new phenomenon destined in due course to work one of the miracles of history and transform the common man into a dynamic factor of political society.

Out of the conquest of the resources of the continent emerged new social institutions peculiar to America, among which none is more nearly unique than the interest-group combinations that constitute our national political parties.

European political parties are conditioned by such relics of the medieval era as a titled nobility, a hereditary monarchy, a professional army, and an established church. Never firmly rooted here, these anachronisms were eventually almost completely eradicated by the Fathers, and in order that there might be no misunderstanding about it, the *faits accomplis* were set down in unmistakable terms in provisions of the Federal Constitution. The absence of these factors in American society produced striking results. Neither challenged nor checked by the dead hand of the feudal past, natural resources and other economic factors exerted an enormous dynamic influence on the development of American society, producing here institutions contrasting with those of Europe. So different, indeed, are American from European political parties that they may be regarded as a distinct contribution to human institutions. It is a significant fact that the Federalists, the only American party that ever attempted to maintain the British social tradition, proved exotic, were sharply challenged at once by indigenous American forces, and persisted scarcely more than a dozen years.

Inasmuch as the exploitation of the New World's resources was the paramount purpose of the settlers, the land speculator has played a major role from the earliest generations. The foresighted and enterprising, if not even unscrupulous, of the early comers to Virginia busied themselves obtaining titles to tracts of choice land far beyond their ability to utilize them and held them for a rise in value. Later comers, unable to purchase at the price demanded, pushed inland toward the foothills and purchased, if they did not "squat" on, less fertile land, remote from convenient river transportation. Here they engaged in grain-production, stock-raising, and hunting. In combination with the streams of settlers migrating southward from the Pennsylvania hinterland they came in the eighteenth century to constitute a distinct society in the piedmont.

These inland pioneers, "backwoodsmen" to the smug coastal planters, multiplied prolifically while they nursed their accumulating grievances against the older settlers. They were handicapped by a gross under-representation in the colonial assemblies and consequently had shifted upon them an inequitable tax burden, despite their poverty and the practical impossibility of converting the products of their isolated holdings into the specie or tobacco demanded by the despised taxgatherer. When, in return for their burdensome taxes, they sought some protection against Indian raids, the tidewater colonists, secure from danger behind the buffer of the frontiersmen, were usually deaf to calls for help. The piedmontese were even chided for having pushed into the wilderness, disturbed the Indians, and interfered with the fur-trading interests of the tidewater planters. The cards seemed always to be stacked against the hapless frontiersmen, and their consequent frustration induced a fierce resentment incomprehensible to the comfortable coastal communities.

In 1676 the embers of frontier discontent burst into the flames of civil war. Fifteen hundred Virginia "redemptioners" annually completed their servitude, came into possession of the fifty acres of land to which they were entitled, and further increased the growing democratic element within the province. Meanwhile the Royal Governor, Sir William Berkeley, and his tidewater favorites were reveling in the graft from special privileges, among which was his monopoly of the Indian fur trade. The Burgesses had been elected in the first flush of the Restoration, and for fourteen years the Governor had stubbornly prevented the holding of new elections. These conscienceless legislators voted themselves a princely *per diem*, which, with allowances for servant and horse, aggregated two hundred and fifty pounds of tobacco daily, and the legislature remained almost constantly in session. The personal greed of Governor and Council imposed other extravagant appropriations upon the colonists, and this tax burden was moreover assessed on the dead level of an indefensible poll tax, whether extracted from the richest planter, the poorest yeoman, or even a landless man. Furthermore, special exemptions from taxation of privileged wealthy officials remind one of the *ancien régime* of pre-Revolutionary France.

When the Indian unrest manifested by King Philip's War in New England had spread south and the savages fell upon the Virginia frontier families, Governor Berkeley was indifferent to demands for summoning the militia against them, for that would disturb the lucrative fur-trading monopoly. Aroused against social injustices almost as much as against the Indians, the inland democracy turned to Nathaniel Bacon, a liberal planter, whose frontier plantation had suffered from a bloody Indian massacre. When the Governor refused Bacon a commission to lead a punitive expedition against the Indians, he acted without one. Denounced by Berkeley for insubordination, he then turned with his faithful adherents against the Governor in a rebellion that produced the temporary social reforms known as "Bacon's laws." But when their leader suddenly died, the movement collapsed, whereupon the Governor and his tidewater partisans took savage vengeance on the leaders of this earliest stirring of the American masses.[1]

In Bacon's Rebellion we encounter the first severe conflict of the social forces in which our two-party alignments are rooted. Like a scarlet thread this controversy between old and new settlements runs unbroken through two and a half centuries of political conflict. "From Bacon's Rebellion to the LaFollette revolt," wrote the late Frederick J. Turner, "there are almost continuous manifestations of sectional contests of East and West, of the frontier and the older areas." [2]

Since pre-Revolutionary groupings of interests were necessarily provincial in scope, we must seek the genesis of our national political alignments in the period when continent-wide movements first took permanent form. So divergent were the major interests of the colonists that they could never agree on a continent-wide central control of such paramount common concerns as the fur trade, the public lands, defense against the Indians or even against such foreign neighbors as the French and the Spanish. Not until the irksome commercial regulations of the British ministry had harassed the merchants

---

[1] See Edward Eggleston: "Nathaniel Bacon, The Patriot of 1676," *Century Magazine*, Vol. XL (1890), pp. 418–35.

[2] *Sections in American History*, p. 196; see also H. C. Hockett: *Western Influence on Political Parties to 1825*, p. 9; V. F. Calverton: *The Awakening of America*, pp. 226 ff.

almost to distraction were the incompatible interest groups of the colonists combined into the improvised association that took up arms to force redress of grievances after polite petitioning had proved fruitless.

When the revenue act of 1764 sought to convert a hitherto frankly regulatory tax into a rigidly enforced revenue-producer, the time-honored practice of smuggling was threatened with extinction. The alarming character of this new departure of the ministry lay in the fact that it would end the illicit traffic with the French and Spanish Indies, the only colonial commerce with a cash balance wherewith to redress the unfavorable balance with the mother country. When, however, the hard-pressed merchants either prompted or permitted Sam Adams to rally the working men of Boston and dump the tea into the harbor, they unwittingly stirred the unenfranchised and hitherto inarticulate masses to self-expression and the challenge of the ruling class. Thus were they releasing the genie that no incantation since has quite sufficed to reconfine. Indeed, less than nine months after Lexington, Tom Paine, a radical patriot pamphleteer, in the clarion call of his *Common Sense* had executed the most astounding single stroke of propaganda in American history. Deeply moved, the masses demanded independence and, to the consternation of the ruling classes, they suddenly converted the Revolution into a popular mass movement. It then fell to the lot of Thomas Jefferson in the glowing phrases of the Declaration of Independence to express the philosophic faith of the elements of American society that were to rally around him a generation later in the first Republican Party.

Beard has written that the Revolutionary soldier might have said: "We are fighting for the plantation owners of the South, the merchants and landed gentry of the North and the free farmers everywhere." Incomplete as is this enumeration of interests, even it contains incompatible elements. Indeed, the patriots were held together in the unstable union of the Continental Congress and the Articles of Confederation only so long as hostilities lasted. Even before the last British soldier had embarked for home, the disintegration of the Revolutionary bloc of interests had set in. The various business interests, despite lack of cohesion among themselves, were already at grips again with the discontented agrarian debtors. Among these latter the hundreds of thousands of grain-growing yeomanry were jealous of the landed gentry, and the frontiersmen had resumed their century-old feud with the tidewater planters. Nor was unity to be found even among these proud aristocrats of the salt-water plantations. A sharp difference as to the propriety of the African slave trade had sprung up between the tobacco-planters of Virginia, eager to dispose of their surplus slaves, and the rice-growers of the deep South, accustomed to look to the African slavers for replenishing their labor supply.

"Happy Days Are Here Again" might have been sung as lustily by patriots in 1781, when couriers raced lathered steeds into every American community shouting: "Cornwallis has surrendered," as it was actually chorused a century and a half later in the lyric written to celebrate the Armistice of 1918. Nor was the subsequent disillusionment in the latter case one whit more poignant than in the former. At first aiming only at redress of grievances, in the end independence instead had been achieved. Now, it was naïvely assumed, Americans would be perfectly free to order their economic and political society as one great happy family. Our history has produced no finer demonstration of the vanity of human hopes and aspirations than the bitter post-war disillusionment of the American Revolutionary era. John Fiske called it the "Critical Period," and the appellation has stuck.

To understand the disappointment of Americans in the 1780's it is necessary to recall that the colonists had sought at first merely to compel the ministry to relax certain irksome trade restrictions. They had been enjoying very substantial advantages and positive benefits within the Empire. Radical elements, however, had insisted upon independence, and its realization in 1781 suddenly confronted Americans with the substantial disadvantages of exclusion from the Empire.

Before the Revolution New England had benefited enormously by the legal requirement that Imperial commerce be borne in "English" vessels, which term included colonial ships. So greatly did this stimulate colonial shipbuilding that British shipping felt its keen competition. The surplus sons of the rocky New England farms poured a steady stream of sailors into the service of the colonial merchant marine, while the towns provided the capital and the captains and pocketed the profits from the sea. But after the Revolution the New Englanders, who had formerly traded freely with the British West Indies, found themselves excluded as foreigners by the very system of Imperial trade regulations from which they had triumphantly freed themselves. New England fishermen suddenly found themselves shut out from the British West Indies market at the same time that they had lost the royal bounties on their product.

At the very time when Americans lost Imperial trading privileges English merchants benefited by the utter confusion of trade policies of the thirteen independent states. The same commercial anarchy that permitted these foreign merchants to dump their commodities on the American markets afforded English shipowners a freedom from the competition of American shipping undreamed of in the old Imperial system. "In the harbor of New York," reported the *Connecticut Courant* of November 12, 1787, "there are now 60 ships of which 55 are British. The products of South Carolina are shipped in 170 ships of which 150 are British."

The Congress under the Articles of Confederation had no power to regulate commerce by means of statutes or taxation, but could make trade treaties. But since the Congress possessed no coercive power to compel the obedience of private persons and lacked the prestige to obtain the voluntary co-operation of the states, its treaties promptly became a dead letter. Accordingly when John Adams, our diplomatic representative in England, broached the subject of a commercial treaty, the ministry parried by asking whether he sought one or thirteen treaties. What assurance could he give that a treaty with Congress would be enforced? Adams could give none.

It was exasperating to American handicraftsmen, in their

homes or in the manufacturing shops that had sprung up to supply the demand during the war, to see British vessels dumping the contents of bulging British warehouses on the American market to be auctioned off for whatever they would bring. Virginia planters who had formerly enjoyed a statutory monopoly in supplying the British tobacco market now found their erstwhile guaranteed customers purchasing elsewhere. The rice- and indigo-planters of Georgia and the Carolinas sadly missed the royal bounties formerly paid for their products, as did also those who had supplied the Imperial fleet with ship timber and naval stores.

In the midst of this flood of misfortunes and indeed as an integral part of it there had descended upon the land a post-war business depression. Except in the limited theater of actual hostilities the latter years of the war had witnessed a feverish prosperity. The rapid depreciation of Continental currency in its brief and fantastic career had been extremely inflationary, shooting prices up to astronomical heights. Even the gold spent by the British army for supplies, and later by the large French expeditionary force that aided the patriots, maintained satisfactory specie prices and produced an era of "good times."

When, however, the Continental currency had run its mad course; when the British and French armies had departed and consequently ceased to purchase further supplies in America; when the flood of British imports dumped here had practically drained the country of specie, then prices struck bottom and the depression was at hand. As always, however, debts were not deflated, but remained to plague and drive to distraction those who had contracted them at inflation prices. Presently creditors everywhere were taking alarm at the strident demands of agrarian debtors for state issues of paper money, as if the disastrous experience with the Continental currency had left that lesson still unlearned. Nor was the peril a mere figment of the imagination when it became possible legally to extinguish a substantial debt with a wad of practically worthless paper money. When the Rhode Island legislature provided severe penalties for refusal to accept their issues of legal tender in payment of debts, creditors literally fled to the country and went into hiding. "For two or three years," wrote President John Witherspoon of Princeton, "we constantly saw and were informed of creditors running away from their debtors, and debtors pursuing them in triumph and paying them without mercy."

When the depression had reached its trough in the middle eighties, the interest groups destined, in due time, to constitute the Federalist combination were all present on the American scene though even the most clairvoyant contemporary could scarcely have foreseen then the potential community of interest among them and the course of events that would ultimately bring them together in concerted action. Gradually, however, there began to develop the belief among these interests that sooner or later there must be established somehow a central authority utterly different from the impotent Congress of the Articles of Confederation, one that could restore the more integrated economic life once assured by the authority of the British Crown.

Here was an idea peculiarly acceptable on sentimental grounds to that very considerable Tory element in America that had weathered the Revolution, since only a minor fraction of the Loyalists had emigrated. There is competent authority for the conclusion that the Constitution could never have been established without "the active and steady cooperation of all that was left in America of attachment to the mother country."[8] So large an element did these Loyalists contribute to the personnel of the Federalist Party when it took form that the opposition, after the fashion of party propagandists even in our own day, sought to fasten the odious epithet "Tory" on the party as a whole.

But it was no sentimental consideration that impelled the fishing, shipping, and commercial interests to perceive promptly the advantage of a central government able to resolve the prevailing economic confusion through commercial treaties and statutes regulating trade. Even the Southern planters, producers of great export staples, were helpless

---

[8] Charles Francis Adams (editor): *The Works of John Adams*, I, 441.

without such a government. Speculators in western lands wanted a government competent to create armies capable of bringing the Indians to terms and rendering their western holdings salable to prospective settlers. To the officers of the Revolution, organized in the secret Order of the Cincinnati, the five years' extra pay voted by the Congress of the Confederation might become something more than just a gesture of goodwill if only there could be established a new government vitalized by taxing power, sound credit, and the ability to convert paper promises into ready cash. Indeed, holders of every type of paper claims against the government of the Confederation helped swell the tide of discussion of some plan for investing the central government with adequate power to promote their purposes.

No one can know how long the momentous issue might have remained unresolved had not the "desperate debtors" (Hamilton's expression, used in the sixth article of the *Federalist*) in Massachusetts, under the leadership of Captain Daniel Shays in the autumn of 1786, sought relief from their intolerable burdens through direct action. Many a Revolutionary veteran had returned from his campaigns only to find his family in the clutches of a stay-at-home, mortgage-shaving profiteer waiting to have him cast into prison for debt. The cutting off of the West Indies trade had knocked the bottom out of Massachusetts farm prices. Moreover the Massachusetts Constitution of 1780, through property qualifications both for voters and for members of the legislature and through an apportionment of representation based upon taxes paid, had securely entrenched property in the state Senate. Not only were the agrarians under-represented, but their natural allies, the workers of the cities, because of property qualifications, were unenfranchised. Thus enthroned, the dominant interests proceeded to exact their pound of flesh. Not content with piling land taxes on debt-impoverished farmers, they superimposed a vicious poll tax that alone provided forty per cent of the state's revenues. Pathetic petitions came from farmers' meetings, protesting that in "the state and county taxes, town and class taxes, the amount is equal to what our farms will rent for" and "many of our good inhabitants are now confined in gaol for debt and for taxes"; but all protests went unheeded by Governor and legislature.[4]

As the Massachusetts farmer saw his cattle driven away by the grasping money-lender, and the sheriff ready to sell for a song the ancestral homestead of sacred memory at the behest of the forecloser of mortgages or the inflexible tax-gatherer, as there loomed just ahead the dread prospect of a debtors' prison, a chamber of horrors in comparison with a present-day jail, his fury broke loose against the personal agents of his persecution, the courts and the lawyers, "who have been more damage to the people at large than the common savage beasts of prey." [5] Revolutionary Captain Daniel Shays reluctantly assumed leadership of the aroused farmers who were demanding abolition of that citadel of wealth, the state Senate, removal of the capital inland, away from aristocratic Boston, and the sale of state lands in Maine, then a part of Massachusetts, in order to reduce the burden of taxation. Nor were they less eager than debtors elsewhere for legal-tender issues of paper money.

With characteristic directness the rebels began breaking up sessions of the courts in order to prevent judgments against them. But when the "army" of two thousand malcontents sought to arm themselves by seizing the Continental arsenal at Springfield, the alarm among the dominant interests spread quickly from Maine to Georgia. General Lincoln wrung sufficient funds from frightened Boston merchants to set the militia of eastern Massachusetts marching. Pursued by cavalry and mounted college boys with hunting suits and horns as if on a lark, the hapless and practically unarmed farmers were dispersed and then tracked down like wild game in the winter snows. Then, when the uprising had been suppressed, the legislature enacted many of the reforms demanded by the rebels.

As in a flash of lightning Shays's Rebellion revealed to the

[4] See S. E. Morison and H. S. Commager: *The Growth of the American Republic* (1937), I, 159, 160.

[5] Quoted by H. C. Hockett: *The Constitutional History of the United States, 1776–1826*, p. 170.

ruling classes everywhere the existence of an element of discontent and potential violence, extending throughout the thirteen states. "What if the potential were to become the actual?" was the dread query that at once began to haunt the men of property. The near panic provided precisely the catalytic element to accelerate the combination of groups that, in due time, made the new Constitution. In 1785 Maryland and Virginia had been perplexed over problems of navigation rights in the Potomac River and Chesapeake Bay and had sent commissioners to confer on the matter at Mount Vernon. A later attempt to get together representatives of all the states at Annapolis for deliberation on problems of interstate commerce had brought together delegates from only five states. But here was laid the plan for the convention to "revise" the Articles of Confederation at Philadelphia in the summer of 1787. Posterity ought to thank Daniel Shays for the deeply concerned and quite determined group of delegates that constituted the roll of the convention.

There sat in the midst of the members when they convened one whose contributions to their deliberations and handiwork was to earn him the merited title of the "Father of the Constitution." James Madison had come to the Philadelphia Convention informed as no other delegate on the experience of the human race with governments from the city states of the ancient world to the nations of his own day. The reflections of political philosophers from Plato and Aristotle to such near contemporaries as Montesquieu and Blackstone were at his tongue's tip, objectified by his personal observations of the practical experience of the governments of the thirteen American states. Out of this erudition he had extracted and synthesized a severely realistic conception of the manner in which governments function.

While other noted Americans were fulminating against the moral obliquity of agrarian debtors and considering the means for suppressing by force all social unrest, Madison with a penetrating insight into the nature of current problems was diagnosing social maladies and seeking appropriate remedies. Who today could give a better analysis of the critical conditions of the 1780's than did James Madison in his letter to Jefferson of March 18, 1786? "A continuance of the present anarchy of our commerce," he wrote, "will be a continuance of the unfavorable balance on it, which by draining us of our metals [specie] furnishes pretexts for the pernicious substitution of paper money, for indulgences to debtors [moratoria], for postponement of taxes. In fact most of our political evils may be traced to our commercial ones, as most of our moral may be traced to our political." Time was to confirm the judgment of Madison when half a dozen years later the sun of prosperity again shone even on the erstwhile rebels of Daniel Shays enjoying once more the good farm prices of a Boston market bustling with the revival of the maritime trade under the government of the new Constitution.[6]

How did this architect of the Constitution, the pre-eminent exponent of its underlying philosophy with respect to pertinent interests and parties,[7] acquire his clairvoyant insight into the dynamics of political society? First, let us look into his social background. His home was in the Virginia piedmont, that "stronghold of democracy."[8] Inhabited by newer families from the North and poor whites pushed westward out of the tidewater, the region contained few slaves. Slavery was, in fact, despised by these farmers, not because of sympathy for the Negro, but because it was the invidious badge of planter superiority. While the climate of opinion prevailing here doubtless determined Madison's social outlook, his ideology was somewhat conditioned by the fact that he was the heir apparent of a prosperous planter family. Had he not inherited a trace of the "ruling class instincts,"[9] his influence might not have been so pronounced in the deliberations of the assembly of notables that framed the Constitution of the United States.

Madison's academic preparation was one of the most fruitful in the records of American statesmanship. Having completed the typical classical course at the College of New Jer-

---

6 See Morison and Commager, op. cit., I, 222.
7 *The Federalist*, Art. 10.
8 C. H. Ambler: *Sectionalism in Virginia from 1776 to 1861*, p. 8.
9 See E. M. Burns: *James Madison*, p. 2.

sey (now Princeton), he remained to pursue graduate studies in political science. The vogue of Montesquieu led him into an intensive study of that philosopher's search for the fundamental causes of social phenomena, but he also delved deeply in Hobbes, Locke, Sidney, Pufendorf, and others. His reading was not at all desultory but guided by the college president, John Witherspoon, who was anything but a closet philosopher. Leader of the Presbyterians in their great contribution to the American Revolution, Witherspoon was one of the signers of the Articles of Confederation. It was a rare stroke of good fortune that placed the future "Father of the Constitution" under the tutelage of one who disparaged book learning for its own sake and who observed that there are many learned men "whom yet we reckon greatly inferior to more ignorant persons in clear sound common sense." [10] It has been said that it is to John Witherspoon that "America owes for what it is worth the philosophy of common sense that permeated its thinking for so long." [11]

Let the present-day specialists in social dynamics who prides himself on a mastery of the new science of interpreting current politics in terms of pertinent interests and pressures humbly peruse Madison's commentary on the factors involved in the then current crisis. Two months before the delegates convened at Philadelphia he set down his observations in a paper entitled "Vices of the Political System of the United States." "All civilized societies," he wrote, "are divided into different interests and factions as they happen to be creditors or debtors, rich or poor — husbandmen, merchants or manufacturers — members of different religious sects — followers of different leaders — owners of different kinds of property, etc., etc. In republican government the majority, however composed, ultimately give the law. Whenever, therefore, an apparent interest or common passion unites a majority, what is to restrain them from unjust violations of the rights or interests of the minority, or of individuals?" [12]

---

[10] John Witherspoon: *Works*, IV, 17.

[11] J. E. Pomphret: "John Witherspoon," *Dictionary of American Biography*, XX, 437.

[12] *Writings* (Hunt ed.), II, 361 ff.

Madison had succeeded in reducing to a clear-cut statement the paramount problem of the framers of the Constitution when they were to assemble. The specific fear that gripped them all was the possibility that a single interest, the "desperate debtors," who undoubtedly constituted a majority of Americans, might act in concert and, by formulating and executing rash policies, wreck the existing social, economic, and political system. It is probable that not one member of the Convention believed in the rule of simple majorities and it is doubtful whether any considerable group of Americans has ever been willing to accept that principle, once its perilous implications have been explored. With all his professions of devotion to "popular rule," even Jefferson feared the "tyranny of majorities." [13] Madison, no doubt, expressed the majority opinion of the convention when he said: "There is no maxim which is more liable to be misapplied . . . than the current one that the interest of the majority is the political standard of right and wrong." [14] He conceived this to signify nothing more or less than that force is the measure of right. The American historian whose studies have been centered on our later experience with this problem concluded that "the more the nation is organized on the principle of direct majority rule and consolidation the more sectional resistance is likely to manifest itself." [15]

Madison did not content himself with merely the concise statement of the problem of majority rule. He believed the convention had within its power the setting up of a system that would permit a natural and automatic check against the peril of a simple majority. His study of Montesquieu had not convinced him that the mechanical device of checks and balances was sufficient; too many American state constitutions with that specific equipment had failed to produce the expected security. That pre-eminent specialist in checks and balances, John Adams, had been given practically a free hand in writing the Constitution of Massachusetts, which, instead

---

13 *Works* (Ford ed.), V, 83.
14 *Writings* (Hunt ed.), II, 366–8.
15 F. J. Turner: *Sections in American History*, p. 314.

of preventing Shays's Rebellion, had almost as much to do with provoking it as the depression itself. But, reasoned Madison, if the geographical scope of government could be extended to a grand republic continental in jurisdiction, the greater variety of interests scattered through its length and breadth would render difficult a combination of factions into a majority bent upon a radical policy.

Thus early in our career as Americans appeared the public determination deliberately to guard against any single radical group seizing the reins of government. In this Madison was the spokesman not only of the Fathers but of unborn generations. It may be set down as an essential American tradition, implicit in the political genius of our people. Something like an instinctive fear of the annihilation of the individual lurks in the background of this profound social conviction. Any threatened American group dictatorship, agrarian, proletarian, sectarian, military, or what not, arouses widespread resentment and is considered a movement foreign to our historical experience, a manifestation of continental European class consciousness, against which distemper the Atlantic Ocean is presumed to have provided a salutary immunity.

Viewed in the retrospect of a century and a half, Madison's calculation as to how combinations of interests would form majorities proved remarkably prophetic. Yet he was in no wise consciously a forecaster of the combinations as political parties.[16] Apparently he assumed that these interests would combine in temporary *ad hoc* coalitions as major issues prompted them and dissolve to form again in a different pattern on another issue. He never dreamed that they would eventually evolve into permanent institutions, each sustained by a cherished tradition, a passionate faith, and sometimes a crusading spirit. The fathers had known no national parties except the personal followings of British politicians, the most notorious of which had been the servile, patronage-seeking adherents of King George III, the "King's Friends" as they had been designated, the party sustaining the ministry whose arbitrary poli-

[16] See A. C. McLaughlin: "The Significance of Political Parties," *Atlantic Monthly*, February 1908.

cies had driven the colonists to revolt. Vice President John Adams merely gave expression to a prevailing opinion when he declared: "There is nothing I dread so much as the division of the Republic into two great parties, each under its leader. . . . This, in my humble opinion, is to be feared as the greatest political evil under our Constitution." [17]

In due time the convention completed its work and adjourned. The ratification of the Constitution by a sufficient number of states was hanging in the balance. Madison was busy collaborating with Hamilton and Jay in writing the series of papers supporting ratification since known as *The Federalist*. In the tenth number of that political classic he recurred to his favorite theme and amplified it when he penned the paragraph that may be considered his greatest contribution to political philosophy. We may assume that all the economic confusion of the "critical period" was still fresh in his mind as he wrote: "The most common and durable source of faction has been the various and unequal distribution of property. Those who hold and those who are without property have ever formed distinct interests in society. Those who are creditors and those who are debtors fall under a like discrimination. A landed interest, a mercantile interest, a moneyed interest, with many lesser interests, grow up of necessity in civilized nations and divide them into different classes actuated by different sentiments and views. The regulation of these various and interfering interests forms the principal task of modern legislation and involves the spirit of party and faction in the necessary and ordinary operation of the government." [18]

With clairvoyant vision the "Father of the Constitution" had perceived the paramount problem of a central government in the United States. It seemed to him that in the new Constitution he had the answer to the great riddle. As one peruses his illuminating exposition, there emerges clear-cut

[17] W. M. West: *History of the American People*, p. 333n.

[18] It is quite evident that Madison did not use the term "faction" in the sense of political parties of the kind existing today. He appears to have had in mind rather the interests or pressure groups, the elements composing our present-day parties. See P. H. Odegard and E. A. Helms: *American Politics*, p. 7n.

the pattern of the historical American process of resolving the inevitable clash of "factions" into the concept and practical reality of "the general good." For example, in the fiftieth number of *The Federalist* he states the formula in terms most explicit: "In the extended republic of the United States and among the great variety of interests, parties and sects which it embraces, a coalition of a majority of the whole society could seldom take place on any other principles than those of justice and the general good." Herein Madison was but the spokesman of the framers of the Constitution, giving authentic expression to their accord as revealed in the political literature of the period.

Half a century of American experience with group combinations under the Constitution afforded John C. Calhoun an opportunity to describe the process (in *A Disquisition on Government*) as he had observed it. Concerning the conflict for political power he wrote: "For this purpose a struggle will take place between various interests to obtain a majority, in order to control the government. If no one interest be strong enough, of itself, to obtain it, a combination will be formed between those whose interests are most alike — each conceding something to the others, until a sufficient number is obtained to make a majority. The process may be slow, and much time may be required before a compact organized majority can be thus formed; but formed it will be in time, even without preconcert or design, by the sure working of that principle or constitution of our nature in which government itself originates. When once formed, the community will be divided into two great parties — a major and minor, between which there will be incessant struggles on the one side to retain on the other to obtain the majority — and thereby the control of the government and the advantages it confers. . . ." [19]

Just a hundred years after Madison had published his prediction as to the interest combinations that would determine public policies F. H. Giddings, in an article analyzing the

[19] *A Disquisition on Government*, in B. F. Wright: *Source Book of American Political Theory*, p. 521.

presidential vote in 1888, concluded that "a numerical majority is not formed and maintained without much conciliation and mutual concession and that while it is far from being that concurrence of all interests that Calhoun desired, it is yet the concurrence of so many that its conduct can hardly become arbitrary without peril of disruption." [20] And such a majority "in a differentiated society, occupying an extended and diversified geographical area is a concurrent majority in composition though by no means a perfect one." [21] If further authoritative confirmation of the essential soundness of Madison's speculation was needed it came in our own day in the conclusion of A. W. MacMahon: "On the formal side this [Madison's forecast, *supra,* p. 25] missed the course upon which politics almost immediately entered. In *essence,* however, his expectations have been realized; diversity, balance and concession (with the immediate security and the long run dangers which attend deadlock and inertia) have been provided in American history by factional divisions [interest groups] within each of the two country-wide organizations." [22]

Whoever would know how a politically gifted people find, among conflicting interests, the common denominators of public policy that make possible government by willing consent could scarcely do better than to study intensively Madison's *Notes,* in which he recorded day by day a summary of the deliberations of the Constitutional Convention. A fairly adequate handbook of practical politics might be constructed from the material there available. Fortunately it was no group of formula-bound philosophers who had gone to work on the problems confronting the convention at Philadelphia, but statesmen accustomed to the give and take of practical politicians.

Some of the delegates were convinced that a system of Federal courts inferior to the Supreme Court would be necessary, while others believed the state courts would suffice. The

---

[20] "Conduct of Political Majorities," *American Political Science Quarterly,* VII, 120–1.

[21] Ibid., p. 131.

[22] *Encyclopedia of the Social Sciences,* XI, 597. Italics mine.

difference was composed by the simple provision that Congress *may* establish inferior courts.[23] The controversy as to whether or not state debts should be assumed was disposed of with the non-committal statement: "all debts . . . shall be as valid against the United States under this Constitution as under the Confederation." [24] Both those who wanted the western territory doomed perpetually to a colonial status and those who, on the other hand, wanted the possibility of full-fledged statehood left open found satisfaction in the simple provision that "new states may be admitted to the Union." [25] Sectional differences lurked in the background of every one of these controversies, and the modern politician who has seen service on a platform committee of a national party convention will detect the familiar practice of finding the formula that ends debate. Here is the perennial pattern of American party politics.

The delegates from the small states were fearful that the large blocks of electoral votes cast by the populous states would enable them to elect the President. It was then pointed out that by voting blindly in their separate states, presumably without any announced candidates, the electors would fail to concentrate a majority on any candidate "nineteen out of twenty times," [26] as Mason calculated the chances. The small states were then placated by the provision that the House of Representatives, casting one vote for each state, would elect the President from the five candidates standing highest in the electoral vote.[27] Under this system, as it was explained again and again, the large states would nominate the candidates in the electoral college, and the small states would elect in the House of Representatives.

We have noted but a few of the scores of compromises of the Constitutional Convention. Extending them would merely

---

[23] Art. III, sec. 1, cl. 1.
[24] Art. VI, sec. 1.
[25] Art. IV, sec. 3, cl. 1.
[26] *Documents Illustrative of the Formation of the Union of the American States,* 69th Congress, 1st Session, House Document No. 398, p. 663.
[27] Art. II, sec. 2, cl. 2.

confirm the conviction that the new instrument was the product of practiced political craftsmen. Their freedom in composing differences was facilitated by the fact that they sat behind closed doors with every member pledged to secrecy about their deliberations. Not until they had adjourned and the proposed Constitution, without commentary, had been published for submission to state conventions did the public know definitely what the delegates had produced.

How was the finished product of the framers received by the public? Most Americans, especially the unenfranchised majority, were indifferent, the potential opposition too tardily arousing themselves to action. What of the proponents? Should we expect to find in them one of those country-wide majority coalitions of "factions" or interests that Madison had calculated could seldom combine "on any other principles than those of justice and the general good"? In short, did the proposed Constitution itself consist of a complex common denominator for just such a combination?

No one need assume that the typical American in 1787 looked at the proposed new Constitution and asked: "Just what do I get out of this?" Then, even as now, men saw with their own eyes and beheld whatever the climate of opinion in which they lived prompted them to see. No doubt they rationalized their sectional, group, and personal interests in terms of the general good. None the less we may be sure this clause caught the approving eye of one while that provision aroused the indignation of another. In the mind's eye we can see the portly merchant seat himself serenely in his great chair, adjust his spectacles, and begin reading his copy. Presently he perceives with the greatest satisfaction that this new plan provides the central government with power to regulate commerce both among the states and with foreign nations by imposts, by statute, and by treaty, all of which, by the way, were to be "supreme law of the land." Moreover, the prevalent interference of the states with commerce was to be terminated by the specific prohibition against their making treaties or laying any but the slightest import or export duties without the consent of Congress. Nor is it likely that this merchant failed to note the power "to provide and maintain a navy," then quite generally regarded as a legitimate instrument of commercial policy. "Here," he may have murmured, "is the answer to our prayers." Whether he said it or not, he no doubt also believed: "What is good for business is good for the country."

Public creditors generally as well as speculators in public securities who caught the scent of potential profits were prompt to perceive the significance of that clause which supplied the fatal omission from the Articles of Confederation, the power "to lay and collect taxes" in order "to pay the debts . . . of the United States." The power "to borrow money on the credit of the United States" was also gratifying, but these holders of government securities found, made to their hearts' desire, the provision: "All debts contracted and engagements entered into before the adoption of the Constitution shall be as valid against the United States under this Constitution as under the Confederation." Here was security against the terror that haunted the public creditors of the 1780's, the dread specter of repudiation. Indeed, creditors, whether public or private, saw insurance also against that twin specter, inflation, in the provision that no state shall "emit bills of credit or make anything but gold or silver legal tender in the payment of debts." The prohibition of any state "law impairing the obligation of contract" should end that curse of the creditor, the stay-law or moratorium.

Nor were merchants and creditors the only interest groups captivated by the prospects held forth by the new Constitution. The fishermen of Gloucester and Marblehead, submerged in an economic degradation as "abject as that of slavery," thought John Adams, and impoverished since the Navigation Acts had shut off the French and Spanish West Indies market for their product and later independence had deprived them also of the English West Indies market, now looked forward with a new hope, which time would fulfill, to the promised Federal control over foreign commerce. Their county consequently voted eight to one in favor of delegates pledged for ratification.[28] Thousands of artisans in homes and manufacturing shops throughout New England and the middle states saw potential protection against foreign competitors in the power to tax imports and regulate commerce. The hopes of merchant shipowners were revived and the votes of shipbuilding mechanics in favor of the Constitution were captured by the promise of contracts for construction contingent upon ratification.

The American yeomanry for the most part opposed ratification of the Constitution as an anti-inflationary document. One outstanding exception to this, however, must be noted. The grain-growers of the fertile Shenandoah Valley, Scotch-Irish and Germans, voted ninety-seven per cent for ratification. The Constitution's assurance of free interstate trade would open the routes to the flour mills of Philadelphia and Baltimore for the passage of their wheat.[29] The great planters of the South favored the Constitution because they were being impoverished by the opportunity the prevailing commercial confusion in the states had given the English merchants to drive a profitable trade. They saw in the expected Federal control of commerce the potential development of domestic shipping and the reopening of the West Indies trade.[30] Moreover, embarrassed by the accumulating surplus of slaves on the already declining tobacco plantations, the Virginia planters welcomed the opportunity to tax at once, and twenty years hence to outlaw, the African slave trade [31] and thereby terminate the continuous deflation of the value of their human stock by the competition of supplies fresh from the jungle.

Several abortive uprisings of slaves in colonial times had been suppressed, but the great planters could never feel certain that there might not come a general servile revolt. Consequently they welcomed the potential security against that peril implicit in the power of Congress to provide "for calling

[28] See Louis M. Hacker: *The United States: A Graphic History,* map, p. 31.

[29] C. H. Ambler: *Sectionalism in Virginia,* pp. 53 ff.

[30] See J. B. McMaster: *History of the People of the United States,* I, 272–3; Ambler, op. cit., pp. 48–52.

[31] Art. I, sec. 9, cl. 1.

forth the militia . . . to suppress insurrections." Nor were
other men of property who had scarcely yet recovered from
the panic into which Shays's Rebellion had thrown them
unaware of the significance of that same clause as a precau-
tion against other than servile "insurrections." A related
clause, granting Congress the power to establish an army,
won the speculators in western land, infested with hostile
Indians. Even that active young pedagogue Noah Webster,
the future lexicographer, then busy publishing his famous
"blue speller" and other school textbooks and threatened with
having them pirated unless copyrighted in every state, would,
like the professional classes generally, no doubt have favored
the new Constitution in any case, but he must have derived a
peculiar satisfaction from the clause that invested Congress
with the power "to promote the progress of science . . . by
securing for limited times for authors . . . the exclusive
right to their respective writings. . . ." [32]

Since rejection by five states would have been fatal the issue
hung in the balance for months. A determined opposition,
consisting largely of the grain-growers outside the Shenandoah Valley, narrowly failed to prevent validating the work
of the Philadelphia Convention. This opposition sincerely
believed the Revolution to have been fought to free local or
state government from a central control. To them the "critical
period" was a figment of the imagination and the Articles of
Confederation provided as much central government as they
cared for. The Constitution on the contrary meant a return
to just such an imperial thralldom as they had won relief
from by seven years of war.[33] Here are the interests soon to
be found presenting a united front against the Federalist
Party and in due time to constitute the rank and file of the
Jeffersonian Republicans.

The loose association of interests — mercantile, shipping,
planting, speculating both in land and in securities, and finally
creditors both public and private — that produced the Con-

[32] See T. J. Norton: *The Constitution of the United States*, p. 65.
[33] See C. A. and M. R. Beard: *The Rise of American Civilization*, I,
299, 300.

stitution is, then, the prototype of the great national political party, of which, indeed, it was in embryo the very first. While these interests clashed at many points, they quickly learned the lesson of American politics: to disregard differences and concentrate on the one thing essential to their several purposes, in this case an integrated, national, economic society of which the *sine qua non* was the central authority the Constitution provided. This fundamental instrument was to these matter-of-fact men merely an elaborate practical device — a means to a great end. "While some have boasted it as a work from heaven," wrote Robert Morris, the biggest business man among the framers, "others have assigned it a less lofty origin. I have many reasons to believe that it is the work of plain honest men and such, I think, it will appear."

Of course, the men who made the Constitution consisted of a ruling class. In the stage of social development then obtaining, no others were competent to devise one capable of cementing sufficiently the then articulate elements of American society. "What proximate test of power can be found," asked the late Associate Justice Oliver Wendell Holmes, "except correspondence to the actual equilibrium of forces in the community — that is, conformity to the wishes of the dominant power?" [34] Fortunately the framers had already developed a sense of responsibility even to elements in society other than their own. After observing, in the Convention, that "the course of a few years would distribute their posterity to the lowest classes of society," the great Virginia planter George Mason declared that "every selfish motive therefore, every family attachment, ought to recommend such a system of policy as would provide no less carefully for the rights and happiness of the lowest than the highest order of citizens." [35] And Madison, in effect, echoed Mason in the statement "that the interests and rights of every class of citizens should be duly represented and understood in the public councils." [36] All of which contrasts strikingly with the contempt for the masses that

---

[34] *Collected Legal Papers*, pp. 224–8.
[35] Max Farrand: *Records of the Federal Convention of 1787*, I, 49.
[36] Ibid., II, 124.

characterized the social outlook of the ruling classes of still
semi-feudal Europe in 1787.

It now remains to be seen how the several social groups attracted by common interests into an unplanned association
presently, under the responsibility of administering the new
government they had created, coalesced into a permanent
combination, developed a consistent ideology, and became
the first of our several national political parties. This did not
come about automatically, but through the instrumentality of
two of the foremost statesmen of human history. The mono-
lithic figure of Washington provided the Federalist Party
with an incomparable centripetal force, inspiring in its nature. We shall see, however, that it was due pre-eminently to
the superb daring with which Alexander Hamilton manipulated the raw social forces of his day that the Federalist Party
was integrated and vitalized into a nation-building institution.

CHAPTER II

THE FEDERALISTS BECOME A POLITICAL PARTY

"HAMILTON *knew that the government could not stand if its sole basis was the platonic support of genial well-wishers. He knew that it had been created in response to interested demands and not out of any fine-spun theories of political science. Therein he displayed that penetrating wisdom which placed him among the great statesmen of all time.*" C. A. BEARD.*

JAMES MADISON had provided the philosophic pattern of the group combination responsible for the Constitution. It fell to the lot of Alexander Hamilton to perform a similar service for the somewhat less inclusive group combination that organized and then administered the new government during the first dozen years under the Constitution. In his origin, background, cast of mind, and philosophic outlook, and as a man of action Hamilton is a contrast to Madison in almost every particular.

Eighteen years before the Battle of Lexington, Hamilton was born on the British West Indies island of Nevis, of good stock, a Scotch merchant father and a French Huguenot mother. At eleven the death of his mother and the financial failure of his father left him practically an orphan in the care of maternal relatives. While he was engaged in clerical work in a general store, a brilliant description of a tropical storm written by the precocious youth created a sensation when published in a local newspaper. As a consequence, relatives sent him to the North American continent for education. Entering King's College (now Columbia University), he distinguished

* *Economic Origins of Jeffersonian Democracy*, p. 131. By permission of The Macmillan Company, publishers.

himself by diligent study and an astonishing mental maturity. Though still in his teens, he became a conspicuous opponent of the ministerial policies presently to precipitate the Revolutionary War. Enlisting in the patriot army, he became Washington's secretary and aide, but fretted under the irksome clerical duties because of a conviction he was never to relinquish that he was destined for a brilliant military career. Finally at Yorktown he was given his opportunity and led in person assaults upon the British redoubts. Meanwhile Madison in his middle twenties, unattracted even by the troops that marched by his plantation, pursued his legislative career.

Madison was to the manner born as a planting aristocrat of the Great Valley. Hamilton, on the contrary, was a social climber, but he climbed fast and far. At the age of twenty-three and only a few weeks before Yorktown, the erstwhile "orphan of Nevis" married Elizabeth, second daughter of General Philip Schuyler, among the richest and most influential of the mighty lords of the Hudson and one of Washington's four major generals. Schuyler's economic interests were capitalistic rather than agrarian. At one time he held $60,000 in government securities and was interested in the financing of banking, manufacturing, and transportation.[1] Hamilton easily assimilated the tradition of this proud aristocratic class and ever after proclaimed it with the peculiar earnestness of the late convert. For generations these landlords of the great river had played the game of politics after the prevailing pattern of English party struggles. Here Hamilton found ready-made the model he deemed so desirable in American politics.

After a scant five months' study of law young Hamilton began practice in New York City and rapidly rose to high rank in the profession. Here he had entered an environment with a peculiar climate of opinion that served to intensify the already aristocratic outlook of the son-in-law of a great landlord. While the Tories of Boston had emigrated with the evacuating British army in 1775, the leading families of New York City, mostly Tories, had, of course, remained during the

---

[1] See J. A. Krout: "Philip Schuyler," *Dictionary of American Biography*, XVI.

half-dozen years the British occupied that metropolis.[2] Fraternizing with British officers and completely isolated from patriotic influences, New Yorkers had become, by the end of the war, the most aristocratic and pro-British of American citizens. Significantly enough, here was the environment in which the Federalists conducted the new government during the first year of its history. It was in this alien atmosphere so congenial to him, despite his undoubted patriotism, that Hamilton nurtured that unbalanced admiration for the British system, social, economic, and political, that he will presently be found utilizing to rationalize the interests and designs of the Federalist group combination.

Like most of his fellow Federalists, Hamilton was so completely isolated from the frontier as to be blind to the most dynamic factors of developing American society. It was his misfortune to have had no first-hand knowledge of what Madison and Jefferson were learning and experiencing in western Virginia, where an emerging democratic way of life was already setting the pattern eventually to receive its literary expression in the phrases of Lincoln, himself a confessed disciple of Jefferson. So Hamilton's social philosophy petrified early with the belief in a society not only static but even stratified, and desirable in America since prevalent in England. The masses, then, were fit only to be ruled. One searches in vain through the many volumes of his *Works* for any concern about uplifting the common man. Protective tariffs would introduce here the English factory system, which provided work for "females and children of tender years," as he was wont to express it. He was eager to herd immigrants into the country in order to provide cheap labor. Having never seen the degenerate slum dwellers of London and Paris, as had Jefferson and Adams, he was not concerned about preventing the reproduction of such conditions here.

Behind the sheltering secrecy of the Constitutional Convention Hamilton had so freely expressed his admiration for monarchy and the British Constitution and his contempt for "the people" that a dozen years later Jefferson was to suggest

[2] J. T. Adams: *The Living Jefferson*, p. 213.

to Madison that he publish his *Notes* in order to ruin Hamilton politically.[3] Even after the new government under the Constitution had been functioning for some time, Hamilton is reported to have acclaimed the British Constitution as the most perfect government that ever existed,[4] and to have asserted that the American Constitution was a "shilly-shally thing of milk and water which could not last and was good only as a step to something better."

Unsatisfactory as the Constitution may have seemed to him as it left the hands of the Philadelphia Convention, Hamilton nevertheless threw the weight of his extraordinary talents into the battle for ratification, writing or collaborating on more than half the numbers of *The Federalist*. By reason and by strategy he, more than anyone else, brought about ratification by the New York Convention. When, in due course, President Washington appointed Hamilton Secretary of the Treasury, he proceeded at once to "administrate" (Madison's term) the Constitution into what he thought it ought to be. Inasmuch as there had never been a distinct central American executive, Hamilton was bound by no compelling American precedents and he consequently turned gladly to the usages and conventions of the English ministerial system. The younger Pitt was just then First Lord of the Treasury and Chancellor of the Exchequer as well as Prime Minister. Hamilton accordingly asked his friends to call him "chancellor of the Exchequer." Washington accepted Hamilton's assumption of the initiative in dealing with Congress, and consequently the President took on something of the separateness of the titular headship of the English King. With a boldness at which even an English Prime minister might have hesitated, the young Secretary began giving directions, even in matters of detail in their respective departments, to Secretary of State Jefferson, Secretary of War Knox, and Attorney General Randolph.[5] The Virginia delegation, the largest of any state representation in

---

[3] See H. C. Hockett: *The Constitutional History of the United States, 1826–1876*, pp. 66, 67.

[4] Jefferson: *Works* (Ford ed.), I, 165.

[5] See H. J. Ford: *The Rise and Growth of American Politics*, p. 82n.

Congress, prevented the establishment of standing committees and insisted instead on referring matters to the department heads. Hamilton eagerly accepted the responsibility thus assigned him by Congress of making his *Reports* on various matters. Through these famous state papers the great Federalist leader was enabled to formulate the policies that were at the same time an expression of his own and the Federalist Party philosophy. So the first great grist of statutes has gone down in history as the program of Hamilton rather than of President Washington.

The "prime minister's" problem was how to get the new government securely established, and he proceeded to execute his daring solution with a fairly breath-taking audacity. The paper Constitution was, of course, by no manner of means self-executing. Even to those who believed wholeheartedly in it, the odds must have seemed to lie heavily against its ever producing a robust government. We have found Hamilton expressing privately his little faith in it. Yet his army experience, his marriage connections, and his clients had put him in intimate association with the interests that at that moment were the most dynamic in America. If only these social forces could be harnessed and hitched to the Federal government, then it might move with vigor and gain momentum. If the merchant shipowners, the public creditors and financiers who were most potent in making the Constitution could become so deeply involved in financing the great adventure that its collapse would threaten them with economic ruin, then the Constitution might function.

Hamilton's opportunity lay chiefly in the paper claims against the government constituting the Revolutionary War debt. They included the loan-office certificates of 1776, the interest indents, issued to pay interest, and the treasury, commissary, quartermaster, marine, and hospital certificates of the respective services issuing them, amounting in all to $42,-000,000. The foreign debt was $11,700,000, and if the state debts later assumed at $21,500,000 be added, the national debt totaled in round numbers $75,000,000.

That the paper Constitution did not automatically establish

the credit of the United States is evidenced by the fact that when Washington was inaugurated President, the above securities were passing current for only a fraction of their face value. Nor would Congress of its own initiative have proceeded at once to provide for payment of these obligations. Channing estimated that not many more than half a dozen members of the First Congress started their sessions with any other idea than that the grand debt would be scaled down as a mere matter of course. "Repudiation" carried no such odious connotation then as now.

When Congress received their "finance minister's" *Report on the Public Credit,* they found it arguing that future emergencies rendered it imperative that the government establish its credit "by good faith and punctual performance of contracts." As a moral obligation the "debt of the United States" was "the price of liberty. . . . The advantage to public creditors from the increased value of that part of their property which constitutes the public debt needs no explanation." America was deficient in fluid capital, but "transfers of stock or public debt . . . are equivalent to payments in specie." This capital would stimulate economic life and restore land values.

After noting the universal agreement to pay the foreign debt "according to the precise terms," Hamilton took cognizance of a current proposal to pay American holders of security only the market value and the remainder to the original holder. This, he argued, would be a "breach of contract — a violation of the right of a fair purchaser. . . . The intent in making the security assignable" had been "that the buyer may be safe in his purchase." Quite naturally, Hamilton persuaded himself that under the circumstances the national debt could be "a national blessing."

The ecstatic praise that conservative historians have bestowed on Hamilton's *Reports* has invested them with something of the sanctity of holy writ. This, unfortunately, has obscured the fact that they were the perhaps unconscious rationalizations of the Federalist interests. It is no disparagement to say that they constituted high grade propaganda.

So completely have the Hamiltonian dogmas of finance captured the public opinion of America that to the typical American of today they would seem more like axioms of sound finance than subjects for debate. Not so to the First Congress, with only a little handful of one-hundred-per-cent "sound credit" representatives. Full funding of the foreign debt with interest was not questioned, but no less a figure than Madison assumed leadership of the congressional opposition to Hamilton's proposal to finance at face value every security but the Continental currency. Madison represented a typically agrarian Virginia constituency, democratic in temper, and could not have remained in politics had he not "represented" his district. Nor need there be any intimation that in parting company with the combination that made the Constitution he compromised his conscience, for he sincerely believed that Hamilton was "administrating" the new government into something quite different from what the Constitution prescribed. So, for the time being, Madison became the chief congressional spokesman of the agrarian, as opposed to the capitalistic, combination of interests.

Madison's tilts with the Hamiltonian forces in Congress resulted in an unbroken succession of defeats. He proposed that in the funding of the Continental debt the holders of securities, largely speculators, should be paid only the market value and the original holders the remainder. It was an impractical and hopeless proposal, losing thirty-six to thirteen in the face of the powerful forces marshalling compact ranks in support of Hamilton's program. Advance information of the Secretary's program having leaked out,[6] enterprising financiers, gambling somewhat on the chances, sent agents by fleet horses and swift sailing vessels into remote sections, especially the South, with abundant cash to purchase at the prevailing ruinous discount the holdings of securities from those who were as yet unaware of their potential redemption at face value. The later bitter disillusionment of those who sold for a song boded ill for the Federalists and was an important factor in the ultimate extinction of the party.

---

[6] Jefferson: *Writings* (Ford ed.) I, 161.

In vain did the opposition counsel delay, hoping for the sentiment of the inland settlements to crystallize among the agrarians. For fear of that very development the Hamiltonians insisted on the necessity of establishing sound credit immediately. With a glance at the speculators in the gallery, Representative Sedgwick of Massachusetts declared that "the ardent expectations of the people on this subject want no other demonstration than the numerous body of citizens assembled within these walls."[7]

Whoever assumes that pressure groups are a recent development should know of the Society of the Cincinnati. When the Continental army was demobilized, the officers founded an extraordinarily exclusive secret society. Only the eldest descendant of an original member might wear the insignia and enjoy the privileges. No wonder Judge Aedanus Burke of Charleston, South Carolina, attacked it on the ground that it established an order of nobility distinct from the plebeians.

By 1787 the Cincinnati constituted the best-organized country-wide interest in America, with a network of state and local organizations. With Washington as their president, the Cincinnati came in time to be even more positively identified with the Federalists than the much more democratic Grand Army of the Republic was with the Republican Party a century later. Whether by accident or design, the members convened in Philadelphia at the time of the Constitutional Convention. Fear that such a compact organization might perpetually dictate the choice of a President is one reason assigned for the rejection of popular election by the convention. A French chargé d'affaires, reporting from Philadelphia, informed his home government that the Cincinnati, aware of the feebleness of the Confederation government and the impossibility of their being paid the extra five years' pay voted them, "proposed to throw all the states into one mass, and put at the head the gallant Washington with all the powers and prerogatives of a crowned head."[8] No wonder the delegates

---

[7] *Annals,* I, 1135.
[8] See Farrand: *Records,* II, 119.

felt impelled to deliberate behind closed doors with such a persistent pressure group so near at hand.

The Cincinnati need not be charged with sinister designs in promoting the Constitution and sound credit. They constituted merely the first veteran organization to employ power and prestige to promote their purposes. They had been "paid" in land warrants and depreciated paper and, in contrast with the privates, were also voted the five years' extra pay. While the poor common soldier had to cash his warrants immediately at a ruinous discount, the officer could often hold his for ultimate redemption at par. Consequently the Cincinnati were one of the most powerful elements of the security group who hoped for a central government able to redeem their paper claims at face value.[9]

The second major item in Hamilton's financial program was his proposal to assume and fund the state debts. Perhaps his most telling point was that, under the Constitution, "a principal branch of the revenue is exclusively vested in the Union and that a state could not impose consumption taxes easily because of the failure of other states to impose like taxes. These state debts were, moreover, largely war debts incurred in the common cause of winning independence and therefore ought to be regarded as Federal obligations. The heart of the matter, from the Federalist point of view, Hamilton could not incorporate in his *Report,* but we find it expressed in the secrecy of a personal letter of a Connecticut Federalist, Oliver Wolcott, Sr., apparently to his son in the Treasury Department: "Your observations respecting the public debts as essential to the existence of the national government are undoubtedly just. . . . *There certainly cannot at present exist any other cement.* . . . If the state governments are to provide for their payment, these creditors will forever oppose all national interests as inconsistent with their interests."[10] Congress proved far less responsive to Hamilton's leadership on the state debts than on the Continental. The remoter agrarian

---

[9] See C. A. Beard: *Economic Interpretation of the Constitution,* p. 38.
[10] George Gibbs: *Memoirs of the Administrations of George Washington and John Adams,* I, 46. Italics mine.

regions were now becoming alert to the threat of the "money power." Patrick Henry had put through the Virginia legislature his resolutions protesting that no clause in the Constitution authorized assumption and proclaiming the "sentinelship" of the state legislature "over the ministers of the federal government." "This," remarked Hamilton, "is a spirit which must either be killed or it will kill the Constitution," and in his extremity he resorted to intrigue to gain his end, perpetrating the first notable piece of logrolling in congressional history. Already Thomas Jefferson, the Secretary of State, was being looked to for agrarian leadership. Only recently returned from France and scarcely yet familiar with current circumstances, he afterward maintained he had been duped by Hamilton's clever appeals for assistance in persuading some Congressmen to support the assumption of state debts in order to save the Constitution and the Union, which were represented to be in critical peril. Hamilton perceived a possible solution of the impasse on the assumption issue by taking advantage of the competition for the location of the permanent capital of the Union. So he persuaded Jefferson, already inclining toward assumption, to induce some of the Virginia Congressmen to support that measure. Since Virginians had paid their state debt and knew that, under the prevailing system of Federal taxes, assumption would require their starting to pay, through consumption taxes, the debts of the less thrifty states, Hamilton's proposal to Jefferson certainly called for a *quid pro quo*. So over the glasses at a dinner the two swung the deal. It was arranged that in return for the votes for assumption of two Virginia Congressmen the capital would be located at some site on the Potomac after a sojourn of ten years at Philadelphia, which latter proviso, by the way, was a factor in winning the unanimous vote of the Pennsylvania delegation for assumption.

Whoever may be curious about the dynamics of American politics then and now may note that the two Virginia Congressmen persuaded to switch from con to pro on assumption were Richard Bland Lee and Alexander White, whose districts bordered the Potomac. No other Virginia constituencies could have been reconciled to the vote so easily as these. White, moreover, had extensive holdings in the upper valley of the river and it later fell to him to be assigned the laying out of the city of Washington.[11] Robert Morris, who won the Pennsylvania delegation to unanimity on assumption, plunged so deeply into the development of the site of the capital that he landed eventually in a debtors' prison. When party alignments became stabilized, Lee and White were Federalists.

Once Hamilton's funding measures were enacted into law, the securities that had passed current at five to twenty per cent of face value rose promptly to par.[12] Since the new Constitution, through Hamilton's funding measures, had put an estimated gain of $40,000,000 in the pockets of security-holders,[13] no one need marvel at the cohesive power of the public debt in cementing the security groups within the Federalist Party.

Hamilton's proposed Bank of the United States was in the best English tradition. The Bank of England had been created by the triumphant commercial interests that had placed William and Mary on the throne just vacated by the Stuart line. Hamilton's bank was to be capitalized at $10,000,000, with all the stock privately owned except $2,000,000 to be subscribed by the Federal government. With branches in key cities, it suggests the great modern chain of banks, and it instantly alarmed the suspicious agrarians, to whom the money power was far more of a terror than today. It was to issue bank bills receivable for public lands, taxes, duties, and postage and in payment of any debt due the government. As a depository and dispenser of Federal moneys it was to be, as John Marshall later held, a governmental agency, but with private citizens owning most of the stock and constituting a majority of the directors. For at least ten years Hamilton

---

[11] See the map plotting pro and con districts on the assumption vote in C. O. Paullin: *Atlas of Historical Geography of the United States,* Plate 112.

[12] Washington had been compelled to use at 20 to 1 the certificates Congress had sent to reimburse him for his expenses as Commander-in-Chief of the army. George Bancroft: *History of the Constitution,* II, 411.

[13] See C. A. Beard: *Economic Interpretation of the Constitution,* p. 35.

had nursed the idea of a national bank as a means of uniting "the interest and credit of rich individuals with those of the State." [14]

Since chartering the bank would require the exercise by Congress of powers not specifically delegated in the Constitution, we have in the controversy over its constitutionality an illuminating illustration of the human propensity to rationalize. The bank bill, thanks to Hamilton's "ministerial" leadership, was put through Congress. President Washington, however, hesitated to sign the measure and sought the counsel of his department heads. Jefferson, sensing the peril to planter and yeoman interests in a "consolidated government" as contrasted with that of a federated union of states, took a firm position against deriving congressional power from constitutional construction. He pointed out that the phrase "general welfare" limited the taxing power and that the bank, while it might be "convenient," was not "necessary" to carry out any specifically delegated power. Washington having sent Jefferson's objections to Hamilton, the latter, in what was virtually a rebuttal by the attorney of the creditor bloc of interests, pounced upon Jefferson's distinction between "necessary" and "convenient," and when he had finished he had whittled away the difference between the two terms so completely that in American constitutional exegesis they have since come to pass as practically synonymous. Moreover, Hamilton managed to derive from a combination of specifically delegated powers "resultant" powers, of which chartering a bank was, of course, one. Thus "loose" versus "strict construction" became a perennial controversy, not, as was long erroneously assumed, between Federalists and Republicans respectively, but instead between the "ins" and the "outs." In a dozen years the Federalists were to protest in vain against the "unconstitutional" annexation of Louisiana by Jefferson.

The direst predictions of the agrarians as to the corrupting effect of the financial program seemed to them to be more than confirmed by the frantic scramble of investors and speculators for the stock of the Bank of the United States. Nor were

---

[14] *Works*, III, 332.

they reassured by the fact that the management of the "sinking fund," which enabled the government to enter the open market and purchase its own securities, was not designed or utilized to reduce the Federal debt on the most favorable terms but, to use Hamilton's own words, "to keep the stock from falling too low in case the embarrassment of the dealers would lead to sacrifices." Thus the Secretary was no doubt strengthening Federalist satisfaction with the government by deliberately supporting the "bulls." "If there are any gentlemen who support the funds and others who depress them, I shall be pleased that your purchases aid the former," he wrote to William Seaton, whom he had commissioned to buy Federal securities on behalf of the sinking fund.[15]

It is difficult to describe Hamilton's career as Secretary of the Treasury without seeming to imply a personal corruption from which even unfriendly historians have absolved him. Not the slightest taint of personal graft tarnished his integrity as a public servant. Sacrificing perhaps the most lucrative legal practice in New York for the $3,500 salary as Secretary of the Treasury he needed none of that economic motivation he found so useful in others in giving an impetus to the new government. In his perception that government in order to be stable must be based upon and serve men's interests, and his frank and courageous application of the principle to the current situation, he manifested statesmanship of the highest order. One wonders what kind of government would have been established if the Fathers had been mere well-wishers and enthusiasts for such an abstraction as the public good instead of men intimately identified with the dominant interests of their time. Considerable moral indignation has been wasted on the Congressmen who voted for the funding system while holding securities and profiting by the consequent rise in value. Beard, whose research qualifies him to speak authoritatively on this subject, discovered that some of the Congressmen holding securities voted against funding. The evidence indicates "that nearly all the members, security holders and non-security holders alike, represented the dominant eco-

[15] See *Works* (Lodge ed.), VIII, 232.

nomic interests of their respective constituencies rather than their personal interests." [16]

H. D. Laswell's characterization of politics as the question of "Who gets what, when, how?" was no less pertinent to the Federalists of the 1790's than the Democrats of the 1930's. For example, the preamble of the first tariff measure gave its purpose as "the encouragement and protection of manufactures." The debates, logrolling, and balancing of interests on this measure set the familiar pattern of tariff-making. Pennsylvanians wanted protection for molasses, rum, and steel. Massachusetts wanted molasses on the free list because of its use in the manufacture of rum, was doubtful about the duty on rum itself, but did not object to protection on steel. The South was willing to have molasses taxed, but not rum and steel. Congressmen from the transmontane districts of Virginia and North Carolina (the Kentucky and Tennessee region) opposed the demand of the coastal merchants for a tariff on salt required by western cattle-raisers, but the inlanders gave in when compensated by protection on hemp.[17]

Manufactures were, of course, in their infancy, but they constituted a distinct Federalist interest to be taken care of. American forges and furnaces as early as 1775 were producing as much bar iron as England and Wales. By 1789 the industrial revolution had by no means arrived and "manufacturer," as the Fathers used that term, signified a handicraft laborer in a shop or home instead of a factory-owner. During the special session of 1789 Congress was almost deluged with petitions for protection, coming from Baltimore, from the mechanics and manufacturers of New York, the tradesmen and manufacturers of Boston, all of which cities had been active centers in promoting the Constitution. The rope-makers, hatters, pewterers, soap-boilers, and tallow-chandlers, wool-card-makers, ship-carvers, sail-makers, cabinet-makers, coach-makers, tailors, brass-founders, and coppersmiths were among the Boston petitioners for heavy duties. These, by the way, were

---

[16] C. A. Beard: *Economic Origins of Jeffersonian Democracy*, p. 195.
[17] See A. M. Simons: *Social Forces in American History*, pp. 109, 110; D. R. Dewey: *Financial History of the United States*, p. 81.

not aristocrats, but workers, and the fact that special protection was laid by this first tariff on such articles as cordage, nails, iron, and glass indicates that this element in the Federalist Party was not ignored.

While we shall find the working classes being attracted largely to the Jeffersonian group combination as it develops, nevertheless it is significant that the Federalists gave their rebuttal to Thomas Jefferson's severe stricture against the working classes of the cities.[18] Federalist journalists pointed out that in America the "working man could escape [from poverty] by taking up land in the west," and that it was "highly probable much higher wages can be afforded to manufacturers and artists than is usually paid those descriptions in Europe, particularly Great Britain."[19] In fact, Harrison Gray Otis rallied to the Federalist Party even the ship calkers and shoemakers who had rioted as radicals during the Revotion. They saw their welfare involved in the growth of American shipping and are thus an early illustration of the tendency of the laborer throughout our history to vote for jobs rather than to constitute a group with distinct class interests. Moreover, even the Federalist Party, though certainly not so complete a cross-section of American society as later major political parties, was, nevertheless, a broader combination of interests than has been generally assumed. Its career was brief because of its fatal neglect of inland agrarian interests, but to dismiss it as merely a group of aristocrats would be as grotesque an over-simplification as to assume that the present Republican Party is simply an aggregation of capitalists. For example, Dixon Ryan Fox discovered that the Negro voters of New York City not only were numerous enough to swing a close election at the turn of the century but were almost all Federalists. Formerly slaves in Federalist homes, they had imbibed Federalist opinions, and when emancipated by their masters who were turning abolitionist, they gratefully supported that party. This allegiance was intensified by the fact that the Jeffersonian workingman, in fear of the competition

---

[18] See *Notes on Virginia,* p. 302.
[19] *Gazette of the United States,* September 7, 1791.

of these freedmen, bitterly opposed the abolitionists.[20]

Since New England contained the strongest elements of the Federalist combination, Hamilton's program rewarded that section handsomely. New England fishermen, who had been reduced to a condition "worse than slavery," found compensation for the loss of the royal bounty on dried codfish by a similar subsidy from the Federal Treasury. The shipowners, who had been almost crowded out of American harbors by English sails, flourished once more under preferential tonnage duties only one fifth as great as those that burdened foreign-built vessels. With such policies providing steadier employment, shipbuilding mechanics and artisans could be loyal Federalists. The maritime interests, dependent upon a relatively unimpeded flow of exports and imports — that is to say, loaded vessels on both the outgoing and the homeward voyage — might have gagged at tariff measures had not the duties laid to protect certain interests been so light that tariff historians hesitate to consider them genuinely protective.[21]

The time was to come, in due course, when the eternal gratitude of Federalist New England to Hamilton was to be given its perfect expression in Webster's classic phrases: "He smote the rock of the national resources and abundant streams of revenue gushed forth; he touched the dead corpse of Public Credit, and it sprang upon its feet." The orator ignored the fact that these "abundant streams of revenue" flowed to a great extent into the pockets of New Englanders. The wealth these Yankees had drawn from the sea through privateering and profiteering had gone largely into the buying of depreciated Revolutionary War securities. By the summer of 1790 speculation was wilder in Boston even than in New York. Five years later Massachusetts citizens were receiving $300,000 annually in interest on United States securities while citizens of Virginia, the most populous state, were receiving only one fifth as much.[22] Many of these new six per cent Federal securities had been obtained by the exchange, at par, of old cer-

---

[20] "The Negro Vote in Old New York," *Political Science Quarterly*, XXX (June 1917), pp. 225 ff.

[21] F. W. Taussig: *Tariff History of the United States*, p. 15.

[22] See C. A. Beard in the *American Historical Review*, XIX, p. 294.

tificates that had been picked up at twenty cents or less on the dollar and consequently represented a twenty-five to fifty per cent annual return on the investment, speculative though it may have been at the time of purchase.

It was these *nouveaux riches* among the New England Federalists who intensified the class animosity of the party toward the common man. Having replaced only recently the old aristocracy of the Tories, who had largely fled with the evacuating British army from Boston, and conscious that their position was not yet securely established, they bitterly resented the stubborn refusal of the masses to accord them the homage and obedience they insisted was due them.[23]

Massachusetts had been groaning under the heaviest debt of any state, the very debt whose burden Boston merchants had succeeded in shifting onto the land and polls of the farmers until Shays led them in revolt. We have seen Hamilton trade a capital site to get the burden of such debts shifted from the states to the nation at large, concealed in consumption taxes. Such was the whisky tax, soon to set the Allegheny slopes aflame with another insurrection. Incidentally, this tax served somewhat to protect New England rum-distillers from the competition of Pennsylvania whisky.[24] Agrarian states, such as Virginia, could hardly reconcile themselves to the policy which required those states that had already discharged their own debts to set about now, through Federal taxation, paying the debts of the less provident commercial states.

The Constitution, the new government, and the Federalists were all three the beneficiaries of the upward trend of the business cycle in the early nineties. By the beginning of Washington's second term the war between France and England had given Federalist shipowners a near monopoly of the neutral carrying trade. It was this war, together with the French Revolution, rising presently to the shrillness of the Reign of Terror, that transformed the opposing alliances of

---

[23] See A. E. Morse: *The Federalist Party in Massachusetts*, pp. 37–8.
[24] See H. C. Hockett: *Political and Social Growth of the United States, 1492–1865*, p. 317.

Federalist and anti-Federalist interests into integrated parties with intensified, though semi-rational, convictions. The sentimental insistence of the agrarians on a declaration of war against England in order to fulfill our obligations to our Revolutionary ally, France, was countered by the Federalist policy of neutrality. The Federalists perceived that England was a nation whose trade we needed far more than she needed ours. We bought one twelfth of her exported manufactures in 1789. Before long much of the customs duties on our imports was flowing through the Federal Treasury into the pockets of Federalist security-holders. The mad agrarians would kill the goose that laid these golden eggs by declaring war on England.

Then England almost forced war through her Orders in Council, under which she seized neutral vessels loaded with grain for France and later the French West Indies. When a New England merchantman dropping into a British West Indies harbor could be fallen on by a band of ruffians, its cargo seized, the vessel dismantled or made captive, the crew imprisoned or impressed into His Majesty's service, all under pretext that it was involved in trade with France, and with no chance for justice in an Admiralty court, even such an Anglophile as Hamilton had to condemn the practice. Atlantic shipping interests were turning to the Republicans, who began to bid for their votes by championing their rights. Shipbuilding suffered and unemployment spread, especially in New England. Under the pressure Congress enacted an embargo and began preparations for war with England. News leaked across the Canadian border that Lord Dorchester, British commander at Detroit, had promised the Indians of the Northwest aid in driving the Americans south of the Ohio. Fortunately it was not known in the United States then that the Lieutenant-Governor of Canada had invaded the Northwest Territory and erected and occupied a fort at the rapids of the Maumee River, where General Wayne was soon to crush the power of the Indians at the Battle of Fallen Timbers, almost under the guns of the British fort.

President Washington sought to avoid war by sending John

Jay to negotiate the differences with England. Jay's trump card, the threat of joining Denmark and Sweden in armed neutrality against England's paper blockade, was ruined by Hamilton's unpardonable admission to the British Minister that the American policy was to avoid European alliances. The inequitable treaty that Jay brought home provided the issue on which our first presidential contest was waged.

Though the treaty of 1783 had obligated the British to evacuate the forts in the Northwest, they still held them as a pledge against the American agreement to enforce the collection of planters' debts to English creditors. The planters had the counter-claim that the British had carried away thousands of their slaves at the close of the Revolutionary War. Speculators in Western lands were convinced that the British occupation of the forts incited the Indians and made their holdings unsalable, while American fur traders were losing half a million dollars annually because of the presence of the British soldiers.[25]

When Jay returned to America with the results of his negotiations, his treaty astonished even the Federalists. Southerners grew furious when they learned that, while their claims for stolen slaves had been ignored, the planters' pre-Revolutionary debts to English creditors were to be paid in full with interest, all in specie, as determined by a mixed commission to sit in London. They recalled that Jay was the statesman who, in 1783, had proposed to trade away their right to navigation of the Mississippi in return for commercial concessions to Northern interests. Now, as a known abolitionist, he was believed to be bartering away the just claims for their stolen slave property in exchange for special commercial concessions to his fellow Federalists.[26] And the maladroit Hamilton merely fanned the flames of passion when he condoned the conduct of the British in carrying away the slaves by arguing that it would have been as odious and immoral a thing as could be conceived of "to have abandoned to their masters

    25 See A. C. McLaughlin: "Western Posts and British Debts," American Historical Association *Reports*, 1894, pp. 413, 418.
    26 F. A. Ogg: "Jay's Treaty and the Slavery Interests of the United States," American Historical Association *Reports*, 1901, pp. 275 ff.

Negroes who had been induced to quit them with the promise of freedom." [27] Jay's suspected vindictiveness seemed proved beyond peradventure by his innocent blunder of consenting to an agreement not to export cotton, not knowing it to be an American export. Nor is this lack of knowledge so remarkable when we recall that the cotton gin, not yet three years old, had yet to exert its stimulus on cotton-production.

There were advantages to some, however, even if none of them accrued to the luckless agrarians. The forts were to be evacuated, to the chagrin of the Indians and the advantage of Northern settlers, speculators, trappers, and fur traders. The shipowners were to have "full and complete compensation" for losses and damage by irregular and illegal capture or condemnation of American vessels, owned, of course, almost exclusively by Federalists. "In short it was through necessity or design or a mixture of both a thoroughly partisan document tender to Northern commercial interests as far as it wrung any concessions at all from Great Britain." [28]

President Washington said that "the cry against the treaty was like that against a mad dog," the opposition condemning particularly the alleged violation of our obligation to France.[29] Jay was burned in effigy, Hamilton stoned for defending the treaty, and the British Minister openly insulted. In Philadelphia, New York, and Boston the treaty was endorsed by chambers of commerce, which were practically Federalist political clubs. In New York the dissenting members of the Chamber of Commerce sought to make it a Tory measure by charging that of the fifty-nine members who supported the treaty, only eighteen had lived outside the British lines during the Revolution.[30]

In 1796 the Federalists elected their last President, John Adams, by the narrow margin of three electoral votes. The burden of the unpopular treaty was almost too much. Fortunately John Adams was not, like Hamilton, pro-British. During the first generation under the Constitution, state legisla-

---

[27] *Works* (Lodge ed.), IV, 398, 419.
[28] Beard: *Economic Origins of Jeffersonian Democracy*, p. 283.
[29] *Writings* (Ford ed.), XIII, 77.
[30] C. A. Beard, op. cit., pp. 289, 290.

tures quite generally chose the electors in a presidential election, and consequently these were not, in the modern sense, popular contests at the polls. Nevertheless, the distribution of electoral votes between John Adams and Thomas Jefferson presents all the appearance of a referendum on Jay's treaty. North of the Potomac Jefferson received fourteen votes in Pennsylvania and four in Maryland. South of the Potomac Adams received one vote in Virginia and one in North Carolina.

The Federalists' days were certainly numbered. The handwriting was on the wall although no Daniel was at hand to decipher and interpret the message. Their remaining years are so intimately involved in the rise of their opponents to power that the discussion of them may be deferred. Why was it such a shortlived party? In answering this question let it be borne in mind that the Federalists never conceived of their group combination as constituting a political party, because they did not believe in such an institution. Representing, at least so far as New England was concerned, a "cordial union between the clergy, the magistracy, the bench and bar and respectable society throughout the State," [31] their combination was dominated by a ruling class that had created public opinion since early colonial times and regarded as indisputable its right to rule. John Adams was but their spokesman when he wrote to his radical cousin, Samuel: "Blind, indistinguishing reproaches against the aristocratical part of mankind, a division which nature has made and we cannot abolish, are neither pious nor benevolent. They are as pernicious as they are false. They serve only to foment prejudice, jealousy, envy, animosity, and malevolence." The Federalists were but perpetuating the early Puritan tradition epitomized by John Cotton's rhetorical question: "If the people be governors, who shall be governed?"

Existing society, as Federalists conceived it, was static and stratified, or at any rate ought to be. Hence Hamilton was to say: "Every institution calculated to restrain the excess of law making and to keep things in the same states in which

---

31 Henry Adams: *History of the United States*, I, 76.

they happen to be at any given period was likely to do more good than harm." The Federalist Party's brief but brilliant career of achievement was due, no doubt, to its adaptation to the status quo of the 1790's. For a brief moment in the long sweep of history it captured a balance of social forces and narrowly missed institutionalizing it permanently. Its leaders failed to see and consequently neglected certain dynamic factors inherent in American society. Indeed Hamilton's program piled rewards unnecessarily on already faithful adherents of the Federalist cause and neglected the essential political tactics of courting other interests capable of providing new recruits. The steady growth of the inland settlements doomed any party obsessed with European concepts of society and politics. When the Reign of Terror came to France, the Federalists were unable to distinguish frontier agrarian opponents from Parisian proletarian sans-culottes. So they railed futilely at the refusal of virile agrarians to submit complacently to the rule of their "betters."

Since the Federalists denied the very legitimacy of a political party, they never openly effected any such party organization as has characterized every other major American party. Utterly abhorrent to them was the idea that the body of Federalist voters had any right either directly or indirectly to choose local, county, or state party committeemen. Their heritage of English social philosophy prevented their establishing an "American" political party organization. A "convention" would suggest the bloody "Jacobins." However, they were compelled to establish their own oligarchical system of party management, based upon the frank assumption of the right of the leaders to rule the party. In Massachusetts the sovereign authority of the party resided in the Federalist legislative caucus, a committee of which appointed the county committees, and these controlled the town committees and through them determined nominations to the legislature and managed the campaigns. All this was clandestine, however, and the very existence of the organization was kept secret, as was their Federalist National Convention of 1808.

This secrecy was due to the fact that the Federalists could

not openly organize since they condemned any organization of their opponents. The Federalists' opponents challenged the status quo; they would overthrow the ruling class, and their activity therefore partook of the nature of a conspiracy, revolutionary in character. Popular sovereignty, as their opponents proclaimed it, also smacked of pernicious French Jacobinism. The leading members of the Federalist Party ought to determine nominations and party business without consulting the common voter of the party, whose implicit obedience was expected. Nor should anyone be misled by the Washington Benevolent Societies, organized as Federalist political clubs. Through charity they sought to hold the allegiance of the poorer classes.

The Federalists succeeded, to their own satisfaction, in making the terms "Federalist" and "patriot" synonymous. When Washington condemned the "self constituted democratic societies," he was expressing the Federalist intolerance of organized opposition. In his "Farewell Address" he clarified this position in the statement that "all combinations and associations under whatever plausible character, with the real design to direct, control, counteract or awe the regular deliberation of the constituted authorities, are destructive of this fundamental principle and of fatal tendency." [32] Shortly before his death he paid unconscious tribute to the growing solidarity of the Republican movement that would overwhelm the Federalists a year or two later. "Let that party set up a broomstick," he wrote to Governor Trumbull, "and call it a true son of liberty — a democrat — or give it any epithet that will suit their purpose and it will command their votes *in toto*." [33] In the same year John Marshall was complaining that nothing debases or pollutes the human mind more than a political party. [34] Surely this ardent Federalist could not have conceived of those professing his political faith as constituting anything so reprehensible as a political party. It was the odious opposition only that answered that description.

---

[32] J. D. Richardson: *Messages of the Presidents*, I, 217.
[33] *Writings* (Ford ed.), XIII, 190.
[34] A. J. Beveridge: *Life of John Marshall*, II, p. 410.

CHAPTER III

THE ANTI–FEDERALISTS

"IT [*the Constitution*] *was, to the masses, something new, vague and awful; something to oppress the poor, the weak, the debtor, the settler; something to strengthen and enrich the already strong and opulent, the merchant, the creditor, the financial interests.*"
ALBERT J. BEVERIDGE.*

THE GENESIS of Jeffersonian democracy is to be sought among the elements that constituted colonial society. Geographically it was rooted in what early historians designated the "Old West," the interior or upcountry of pre-Revolutionary America. This long strip of back country extended from Maine to Georgia, with perhaps a million inhabitants on the eve of the Revolutionary War. Similarity of conditions along this western fringe of settlement had produced a society with common characteristics and ideas. Recruited from migrant mechanics and the poorer whites of the older settlements as well as immigrants from Europe, especially the Scotch-Irish, these settlers had purchased or squatted upon the holdings of land speculators. Since they were debtors to the towns, their conscious identity of interests was manifested by intense animosity against the older settlements.

These backwoodsmen had been profoundly stirred by the religious revival known as the "Great Awakening" of 1740. Denominationally they were adherents of the dissenting sects, Presbyterian, Baptist, and Methodist, and in most colonies had been embittered against the established churches, Congregational in New England and Episcopal in the South, which they were taxed to support. In North Carolina no mar-

---

* *John Marshall,* I, 37. By permission of Houghton Mifflin Company, publishers.

riage was legal unless celebrated by one of the very few Anglican clergymen there. The widely circulated rumor that an Anglican bishopric was about to be established in America was one of the minor provocations of the American Revolution. The "popish" symbols that dissenters had fled across the Atlantic to escape were about to pursue them into the very wilderness. The political color of these dissenters was evident enough when the free-thinker Jefferson paid, out of his own pocket, the salary of the first Baptist missionary in Illinois in recognition of his service in organizing churches of the democratic order on the frontier.[1]

The most important single ethnic group in the colonial democracy was the Scotch-Irish. These extraordinarily virile people had come to America already hardened by pioneering and border warfare. Migrating first to northern Ireland early in the seventeenth century, they had served as a Protestant buffer against the Catholic Irish. They transformed the wild moorlands of Ulster into cultivated fields and gardens and established flourishing linen and woolen textile industries. But when competing English industries had induced Parliament to outlaw their products and rack-renting landlords had provoked civil war, a tide of migration to America set in. The flood of immigrants alarmed Cotton Mather and John Winthrop, but they passed on promptly to the Massachusetts border.[2] Strange to say, they contributed in time more to the New England population than the Puritans themselves, and since New England did not develop its peculiar traits until after the influx of the Scotch-Irish, they played their part, too, in the making of the "New England Yankee."[3]

In even greater numbers these Scotch-Irish poured into Pennsylvania, to the vexation of the proprietors. "It looks as if Ireland is to send all its inhabitants hither, for last week not less than six ships arrived, and every day two or three arrive also," wrote James Logan, Penn's secretary, in 1729.[4]

---

[1] Claude Bowers: *Jefferson and Hamilton*, p. 145.

[2] See S. P. Orth: *Our Foreigners*, pp. 10, 11.

[3] H. J. Ford: *The Scotch-Irish in America*, pp. 523, 524.

[4] Quoted by Morison and Commager: *Growth of the American Republic*, I, 55.

As incorrigible squatters they took possession of the proprietors' frontier land, defending their appropriation with the pious observation: "It was against the laws of God and of Nature that so much land should remain idle while so many Christians wanted to labor on it." [5] In eight years squatters, mostly Scotch-Irish, took possession of 400,000 out of the 670,000 acres occupied in that time. From Pennsylvania thousands of them along with migrating Germans pushed southward along the plateau terraces of the Blue Ridge, through Maryland, the Shenandoah Valley, the Carolina and Georgia uplands, until the whole back country from Maine to Georgia became "the skirmish line of the Scotch-Irish taking possession of the wilderness." [6] John Fiske estimated that by the time of the Revolution they constituted one sixth of the population, but as a factor in our political history they exerted an influence out of all proportion to their numbers.

The Scotch-Irishman became the typical frontiersman, "the long-limbed pioneer, with the long knife, the long gun and the long memory." An orthodox Calvinist, he was severely dogmatic, emphasizing the Old rather than the New Testament.[7] To him the Indians were heathens to be smitten like Canaanites and their lands appropriated by the Chosen People.

After the French and Indian War the British ministry decided to set aside the West as a vast Indian reservation. The consequent establishment of the Proclamation Line around the headwaters of the Atlantic rivers as a western limit of settlement enraged the frontiersmen at such tenderness toward the savages. It was this ministerial policy, indeed, that made allies of frontiersmen and tidewater planters on at least one issue, thus foreshadowing the Jeffersonian Republican combination a generation later. The planter grew his tobacco under conditions of high fixed costs on soil undergoing rapid depletion, but was compelled by law to sell it only in the manipulated English market. Victims of adverse circumstance,

---

[5] Quoted by Morison and Commager: *Growth of the American Republic*, I, 56.
[6] S. P. Orth, op. cit., p. 12.
[7] Carl Wittke: *We Who Built America*, p. 54.

nearly all the great planters sought to recoup their declining fortunes by the fur trade and speculation in Western land. Suddenly the Proclamation Line denied this opportunity for relief, and when Parliament's Currency Act vetoed the agrarian demand for cheap money, economic ruin seemed inescapable.[8] No wonder Virginia was to have fewer Tories than any other state during the Revolution and at the end of the century, in the Second Revolution, the leadership of the state overthrew the pro-British Federalists and established the Virginia dynasty.

As early as 1760 Virginia already had a genuinely democratic party. As a group combination it consisted of small farmers along the upper rivers, tobacco-growers from the ridges between, and hunters and trappers from the slopes of the Alleghenies all from the twenty-one western counties of the colony, with whom were combined the hitherto inert and unorganized mass of small proprietors and slave-owners in the old counties.[9]

The combination grew under the superb political leadership of Patrick Henry. As an impressionable youth Patrick had gone with his mother to hear the soul-stirring revival sermons of Samuel Davis, the greatest of the Southern New Light Presbyterian preachers and an outstanding leader of the democratizing "Great Awakening." Rousing revival exhortations made their indelible mark on pioneer oratory and, in a very true sense, determined the style of the Western stump speech, with Henry as its greatest exponent. At eighteen the young orator married and settled down on three hundred acres of half worn-out land nearly ten miles from river transportation — circumstances sufficient to make a radical out of even a less erratic and emotional genius. Within three years of admission to the bar he had managed 1,185 suits of poor piedmontese clients, usually winning his cases. Meanwhile he had championed the cause of the Presbyterians against the established church, and presently that of the other dissenting sects also, the Baptists and Methodists who were pushing into

---

[8] See L. M. Hacker: *The United States, A Graphic History*, p. 28.
[9] W. E. Dodd: *Statesmen of the Old South*, p. 19.

the hitherto exclusively Episcopalian tidewater parishes, where their ministers persevered despite even imprisonment. The middle class of the whole colony was rallied by Henry against the ruling tidewater oligarchs. Elected to the colonial legislature, he struck boldly at the corruption of aristocratic officials and obtained the conviction of some conspicuous members of proud tidewater families. When the oppressive measures of the British ministry aroused New England, Henry seized the opportunity to push hesitant Virginia planters toward open revolt.

The upcountry of North Carolina was the region of the most extremely democratic habits in the colonies. "They are rarely guilty of Flattering or making any Court to their governors, but treat them with all the Excess of Freedom and Familiarity," wrote William Byrd II concerning them. The piedmont of South Carolina has been described as the melting-pot of German, Swiss, Scotch-Irish, English, and Welsh dissenters, all with leveling ideologies.

Far to the north, democracy was represented by the irrepressible Green Mountain Boys, up in arms even before hostilities against England broke out, resisting the claims of the New York Governor and landlords to what is now Vermont. Within the colony of New York, as elsewhere, the excitement over the Stamp Act was taken advantage of by discontented elements, who were not in the least concerned about stamps, but who exerted pressure for redress of their own grievances against colonial aristocrats. Typical was the case of the tenants of Westchester and Dutchess counties in New York who refused to pay the patroons their rent and marched, five hundred strong, to New York City to participate in the "Stamp Act" rioting.

Pennsylvania, with the largest non-English stock of any colony, was the promised land of the poor and discontented of Europe. The 90,000 thrifty German farmers were natural allies of the Scotch-Irish against the autocratic proprietary government of Penn's heirs. The Quaker aristocracy, centered in Philadelphia, was too socially exclusive to admit even Benjamin Franklin, who became the political leader of the under-represented and consequently overtaxed agrarians. "Those to the westward," commented a contemporary, "look upon the people in any of the commercial towns as little better than swindlers while those of the east consider the western members a pack of savages." [10] Here, as elsewhere, the discontented took advantage of the quarrel with the British ministry to force redress of domestic grievances. No one can say how long the Revolutionary War might have continued with the patriots professing loyalty to the King while fighting to compel the ministry to revise its policies, had not Tom Paine let loose his tirade against George III. His *Common Sense* appealed powerfully to the debtor element and "contained even more dynamite than Thomas Jefferson." [11] It served suddenly to arouse radical democratic elements throughout America and crystallized sentiment for independence. In Pennsylvania the Scotch-Irish frontiersmen, combining with the lesser German farmers and the unenfranchised masses of Philadelphia who began peremptorily to assume the voting privilege, overwhelmed the Quaker and wealthy German oligarchy. Then they forced the making of the most radically democratic state constitution of the Revolutionary War period with a liberal elective franchise and fair representation for the western counties. They instructed the Pennsylvania delegation in the Continental Congress to support independence, which powerfully affected the issue pending in other states.[12] Indeed, it was at this point that the Revolutionary movement became vitalized by the merging into it of a hitherto lukewarm element, the mass of debtors, who through extra-legal committees of correspondence now took charge of local government in all the states.[13]

It is not an unreasonable approximation of the truth to say that these militant elements of the Revolutionary or Patriot Party were the forerunners of the Anti-Federalists and eventu-

---

[10] Quoted by Morison and Commager, op. cit., I, 58.

[11] H. C. Hockett: *Constitutional History of the United States, 1776–1826*, p. 169.

[12] See J. F. Jameson: *The American Revolution as a Social Movement,* p. 20; H. J. Ford, op. cit., p. 526.

[13] See R. G. Usher: *The Rise of the American People*, p. 114.

ally contributed the rank and file of the Jeffersonian Republicans. The officers of the Continental army, largely gentry, may have joined the Cincinnati and become Federalists, but the common soldier who had carried the musket usually gravitated into the ranks of the Jeffersonians. The evidence is clear that, on the whole, the Revolutionary Party was the party of the plain people as distinguished from the aristocracy.[14] Everywhere small debtors joined the revolutionists, embittered by the deflationary statutes of the creditor-dominated English Parliament, which forbade colonial issues of paper money. The elements aroused by the "Great Awakening," and indeed dissenters generally, were likely to be Patriots. So very obvious was the contribution of the Scotch-Irish that the war was sometimes half seriously known as "the Presbyterian Revolution."[15] Presbyterian churches especially suffered from the vandalism of the British army, and if the redcoats found a home containing a metrical version of the Psalms and a large Bible they were likely to conclude that it belonged to a rebel.[16] Lecky declared that the evicted Ulster tenants of Lord Donegal formed no small part of the armies that severed the New World from the British Crown. Certainly the British agents who, late in the war, thought to bribe the miserable patriot soldiers, mutinying to collect arrears in pay, encountered the stone wall of the inflexible Scotch-Irish in the Continental army.

The Patriot, Whig, Popular, or Revolutionary Party regarded the surrender of Cornwallis as signifying the triumph of their decentralizing objective. They had defeated the British design of establishing a more vigorous central authority, so offensive to popular and debtor interests. The states began functioning as independent nations. Virginia ratified a treaty with France. Nine of the states had built navies, and all had armies of their own. Most of them laid tariffs and enforced embargoes. All coined money and issued paper currency. This was exactly what the Revolutionary Party wanted, not a central national government. Post-war North Carolina

14 J. F. Jameson, op. cit., p. 25.
15 L. D. Baldwin: The Whiskey Rebels, p. 18.
16 J. F. Jameson, op. cit., p. 143.

presented a typical situation. Lukewarm patriots, uniting with outright Tories, constituted a compact and powerful party that desired to substitute a strong national government as in the old royal regime in order to check popular state governments. Tory refugees, confident of the success of this nationalist movement, came slipping back. The Whigs or Patriots were resolute in the determination that this combination should not get control.[17]

The rank and file of the Patriot Party took no part in the making of the Constitution. Their great leader, Patrick Henry, refused the proffered appointment on the Virginia delegation to the Philadelphia convention, averring that he "smelt a rat." Incidentally, he lacked the cash to defray his expenses at the convention. Consequently, when the framers had completed the document and made it public in the fall of 1787, the "Patriots" promptly focused attention and hostility on the powers delegated to Congress. They who had destroyed the authority of King George in America were determined to prevent the enthronement of King Congress. Leaders of the old Patriot Party such as Samuel Adams of Massachusetts, Melancthon Smith of New York, and Patrick Henry and George Mason of Virginia were convinced that the new fundamental instrument would sacrifice all the Revolution had been fought to win,[18] since the party had been an anti-national movement. The masses were convinced that the ratification of the Constitution would mean "the triumph of the legitimate successors of the Anti-Revolutionary Party of 1775."[19]

We need not picture the common man of 1787 sitting down to study the Constitution. Often he could not read at all. He was more likely to get his information, such as it was, from the emotional harangues of frontier "rabble-rousers." Appeals to prejudice were, if possible, more potent political tactics then than now. It was easy enough to arouse the fears of the "Kennebec squatters" that Massachusetts would summon the

---

[17] W. E. Dodd: "Nathaniel Macon in Southern History," *American Historical Review*, VII, 655.

[18] See R. G. Usher, op. cit., p. 179.

[19] Judge Chamberlain, in *Papers of the American Historical Association*, III, No. 1.

military forces of the new government to evict them.[20] Shays's
"rebels" knew the Constitution was not designed for their
benefit, and nearly a score of them were elected and deliberated as delegates in the Massachusetts ratifying convention.[21]
Delegate John Holmes expressed a majority opinion of the
hinterland when he warned the Massachusetts convention
that the Constitution gave Congress the power to "institute
judicatories" like "that diabolical institution, the Inquisition."
"Racks," he shouted, "and gibbets may be amongst the most
mild instruments of their [Congress'] discipline." [22] Up-state
New Yorkers, whether great landlords or mere yeomen, were
dead set against the threatened shift of the tax burden upon
them if the port duties of New York City were to be diverted
from the state to the Federal Treasury. What kind of opinion
of the new Constitution could the Scotch-Irish of Pennsylvania be expected to hold when every one of the eight Pennsylvania signers of it lived in Philadelphia, that city of sharp-
ers, Shylocks, and oppressors of agrarians? So also the South
Carolina hinterland discovered that all four of their state's
signers were aristocrats of Charleston. And a Baptist preacher
in his backwoods log church, campaigning for election as a
delegate to the North Carolina ratifying convention, shouted
that "the proposed Federal city would be a fortified fortress
of despotism. . . . This, my friends, will be walled or fortified. Here an army of 50,000 or perhaps 100,000 men will be
finally embodied and will sally forth and enslave the people
who will be disarmed." [23] It is indicative of frontier sentiment
that one of his audience who undertook to controvert the
minister's statement narrowly escaped being mobbed.

Any constitution so positively the product of the coastal
communities was bound to be more than suspect to begin
with in the opinion of the congeries of interests constituting
the popular element. A map locating the homes of the signers
of the Constitution reveals the remarkable fact that thirty-

[20] A. E. Morse: The Federalist Party in Massachusetts, pp. 43–4.
[21] See O. G. Libby: Geographical Distribution of the Vote of the Thirteen States on the Federal Constitution, 1787–8, p. 13.
[22] A. J. Beveridge: Life of John Marshall, I, 346.
[23] Ibid., I, 291.

five of the thirty-nine lived adjacent to salt water. The delegates to the ratifying conventions in the several states were elected on the same pattern of inequitable representation as the legislatures, and consequently the regions where the opposition lived were greatly under-represented.[24] It should not be assumed that the back country rose *en masse* against the Constitution. They were, to a large extent, uninformed, misinformed, or ignorant of the new fundamental instrument, and from two thirds to three fourths of those eligible failed to vote for delegates to the state conventions. This, however, did not affect the results, since almost no proponents of the Constitution were elected from the interior. The natural allies of this inland opposition, the mechanics and artisans of the coastal communities, were mostly unenfranchised. On the whole those of the opposition were handicapped by the fact that they were fighting a definite proposal promoted by a powerful set of interests. They had no alternative to offer, but were merely opposed to the Constitution submitted.[25] The advocates of the Constitution, by snatching from the opposition and appropriating the term "Federalists" for themselves, concealed their own consolidating tendency. Thus by "virtue words" and artful propaganda did the pros outwit the cons.[26]

No higher tribute can be paid to the political morality of the Americans of 1787 than the fact that the bitter conflict over ratification in the several states left no irreconcilable groups. It was concerning the new Constitution that Woodrow Wilson wrote: "Indeed, after its organization little more is heard of the party of opposition; they disappear so entirely that one is inclined to think, in looking at the party history of that time, that they had been not only conquered but convinced as well." [27] The Anti-Federalists were never a national party in the true sense of the term. In the several states they had struggled in vain to prevent ratification of the proposed

---

[24] A. M. Simons: *Social Forces in American History*, p. 98.

[25] H. C. Hockett: *Constitutional History of the United States, 1776–1826*, p. 225.

[26] Ibid., p. 256.

[27] *Congressional Government*, p. 2.

Constitution, but had no opportunity then to form a nation-wide combination. However, we must watch these back-country, land-hungry squatters and cultivators of small, grain-growing farms, these hunters and trappers of the Allegheny slopes and transmontane forests, as their fears and animosities mount over the Hamiltonian financial program and as they coalesce into a typical American party.

Hamilton's *Report* on the Public Credit [28] was, on the surface, merely a frank presentation of a proposed program, but agrarians in the House promptly perceived its potential impact on their interests. As the successive proposals — funding the Continental debt, assumption of the state debts, a Bank of the United States, the excise on whisky — were debated and became statutes, the opposition of the agrarians increased and the debates reveal their unconscious search for and gradual discovery of the dogmas suitable as common denominators to combine their heterogeneous interests. Nor was this so difficult since the great planters south of the Potomac no less than yeomanry everywhere were struggling with tax-gatherers and creditors. Virginia tobacco culture had seen its best days years before the Revolution, and the ultimate payment of the pre-Revolutionary debts of the planters to English creditors had apparently been practically required by the treaty of 1783. It was on a common basis as distressed fellow debtors that planter and yeoman saw eye to eye on the Federalist financial legislation.[29] Thus the debtor complex became the most important common characteristic of the groups coalescing into the emerging Jeffersonian Republican Party.

So the agrarians concentrated their attack on the threatening money power. Their first congressional spokesman, Representative James Jackson of Georgia, turning to English history for illustration, pointed out that the English national debt had been established to create a "monied interest in favor of the Prince of Orange in opposition to the landed interest which was supposed to be in favor of the King who had abdicated the throne. I hope there is no such reason existing here;

---

[28] See *supra*, p. 34.
[29] See Richard Hildreth: *History of the United States*, II, 348–50.

our government, I trust, is firmly established without the assistance of stock-jobbers." [30]

Hamilton, however, thought otherwise. His financial proposals were, of course, incomprehensible to agrarians, both great and little, as concepts of the public good. The tobacco-planters not only despised commerce, socially ostracizing "tradesmen," but they had a contempt even for private debts, which obligations they inherited as a matter of course with their declining plantations. Nor had they any less compunction over compounding, if not repudiating, public than private obligations. Creditors in either case were their enemies. The incubus of planter debts to English creditors goes far to explain the anti-English attitude of Virginians. New England was almost as much an obsession to them as old England and for identical reasons — commerce and finance.

No one can understand the vehemence with which the Virginia planters condemned every cardinal feature of the Federalist program who does not first get a clear conception of the peculiar pattern of their economic thought. They were readers of the French Physiocrats, whose dogmas grew out of the experience of the landed nobility of France. There was sufficient similarity between the circumstances of the landed aristocracy of France and that of Virginia to enable the latter to rationalize their own interests in terms of the economic philosophy of the former. "Quesney taught that land was the unique source of wealth. '*C'est donc la terre qui paye tout.*' Human society is divided into the 'productive class' of husbandmen, the 'proprietor class' of renting landlords and the State, and the 'sterile class' of merchants, manufacturers, bankers, and public creditors, parasites on the land. Dr. Price in his *Observations* which might well have served Jefferson as sailing directions, warned Americans against the danger of foreign commerce and banks. And the Abbé de Mably exhorted Georgia to erase the ship from its state seal lest the rising generation be seduced by such ideas of false prosperity." [31]
So it was only natural for Jefferson to suggest that the Ameri-

---

[30] *Annals*, I, p. 1214.
[31] S. E. Morison: *Oxford History of the United States*, I, 158.

can states ought "to practice neither commerce nor navigation but to stand with respect to Europe precisely on the
footing of China." [32] It merely reinforced the Jeffersonian Republicans' prejudices to be able to turn to that French philosophy which held that "the body politic would naturally
comprise as full-fledged citizens only the possessors of landed
property and the large scale farmers who direct it." [33]

These economic doctrines were not mere academic reflections. To the planters they were settled convictions and economic axioms and as such not open to discussion. It did not
matter in the least that these dogmas made "parasites" of
practically all Federalists. So much the better, for they deserved the opprobrious epithet. Without any recourse to
French philosophy, the little agrarians one and all held firmly
the delusion that the farmer was the sole producer. When
Thomas Jefferson in 1782 had seriously written: "Those who
labor in the earth are the chosen people of God, if ever he had
a chosen people," [34] he struck a moral if not a religious keynote for the combination he was to rally a dozen years later.
Here was a common denominator of opinion almost as universally acceptable to the Republicans as it was absurd to the
Federalist interest groups.

The philosopher of the agrarian opposition and ultimately
of Jeffersonian Republicanism was a Virginia planter, John
Taylor of Caroline, whose home became a rendezvous of
Southern Congressmen traveling to and from the sessions. He
outdid even Jefferson in his super-extravagant opinion that
God had "prescribed the agricultural virtues as the means for
. . . admission . . . into heaven." [35] Taylor reached the conclusion that, historically, the masses had always been exploited by the classes, royal, ecclesiastical, or feudal, through
appeals to "loyalty to the throne or altar." He saw Hamilton's
policies creating a new class, through inflated paper, bank
stock, and protective tariffs, by means of slogans of "public

[32] Writings (Ford ed.), IV, 104.
[33] G. Weulersse: "The Physiocrats," Encyclopedia of the Social Sciences,
V, 349.
[34] Notes on the State of Virginia, p. 302.
[35] Quoted by Avery Craven: The Repressible Conflict, p. 22.

faith," "national integrity," and "sacred credit," exploiting
and filching wealth from labor, especially that on land.[36]
"Paper could not rule the nation equitably unless it were distributed proportionally to population. Then Virginia ought to
hold $22,000,000 but had only $1,000,000 in the hands of 100
persons. Massachusetts probably had her proper proportion
but it was held by 1000 individuals. Under paper government
only 100 persons in Virginia have really any political existence." [37] Agrarians were practically unanimous in believing
with Taylor in 1793 that the Federal government was "a class
government in which landlords, merchants and artisans were
not truly represented." [38]

Virginia was the most populous of the states, and when
Hamilton's fiscal policy, built upon the temporarily invincible
Federalist bloc of interests that ran the government, prevailed,
it "bore hard on her spirit to see the scepter of power taken
from her hands." [39] It added insult to injury that, through imposts, debt-free Virginia would pay the assumed debt of less
provident Massachusetts, and moreover pay it ultimately to
sharp speculators who had purchased the securities for a
song and largely from financially pinched agrarians. The
South perceived that, since the bulk of Federal revenue was
from imposts, they contributed far more heavily to the Federal Treasury than economically more self-contained New
England. Thus did the system force "God's chosen people" to
pay tribute to the New England "parasites."

The bank controversy over "expressed," "reserved," "implied," and "resultant" powers obscured for a century and
a quarter the genuinely significant conflict of economic ideologies involved. Southern planters had become hard-money
men, believers in a specie medium of exchange. Had they not
had their experience with paper currency? Jefferson had once

---

[36] See C. A. Beard: *Economic Origins of Jeffersonian Democracy*, Ch.
xiii.

[37] John Taylor: *A Definition of Parties, or the Political Effect of the
Paper System Considered*, p. 5.

[38] C. A. Beard: *Economic Origins of Jeffersonian Democracy*, p. 205.

[39] J. S. Bassett: "The State of Society," *Social and Economic Forces in
American History*, p. 166.

sold a farm to pay a debt and obtained enough to buy an overcoat.[40] And now this Bank of the United States would issue paper currency, which Virginians assumed would again drive specie out of the country, with the attendant distress. Of course bankers too were "parasites," and it was almost impossible to get Virginia to authorize even a state bank.[41] What would Virginians say of a monster central bank, a monopoly chartered under an unexpressed congressional "power," capable of planting its branches within the confines of "sovereign" states to prey upon their citizens? Planter objections were quite naturally expressed in terms of labor. "Banking," wrote the greatest of the Republican philosophers, "in its *best* view is only a fraud whereby labor suffers the imposition of paying an interest upon the circulating medium. . . . The loss is the same, whether a daring robber extorts your property with his pistol at your breast or whether a midnight thief secretly filches it away."[42] That this represented Jefferson's opinion may be gathered from his statement: "Banking establishments are more dangerous than standing armies." The orgy of wild speculation in stock of the Bank of the United States confirmed the conviction of agrarians that Hamilton had fortified the powers that prey upon the virtuous.

Americans had been almost unanimous in their rejoicing over the fall of the Bastille. They interpreted the overthrow of the Old Regime in terms of their own struggle for freedom and independence. But as the tumult of the Parisian mobs grew shrill, American conservatives became at first concerned and then alarmed. The declaration of war on England, the guillotining of many of the nobility, the King, and then the Queen, threw them into a near panic, especially since the American masses applauded each new outrage more vehemently than the last. To make matters worse, there came the officious young French Minister Plenipotentiary Edmond Genêt, who landed at Charleston, South Carolina, and was welcomed with the wildest enthusiasm. There he presided at

[40] J. T. Adams: The Living Jefferson, p. 342.
[41] W. G. Sumner: History of Banking in the United States, p. 20.
[42] John Taylor: An Enquiry into the Principles and Tendency of Certain Public Measures (1794).

the founding of a Jacobin Club and left a trail of new ones behind him as he made his tumultuously triumphant journey to Philadelphia, where another club was founded within the week of his arrival.

The French war against England had raised the question of our treaty obligation to defend her West Indian possessions. The lack of an American navy rendered this academic, whether or not the treaty required it. Washington's neutrality proclamation nevertheless created a storm of resentment on the part of the "Gallo-maniacs" because it defeated the French hope of using our harbors as bases for privateering. Vice President Adams said that "ten thousand people in the streets of Philadelphia, day after day, threatened to drag Washington out of his house and effect a revolution in the government, or compel it to declare war in favor of the French Revolution and against England"; and in his opinion only the yellow-fever epidemic frustrated their purpose.[43] Judges, however, were intimidated against enforcing neutrality. The Jacobin Club of Boston encouraged the French consul to defy the United States marshal there and instigated a piratical attack by the frigate *La Concorde* on a merchant vessel owned by Federalists.[44] General Anthony Wayne from the trackless wilderness of the Northwest reported that the baneful French leaven, fermenting in his legion, threatened its discipline.[45]

Nor should these Jacobin clubs be dismissed as mere exotic organizations. Americans had developed the habit of almost spontaneous organization since early in the pre-Revolution controversy with the British ministry. Committees of correspondence had sprung up in many communities as early as 1763, but became a continent-wide network on the eve of open hostilities. Township committees corresponded with one another, usually within the county. Members of the local committee formed a county committee, as is frequently the case today when the local precinct party committeemen collectively constitute the county central committee. Our pres-

---

[43] *Works*, X, 47–8.
[44] See S. E. Morison: *Harrison Gray Otis*, I, 50.
[45] A. E. Morse: *The Federalist Party in Massachusetts*, p. 68n.

ent party organization is the lineal descendant of the Revolutionary committees of correspondence.[46] The Revolutionary county committees of correspondence communicated with one another throughout the province and had provincial committees in touch with each other throughout the thirteen colonies or states. The Continental Congress was considered a grand committee of the whole system, thus completing what has been called the "Revolutionary machine." By extra-legal methods the local committees enforced the policies of the Continental Congress.[47]

As long as Washington remained available for the presidency, the opposition could not hope to capture control of the government. Late in Washington's first term, however, Jefferson was already unostentatiously arousing the masses, mobilizing, drilling, and leading them so successfully that Fisher Ames expressed the Federalist concern with the observation: "The discipline of the party [Jefferson's] is as severe as the Prussian and deserters are not spared." [48] This meant that the superb Virginia politician was busy with the courthouse cliques, organizing them on the familiar pattern of the revolutionists of the 1770's. With characteristic secrecy the sage of Monticello gathered Virginia leaders at his home whenever court brought them to the neighborhood and his purpose would therefore not be suspected.[49] Soon the Jeffersonians, in contrast with the Federalists, had a network of organizations extending throughout the land.[50]

It was the whisky excise that brought party conflict to the verge of civil war. Excepting the very few able to bribe the Spanish officials after running the gantlet of hostile Indians along the river banks, Western grain-growers found the Mississippi River closed to them. They solved the problem of transportation by concentrating twenty-four bushels of rye

46 See H. J. Ford: *The Rise and Growth of American Politics*, p. 68.

47 See American Historical Association *Reports* 1901, I, 257.

48 Quoted by Claude Bowers: *Jefferson and Hamilton*, p. 151.

49 W. E. Dodd: *Statesmen of the Old South*, p. 49; Edward Channing: *History of the United States*, IV, 224.

50 See Jesse Macy: *Political Parties in the United States, 1846–1861*, pp. 32–3.

into sixteen gallons of whisky, which, in two eight-gallon kegs, could be packed on a horse to the East, where "Monongahela rye" commanded double the price at Pittsburgh. In the West it passed as currency, even the good minister's salary being paid in "old Monongahela rye." [51] Hamilton's serene assumption that this excise was merely a tax on a luxury erred doubly. To the typical pioneer whisky was considered a "necessity" as well as a medium of exchange. It was his means of paying for the absolutely necessary iron, salt, and other things the frontiersman could not produce. Then, too, the excise-collector demanded "cash" — that is, specie — while whisky itself was the frontiersman's "cash." Thus the excise seemed to be a tax on money itself. Every autumn a packhorse train wound eastward from each neighborhood with whisky, furs, and skins to be traded for salt and iron. On the trip they visited friends, gathered political gossip, and brought home news of political developments. [52]

Hamilton had been warned that the whisky tax would embitter the West, but he persisted and had his way with Congress. Not only did it array the West against the East, but it set the little against the big distiller, who seemed to be favored by the Federalist excise. The large distillers welcomed the whisky tax because it would cut out the competition of small distillers who could not afford to pay the tax and who were thus compelled to use the plant of the large distiller. [53] This accounts for the mobs wrecking the larger stills whose owners had paid the tax. Lawyers who aided the big distillers came in for their share of condemnation and persecution.

The excise was one more count of the frontiersman against the hated East. We have already seen that the tax served as protection for the rum of New England manufactured by Federalists. [54] Moreover, the Eastern farmer who bought his whisky instead of making it did not consciously encounter the inquisitorial tax. [55] The West wanted the burden of taxation

---

[51] L. D. Baldwin: *The Whiskey Rebels*, pp. 25–6.
[52] Ibid., pp. 11–12.
[53] H. M. Brackenridge: *History of the Western Insurrection*, p. 17.
[54] *Supra*, p. 45.
[55] See F. L. Paxson: *The American Frontier*, p. 106.

put on land instead of consumption, but the political weight of the big landowners prevented this.[56]

That the Whisky Rebellion vitalized latent opposition to the Federalist interests is evident from the malcontents' prompt perception of the connection between the excise and the assumption of state debts. Nothing could shake their conviction that the tax was laid at the behest of speculators in state securities and big property-owners, eager to shift the burden of the assumption of state debts to the shoulders of consumers and little agrarians.[57] They saw their specie drained away to the East for the benefit of speculators and manufacturers. Nor did they need the aid of French Physiocrats to convince them that they were being made tributary to "parasites."

Was this what the Scotch-Irish had fought the Revolution to achieve? The West had poured out the blood of its men, women, and children, they argued, and now the fruits of victory were accruing to the despised moneyed class of the East.[58] It was an egregious Federalist blunder to have appointed as excise-inspector of western Pennsylvania General John Neville, a conspicuous speculator in the securities of the funded debt. Apparently the conqueror was coming in person to extort tribute from the vanquished. Committees of correspondence, the traditional organs of American revolutionists, sprang up in the disaffected regions of western Pennsylvania where some five thousand stills, one fourth of the total in the United States, were concentrated. Stills of owners paying the tax were wrecked and General Neville's home was sacked. Thus were the Federalist Party and the government itself defied. Hamilton gleefully urged military suppression on the reluctant President, seeking thereby to fix the stigma of disloyalty upon the opposition party and thus to convict Gallatin and Brackenridge of treason.[59] So would the "democratic societies" be smashed in Pennsylvania and discredited everywhere.

---

[56] L. D. Baldwin, op. cit., p. 10.
[57] Ibid., p. 67.
[58] See ibid., p. 3.
[59] Russel J. Ferguson: *Early Western Pennsylvania Politics*, pp. 126–9.

The army of 15,000 militiamen pillaged and ravaged their way westward, finding no insurrection, but almost creating one by their conduct. Citizens merely wanted as witnesses were seized in their beds and marched through the snow to concentration camps. That captured prisoners were taken to Philadelphia and paraded before hooting mobs did not sweeten Western feeling for Easterners or win Federalist recruits any more than did Hamilton's insistence upon executions. Slipping Federalist prestige was momentarily enhanced in other sections but in the long run it proved to be a Pyrrhic victory. The wild predictions made when ratification of the Constitution was pending that the Federal government was being created to use military force against the people seemed to the whole back country to be realized. Hamilton had more than shaken the mailed fist; he had used it against the agrarians, and they never forgot it.

The whisky rebels, however, had learned their lesson. Direct action is not the American way of solving a problem of policy, for it alienates important elements in society. Instead the agrarians resolved as never before to persevere in their determination to oust from the seats of authority the dominant interests, take possession of the Federal government themselves, and administer it in their own interest. We shall see how this was done under the leadership of Thomas Jefferson at the head of the Republican Party.

Hamilton had perceived precisely the motivating means by which to unify the non-agrarian interests — the "rich, the well born and the good" — already the ruling class in their several communities. In this he was scarcely pioneering, for he followed the old familiar pattern of British political practices. Utterly different was Jefferson's problem. Despite conspicuous exceptions, it was chiefly the less prosperous, the unprivileged, and even the unenfranchised he was to combine into a party, and for this project no precedents were at hand. How the creative genius of our first indigenous politician-statesman devised the means for the making of a genuinely American party constitutes, as we shall see, a fascinating episode of our party history.

CHAPTER IV

THE JEFFERSONIAN REPUBLICANS

"Jefferson had captured Henry's party in Virginia, rejuvenated it, formed allies for it in the Carolina upcountry and then made it national. And it was this growing section of the South, the populous border region, now spread into Tennessee and Kentucky and Ohio, Presbyterians, Baptists and Methodists, considered in denominational terminology, that contributed the ideals which made Jefferson's first four years unparalleled in American history and which caused his policy to prevail even in New England." W. E. Dodd.*

Thomas Jefferson was but the first of the succession of notable political chieftains American society has produced through the opportunity it affords a leader first to become the spokesman of the interests and ideals of a section and then, by means of intersectional and intergroup understandings, to build up a winning national following.[1] The son of a pioneer settler of one of the western counties of Virginia, young Jefferson grew up among frontier democrats, small proprietors, clad in buckskin breeches, Indian moccasins, coonskin caps, and hunting shirts without coats. After being tutored by a frontier Presbyterian schoolmaster he entered William and Mary College at seventeen, where he won the unique distinction of being regarded the homeliest youth in the school. Until he started for Williamsburg he had never seen a collection of houses that could be called a village, and to his dying day he remained a "western man with eastern polish." His sympathies were never with the great planters who aped the

---

* *Statesmen of the Old South,* p. 54. By permission of The Macmillan Company, publishers.
[1] Cf. F. J. Turner: *Sections in American History,* p. 183.

English squires, but with the farmers, trappers, and hunters of the western counties, whose cause he championed so effectively as never to be forgiven by the salt-water aristocracy. Yet as a great planter himself he possessed an essential qualification for leadership of the gentry along with the humbler elements of the old Anti-Federalist combination.

Jefferson, then, emerged out of that inland democratic society of which Hamilton and the Federalists generally were only faintly aware and whose dynamic character they certainly never accurately appraised. As a practical politician Jefferson started with Patrick Henry's party in Virginia, which had fallen into his hands, and to this he managed to attach the fierce democracy of the back country of the Carolinas.[2] These Southern backwoodsmen, Scotch-Irish Presbyterians and German Lutherans, had migrated, often *en masse*, through the Appalachian valleys from distant Pennsylvania. The new upland cotton-raisers of the Carolinas were making common cause politically with these newcomers, and the religious fundamentalism of the inlanders gave them at least one bond of union with their aristocratic coastal enemies in that they all hated change. A distinguished publicist laments that "this coastal aristocracy voted for Jefferson, thereby completing the pattern which has plagued the Democratic party to this day."[3] For better or for worse, such are the patterns of the party combinations that American social forces have almost automatically produced throughout the history of our major parties.

Before the end of the century the non-slaveholding surplus population of these Southern backwoods communities was already pouring through Cumberland Gap into Tennessee, Kentucky, and southern Ohio and populating new communities with ardent Jeffersonians. Federalists had established the Marietta and Cincinnati nuclei in Ohio, and as late as 1799 the territorial legislature cast only five dissenting votes against a complimentary address to President Adams. Presently the migration from the south across the Ohio River

---

[2] See *supra*, p. 56.
[3] Herbert Agar: *The Pursuit of Happiness*, p. 67.

had so changed their political complexion that in 1804 Marietta went Republican by a large majority, the Federalists in sheer despair casting blank ballots.[4] In the very sparsely settled new state of Ohio the Federalists had only 364 of the 2,957 votes cast for President in 1804.[5]

Hamilton's financial program had alienated most of the great Southern planters from the group combination that produced the Constitution. Speculation in securities was especially reprehensible in their eyes, although almost none of them had any compunction of conscience against speculating in land, obtained through governmental favors and constituting the only other type of property subject to great fluctuations in value.[6] Of course they had no sympathy with the piedmont statesmanship which had proclaimed the equalitarian doctrines of the Declaration of Independence and given them practical application in the abolition of primogeniture and the disestablishment of the church in Virginia. Consequently the union of tidewater planter and inland farmer was not a natural one and persisted only because the gentry provided most of the leadership and the issues of radical democracy were not stressed by the Virginia dynasty. This arrangement satisfied the planters, whose "ideal was an agricultural community settled in its habits and steady in its ways, requiring no more apparatus of government than would suffice to subject the common people to the magisterial supervision of their natural protectors — the landed gentry." [7] This was a type of "democracy" that the planter, with his slaves forever disfranchised, could easily accept. Recognizing the superior cultural equipment of the gentry, the lesser agrarians generally accepted their leadership in the common cause of battling mercantile capitalism.

"In Pennsylvania," wrote Albert Gallatin, its leading Republican statesman, "not only have we neither Livingston nor Rensselaer, but from the suburbs of Philadelphia to the banks

    4 H. C. Hockett: "Federalism in the West," Turner Essays in American History, pp. 124, 127.
    5 C. O. Paullin: Atlas of Historical Geography of the United States, p. 93.
    6 See J. S. Bassett: The Federalist System, p. 45.
    7 H. J. Ford: The Rise and Growth of American Politics, pp. 103–4.

of the Ohio I do not know a single family that has any extensive influence. An equal distribution of property has rendered every individual independent, and there is among us true and real equality." Here is but another illustration of the principle that America is politically democratic because it first became economically democratic through the wide dispersion of the ownership of land, again confirming the opinion of Aristotle that the form of the state is chiefly determined by the character and distribution of the ownership of property. Pennsylvania, indeed, set the pattern of the social and political character of the Northwest Territory, and Gallatin's description of it might have applied to the whole Northwest a generation or two later. So thoroughly democratic was Pennsylvania that it supported the party of Jefferson and then of Jackson until the Civil War, excepting the candidacies of W. H. Harrison and Zachary Taylor.

The frontier environment of New York was no less potent than that of the South in producing Jeffersonian Republicans and indeed converting migrating Federalists to the democratic faith. New England settlers swung the state to the Federalists only until they became conditioned by their frontier environment, whereupon they too became Jeffersonians. The frontier within New England had a set of interests and a consequent climate of opinion that inclined its inhabitants strongly to Jeffersonian Republicanism. The party strength lay in an irregular belt extending across northern New England and interrupted by Federalist regions where river communications fostered commercial interests. The interior of Maine, northern and central New Hampshire, the Green Mountains of Vermont, and the Berkshires of Massachusetts were inland Republican areas.[8]

The New England Republican was anti on a long list of issues, but primarily as a debtor. He depended for credit on the village store, whose proprietor owed the seaboard merchant, who imported on credit from the English exporter.[9] Much of the farmer's animosity was accordingly directed

---

[8] W. A. Robinson: *Jeffersonian Democracy in New England*, p. 169.
[9] Kendall's *Travels*, II, 289. Quoted by W. A. Robinson, op. cit., p. 100.

against the ultimate British creditor, and the New England agrarian, as befitted a Jeffersonian, was decidedly anti-British, fortified in this attitude by the tradition of Lexington, Concord, and Bunker Hill.

New England agrarians hated the navy and on this count also fitted into the Republican Party. It made the merchants a privileged class at the expense of the people who paid for it in taxes. "To the farmer it is of no importance who brings his merchandise" sounds like a sentence from a philippic of John Randolph, the Virginia planter, but it is extracted from a New England Republican newspaper of 1807.[10] No less than Virginia planters did these Republicans consider their political opponents "parasites." A Republican address to Connecticut voters in 1798 declared that "there are two classes of people, the mechanics and farmers who produce goods for the community and others living by cunning — merchants, speculators, priests, lawyers and government employees." [11] Perhaps in a bid for the votes of urban artisans and mechanics this economic doctrine goes a step beyond that of Virginia since it admits non-agrarians to the producing class.

It was charged that the banks were utilized as Federalist instrumentalities to compel conformity to the policies of the owners of capital.[12] Agrarian bitterness against lawyers had persisted since Shays's Rebellion, and very few of that profession were Republicans. The judiciary was considered completely under Federalist control. Joseph Story, a Jeffersonian Republican until, as a Justice of the Supreme Court, he fell under the spell of Marshall, could testify how difficult it was for a Republican jurist in eastern Massachusetts. In 1806 the *American Mercury* pretty completely catalogued Republican antipathies, maintaining that Connecticut Federalism "had secured in its interests the college, the clergy, the bar, the monied institutions, the religious and literary societies and most of the press. It has complete annual control over the military and judiciary departments." [13]

10 Quoted from *American Mercury* by W. A. Robinson, op. cit., p. 100.
11 Ibid., p. 111.
12 Ibid., p. 103.
13 W. A. Robinson, op. cit., p. 110.

In sectarian terms the New England Republicans were Baptist, Presbyterian, Methodist, and other dissenters seeking to break the hold of the established Congregational Church on politics and secure religious freedom and they accordingly looked to the leadership of Jefferson the disestablisher. Their antipathy extended to Harvard and Yale, especially the former because of its "heretical" teachings and Unitarian leanings. Congregational ministers had damaged their prestige by pro-British sympathy, and from 1795 until after the War of 1812 complaints on this score came from the Republicans. The sectarian connection with party politics is strikingly illustrated by the fact that, when the New Hampshire statesman William Plumer rejected Calvinism and was converted to the Baptist faith, he rejected Federalism and became a Republican. Under the circumstances the Episcopalians paradoxically became dissenters, and Turner pointed out that the key to the internal policies of New England during this era was the alliance between the Episcopalians and other dissenters against the established clergy and the Federalists.[14]

New England Republicans were bidding for allies among the urban mechanics and laborers, whose emerging class consciousness was already finding expression in strikes. Here were the tumultuous elements that flocked into the Jacobin clubs of the cities. Nantucket, Cape Cod, Portsmouth, Salem, and Marblehead, sailor towns, showed a tendency toward Republicanism; Federalist merchant-shipowners may have been disposed to tolerate the British capture of ships of neutrals, but not so the sailors who manned the vessels and keenly resented impressment.

How did Jefferson knit these scattered and none too congruous elements into a single party? On many matters leader and followers were poles apart. While he hated war, his frontier partisans, particularly the Scotch-Irish, were eager for it. A free-thinker and a deist, he was the idol of religious fundamentalists whose descendants today legislate "evolution" out

---

[14] A. B. Hart (editor): *Social and Economic Forces in American History*, p. 196.

of the public schools. Illiterate backwoodsmen saw in this scholarly gentleman the messiah of a democratic faith. Here was indeed a statesman who believed that most farmers, whether great or small, are honest and that most other people are not, and, moreover, that England is not to be trusted. This was the common point of union in every faction of Jeffersonian Republicanism.

Like all our major political parties this earliest one to organize constituted a loose federation of local parties. Without precedents to guide him, Jefferson set out to negotiate the necessary connections and understanding among them. In 1791, accompanied by Madison, he had made the famous "botanizing" excursion to New York State out of which grew the alliance between the planters of Virginia and the professional politicians of New York, among whom was Aaron Burr, leader of the Sons of Tammany. This intersectional entente set the practically permanent pattern of the party. These two statesmen-politicians extended their journey into New England, conferred with state leaders, and knit the local followings into the Republican coalition. When, in the presidential election of 1792, electors in several Southern states, after indicating their choice of Washington for President, cast their second votes for George Clinton, we have evidence that Jefferson's and Madison's "excursion" was bearing its legitimate fruit. National party management was emerging. By 1800 the Republican intention to support a Virginian, Jefferson, for President and a New Yorker, Burr, for Vice President resulted in a demonstration of party regularity almost disastrous in the tie vote produced.

Let no one assume that two organized parties, Federalists and Republicans, had faced each other in 1796 on the issue of Jay's treaty. So ill-defined were parties as yet that Jefferson, expecting a tie vote in the electoral college, and election by the House of Representatives, wrote to Madison: "in that case, I pray you and authorize you fully, to solicit on my behalf that Mr. Adams may be preferred . . . let those come to the helm who think they can steer clear of the difficulties. I have no confidence in myself for the undertaking." [15] Indeed, the election seemed more like a contest between the pro-French and the pro-English than a presidential campaign between Republicans and Federalists. The French Minister, Adet, toured New England in support of Jefferson, assuring Republicans the French would never abandon them, while they in turn urged France to continue destroying American commerce in order to force merchants to support Jefferson. Incidentally Jefferson considered the carrying trade in belligerent goods an illegitimate business that deserved to be pillaged by French privateers. Adet went so far as to publish letters in the Republican journal the *Aurora* giving the American people to understand they must either elect Jefferson or prepare for a French war. He hoped thereby to steer Pennsylvania Quakers into the Republican ranks.

The magic spell France had cast over the Republicans was suddenly broken by President Adams's coup in submitting to Congress in April 1798 the report of our commissioners to France on the sensational X Y Z affair. These envoys had sought to compose the differences between the United States and France and to restore the diplomatic relations broken off by France when that nation learned of Jay's treaty. Simulating a hesitancy to reveal the contents of the commissioners' report, the wily Federalists had lured the Republican Congressmen into a trap — the introduction of a resolution demanding publication of the report. As the news spread throughout the land that the French Directory had required a bribe as a preliminary to opening negotiations, a roar of indignation arose and Americans almost unanimously became anti-French. French flags, cockades, and customs suddenly vanished and both Congress and the President prepared for war. That autumn the Federalists made marked gains in the congressional and state elections.

Then the Federalists proceeded to enact statutes that betrayed not only their ruling-class consciousness but even their conviction of the illegitimacy of political parties. The Alien

15 *Writings* (Ford ed.), VII, 91 ff.

and Sedition Acts were designed to suppress Republican editors and pamphleteers of French, British, and Irish nativity — "foreign liars," the Federalists called them. One New England Federalist sojourning in Pennsylvania wrote home of the numerous Irish there as "the most God provoking Democrats on this side of Hell." The Federalists were, in fact, a nativist party, and immigrants naturally gravitated to the party of the underdog and opposition to the government. Republican politicians were already learning to court their favor, a practice of which the Federalists were inherently incapable. They decided instead "to strike the evil at its roots and destroy the foreign vote." [16] So the period of residence required for naturalization was increased from five to fourteen years, during which period the President was empowered to deport any alien he judged to be "dangerous to the peace and safety of the United States." Having provided for subduing the aliens, the fatuous Federalists turned to the native Republicans and, in the Sedition Act, provided for fines and imprisonment as penalties for seditious utterances or writings against the President or Congress. Such latitude did this afford the courts that partisan Federalist judges applied it with savage severity against Republicans for relatively innocent remarks.

How were the Republicans to defend themselves against such an arbitrary exercise of legislative and judicial power? Since Congress had not even been delegated power to enact the Sedition Act, but the first amendment even forbade "abridging the freedom of speech, or of the press," Republicans promptly denounced the act as unconstitutional. But how convert this opinion into an authoritative determination? The Supreme Court had not yet established judicial annulment and, in any case, its personnel consisted of Federalists, some of whom on circuit had applied the act with extreme severity, accompanied with stump speeches from the bench under the guise of charges to the jury. Jefferson and his colleagues began groping for a way to counteract

16 S. E. Morison: *Harrison Gray Otis*, I, 108.

congressional "tyranny," and the outcome was the Virginia and Kentucky Resolutions.

The Republicans needed a device for appealing to public opinion, later to be supplied by party platforms. They resorted to the not altogether new practice of resolutions by state legislatures, and Virginia passed a set protesting against the obnoxious statutes. It was planned to have the legislature of South Carolina pass similar ones, but the elections following the X Y Z outrage had given the Federalists too much strength there, and the Kentucky legislature instead was used. Both sets of resolutions declared the Alien and Sedition Acts unconstitutional and proposed a method of challenging the execution of Federal statutes deemed invalid. The then novel theory was advanced that the Constitution was a compact between sovereign states. These constituted the principals, whose agent the Federal government was. Whenever the agent exceeded the authority delegated, each state, according to the Kentucky Resolutions, or "the states," according to those of Virginia, may determine the remedy and apply it. These resolutions were in the nature of what would today be called "trial balloons." It had been hoped that the legislatures of the sister states would concur and a decisive check be thus established against Federal "usurpations" of power. Instead only seven states replied at all, and those unanimously to the effect that the Federal statutes questioned were constitutional. This, however, was no referendum indicating current popular opinion since the legislatures reject. ing the resolutions were of a Federalist complexion representing the early reaction against the French in the fall elections of 1798.

The Virginia and Kentucky Resolutions became the political bible of the Jeffersonians by 1800, and for a generation the undisputed articles of faith of the overwhelming majority of Americans.[17] Let it be remembered that they came respectively from the pens of the "Father of the Constitution" and the author of the Declaration of Independence. Since they

---

[17] See Henry Adams: *John Randolph*, p. 35.

reversed the Federalist pattern of constitutional theory, Henry Adams wittily declared: "The Constitution of the Republican party was the Federalist Constitution read backwards, like a mediæval invocation of the devil." [18] At any rate Americans had again become involved in a domestic issue and had, for the moment, forgotten to think of themselves as pro-English or pro-French, which was no small gain.

The preparations against France might have been called Hamilton's war, so much did he have his heart set on hostilities. As the march of fifteen thousand armed men against the whisky rebels had once before revived the declining fortunes of the Federalist Party, so might a war with France give it a new stimulus. Emulating the then rising Corsican corporal, Hamilton by letters conveyed his desires to Congressmen: War with France by the summer of 1798, a permanent standing army, and the invasion of the bordering Spanish possessions, Florida and Louisiana. Then, in co-operation with the Venezuelan patriot Francisco de Miranda, the allied American army and British fleet would liberate Spanish America and annex Florida and Louisiana as our share of the conquests. With such magnificent trophies would another Bonaparte return in triumph. The wavering West, grateful for a Mississippi River freed at last, would be securely attached, not only to the United States, but to their benefactors, the Federalists. Thus would the Jeffersonians again be discomfited, as in 1794, and the rule of "the rich, the wellborn and the good" be firmly re-established. Suddenly, however, President Adams made an incredible *volte-face* that completely blasted the dream. Without consulting party leaders he decided on peace and resumed diplomatic relations with France. Hamilton, in the bitterness of his disappointment, turned on Adams and thereby disrupted the already tottering Federalist Party with factional bickering.

Even the unfought war gave the Republicans the campaign issue of Federal expenses needlessly doubled in four years. The direct tax on land and houses, graduated according to

---

[18] Henry Adams: *John Randolph*, p. 57.

the number of windows, provoked Pennsylvanians into an insurrection led by John Fries, who was apprehended, tried, convicted of treason, and pardoned by the President. Southern planters felt keenly the tax of fifty cents a head on slaves. Since wealth in securities, shipping, mercantile establishments, and factories absolutely escaped taxation, the "parasitic" Federalists had simply exempted their own peculiar types of wealth and as usual loaded the burden on the agrarians. Even that partisan Federalist, Gouverneur Morris, admitted that the "Democrats and their demagogues have had just complaint of the manner in which money is raised; and our expenditures are so far from economical that no applause is expected on that score." [19] Adams's courageous decision for peace worked against the Federalists, since it enabled the Republicans to argue that the obnoxious taxes had never been necessary.

As the presidential election approached, the score against the luckless Federalists steadily mounted. A typical instance will illustrate their shortsightedness in using the Sedition Act even in Republican territory. Jedediah Peck, an unlettered upcountry New Yorker, because he had circulated a petition for the repeal of the Alien and Sedition Acts, was arrested at the instigation of Judge Cooper (Father of the novelist) and carried two hundred miles through disaffected territory to New York City for trial on the eve of state and national elections. "A hundred missionaries, in the cause of democracy," wrote J. D. Hammond, a contemporary New Yorker, "stationed between New York and Cooperstown, could not have done so much for the Republican cause as this journey of Jedediah Peck from Otsego to the capital of the state." [20] Aaron Burr missed no opportunity to make capital out of this *faux pas*, and New York for various reasons never cast another electoral vote for a Federalist candidate.

President Adams attributed the loss of Pennsylvania and consequently the election of 1800 to General Washington's refusal in 1798 to grant an officer's commission to the Penn-

---

[19] *Life and Correspondence of Rufus King*, III, 252.
[20] *History of Political Parties in the State of New York*, p. 132.

sylvania pastor-politician and Revolutionary general Peter Muhlenberg, whose prestige in Pennsylvania was second only to Washington's. "And what was the consequence?" asked Adams, and then answered his own question. "These two Muhlenbergs [Peter and Frederick] addressed the public with their names both in English and German, with invective against the administration and warm recommendations of Mr. Jefferson. . . . The Muhlenbergs turned the whole body of the Germans, great numbers of the Irish, and many of the English. . . ." [21]

Republican campaign tactics in 1800 were shrewdly adapted to section and interest. Propaganda was scarcely needed among the lesser agrarians and the frontiersmen. The great planters were gently reminded that the Republican leader was himself a slaveholder. Jefferson shrewdly toned down his earlier strictures concerning the "mobs of great cities" who "add just so much to the support of pure government, as sores do to the strength of the human body." [22] "I had in mind," he explained, "the manufacturers [laborers] of the old countries, at the present time, with whom the want of food and clothing necessary to sustain life, has begotten a depravity of morals." [23] It may have been unnecessary, many mechanics of Boston, New York, Philadelphia, and Baltimore having already been impressed by Jefferson's attack on the "aristocracy of wealth." Certainly the vituperation of the New England clergy and press served only to reinforce the faith of the underdog in the Republican leader.

The Republican candidates, Thomas Jefferson and Aaron Burr, tied in the electoral college, and the House of Representatives had to elect the President. It might be recalled that this was, of course, a lame duck House and, moreover, a Federalist one elected in the heat of the anti-French hysteria. There was considerable Federalist conspiring to elect Burr, who did indeed receive the vote of every New England congressional delegation except one, which was evenly divided.

---

21 *Works*, IX, 633–4.
22 *Notes on the State of Virginia* (1782), p. 302.
23 *Writings* (Ford ed.), III, 269.

Burr, however, refused resolutely to come to any advance understanding with the Federalist leaders, while they obtained from Jefferson his views and were sufficiently satisfied finally not to obstruct his election.

If, as has been said, "New England Federalism was not so much a body of political doctrines as a state of mind," [24] certainly it must have been almost a pathological one. Chief Justice Ellsworth in a charge to a Massachusetts grand jury had denounced "the French system mongers, from the quintumvirate at Paris to the Vice President [Jefferson] and the minority in Congress as apostles of atheism and anarchy, bloodshed and plunder." No wonder nervous women hid their Bibles before the new President could confiscate them. Fisher Ames was convinced that unless the popular movement could be checked we would soon see here what he pictured in his mind's eye in the mobs in France, "the dismal glare of their burnings and scent of the loathsome steam of human victims offered in sacrifice." [25] And while his "health was poor, if the Jacobins made haste he might yet live to be hanged." Timothy Dwight, in July 1801, saw the "country governed by blockheads and knaves," and as a consequence "the ties of marriage . . . severed; our wives and daughters thrown into the stews; our children cast into the world from the breast and forgotten, filial piety extinguished." [26]

Much of the outcry against Jefferson was symptomatic of the fact that the power of established Congregationalism, practically synonymous with New England Federalism, was slipping. Blind to the social forces that were transforming American society, these churchmen preferred a simplified explanation, a personal devil, and Jefferson served them perfectly for this purpose. Unquestionably the class cleavage in New England was intensified at the turn of the century. Federalists and Republicans avoided each other on the street and in society, and they even had their separate taverns. The Federalists, for the time being, constituted an irreconcilable

---

[24] Allen Johnson, *Union and Democracy*, p. 161.
[25] Henry Adams: *History of the United States*, I, 83.
[26] *An Oration* (Hartford, 1801), p. 26.

minority. The persistence of such a dissident group threatened not only the permanence of the Union but the integrity of society itself. They had, however, an economic power and prestige that could not be ignored by the Republicans.

That Jefferson possessed the prescience to perceive the peril is one of the fortunate accidents of American history. Certainly he understood the Federalists better than they understood either themselves or the Republicans. Once in power, he manifested an acute awareness of the fact that Federalists no less than Republicans constituted part of his nation-wide constituency. Hence the statement in his inaugural address that astonished political friend and foe alike: "We are all Republicans, we are all Federalists." Yet it was a Republican document so universal in its statement of fundamental principles that it stands to this day second only to Lincoln's Gettysburg Address as a classic statement of the democratic faith. Federalists searched its sentences in vain for any sign of an attack on their interests. That staunch old Federalist, Henry Knox, Washington's Secretary of War, was impelled to congratulate the new President on his address. "The great extent of our country and the different manners of the respective parts claim forcibly the superintendence and direction of an enlarged mind to consolidate the interests and affections. And if you should happily affect [sic] this much to be desired object an imperishable fame will be attached to your character." Jefferson confided to a private correspondent the main purpose of his conciliatory address — to win back the Republicans stampeded to the Federalists by the hysteria of 1798.

The inaugural pledge of the "honest payment of our debts and the sacred preservation of the public faith; encouragement of agriculture and of commerce as its handmaid," gratified Federalists at the recognition of commerce even as a "handmaid," and the subordination of commerce no doubt pleased agrarians. Hamilton, who had advised Federalist Congressmen to support Jefferson rather than Burr because of his essential conservatism, regarded the inaugural "as virtually a candid retraction of past misapprehensions, and a pledge to the community that the new President will not lend himself to dangerous innovations, but in essential points tread in the steps of his predecessors." The paradox in Jefferson that made him peculiarly fitted to rule during the transition from a merchant-capitalistic to an agrarian regime is aptly put by Beard: "His academic views assiduously circulated by his partisans pleased the temper of the agrarian masses and his practical politics propitiated rather than alienated the capitalistic interests." [27]

Visitors at the executive mansion, however, promptly detected a shift from the Massachusetts climate of opinion to that of Virginia. No longer was a national debt a national blessing, but rather, as seen through agrarian eyes, a mortgage; the more promptly paid, the sooner the emancipation from the sinister power of the money-lender. So government expenditures were reduced $3,700,000 a year, leaving a revenue surplus of $7,000,000 each year to be applied to the debt. Mountaineers were rewarded with the repeal of the whisky excise. Political prisoners serving sentences under the detested Alien and Sedition Acts were promptly pardoned. Agrarian fear of militarism, aroused by the recent preparations, was allayed by the reduction of the standing army to a mere Republican "police force" of 2,500 men. All the ships of the navy excepting thirteen were sold, but those remaining were presently used with startling vigor to protect American commerce from Tripolitan pirates, a reversal of the tribute-paying practice of the Federalists and altogether disconcerting to the commerce-hating Republicans.

Something more than Jefferson's desire to placate dissident Federalists checked the execution of the Republican program. No matter how well they cohered as an opposition, once in power the party group combination demonstrated Madison's principle that a nation-wide majority can agree only on a moderate program. The extremists, for example, would have abolished the mint and used only foreign coins, since even the one national coin in common use, the copper cent, was

---

[27] *Economic Origins of Jeffersonian Democracy*, p. 467.

a perpetual reminder of national supremacy over state "sovereignty." The "midnight judges" created by Congress and the President after the election and designed to pack the judiciary with Federalists were promptly disposed of. But Republican coherence broke and failure of conviction resulted in the impeachment of Supreme Court Justice Samuel Chase, despite his having gone so far in a sedition trial as to require the striking from the jury panel of "any of those creatures or persons called democrats." [28] The break in Republican discipline was never fully repaired and the insecurity of the artificial alliance between Virginia and New York was evident enough. The Northern non-agrarian Republicans feared the charge of revolutionary attacks on the Constitution too much to tamper with the judiciary. Jay's treaty was left intact and New England fishermen were not deprived of their bounties.

Once in power, the Republicans never molested the sources of danger at which they had trembled as the party of the "outs." In contrast with his predecessors, whose autocracy he had criticized, Jefferson was the first President to begin an administration as the unchallenged master not only of the executive but even of the legislative branch, through personal partisans as Speaker of the house and chairmen of congressional committees. Apparently the "people's President" could do no wrong. At any rate so it appeared to the fuming Federalists. Nor need the Constitution any longer be so strictly construed now that its real friends were in power. Annexing Louisiana looked especially unconstitutional to Federalists since doubling the area of the West merely meant so much more of the environment that converted even their own migrating children into Jeffersonians. Moreover, the annexation played havoc with the doctrine of state rights and compelled Jeffersonians to eat millions of their own words against "consolidation" and the national sovereignty inherent in the treaty-making power used for that purpose. Even more inconsistent was the Republican legislation to enforce the embargo, which Henry Jones Ford considered "a greater interference with

---

[28] Morison and Commager, op. cit., p. 293.

the ordinary privileges of citizens than would have been necessary in exercise of the war powers." [29]

The Federalists approached the election of 1804 with the forlorn hope of capturing the consolation prize of the vice-presidency in the confusion of the "blind" voting required by the original Constitution, only to have it dashed by the adoption of the twelfth amendment, with its provision that henceforth ballots must be cast specifically for President and Vice President. With Republicans leaving the Bank of the United States untouched and the navy still afloat even if reduced, many Federalists saw no sense in continuing the contest. In the election of 1804 only fourteen electoral votes were cast against Jefferson. "I declare to you," wrote the melancholy Fisher Ames, "I fear Federalism will not only die, but all remembrance of it will be lost."

Then came a turn that revived the hope of despairing Federalists. War between France and England had broken out again, and seizure of neutral vessels as well as impressment of our seamen was resumed. Yet so profitable was the trade that Federalist shipowners were glad to take the risks. The loudest lamentations over the losses at sea came from farmers, who lost nothing. The Republican agrarians, convinced that the belligerents needed our foodstuffs so much that they could be forced into granting us freedom of the seas, resorted to an embargo. In a single year exports fell off eighty per cent and New England prosperity was ruined. McMaster estimates that 55,000 sailors and 100,000 laborers and mechanics were thrown out of work. Recent Republican converts began returning to their old allegiance, and the Federalist Party experienced what it mistook for a resurrection. [30]

The awkwardness of the Republicans in preparing for the danger of war was due to their deep-seated distrust of a professional army and navy. Jefferson's proposal to Congress was to lay up the frigates the Federalists had built and construct two hundred small sailboats, each with a single gun mounted

---

[29] *Rise and Growth of American Politics*, pp. 131, 132.
[30] See H. C. Hockett: "Influence of the West on the Rise and Fall of Political Parties," *Mississippi Valley Historical Review*, IV, 455.

in the stern. Designed solely for coast defense, they were purposely unsuited for protection of commerce. They were to be kept in sheds until invasion was threatened, when they would be thrust into the water and manned by volunteers, somewhat after the manner of a village fire department. The mirth of the Federalists was unrestrained, since the largest boat was only seventy-five feet in length, but "their construction by numerous petty ship builders made votes." [31] Later, when the *Leopard* disabled the *Chesapeake*, Jefferson obtained an appropriation of $850,000 for 188 more of these little boats and ordered three more large naval vessels laid up. Nathaniel Macon, Speaker of the House, and intimately connected with the non-intercourse legislation, came from a lonely North Carolina farm remote from traveled highways and was representative of a large segment of the Jeffersonians. He wanted no navy because it would be manned by New Englanders and would put power in their hands. Whenever our shippers ran the blockade carrying the trade of belligerents, they could expect no protection from him. "I for one," he declared, "will not mortgage my property and my liberty to carry on this trade." [32]

Since the prevalent public opinion then was that a public office was a species of private property and removal from it a deprivation of property rights, as Jefferson was to discover when he removed Elizur Goodrich from the collectorship of New Haven, a turning of the "rascals" out *en masse* would have been impracticable. Let no one be astonished, however, to learn that this practical-politician President made a Federal supervisor out of James Linn, the former Congressman who had cast the deciding vote in 1801, shifting the New Jersey delegation to Jefferson and ensuring his election as President. Social solidarity ensured the easy rule of the gentry in the South without resort to patronage, but Jefferson did not hesitate to employ his appointing power for party purposes in Pennsylvania and New York. Nor was he averse to suggest-

---

[31] Morison and Commager, op. cit., I, 297.
[32] See W. E. Dodd: "The Place of Nathaniel Macon in Southern History," *American Historical Review.* VII, 608 ff.

ing "a judicious distribution of favors" to the Bank of the United States in order "to engage the individuals who belonged to them in support" of the administration.

Jefferson's presidential career closed with an anticlimax. By 1807 the Republicans had governors in every New England state except Connecticut, but a year later they lost every one of them. Two months before laying down his presidential duties Jefferson, in the expectation of making the embargo effective, persuaded Congress to pass the Force Act empowering Federal agents to seize, without warrants, goods suspected to have a foreign destination, thus reminding New Englanders of the infamous writs of assistance. At this point the President's partisans revolted in New England, whence protests and threats of secession poured in, and the administration trembled under the impact of the town meetings, as Jefferson admitted. New York Republican leaders challenged the President's party leadership by nominating for President George Clinton, in place of Jefferson's choice, the heir apparent, Madison. And the President's fellow Virginians, "the Quids," under the inspiration of John Randolph, presented James Monroe as their candidate against Madison.

Unquestionably the disintegration of the Jeffersonian Republicans was now forecast. The tobacco plantations that had nurtured the statesmen of the Virginia dynasty were lapsing into ruin, wherefore their three great Presidents died practically impoverished. Other hands would soon itch for the scepter. Pure Republicans such as John Randolph's "Quids" would no longer compromise with patronage-seeking Middle-State politicians. And these politicians in their turn refused to support the mad agrarian policies that ruined their opportunity to command votes at home. New England's lower-income groups, convinced by the embargo that their own well-being could scarcely be separated from the prosperity of the merchant-capitalists, gave evidence of approaching New England party solidarity. The interior grain-growers, far and near, most devoted of Jeffersonians, multiplied prolifically against the day when they would hold the balance and dominate elections and policies.

Before Madison had been President two years, the policy of temporizing with England produced the first congressional tidal wave in American history. The whole long frontier of land-hungry pioneers fretted over the Indians that encumbered choice land. In the South the native tribes inhabited the black belts coveted by the enterprising cotton-planters. New farm land was also needed for the innumerable sons of the virile inland yeomanry of the North. There was alarm over the Illinois prairies, too tough to be turned by pioneer plows and deemed sterile since they grew no trees. If this was the western limit, then migration must push northward as soon as Canada could be conquered. Hunter, trapper, and fur trader united on the project to wipe out powerful British competition. The entire frontier was bitter over the British policy of keeping Indian chiefs on pension rolls to stir up strife with the settlers, and the West was a unit in the conviction that the redcoats were back of every Indian atrocity. The section also blamed the British for the depression in the Mississippi Valley. Soldiers of the Revolution had settled in the West without forgetting their traditional enemy, and among them the implacable Scotch-Irish were numerous.[33]

It was, then, an intensely anti-British sentiment that the "tidal wave" had swept into the new Congress that met in December 1811, determined to end at once the temporizing foreign policy of the Virginia dynasty. This was the purpose with which Henry Clay, just elected Speaker, as chief of the "War Hawks," confronted the Virginia dynasty in the person of President Madison. Madison had lost his New York allies, George Clinton having even challenged him as a presidential candidate. Where would he find new allies? Older Jeffersonians were only feebly nationalistic and scarcely felt the sting of British insults. The strongest delegation in Congress now was the South Carolinians, with the Kentuckians not far behind, and both dominated by the war-mongers. With these the harassed Madison was compelled to come to agreement

---

[33] See George R. Taylor: "American Discontent in the Mississippi Valley Preceding the War of 1812," *Journal of Political Economy*, August 1931.

as the price of a second term. At any rate this man who could not be "kicked into a fight" reluctantly recommended a declaration of war and then the congressional caucus approved his candidacy, which was tantamount to re-election. Thus the Republican Party ventured on the war that was incidentally to wipe out their political opponents and give Americans a taste of one-party government.

There is a debt of gratitude the Jeffersonians have yet to pay to Alexander Hamilton. They themselves could never have established the new government to which they fell heir in 1801. Their forerunners, the Patriot Party of the 1770's, had waged the Revolutionary War as an anti-national movement. During the "Critical Period" their drive for paper currency and stay laws had proved socially disintegrating in tendency, as shown by Shays's Rebellion. It was Hamilton who had managed to integrate the then dominant elements in American society into the party that gave the new government, under the Constitution, a commanding prestige and authority in every section of the Union. This firmly established and efficiently functioning government was the unintended bequest of the competent Federalists to the Jeffersonians, who soon learned, as we have seen, to divert the magnificent instrument to their own particular ends.

CHAPTER V

ONE–PARTY GOVERNMENT

"Now is the time to exterminate the monster called party spirit. By selecting characters most conspicuous for their probity, virtue, capacity and firmness, without any regard to party, you will go far to, if not entirely, eradicate those feelings, which, on former occasions, threw so many obstacles in the way of government: and perhaps have the pleasure of uniting a people heretofore divided. . . ." ANDREW JACKSON to President-elect Monroe in 1816.

W E are about to behold an administration of the Jeffersonian Republicans, who after conducting the War of 1812 with incredible ineptitude, emerged from the conflict covered with glory at the very moment when their Federalist opponents experienced irreparable ruin. Left unchallenged masters of the political field after 1816, the Republicans were to discover presently the disintegrating effect on a multi-group party of the disappearance of a common enemy, a vigorous political opposition. The "War Hawks" of 1811–12 evolved in the post-war period into super-nationalists, literally contemptuous of the prescriptions of the Constitution and irrepressible in their determination to convert the Federal government into a paternalistic institution providing a powerful standing army, a great navy, a new Bank of the United States, government-built roads and canals, and protective tariffs. Here, however, was a program that stirred in the hearts of the older Jeffersonians memories of the Virginia and Kentucky Resolutions — the bible of the original Republicans, which had proclaimed the anti-national dogma of state rights. In little more than a decade this ideological clash was to produce two distinct factions of the Jeffersonian party, the National Republicans and the Democratic Republicans, from which were to evolve in due time the Whig and Democratic parties of the thirties.

Eventually, then, the Federalists were to behold their ideal of a partyless or one-party government achieved not, as they had so fondly hoped, by eradicating the opposition, but instead by the gradual dispersal of their own forces and their leaving the field to the triumphant Republicans. The pre-war policy of non-intercourse and embargoes had baffled the party of mercantile capitalism, but war against their chief customers induced a madness that led to their ruin.

Possessing the bulk of the nation's financial resources, these New England Federalists deliberately refused to finance the war and presently placed the government in a desperate financial predicament. Nor would the New England states contribute their militia for the conquest of Canada and the consequent creation of new agrarian states, with increased congressional delegations and votes in the electoral college certain to reduce their own section to a still more hopeless minority. So disaffected, indeed, did New Englanders become that the British navy refrained from blockading their coast until almost the end of the war, and news of allied — that is to say, British — victories across the sea were celebrated by the fatuous Federalists. Commodore Stephen Decatur even complained that blue-light signals, set on dark nights to warn British war vessels, had prevented his running the blockade and putting out to sea from New London in 1813. Never were these luckless partisans to hear the last of the opprobrious epithet, the "Blue Light" Federalists. In the fall of 1814 their discontent culminated in the convention of delegates at Hartford, assembled to air their grievances and to seek means of redress. Fortunately the extremists among them, the Essex Junto, stark disunionists, were in the minority and the resolutions adopted, consisting of the proposal of some amendments to the Constitution, sound moderate enough today. Collectively they constitute the swan song of the Federalist Party.

While the Hartford Convention deliberated, the American

cause grew day by day more desperate. The army was un-paid, the Treasury was empty, the British fleet had captured, sunk, or bottled up our entire salt-water navy and had clamped down an air-tight blockade on our Atlantic ports. The Capitol and the Executive Mansion had been burned by the British. An expeditionary force of Wellington's presumably invincible peninsular veterans, equipped at the cost of a million pounds, was known to be en route to New Orleans. New England Federalists, in their innocence, were positive that these forces could never be stopped by the raw rabble of Southwestern militiamen. The nation's extremity presented what seemed to be a lucky break for the New England Federalists, an opportunity at long last to wring from the hard-pressed Republican administration consent to a set of reasonable constitutional amendments.

The modest formula devised by the Hartford Convention was that of a minority veto on the agrarian power through the familiar requirement of an extraordinary majority in Congress for establishing policies deemed inimical to New England. Thus it was proposed that a two-thirds majority be required for the admission of states since in the future all new states seemed destined to be agrarian, which is to say, Republican. Embargoes would be limited to sixty days, and the interdiction of foreign commerce was to require a two-thirds majority of both houses of Congress. Except in case of invasion, the two-thirds vote was to be required also for a declaration of war, a provision that would have easily prevented the detestable War of 1812. In order to deprive the planters of the extra Congressmen and presidential electoral votes derived from counting three fifths of the slaves in apportioning representation, it was proposed that henceforth only free persons be counted for that purpose. A thrust at the Virginia dynasty was implicit in the seventh resolution, providing that "the same person shall not be elected President of the United States a second time; nor shall the President be elected from the same state two terms in succession."

With the confidence of emissaries on a mission that could not fail, the commissioners bore their resolutions to the capital for submission to Congress as proposals for amendments to the Constitution. Unfortunately they drew near Washington just at the moment when the news of the unexpected treaty of peace along with the tidings of Jackson's crushing defeat of the magnificent British army at New Orleans had converted a despondent people into a nation of rejoicing madmen. Realizing they could not make themselves heard in the midst of the tumult of the celebrations, the commissioners slunk away into oblivion. Instantly the discredited Madison's administration acquired an unearned prestige and the Hartford Convention an unmerited odium which the jubilant Republicans promptly applied to Federalists generally. The party never recovered from the damage done to its reputation by the current impression of treason that its enemies managed to fasten upon it. A year after the close of the war the Federalists nominated their last presidential candidate, Rufus King, who received only 34 electoral votes to Monroe's 183.

In its after-effect the War of 1812 gave the morale of the American people an almost miraculous lift. Promptly forgotten were the disastrous campaigns, the miserable fumblings of incompetent commanders, the burned Capitol and White House, the inflexible British blockade of our coast, the driving of our navy from the seas, and the failure not only to conquer Canada but even to obtain in the treaty the concession of a single right claimed in the declaration of war. Instead there was to be cherished only such memories as those of Lundy's Lane, of New Orleans and the Thames, and of the naval triumphs on Lake Erie and Lake Champlain. Again, according to tradition, proud Britain had been humbled by the irrepressible Republic of the Western World. A transient conviction of intense nationalism took possession of the American people such as was not to be seen again in many a decade. Under its vitalizing influence disciples of Thomas Jefferson were, for a brief season, to exceed Alexander Hamilton and his Federalists in their palmiest days as exponents of broad construction of the Constitution. Typical of the prevailing ecstasy was the opinion of John C. Calhoun that a discussion of the "constitutionality" of chartering a second Bank of the United States would be a "useless consumption of time."

During Monroe's first term all but the irreconcilable Federalists moved over into the Republican column and were presently modifying that party's agrarianism by the pressures of once Federalist interests. Indeed, the Republican Party, in time, "became almost as much a party of business groups as the old Federalist party had been," [1] thus confirming John Taylor's dictum that the business interests were devoid of principle and would combine with any party. It was an outstanding Federalist leader, Josiah Quincy, who gave utterance to the poignant lament that the Republicans had "out-Federalized Federalism." Even that staunch Federalist, John Marshall, had been tempted to vote for Madison, but he repressed the impulse and cast no vote for President from 1800 to 1824, when he voted for John Quincy Adams.[2]

In the absence of an opposition the Republicans gradually lost their party discipline and their organization on a national scale. There is no better evidence of the disappearance of the old party alignments than the fact that Republican newspapers in 1816 reprinted in support of the second Bank of the United States Hamilton's argument for the first bank. This was simply using, in support of a Republican measure in 1816, the identical Federalist reasoning of 1791 that had aroused the opposition then and even contributed to the origin of the Republican Party. Thus cavalierly was Jefferson's historic opinion against the chartering of the first bank, including his classic statement of the dogma of strict construction, given the *coup de grâce* by his own disciples. And to make the topsy-turviness of politics complete, Webster and other Federalists opposed the chartering of the new bank.

When the time came to nominate presidential candidates in the spring of 1820, there were invited to the congressional caucus not only Republicans but all Congressmen who saw

---

[1] B. B. Kendrick: "Agrarian Movements," *Encyclopedia of the Social Sciences*, I, 504.
[2] See W. E. Dodd: *Statesmen of the Old South*, pp. 70–1.

fit to attend. Even the old New England Federalists were satisfied with Monroe, and the incorporation of Federalists within the Republican fold seemed to be practically complete. The Massachusetts presidential electors in 1820 consisted of seven old-line Republicans and eight former Federalists, among whom were ex-President John Adams and Daniel Webster; and all, of course, voted for the re-election of Monroe.

It had now become as fashionable for Republicans as it once was for Federalists to disparage political parties as such. Paradoxical as it may seem, it was that later prince of partisans Andrew Jackson who was to give authentic expression to this prevailing sentiment in a letter of advice to President-elect Monroe in 1816. Concerning the choice of cabinet members he advised: "In every selection party and party feeling should be avoided. Now is the time to exterminate the monster called party spirit. By selecting characters most conspicuous for their probity, virtue, capacity and firmness, without any regard to party, you will go far to, if not entirely, eradicate those feelings which, on former occasions, threw so many obstacles in the way of government; and perhaps have the pleasure of uniting a people heretofore politically divided. The chief magistrate of a great and powerful nation should never engage in party feelings. His conduct should be liberal and disinterested, always bearing in mind that he acts for the whole and not a part of the community. By this course you will exalt the national character and acquire for yourself a name as imperishable as monumental marble. Consult no party in your choice." [3]

Monroe reciprocated the sentiment in a letter to Jackson, writing: "We have hitherto been divided into two great parties. That some of the leaders of the Federalist party entertained principles unfriendly to our system of government, I have been thoroughly convinced; and that they meant to work a change in it, by taking advantage of favorable circumstances, I am equally satisfied." [4]

---

[3] James Parton: *The Life of Andrew Jackson*, II, 362.
[4] Ibid., II, 362.

Intimately related to the disappearance of political parties was the concurrent decline in the significance of the presidential office. Since the President is the focus of American party conflicts, under the circumstances then obtaining the office sank to comparative insignificance. It was no snap judgment of R. V. Harlow's that "Madison could scarcely have played a less significant part during those eight uncomfortable years if he had remained in Virginia." [5] Had the office then possessed its present pre-eminent importance, Monroe could not have been re-elected without opposition in the midst of the nation-rocking controversy over the admission of Missouri to the Union and just as the economic depression starting in 1819 was spreading disaster throughout the length and breadth of the land. Since then no President has been re-elected following a term of his in which a depression began. During this quarter of a century not only had Congress overshadowed the President, but it had, in every case, determined the choice, either directly through election by the House of Representatives or through nomination by the congressional caucus, which in the absence of any significant opposition was tantamount to an election.

The revival of a two-party alignment was involved in the fact that the Virginia dynasty had now run its course. The tobacco plantation of the Old Dominion had produced its last outstanding statesman-President. Powerful interests in other sections were ready to bid for the stakes of power inherent in the presidential office. Their particular candidates were about to engage in a severe competition for the presidency. Universal manhood suffrage had swept the frontier, forcing the older settlements to consider its adoption in the hope of discouraging somewhat the tide of western migration. The aspirant to the presidency was now compelled to adapt his appeal to a rapidly expanding electorate in which the common man was becoming a distinct force. No longer would the congressional caucus that had so long maintained the Virginia dynasty by mechanically promoting the Secretary of State to the presidency be complacently accepted. Nor could the legislatures

---

[5] *The History of Legislative Methods in the Period before 1825*, p. 196.

of half the states hope to continue much longer to choose presidential electors instead of permitting the people to elect them.

With the restoration of a free competition for the presidency in the middle twenties, aspirants were being compelled to search for issues or combinations of them with a nationwide popular appeal. The most ingenious of these was the so-called "American System" of Henry Clay, which he began to formulate soon after the Peace of Ghent in 1815. The end of the war marked the beginning of a new era, in which Americans stopped calling each other "Anglomen" and "Gallomaniacs." The colonial psychology had given way to a conviction of genuine American independence. Public opinion found its focus on the domestic issues of currency, banking, tariff, transportation, public lands, and western migration. The dogma of state rights proved unsuitable for dealing with these problems, and national needs now induced the resurgence of nationalism, already noted.

The war and its aftermath had demonstrated so convincingly the vulnerability of American prosperity that Henry Clay believed his fellow countrymen were ready for a planned national economy based on a protective tariff. Nor should it be assumed that this plan was merely the revival of an old Federalist dream. The center of gravity in that party combination had been the merchant shipowners of the Atlantic ports from Boston to Charleston. These men certainly wanted no artificial restrictions placed on either incoming or outgoing cargoes. As shipowners they did not relish the early protection of hemp, cordage, flax for sail duck, and iron, all used in shipbuilding. Nor did they welcome the establishment of industries here that could not fail to reduce their import trade. When Henry Clay presented his American System he found himself in controversy with the champion of the New England shipping interests, the Federalist Daniel Webster, who could see nothing "American" about it.

It is one of the paradoxes of our history that it was the Jeffersonian agrarians who had firmly, though unwittingly, established American manufactures. "Never," wrote Henry

Adams, "was the country so racked to create and support monopolies as in 1808, 1809 and 1810 under Southern rule and under the system of the President who began his career by declaring that if he could prevent the government from wasting the labor of the people under pretense of protecting them they must become happy. . . . American manufactures owed more to Jefferson than to Northern statesmen who merely encouraged them after they were established." [6] Then followed the air-tight blockade by the British navy during the war, providing a more thorough protection than any set of import duties. Under the circumstances capital ceased going into ships and went instead into factories, especially textile mills utilizing the water power along the fall line.

This peculiar kind of "protection," incidental to the War of 1812, ended in 1815 when British merchants began "dumping" the contents of their warehouses, accumulated during the long Napoleonic Wars. One of their vessels would dock at an American port and begin auctioning off its cargo at any sacrifice necessary to dispose of it. This "cheated" the American merchant out of his function as a middleman and allied him with the factory-owner and the handicraftsman, all of whom now began deluging Congress with petitions for taxing these auctions to death.

John C. Calhoun, one of the most ardent of the nationalists, expressed the conviction that protection "would make the parts adhere more closely" and that "it would form a new and most powerful cement." [7] He declared "he had often heard it stated both in and out of Congress that the effect of the War in stimulating manufactures would indemnify the country for all its losses." [8] Incidentally there were experimental mills struggling to get established in the Carolinas and no one could then foresee that the mad rage for cotton-planting would soon prevent the hoped-for development of Southern industry. Madison caught the vision of national self-sufficiency, with Northern manufacturers complementing South-

---

6 *History of the United States*, V, 19, 20.
7 Morison and Commager, op. cit., I, 335.
8 J. P. Gordy: *History of Political Parties in the United States*, II, 327–8.

ern agriculture and America independent of foreign supplies, the tariff uniting the sections in a bond of economic interest.[9] When Thomas Jefferson, by no means immune to the prevailing contagion, was saying: "We must place the manufacturer by the side of the agriculturist," Henry Clay could well believe the omens were indeed auspicious for his American System.

Post-war economic trends followed the familiar pattern of a boom, a panic, and then a devastating depression.[10] Thirty-four-cent cotton shot the price of even uncleared Southern land up to fantastic figures. The easy credit policy of the new Bank of the United States stimulated manufactures and feverish land sales in the West. Then when the panic of 1819 created a money stringency, the Bank acquired millions of acres of land through foreclosures against helpless farmers and thereby became to the agrarian West the symbol of monopoly and the money power. Farmers who had generally enjoyed good prices since the beginning of the European wars in the 1790's had overexpanded and they now found their markets glutted. Grain-growing had run riot in the relatively isolated Ohio Valley, and by 1824 corn at Cincinnati was worth 8 cents a bushel, wheat 25 cents, and flour $1.25 a barrel, and grain was consequently left to rot in the fields.[11] Europe's demand for cotton continued, but the price steadily declined. In South Carolina horses and plows were being discarded and planters went medieval by having whole fields spaded up by the cheaper slave labor.[12]

Under the circumstances the demand for protective tariffs began coming in from such divergent directions as the cotton mills of New England and the Carolinas, the iron works of Pittsburgh, the hemp fields of Kentucky, the sheep pastures of Ohio and Vermont, and the grain lands of central New

[9] Letter to H. Clay in *Writings* (Congressional edition), IV, 567.

[10] See the graph of the Cleveland Trust Co. in L. H. Hacker: *The United States, A Graphic History*, p. 199.

[11] See F. W. Van Meter: *Economic History of the United States*, pp. 252–3.

[12] See W. E. Dodd: "The Making of Andrew Jackson," *Century*, CXI, 533.

York — all of which also required highways and canals. "If the Americans of the first years of the nineteenth century," wrote C. C. Arbuthnot, "could have called forth an institution like the present Wall Street they would have regarded it as the greatest of blessings." [13] In the 1820's it was realized that the Federal government through its taxing power was then the one great capital-accumulating agency. Why might it not construct the needed highways and canals? Not only was the situation ripe for a practical American politician, expert in the employment of such issues, to combine sections and interests, but an extraordinarily ambitious and self-confident one was at hand.

A native of Virginia, young Henry Clay had migrated to frontier Kentucky, grown up with the community, and, like Lincoln later, whose exemplar he was to be, deliberately cultivated an inherent talent for politics. Law was then the highroad to political preferment, and Clay so fascinated his juries that it was said no person ever hanged where he spoke for the defense. Perused in cold print today, his speeches seem tame, but so magnetic was the personality of this master of men that for five decades he led Kentucky emotions and reason captive. "In his understanding of human nature, in his ability to appeal to the common reason, and in his absolute fearlessness in stating his convictions, he was unexcelled by any of his contemporaries." [14] Having served his legislative apprenticeship in the Kentucky lower house, he came in 1811 to the national House of Representatives, there to be elected at once to the speakership, where his mastery was to be impressed no less on the incorrigible John Randolph than on complaisant President Madison, whom we have seen obliged to come out for war with England as virtually the price of a second term.

Clay's well-matured exposition of the American System, set forth in the House of Representatives as the presidential com-

---

[13] "The Economic Interpretation of Present Politics," *Popular Science Monthly*, LXXXI (1912), 185.
[14] E. M. Coulter: "Henry Clay," *Dictionary of American Biography*, IV, 179.

petition of 1824 developed, resembled that of the "Open Door at Home" revived by Charles A. Beard more than a century later. "Now our people," declared Clay, "present the spectacle of a vast assemblage of jealous rivals, all eagerly rushing to the seaboard, jostling each other on their way, to hurry off to glutted foreign markets the perishable produce of their labor. The tendency of that policy, in conformity with which this bill is prepared, is to transform these competitors into friends and mutual customers, and, by reciprocal exchange of their respective productions, to place the confederacy upon the most solid of all foundations, the basis of common interest." [15] The presidential aspirant counted on attaching to himself practically every section and interest in the nation. Through adequate protection there might be created the home market for farm products on the one hand and for manufactured products on the other. Reduced prices of the output of factories, once they were firmly established, was held forth. Revenues from tariff duties would finance the network of canals and highways required for this internal traffic.

The Middle and Ohio Valley states, realizing that the European market was now gone beyond recall, had developed an almost childlike faith in the protection of wool, hemp, flax, wheat, and corn. The frustration of Ohio Valley farmers at seeing their marketable surpluses rot for lack of transportation united them on internal improvements as on no other issue. Already there were, according to McMaster's estimate, 2,000,000 factory workers becoming impressed by the argument for protection as a maintainer of wages and a means of keeping the mills running. If only Clay could manage to convince the farmers, shepherds, road and canal contractors, factory-owners, mill hands, and handicraftsmen of a common interest in his American System, the grand prize of the presidency might be his reward.

Unfortunately for Clay, the post-war nationalist enthusiasm had already spent its force when he presented his for-

---

[15] F. W. Taussig (ed.): *State Papers and Speeches on the Tariff*, pp 312–13.

mula, and the South never found it acceptable. The cotton-planters wanted no restrictions on the free flow of foreign trade in and out. Moreover, nature had provided their states with magnificent systems of river transportation. Not only would protection favor particular industries, but the planter was convinced that he would, as John Randolph put it, "only get much worse things at a much higher price," [16] and the funds extracted from him at the detested custom house would be used to construct Northern canals and highways. In short, it was, to the planters, a system of vicious class legislation. Nor was the West swept off its feet by the Clay formula. After all, its appeal was to the intellect and not to the feelings. "Its acceptance carried no intoxication" and "could not be adapted to the western style of exhortation." [17] Confronted by the dynamic personality of Old Hickory, then emerging as a presidential possibility, the emotion-starved pioneer lost interest in Clay's elaborate argument.

The West had taken, in the early twenties, a keen interest in discussing the relative strength of the followings of Clay and Jackson. The section was ready for a leader who could sense, phrase, and symbolize the needs of the depression-vexed West as well as those of the Eastern urban masses now beginning to stir uneasily under their social subordination. Clay's essay at this was his American System. What had others to offer in this first free-for-all competition for the American presidency? In 1822 *Niles' Register* found sixteen or seventeen candidates, but a year later only half a dozen remained in the field. Easily first among these was William H. Crawford, Secretary of the Treasury, whose candidacy enjoyed the blessing of no less a notable than the aged Jefferson himself. Macon, Madison, Randolph, Van Buren, and Marcy also backed him and he was given the formal nomination of the congressional caucus which made him the official party nominee, the candidate of the regular Republican politicians. Regionally regarded, he was the candidate of the cotton-planters, who were insisting upon the removal of the Indians from

---

[16] *Annals*, 14th Cong, 1st session, p. 687.
[17] F. L. Paxson: *The American Frontier*, pp. 253–5.

the fertile black belts. Ideologically he was the legatee of the Jeffersonian tradition, standing on the extreme ground of the Kentucky Resolutions with their "rightful remedy" of "nullification." [18] The wide appeal of these Resolutions was evident from the fact that the legislature of Ohio was just then using them in its protest against the Supreme Court decision that it could not tax the branches of the Bank of the United States located in Ohio.

Crawford revealed the regional candidate's typical reaching out for a nation-wide union of interests in his support of moderate tariffs and the maintenance of the Bank of the United States. Presently it was Crawford against the field, which "ganged up" on him and proceeded to "smear" him as the candidate of the "undemocratic" congressional caucus, while other candidates were nominated instead by state legislatures presumed to be more immediate agents of the popular will. In any case Crawford was eliminated by a paralytic stroke in the midst of his campaign.

That Andrew Jackson should even be considered for the chair so long occupied by a line of distinguished Virginia statesmen seemed at first thought utterly preposterous to most men, not even excepting General Jackson himself. "Do they think I am such a damned fool as to think myself fit for the presidency?" he asked in 1821 when for the first time he saw his name mentioned in that connection in a newspaper. "No, sir," he continued, "I know what I am good for. I can command a body of men in a rough way, but I am not fit to be president." [19] Yet the smoke of the Battle of New Orleans had scarcely more than cleared away when his availability had been perceived by one of the keenest practical politicians of that day. In 1815 Aaron Burr, eager to find a candidate around whom might be rallied the forces to overthrow the Virginia "oligarchy," had suggested Jackson in a letter to his own son-in-law, Joseph Alston.[20]

---

[18] See Alexander Johnson: *American Politics*, p. 104.
[19] J. P. Gordy, op. cit., II, 532.
[20] W. G. Sumner: "Politics in America, 1776–1876," *North American Review*, CXXII, 47.

It was the depression of the twenties that had provided the seed-bed of what has since come to be known as the Jacksonian movement. Keen political observers perceived deep-seated stirrings of both the rural and the urban masses accentuated by the prevailing hard times. A profound conviction that the ruling class had betrayed the people's interests was taking possession of the common man. A new species of politicians expert in canalizing mass movements began to emerge and sweep the horizon in search of a national leader. That a man of Jackson's background should be called upon for this purpose would have seemed preposterous to any but these new politicians. This Nashville ex-judge, sound-money man, and creditor distinctly distrusted the turbulent masses and had habitually sided with the haves and against the have-nots.[21] Nevertheless the "Nashville Junto" of designing politicians decided to ignore the party machinery, on which, in any case, the Crawford men had an iron grip, and boldly proclaim their fellow citizen as the hope of the underdogs, the champion of the masses then groping for leadership.

Ever since his victory at New Orleans there had not been a more widely known celebrity in the United States than General Jackson. To the depression-frustrated ordinary citizen, whether urban worker, yeoman, or frontiersman, he was a veritable miracle-worker, invincible in battle against Indians, British, or "hard times." Even the illiteracy of voters worked to his advantage, because, as one of his supporters wrote in a letter, "they are illy acquainted with the character and qualifications of the other candidates" and need no education to know of "the glorious exploits which have crowned the career of Jackson." [22]

Nor was Andrew Jackson in 1824 by any means a mere novice in politics. The general, passing down the tense lines in the pitch darkness of one o'clock in the morning before the Battle of New Orleans and picking out by voice and calling by name the soldiers who spoke to him, whether he realized it or not was already practicing the great art. Called upon to

---

[21] See Marquis James: *Andrew Jackson*, p. 345.
[22] Quoted by M. James, op. cit., p. 384.

give his opinion of the tariff measure pending in the campaign year of 1824, he wrote with an eye keenly alert to all the interests concerned: "So far as the Tariff before us embraces the design of fostering, protecting, and preserving within ourselves the means of national defense, I support it. . . . Providence has filled our mountains and our plains with . . . lead, iron, and copper, and given us a climate and soil for growing hemp and wool. These being the grand materials of our national defense, they ought to have extended to them . . . protection, that our manufacturers and laborers . . . may produce within our own borders a supply . . . essential to war. . . ." [23] What candidate in any decade could, with such verbal economy, make a neater bid for the support of seven different interests and, at the same time, base his argument on the universal and fundamentally sound argument of national defense?

Measured by experience, learning, intelligence, and sheer devotion to the public interest, John Quincy Adams was best fitted of all the competitors for the presidency in 1824. Moreover, according to established precedent he was the heir apparent to the high office. As Secretary of State he occupied the position from which every President for almost a quarter of a century had been promoted. "I am a man of reserved, cold, austere and forbidding manners," confessed this unbending Puritan; "my political adversaries say, a gloomy misanthrope; and my personal enemies an unsocial savage." [24] Despite these handicaps here is the candidate who in the end captured the grand prize. Nor was this capable statesman utterly innocent of the game of practical politics. He gave dinners, owned a newspaper, found loans for its editor and public printing for its support.[25]

Since Adams's views corresponded closely with Clay's American System, their candidacies tended to split the vote of the interests soon to form the National Republican Party. When the results of the balloting in the fall of 1824 were

---

available, it was seen that Adams had captured all the counties in New England and those in New York and Ohio wherever the New England stock predominated. Some scattered counties in New York and Missouri gave Clay majorities, but his strength, though far from uniform, lay largely in the Ohio Valley. It is his American System that gives the key to the peculiar configuration of the pattern formed on the map by the counties carried by Clay.[26] Shippers dependent on the Ohio River could use it only when the flow was adequate, which led to such glutting of the New Orleans market that farmers, as has been said, let their grain rot in the fields rather than sell at ruinous prices. Consequently Clay's "home market" and internal-improvement formula became a veritable obsession of the Northwest. Indeed, it seemed so specially designed for the Ohio Valley that its appeal was weakened elsewhere.[27] Clay suffered in some communities where the Bank of the United States had foreclosed on depression-stricken farmers, because he had defended the bank before the Supreme Court in the famous Osborne case.[28] This was the decision that had prevented the legislature of Ohio from exacting a tax of $50,000 on each of the two branches of the bank located in the state.[29] Still others opposed Clay in his own section because of the persistent rumor that he was playing second fiddle to the extremely unpopular caucus candidate, Crawford, and would throw his support to that candidate if the House had to elect the President.[30] So distinctly was Clay a regional candidate, and moreover in a section where Jackson was a competitor, that he won only 37 electoral votes.

Jackson's astonishing showing was due to the support of his fanatically devoted fellow Scotch-Irish scattered throughout Pennsylvania, the upland South, and the entire West south of the Mississippi and St. Lawrence divide, the Germans of Pennsylvania and Ohio, and everywhere the under-

[26] See map in C. O. Paullin, op. cit., Plate 103.
[27] See E. H. Roseboom: "Ohio and the Presidential Election of 1824," Ohio Archæological and Historical Society Publications, XXVI, pp. 163, 167.
[28] Osborne et al. v. The Bank of the United States, 9 Wheaton, 738.
[29] See E. H. Roseboom, op. cit., p. 194.
[30] See Roseboom and Weisenburger: History of Ohio, p. 145.

dog marshaled by Jacksonian politicians who knew how to utilize the popular ferment of the twenties. Jackson's vote in the electoral college was 99 to 84 for Adams, while Crawford received 41.

In case of the failure of any candidate to obtain a majority in the electoral college, one of the highest three would be elected by the House of Representatives, with each state casting one vote as the Constitution prescribed. Clay was, of course, disappointed at his exclusion, for he must have considered his chances good in an election by the House, of which he was the Speaker and in which, of course, he possessed an enormous influence. As it now turned out, he and his following in Congress consciously held a balance of power between Jackson and Adams and were thus in a position to determine the next President. For weeks Clay seemed undecided whether to express his loyalty to the West by supporting Jackson or, for his own future advantage, to endeavor to eliminate his Western rival by supporting Adams. Whatever his motives, his influence ultimately made Adams President, and since the views of the men were so similar on the American System, the action might be regarded as logical and indeed the fulfillment of what amounted to practically a referendum on the paramount issue of the campaign of 1824.

To the Jackson men there was nothing at all logical about the election of Adams. None of them doubted that the House had been morally bound to elect the one who ranked first in the electoral college. Then, too, it was argued that the popular vote carried a like mandate. Even though the legislatures and not the voters had chosen the presidential electors in half the states and despite the fact that in only four states had the electorate voted on all four candidates, nevertheless, for the first time in our history, estimates of the total popular vote for each candidate were published. These seemed to indicate that Jackson had received a plurality of forty-two per cent of the votes. The reaction of the masses to the publication of these data betokened the new force in American politics. Jackson's followers, among whom the Scotch-Irish were most partisan, maintained that the House had flouted their cherished doctrine of popular sovereignty. It was as their peculiar spokesman that Jackson eventually was to recommend the popular election of the President in every one of his eight annual messages to Congress. We have here in fact a germinal dogma of emerging Jacksonian Democracy and it was to be dinned into the ears of the public daily during the four years of Adams's presidency.

Thurlow Weed has given us the opinion of a contemporary expert in party politics that the new President was no practical politician. "Mr. Adams," said he, "during his administration failed to cherish, strengthen, or even recognize the party to which he owed his election; nor as far as I am informed, with the great power he possessed did he make a single influential friend." [31] Adams had indicated a willingness to have Andrew Jackson considered the vice-presidential candidate with him "on correct principle – his fitness for the place, the fitness of the place for him and the peculiar advantages of the geographical situation." [32] Utterly oblivious of the incipient renaissance of political parties, he offered cabinet appointments to all his rivals for the presidency, only to be repulsed by all except Clay, whom he made Secretary of State. This appointment proved to be a fatal error since it served only to confirm the conviction of the Jacksonians that Clay had made a "corrupt bargain" whereby he would make Adams President in return for his own appointment to the office of Secretary of State. The significance attached to this appointment was due to the fact that the office had become the established stepping-stone to the presidency, so the cry at once arose: "Clay is in the succession." The Jacksonians stubbornly insisted that Adams was thereby dictating the choice of his successor to the "sovereign" people – or, at any rate, assuming to do so.

Ill fortune dogged every move of President Adams during his four miserable years in the White House. His first annual message seems commonplace today, but it rent the country

---

[31] Quoted by E. M. Carroll: *Origins of the Whig Party*, p. 13.
[32] *Memoirs*, VI, 241–2.

asunder. The President's grandson, Brooks Adams, saw in it a revival of Washington's dream of tying the West to the East with a system of canals, thereby checking the growing sectionalism of the North and South by diversifying the industries of Virginia and Maryland.[33] Adams's message proposed canals, highways, harbor improvements, a stronger navy, military schools, a strengthened militia, a national university, and an observatory, all at Federal expense. This terrifying program, in the opinion of W. B. Giles, published in the Richmond *Enquirer*, created "a crisis involving the liberty and happiness of all future ages." [34] Nor did the President's message catch the popular favor even of the North, where it was only reminiscent of a post-war nationalism that had already subsided, and prophetic of an enthusiasm for the Union yet to develop and find classic expression in Webster's sonorous periods.

A "minority" President who would remove no enemy from office, not even his Postmaster General, busy employing patronage against him, who prevented his supporters from copying the public record of the court-martial decision on the six militiamen Jackson had executed, for fear it "would be construed as a measure of hostility against General Jackson," [35] but who persisted with inflexible Puritan sternness in the performance of his duty, simply played into the hands of the anti-Adams men. These had no scruples against arousing the pioneer's prejudice against the administration's unprecedented expenditures of $14,000,000 in four years of peace. The absurd rumor that part of this money had been spent on a billiard table installed in the White House for the amusement of the President's son set Western tongues wagging.[36] The Scotch Presbyterians scarcely knew whether to be more incensed over the waste of taxpayers' money or the sin of the game, but thrifty Pennsylvania Dutch puzzled over no such alternative. It was in fact a four-year "smear" campaign in which

---

[33] See Henry Adams: *The Degradation of the Democratic Dogma,* Ch. i.
[34] J. P. Gordy, op. cit., II, 566.
[35] J. Q. Adams: *Memoirs,* VII, 275.
[36] See Roseboom and Weisenburger, op. cit., p. 147.

the Jacksonians converted "a personal prejudice into a political force that was positive, aggressive and effective." [37] So contemptible, in fact, was the propaganda employed that one distinguished recent historian wondered whether it would not have been more honorable for Jackson to have lost than won in 1828.[38]

John Quincy Adams was the first of our Presidents to be confronted by a Congress deliberately organized against the administration. Clay's alleged "corrupt bargain" was aired *ad nauseam*, and filibustering against the President's measures was unblushingly carried on. The crowning device intended to overwhelm Adams was the Tariff Act of 1828. It was an over-clever politician's intrigue for snaring votes, which, as crabbed John Randolph averred, "referred to manufactures of no sort or kind except the manufacture of a President of the United States." The stake was the protectionist vote of Pennsylvania and the West. Jacksonian politicians, with diabolical ingenuity, framed a high-protection bill so loaded with provisos damaging to New England's interests as to invite the Adams men to vote it down. If they did so, the Pennsylvania protectionists would be turned against Adams, while if the measure passed, the Democrats were the champions of protection anyhow. If the tossed coin came up tails, Adams lost; if it turned up heads, Jackson won.[39] To the discomfiture of the Jacksonian politicians, the New England Congressmen accepted the measure, and when passed, Adams signed it.

The transformation of these anti-Adams men into Jacksonian Democrats constitutes a landmark in the history of American party politics. The traditional revolutionary machinery of the committees of correspondence was utilized in order to overthrow the ruling class. The Jacksonian politicians organized the now enfranchised masses through conventions, caucuses, and committees down into the county, the town-

[37] R. C. Buley: *The Political Behavior of the Old Northwest, 1820–1860*, p. 412.

[38] E. Channing: *History of the United States*, V, 376.

[39] See F. W. Taussig, op. cit., pp. 95 ff.; J. P. Gordy, op. cit, pp. 593–5.

ship, and even the rural school districts.[40] National politicians were learning to weave the local sectional and class interests into intricate national patterns. "Their cross sections instead of displaying a few simple colors, were a jig-saw puzzle of radicalism and conservatism, national and state rights, personal loyalties and local issues. Party strategy was directed toward accumulating as many bundles as possible; and statesmanship was the art of finding some person or principle common to all the bundles that would make them forget their differences and in union find strength." [41]

On a national scale the politician *par excellence* of his generation was Martin Van Buren, who perfected his art in the severe competition of the factions in New York politics. "Few men in American life," wrote Turner, "so united the ability to make political combinations and the power of critical analysis of underlying principles. Suave and conciliatory, Van Buren was perhaps the highest type of New York politician. He rose to national greatness and achieved a reputation as a statesman by his ability to think in national terms, to formulate Democratic party principles that remained substantially unchanged down to recent years and at times to make decisions hazardous to his career and to abide by them." [42]

In 1824 Van Buren, with exemplary party regularity, had managed the campaign of the caucus candidate, W. H. Crawford. Three years later, with the opportunism of the practical politician, he saw in Andrew Jackson the chieftain to rally the heterogeneous anti-Adams forces and was working on an alliance, as he put it, between "the planters of the South and the plain Republicans of the North" based on party principles, because otherwise "geographical divisions founded on local interests, or what is more, prejudices between free and slave holding states will inevitably take their place." [43]

---

[40] H. J. Webster: "History of the Democratic Party Organization in the Northwest," Ohio Archæological and Historical Society *Publications*, XXIV, Ch. i.

[41] Morison and Commager, op. cit., I, 447.

[42] F. J. Turner: *The United States, 1830–1850*, p. 118.

[43] Letter of Van Buren to Thomas Richie, January 13, 1827, quoted ibid., p. 35.

W. H. Crawford, convalescing but unquestionably now out of the running, threw his support and the weight of the cotton-planting interests to Jackson in the confidence that the champion Indian-fighter would clear the natives from the potential new cotton lands, whereas Adams had sent a regiment of Federal troops into the "sovereign" state of Georgia in order to protect the Indians from the rapacity of the planters. The tobacco-planters of the upper South were ready to ally themselves with the cotton-planters in the common expectation that Jackson would overthrow the tariff-privileged industrialists attached to Adams. Moreover, Jackson was himself a slaveholder, opposed to a President avowedly unfriendly to the institution of slavery.[44]

One outstanding aspirant remained to be disposed of before Jackson would have a clear field as the candidate of the anti-Adams men. This was John C. Calhoun, upon whom the caucus had concentrated as the vice-presidential candidate in 1824 and who had then accordingly decided to bide his time for four years. Now he too, like the Jacksonians, was cultivating Pennsylvania, whence his Scotch-Irish ancestors had long ago migrated to the Carolina uplands. His grandfather had been slain by Indians incited by British agents, and a Tory had killed an uncle of his. Educated at Yale, this uplander next managed to ally himself by marriage with the coastal planting aristocracy and then by twisting the British lion's tail to win a seat in Congress in time to become an outstanding "War Hawk." The end of the War of 1812 found no more extreme nationalist and loose constructionist than John C. Calhoun, and as the chief spokesman of the piedmont he championed protective tariffs, internal improvements, and rechartering of the Bank of the United States. By the middle twenties he was still relying on his reputation as a protectionist as well as his Scotch-Irish kinsmen and their connections in cultivating a Pennsylvania-Southern alliance to further his presidential candidacy.

The stratagem by which this lone remaining competitor

[44] See F. J. Turner, op. cit., p. 33; W. E. Dodd: "Andrew Jackson and His Enemies." *Century*, CXI, 735.

against Jackson among the anti-Adams men was disposed of illustrates the developing technique of American party politics on a national scale. "Old Hickory," aged sixty-one, kept insisting that he was a very old man, in very poor health, and in any case he could not hope to live very long. Here was the opportunity of his managers to handle Calhoun if only Jackson would co-operate. So the aged candidate let it be rumored that he practically had one foot in the grave, might not even live through the year, and in no case would think of more than a single term. It was an extraordinarily good bait, for, under such circumstances, re-election to the vice-presidency became extremely attractive to the ambitious Calhoun as the almost certain road to the presidency in four years at the most, and possibly within a single year. Accordingly he made the fateful decision to cast his fortunes with the forces of Jackson, under whose leadership a united front could be presented.[45] The person of Jackson now provided the sole positive unifying factor of the anti-Adams groups, which, while constituting a somewhat party-like coalition, came for the time being to be called the "Jackson men."

Nor was the pro-administration combination any less embryonic as an emerging political party than the opposition. The pronounced tentativeness of the alignments is revealed by the fact that, late in the Adams administration, William H. Crawford was urged upon the President as a suitable running mate in the approaching election. The administration supporters were as yet no more than the Adams-Clay faction of the Republican Party and were usually designated merely as the "Adams men." It, too, was then merely a quasi-party group combination that could count on the support of practically every county in New England and the coastal communities south of it as far as Baltimore. Western New Yorkers of New England descent were "Adams men," as were indeed the conservative communities generally throughout the West. Conservatism was the keynote of the administration combination. "In the main the men who supported the administra-

---

[45] See W. E. Dodd: "The Making of Andrew Jackson," *Century*, CXI, 538.

tion were those who feared the rough ways of plain men, the ideas of equality and popular initiative so dear to the American heart." [46] This was evident even in the deep South since the Adams supporters there outvoted Jackson men in the counties where slaves were most numerous and the greatest cotton-production was reported,[47] thus foreshadowing the center of gravity in the future Whigs of the South — that is to say, the greater planters. In 1828 the Adams-Clay men adopted the party designation of National Republicans, in which the qualifying adjective was peculiarly appropriate for a party so pronouncedly paternalistic. When, however, half a dozen years later it became necessary to welcome as allies every description of person alienated from Jackson, even devotees of state rights, they prudently dropped the "National" and even the "Republican" and became simply Whigs.

One striking element in the Jacksonian aggregation was a group of notable ex-Federalists. Adams had originally been a Federalist, but in 1808 he had affiliated himself with the Republicans, for which he was bitterly denounced as a traitor by the die-hard Federalists. In 1816 Jackson had written President-elect Monroe urging him to appoint as Secretary of War a conspicuous South Carolina Federalist, William Drayton. This correspondence was confidential for several years, but when Jackson began to be promoted for the presidency one of his managers, Colonel William B. Lewis, began with consummate skill to permit knowledge of the correspondence to "leak out" where it would do the most good.[48] As this information became disseminated by the grapevine, it produced the intended result of winning over Federalists outside of New England to the Jacksonians. Conspicuous among them were Roger B. Taney of Maryland and James Buchanan of Pennsylvania. Nor should William Drayton himself be forgotten, for he became an outstanding leader of the South Carolina anti-nullification forces in support of Jackson in 1832.

---

[46] W. E. Dodd: *Expansion and Conflict*, p. 15.
[47] See F. J. Turner: *United States, 1830–1850*, p. 36.
[48] See M. James, op. cit., p. 375.

Andrew Jackson then entered upon the presidency in 1829 carrying a mandate from the original "Jackson men," consist· ing of the farmers growing grain on nearly self-sufficient small holdings, the cotton-planters of the lesser plantations, the tobacco-growers of the upper South and the declining tide-water plantations, the old democracy of New York and Pennsylvania both rural and urban, as well as almost the entire piedmont, and everywhere the professional anti-Adams politicians, predominantly original Crawford men who had passed over with their chieftain into the Jacksonian camp in the late twenties. There was as yet no party platform — in fact, not even a real party. Nevertheless there was somehow disseminated the semblance of a program, a set of implied understandings. Jackson would get the Indians out of the way of the Southern cotton-planters and the Northwestern grain-growers; the appetite for free homesteads was going to be satisfied even if it required war with England and Mexico; and inland farmers, it was assumed, would have improved transportation at Federal expense. So well had Jacksonian politicians managed their propaganda that Pennsylvania manufacturers like Samuel D. Ingham "expected the hero to raise the tariff everytime he touched it," [49] while at the same time South Atlantic planters believed the Tennessee cotton-planter as President would counteract the pressures of the privilege-seeking Northern industrialists.

[49] W. E. Dodd: "Andrew Jackson and His Enemies," *Century*, CXI, 736.

CHAPTER VI

JACKSONIAN DEMOCRACY

"PRESIDENT VAN BUREN *inherited from Jackson an organic party whose dominant note was equality and whose common tendency was westward expansion. Eventually this Democratic party became an instrument of the slaveholders, but in the thirties it was a well-balanced alliance of North, South, and West. Shortly, it became identified with state rights, but in 1837 the sturdy nationalism of Andrew Jackson was dominant. 'Old Hickory' had caught the imagination or catered to the appetite of Southern yeomen and petty planters, of pioneer farmers in the Northwest, German and Irish immigrants in the Northern states, and plain country folk in New England and New York.*" S. E. MORISON and H. S. COMMAGER.*

We have seen that the economic distress of the early twenties had stirred in the American masses a spirit of social unrest. A deep-seated conviction that the Eastern squirearchy which had so long dominated the government had betrayed its public trust and ignored the people's interest began to take possession of ordinary men and women. The common man in the East no less than in the West was losing that inferiority complex imposed upon the European masses by the regimentation of the feudal system. Instead he was beginning to perceive the possibility of the theory of popular sovereignty becoming a functioning reality. Here was a social phenomenon of the profoundest significance, not just to academicians, but also to practical politicians who live to exploit the opportunities inherent in emerging popular movements.

---

* From *The Growth of the American Republic*, I, 449. By permission of the Oxford University Press, publishers.

It was because discerning men saw the possibility of polarizing these inchoate impulses of the people by means of the personality of a fascinating military figure that the "rise of the common man" came to be known as the Jacksonian movement.

The nucleus of Jacksonian Democracy was an ethnic group, the Scotch-Irish stock, to a man intensely proud of their kinsman chieftain. Though but a minority element in the party combination, the intensity of their convictions, coupled with an inflexible tenacity of purpose, enabled them to shape the party into almost a perfect expression of the peculiar genius of their people. These were the descendants of the unfortunates we have seen harried from their Ulster homes and finding refuge in the American wilderness, where they nursed an undying hatred of their British persecutors. The rifles that blazed across the cotton-bale breastworks at New Orleans on January 8, 1815 and mowed down the red-coat lines were to them but the avenging instruments of a just God in the hands of the faithful. Jacksonian Democracy knew no stronger emotional bond of unity than its universal hatred of the British. It was peculiarly appropriate that the 8th of January became the fixed date of the annual party banquet.

Having flooded the back country of Pennsylvania, the surplus progeny of these Scotch-Irish, along with English and German migrants, trekked south through the valleys of the Blue Ridge Mountains, scattering their cabins all the way to their southernmost extremity. Some became the Southern mountain folk, dwelling in isolated communities, mostly "above the thousand-foot contour," the offspring of their crowded cabins pushing farther and farther up the steep slopes. They shared with the yeomanry of the valleys a dislike of the aggressive cotton-planting aristocrats and could be won over to their political allegiance only by the practiced arts of consummate party leadership.

Having populated the piedmont and the Appalachian slopes, before the end of the eighteenth century this human tide began pouring through the mountain passes and dispersing fan-like into the valleys of the Cumberland and the Tennessee in the face of the bloody resistance of the Indian tribes, incited by British agents. Nor did this mighty migration spend its force before it had overflowed into the deep South as well as northward across the Ohio toward the headwaters of the streams that flow southward into that river. As expert woodsmen these migrants judged soil by the type of timber it bore. They accordingly shunned the prairies of the old Northwest on the erroneous assumption that they were as undesirable as the Southern pine barrens. In any case their primitive plows could not have broken the stubborn turf, and thus nature determined a northern boundary of Jacksonian Democracy so decisively that "in Illinois a map of party groupings looks like a map of the original forest and prairie areas with the glacial lobe extending from Lake Michigan clearly visible." [1]

These pioneers from the South were non-slaveholders who had found difficulty adjusting themselves and their families to their planter neighbors and so fled to the free Northwest in order to spare their children the stigma of the competition of freemen with slave labor.[2] They became, in time, substantial wheat-, corn-, and pork-producers, supplying their staples to the great Southern single-crop plantations. This trade established one of the firmest economic ties that bound the Ohio Valley to the deep South. Having their "home market" in the South, they had little interest in Clay's American System. They constituted no small part of that grain-growing element so essential to the success of Jacksonian Democracy. Little wonder, then, that when the Civil War suddenly cut off this Southern market, the counties of southern Ohio, Indiana, and Illinois came to constitute the backbone of the Peace Democracy.

Widely dispersed though this original Pennsylvania stock had become, they managed through blood relationship, letter-writing, and visiting to maintain a remarkable homogeneity

---

[1] F. J. Turner: *Sections in American History*, p. 188.

[2] See A. B. Hart (ed.): *Social and Economic Forces in American History*, p. 256.

of customs, interests, and thought. The dogmas of the covenanting Scotch-Irish Presbyterians provided the pattern of popular sovereignty with which to rationalize the *fait accompli* of pioneer democratic society. They who had spurned the authority of both prelate and pope, under the conviction that the body of believers constituted the true sovereign authority in the government of the church, would brook no pretense of autocratic political authority assumed by a ruling class. By 1830 not only had Pennsylvania and its irrepressible migrants become worth bidding for by calculating politicians, but they had even put one of their own North Ireland stock in the presidential chair and had established a new political party.

In the Northeast the pattern made on election maps by the Jacksonian counties resembled that of the earlier Jeffersonians. Thus the partisans of Old Hickory dominated the hinterland of Maine, New Hampshire, Vermont, and northern New York.[3] As elsewhere, these Northern Democrats were strongest in the counties of lower land values. In the Berkshires and in the less prosperous towns throughout Massachusetts the Jacksonians carried the elections. Fellow partisans of theirs were the poorer seafaring folk and the urban laboring class of carpenters, masons, and ship calkers as well as an already teeming element of pick-and-shovel Irish immigrants.

Even as early as 1827 there was an Irish district around Broad Street in Boston. Whig politicians were at first disposed to ignore these newcomers. Presently, however, their native-labor Whig following forced the party into an unequivocal anti-Irish policy. Thereupon Jacksonian politicians, with characteristic opportunism, countered the Whigs by gathering the sons of Erin into the Democratic Party by representing President Jackson, with some semblance of plausibility, as the champion of the poor against the rich.[4] When, in the forties, the Irish supplanted native labor in the Merrimac textile mills, the mill towns showed a tendency to shift

---

[3] See A. B. Hart, op. cit., p. 250.

[4] See A. B. Darling: "Jacksonian Democracy in Massachusetts," *American Historical Review*, XXIX, 283.

from the Whig to the Democratic tickets. By and large, New England Democracy represented a protest against an aristocracy of fashionable society, religious liberalism, capitalism, and smug conservatism. These protesters consisted of "country folk, fishermen and the poorer classes generally who sought a change in the established order of society." [5]

New England Democracy was distinctly conditioned by a debtor complex. A poor farmer, whether setting up a son or daughter in life or pinched financially by a crop failure, presently found his farm mortgaged to a Boston insurance company, and as a consequence New England Jacksonians railed against Boston and State Street. Moreover, this animosity was intensified when, in 1841, the Western Railroad was completed to the Hudson. Thus, through the Erie Canal, the Boston market was opened to the cheaper Western foodstuffs, and many a poor Massachusetts farmer was thereby driven to the wall. As if this competition were not enough, the Whig legislature taxed the luckless farmers in order to service the state bonds issued to provide credit to the promoters of the railroad that was ruining them. New England Democrats who accumulated sufficient capital tended toward commerce instead of manufacturing and imbibed the free-trade doctrines of the Boston mercantile families. As consumers the rural Democrats, like the Southern cotton-planters, felt the burden of tariffs, and until the middle of the century a strong Calhoun faction was found in Massachusetts.

Religious orthodoxy was as intimately related to the Jacksonians as it had been to the Jeffersonians. In 1816 the Presbyterian Republicans, having captured the New Hampshire legislature, proceeded to oust the Congregational-Federalist trustees of Dartmouth College and to reorganize the board, making it subject to state control, only to be frustrated in their purpose by the remarkable opinion of John Marshall in the Dartmouth College case.[6] Jacksonian leaders were educated at Baptist Brown University, not at heterodox Uni-

---

[5] Ibid., p. 272.

[6] See Robert E. Cushman: *Leading Constitutional Decisions* (1941), pp. 145–6.

tarian Harvard, which instead served the Whigs.[7] Leadership no less than the rank and file of New England Democracy was provided by the dissenting and orthodox Presbyterians, Baptists, and Methodists. Nor were these three sects in the West less Democratic or for that matter less orthodox. It was indeed with something of a touch of dramatic propriety that, a century later, William Jennings Bryan, the greatest of all the latter-day evangelists of Jacksonian Democracy, died in armor fighting the foes of fundamentalism.

As the party of the common man, New England Jacksonians were organized in clubs and local associations. The tactics of Democratic party leaders were conditioned here by the presence of a strong Whig — that is to say, conservative — opposition, amounting in most communities to a majority. In order to keep their more moderate members from deserting to the Whigs, Democratic politicians sought to temper the radicalism that characterized their party by holding back from assaults on the credit system. New England extremists, encountering the caution of conservatism in both the major parties, turned to third parties, with the quite natural consequence that the Anti-Masons in the thirties, the Free-Soilers in the forties, and the Know-Nothings in the fifties in turn ran rampant among the humbler folk of rural New England.

If exception is made of the indefatigable Pennsylvania Dutch, the Democracy of the Middle Atlantic states was strongest in the forested and hilly sections and elsewhere in the regions of lower land values. By the middle of the century the small grain- and hay-growers were still the most important factors in New York and Pennsylvania politics. Since these great pivotal states held a balance of power in the Democratic Party combination, the national managers of the party could not afford to ignore these strategically situated interests, to which fact Van Buren and Buchanan owed their national recognition.

New York urban Democracy was growing by leaps and bounds owing to the swelling tide of immigration, particu-

---

[7] A. B. Darling, op. cit., p. 274.

larly of the turbulent Irish. Such of these as did not hasten
to the interior to labor on canal and railroad construction
crowded into the poorer city wards. They brought with them
an inherent hatred of aristocracy and the very party designation "Democratic" beckoned to them. It suited them perfectly that the Jacksonians had championed universal manhood suffrage and easy naturalization. By 1820 Tammany was
already Irish.[8] Democratic politicians readily played upon
the Irishman's chief obsession by twisting the British lion's
tail in season and out of season. The tradition of the American Revolutionary battle for freedom against British "tyranny" made Irishmen fellows with the patriots of Lexington
and Bunker Hill. Nor was it only the humble immigrant in
New York City who adhered to Democracy. The booming
foreign trade there facilitated by the excellent harbor and
connection with the West via the Hudson and the Erie Canal
made the commercial interests of the metropolis inhospitable
to the brake of protective tariffs and hence inclined to the
Jacksonians.

In the deep South, after the party purge of the great planters effected by Jackson's proclamation against the nullificationists, Democracy included the ever faithful petty planters,
owners of few if any slaves, and the grain-growing farmers, even more ardent Jacksonians there than were their kinsmen north of the Ohio. Georgia Democrats, for example, were
faithful to the party largely because they were the non-slaveholding farmers of the mountains or of the pine barrens or
even in the cotton belt, and all of them were traditionally
antagonistic to the great planters, who were mostly Whigs
until mid-century.[9] It did not soften the animosity of these
poorer folk to have been edged off the black cotton lands by
the pressure of high prices per acre paid by the prosperous
planters. They were crowded away in communities with poor
soils, and their lower incomes were reflected in slight if any
schooling facilities and the consequent high illiteracy that
distinguished Jacksonian counties in the South. They resented

---

[8] Carl Wittke: *We Who Built America*, p. 159.
[9] See U. B. Phillips: "The Southern Whigs," *Turner Essays*, p. 212.

the fact that the great planters of the black belts exerted a political power magnified by the counting of slaves in the apportioning of representation in the legislatures. Southern Democrats in the state legislatures accordingly harassed the great planters with their pressure for elimination of the property qualifications for voting, for prison reforms, the abolition of imprisonment for debt, the establishment of free public schools, and legislative apportionment based on the number of free whites. Andrew Johnson, an indomitable champion of the underdog, in 1842 introduced in the Tennessee legislature a resolution providing "that the basis to be observed in laying the state off into Congressional districts shall be the voting population without any regard to the three-fifths rule of the negro population." [10] These Southern Democratic Congressmen to a man backed Jackson on his bank veto and his proclamation against the nullificationists. But they were not successful in their state programs of social reform until Federal armies had overthrown the planting aristocracy, whereupon, in conjunction with the carpetbaggers, they obtained state constitutions so satisfactory as to stand long after the era of Reconstruction had ended.

In the combination that elected Jackson in 1828, the tidewater planters of Virginia and the Carolinas constituted an incongruous element as insecurely attached as the Virginia planters had been to the coalition of groups that produced the Constitution. These tobacco-, rice-, and cotton-planters bitterly denounced President Adams's paternalistic program and despised the New England complex of interests. They accordingly turned to Jackson, a fellow slaveholder, in the hope that he would check the trend of the American System toward the loose construction of the Constitution. Yet these coastal aristocrats must have had their misgivings, for they were intolerant of popular sovereignty and mass majority rule — the reign of "King numbers" as John Randolph contemptuously denounced it. They were compelled in 1828, however, to make their choice between Jackson, the chieftain of the tu-

---

[10] John Savage: *The Life and Public Services of Andrew Johnson*, p. 140.

multuous Western democracy, and John Quincy Adams for a second term. Perhaps they consoled themselves with the idea that they were still "Republicans" since they "rejected the name of democrat which had obtained in the North and it was never until the election of 1840, that decent persons could willingly stomach the name." [11] So from the Potomac to the Chattahoochee there was a bloc of Congressmen and political leaders counting on Jackson to check the rising Northern industrialists.

What was it that bound together, temporarily at least, in a common purpose this heterogeneous aggregation? In the first place Jacksonian Democracy was pre-eminently a party of the antis, even if the only point on which every last Jacksonian agreed was opposition to John Quincy Adams. President Adams's program, as set forth in his inaugural address and first annual message to Congress, was a positive one calling for an unprecedented exercise of national power. The party battle of 1828 was between the pros and cons on a constructive program — Adams's proposal to use Federal power to promote industry, trade, transportation, and scientific discovery.

The typical Jacksonian Democrat was intensely anti-British, or, to view the same fact obversely, he was thoroughly American. The Federalists had been pro-British and the Jeffersonian Republicans pro-French. The Jacksonians, however, were free from any colonial complex and consequently they constituted the first genuinely American party. It is a significant fact that the counties where Jacksonians predominated had been settled largely by non-English stock — the Scotch-Irish, the Germans, and the strictly Irish. There were to be found in practically every Western community veterans of the Revolution, venerable men who treasured and transmitted the cherished tradition of the battles against the English and the Tories. Moreover, the old animosity was sustained and intensified by the constant warfare with the Indians as the frontier was pushed ever westward. With Indian chiefs pen-

[11] From a review of Francis Lieber's *Political Ethics,* in the *Southern Quarterly Review,* October 1847.

sioned by the English, frontiersmen could scarcely be blamed for regarding the English and the Indians as virtually allies. In 1812 all pretense was cast aside and the two became actual allies. It was the British-Indian menace in the Southwest that Jackson finally crushed at New Orleans, as Harrison had already done for the Northwest at Tippecanoe and the Thames. So it was not utterly irrational for Westerners to attribute every Indian atrocity to the English and to lump them and the savages together. It is scarcely an exaggeration to say that Jacksonian Democracy almost institutionalized this anti-English feeling.

Though no Indian menace motivated their animosity, New England Jacksonians too were anti-English. Here the tradition of the minutemen of Lexington, the defense of liberty by the "embattled farmers" against English tyranny, persisted, particularly in the rural towns. Among the humbler urban elements, the impetuous Irish immigrants lost no time in becoming ardent partisans of General Jackson, who had scourged the English troops so mercilessly at New Orleans. As predominantly a debtor class, New England Jacksonians perceived that their ultimate creditors dwelt in London and they accordingly hated the recipients of the tribute money extracted from them through grinding necessity by the Shylocks across the sea.[12]

Stripped of its incongruous elements, which presently deserted it, Jacksonian Democracy was an anti-monopoly party, the enemy of special privilege. The whoop and hurrah of the movement afforded a wholesome psychological release of the accumulated resentments of Western small farmers and Eastern urban underlings. Everywhere the less prosperous had been wont to attribute their ill fortune to the ruling oligarchy that had run the government in its own interest. For this ailment of the body politic the common man had a sovereign remedy, and he now purposed to administer the medicine to the patient in person. The masses that poured into Washington for Jackson's first inauguration and literally took pos-

---

[12] *Supra*, p. 102.

session of the White House manifested an awakened class consciousness and celebrated a triumph. It was as their authentic spokesman that President Jackson was to say that "a monied aristocracy of the few" warred "against the Democracy of numbers; the prosperous to make honest laborers hewers of wood and drawers of water to the monied aristocracy of the country through the credit and paper system." [13]

"Equal rights for all, special privileges for none," became the appropriate slogan of the party. It proclaimed the "liberty of men owning independent means of livelihood," which "ideal was most fully realized in the America of the 1820's and 1830's. . . . At least eighty per-cent of the people, excluding the South, were independent property owners, mainly small farmers." [14] In our day, when private corporations are so common as to seem a part of the order of nature, it is difficult to comprehend how reprehensible they seemed to the pioneer. To the typical Jacksonian it was but a piece of legalized villainy to give the special privilege of doing business collectively to a group of stockholders while exempting them personally from all legal responsibility, monetary or otherwise, for the conduct of the business. Banks constituted a particularly vicious species of corporation, and in mid-century Jacksonians practically drove banks out of Illinois, Wisconsin, Iowa, and Missouri. Jackson cemented his democratic following more securely than ever when he administered the death blow to that super-corporation the Bank of the United States.

When Chief Justice Roger B. Taney, speaking for Jackson's rejuvenated Supreme Court, held that, in incorporating a company to build a toll bridge across the Charles River, Massachusetts did not thereby create a monopoly, but might later incorporate a competing bridge company,[15] the judge was but giving expression to a consensus of opinion among

---

[13] Quoted by Avery Craven: *Democracy in American Life*, p. 63.
[14] Lewis Corey: "The Crisis of the Middle Class," *Nation*, August 4, 1935, p. 176.
[15] *The Charles River Bridge Co.* v. *Warren Bridge Co.*, 11 Peters, 420 (1837).

Jacksonians, to the joy of little and the consternation of big businesses. It was to be expected that the party should resist the licensing of the traffic in liquor as well as in other commodities. Moreover, the party's resistance to such sumptuary legislation was unavoidable in an aggregation including such joyous livers as the Irish and the Germans, to say nothing of some of the older stocks. When in 1828 a Massachusetts statute forbade the sale of liquor in less than fifteen-gallon lots, Democracy arose in its wrath to end such discrimination against the poor man and saw to it that the Whig Governor, Edward Everett, who had sponsored the act was defeated for a second term.[16]

The golden age of Jacksonian Democracy extended only from the early thirties, when many of the great planters had deserted to the Whigs, until the late forties, when many of them returned and, in union with the lesser planters, converted the party into an agency of the slavocracy. It was during this earlier and happier era that Alexis de Tocqueville visited America and, with the keen eye of a political scientist, observed that "nothing struck me more forcibly than the general equality of condition among the people. I readily discovered the prodigious influence which this primary fact exercises on the whole course of society; it gives a peculiar direction to public opinion and a peculiar trend to the laws; it imparts new maxims to the governing authorities and peculiar habits to the governed." [17] During the dozen or so years that Democracy was truly Jacksonian, party members found the formula for rationalizing this economic and social equality in the white-hot phrases of Jefferson's Declaration of Independence, to which they pledged allegiance in their party platform until the influence of the planters in the Democratic national conventions dictated otherwise. Party politicians had found in its natural rights the ideological pattern for allying the humble urban folk of the East with rural democracy everywhere.

The new delegate system of county, congressional district,

16 A. B. Darling, op. cit., p. 217.
17 *Democracy in America* (New York, 1828), I, 1.

state, and national conventions became the means of implementing the Democratic doctrine of popular sovereignty as well as the instrument for overthrowing the ruling class. The Jeffersonians had revolted against too much government, but the Jacksonians revolted against government by an unfaithful oligarchy. The most dynamic element in the Jacksonian combination was the politician who discovered in the spoils system the means of purging the civil service of the oligarchs as well as a way to reward "deserving Democrats." Here was a practical application of the party slogan: "One man is as good as another." No longer would the common man seeking a government appointment be dismissed with the contemptuous remark: "You ought to know your place." If only the educated were eligible, then office-holding was the special privilege of an élite who could afford an education. To no small degree the Jacksonian movement represented a revolt against the cultural hegemony of the East, which section was believed practically to have monopolized the civil service. So Jackson reformed the civil service by opening the door of opportunity even to the illiterate, who constituted no inconsiderable portion of his vast following.

This underprivileged, unschooled element of Jacksonian Democracy gave a peculiar turn to the campaigning of Western candidates. "Stump speaking developed into an art and cajolery a profession, while whisky flowed freely at the hustings. The politicians could most easily attain their object by appealing to the prejudices of the masses. Colleges were said to exist for the rich and the ignorant were asked to elect the ignorant because enlightenment and intelligence were not democratic." [18] In sections of the Southwest the candidate felt impelled to caution his wife and daughters against wearing fine clothes and some candidates canvassed on foot in order to avoid the appearance of opulence and the invidious social distinction implicit in the ownership of a horse. Year after year Democratic candidates baffled their Whig oppo-

---

[18] T. P. Abernethy: "Andrew Jackson and Southwestern Democracy," *American Historical Review*, XXXIII, 70.

nents by the proficiency with which they exploited the persecution complexes of the masses.

The dominant urge of the Jacksonian Democrat, whether
petty planter, yeoman, or artisan, required for its satisfaction
the speedy distribution of the public lands, contrary to President Adams's business-like program for their settlement.
Jackson proposed, as Adams put it, "giving away the national
inheritance to private land jobbers, or to the states in which
they lie." Indeed ex-President Adams perceived that the
Webster-Hayne debate "was one of the earliest results of the
coalition between the South and the West to sacrifice the
manufacturing and free labor interests of the North and East
to the slave holding interest of the South by the plunder of
the public lands surrendered by the South to the new Western
states. . . . The Jackson Administration had been formed
upon this combination and had drawn New York and Pennsylvania into its vortex." [19] In plain terms, the South purchased thirty years of low tariffs by throwing the public lands
to the Westerners. Nor was this vast public domain sufficient
for the insatiable Jacksonians. From the back settlements of
New England to the farthest Western frontier they all believed
in conquest and annexation, an urge idealized in the Democratic slogan of "manifest destiny" and realized in the vast
acquisitions of territory as a consequence of the Mexican
War.

How was Andrew Jackson maneuvered into the leadership
of the mass movement to which he contributed his talents and
his name? In the 1790's he had been engaged in business and
his interests were developing in him the capitalistic outlook
that a generation later was to characterize his Whig antagonists. His intimate Nashville associates were men sometimes
stigmatized as "Federalists." Certainly no one could then
have foreseen the future champion of the debtor masses in this
aristocratic-minded judge, this anti-inflationist with his pronounced creditor complex. He was a land speculator and
dealer in horses, slaves, and general merchandise when the
panic of the early nineties practically wiped him out. Turn-

[19] *Memoirs,* IX, p. 235.

ing to cotton-planting, he prospered and gradually came to see public affairs through the eyes of an agrarian. Falling into the tradition of Thomas Jefferson and John Taylor, he developed a hatred of monopolies of every description, banks among them, and above all the Bank of the United States.

It was with the eyes of the great and not the petty planter that Jackson had come to view public issues. The Hermitage was one of the finest mansions of the West and as the domicile of a Democrat it was to amuse the Whigs of the 1830's no less than did Hyde Park the Republicans of the 1930's. Utterly innocent of speculative philosophy, Jackson never developed a hard and fast social ideology such as that which had made the leadership of Hamilton so unadaptable and so transitory. This super-pragmatist, like every other highly successful national politician from Jefferson through Lincoln to the two Roosevelts, was an astute opportunist who consequently never ceased to learn and grow. He could "by intuition scent the course the public mind would take particularly in the West." [20] "Professing to be servants of the people," Jackson and his advisers "were adept in interpreting the people's mind to the people themselves. Thus they succeeded in leading where they seemed to follow." [21] Jackson too might have said as Lincoln did near the end of his career: "I have not shaped events but events have shaped me." Social forces created the Jacksonian movement, and previous to his election to the presidency Jackson had not contributed one idea to it. An outstanding self-made man, he was put in the White House by the national constituency of self-made men. The pioneer, absorbed in his struggle with nature, had no time for the abstractions of Clay's American System, but he "was taught to think politics in terms of Andrew Jackson. Through the personality of 'Old Hickory,' successfully exploited by party politicians, the apathetic voter was energized into political activity." [22]

20 W. E. Dodd: Expansion and Conflict, p. 37.

21 H. C. Hockett: Constitutional History of the United States, II, 83.

22 Allen Johnson: "The Nationalizing Influence of the Party," Yale Review, XV, 290.

In the presidential office the former border captain took counsel with the coterie of professional politicians he had gathered about him and at once demonstrated a dexterity in practical politics that baffled his ablest Whig opponents. Perceiving that the day of the "common man" had dawned, he boldly proclaimed his chief function as that of a "tribune of the people," thereby setting the pattern to be followed by outstanding Democratic Presidents ever since. Nor did he relax the vigilance of his search for issues that would hold securely to the party combination even its most incongruous elements, and of these the least certain were the tidal planters.

As the spokesman of the coastal planters, John Tyler had expressed their views in the prediction that Jackson would "come in on the shoulders of the South, aided and assisted by New York and Pennsylvania," and "must surround himself by a cabinet composed of men advocating to a great extent the doctrines so dear to us." When instead the President, recognizing that the center of gravity in his party lay in the West, turned toward advisers from that section, Governor Floyd of Virginia complained: "He gave himself up to the opposite party, was willing to take any course that would keep him in a majority." Confronted with the problem of these disillusioned tidal planters, Jackson set about to recover their allegiance and presently perceived his opportunity. The planters of both the Atlantic and the Gulf states were supplied with magnificent systems of river transportation and frowned upon any Federal expenditures upon an internal system of transportation. The President then, carefully calculating party gains and losses, decided to risk the wrath of the inland grain-growers in order to placate the planters of the seaboard staples. His strategy was to make a spectacular veto of some insignificant internal improvement project that would strike at the heart of Clay's system with as little sacrifice as possible of his Western following.[23]

Jackson accordingly besought his ablest political adviser, Secretary of State Van Buren, to discover among pending

---

[23] See Preface, p. v.

internal-improvement measures one whose veto would disappoint the fewest voters. There was guile in the Little Magician's selection of the bill authorizing Federal subscription of stock for a twenty-mile highway known as the Maysville Road, lying entirely in Clay's state. Disregarding its value as a link in the long post road to New Orleans, Jackson pounced on its local character as not satisfying the constitutional requirement of promoting the "general welfare." A map showing the roll call on this measure by congressional districts reveals a party vote, support of the measure coming from the former Federalist areas of communication, and opposition from the sections of Van Buren's alliance of North and South.[24] Incidentally, in his veto, the planter President was expressing a personal antipathy against road contractors who seemed to him to be raiding the public Treasury and who were usually Clay men or National Republicans. Land speculators too were exerting their pressures and a saturnalia of log-rolling for local roads seemed imminent.

Jackson's Maysville veto served to define sharply the developing two-party alignment. The consequent considerable defection from the Democratic ranks induced Clay to meet the President's challenge by launching his own candidacy for the election two years hence. Yet to Jackson's astonishment the veto was applauded even where least expected. Pennsylvania and New York were constructing state canals and highways without Federal funds. Though the National Republicans gained in Kentucky and Ohio, the latter state also was constructing its own system of canals connecting the Ohio River with Lake Erie, and Jackson's losses there were less than might have been expected.[25] Nor had Jackson miscalculated in his expectation that the veto would gratify the planters.

Even more remarkable than the Maysville Road veto was that of the bill to recharter the Bank of the United States. It was an unparalleled example of the national politician's

---

[24] C. O. Paullin, op. cit., Map on Maysville Road Bill, Plate 114.
[25] See S. R. Gammon: *Campaign of 1832*, p. 63; Roseboom and Weisenburger, op. cit., p. 151.

skill in utilizing an official act to make a mass popular appeal. In the incomparable phrasing of his Attorney General, Roger B. Taney, soon to succeed the aged John Marshall as Chief Justice, the veto message argued that the bank was a monopoly, unnecessary, inexpedient, unconstitutional, and injurious to the country. The veto aroused the prejudice of the state banks against the super-bank as well as the poor man's envy of the rich. Nor was the opportunity missed to incite the nationalistic prejudice against foreign — mainly English — holders of stock in the bank. ". . . The President's argument was directed to the voters, with such plausibility as to lead them to believe that he was expressing their own half-formed thought. Many a voter, after reading the message, must have exclaimed, in effect, 'By gum, he's right!' " [26] In order to get a campaign document at public expense a Democratic Congressman moved the printing of 16,000 copies of the message, and the National Republican opposition eagerly supported the proposal under the illusory conviction that the publicity would irreparably damage Jackson on the eve of his campaign for re-election. As if this were not enough folly, the bank also printed thousands of copies more. The great bank had irritated state banks by presenting their circulating notes promptly for redemption, thereby compelling them to maintain an adequate reserve at the same time that they "took hard money out of the community." This practice checked currency expansion and tended to depress prices, to the dismay of the mortgaged agrarians. Worse still, as we have seen, the bank had acquired considerable land through foreclosures and moreover had, by its lending policy, favored the land speculator rather than the actual settler, since the former was likely to enjoy a better credit rating than the latter.

Jackson was no less calculating and sagacious politically in dealing with the Nullification issue. In this battle of the giants the President's chief antagonist was Vice President John C. Calhoun. We have already seen the South Carolina statesman as a super-nationalist subscribing to every essential item that

---

[26] H. C. Hockett, op. cit., II, 85.

later went into Clay's American System. By the middle twenties, however, this ambitious leader faced political extinction at home. South Carolina leaders, including the judiciary, were turning hysterically anti-protectionist. Boycotts of Northern manufacturers and farmers suddenly became fashionable. One judge refused to eat Irish potatoes since they were raised in the North, and another preferred to live on snowbirds rather than feed on Kentucky pork, and to cover the circuit on foot rather than ride a horse from protectionist Kentucky.[27] The tidal planters, facing economic ruin and stubbornly ignoring the real cause of their woes in the competition of the black virgin soil to the west, turned vindictively on the South Carolina champion of protection, John C. Calhoun.

In sheer self-defense the hard-pressed Calhoun met his personal crisis by inventing a formula that was a near miracle of the politician's ingenuity. Turning to the Virginia and Kentucky Resolutions, which were fundamental doctrines of the Republican Party and for many years the undisputed political faith of a vast majority of Americans,[28] not excluding the Federalists of 1812, he undertook to implement their implicit nullification with specific and practicable apparatus. In order to give this the sanctity of the Constitution he made the amending process a principal element in its structure. Substantially his proposal amounted to a procedure by which a state could suspend within its bounds the enforcement of an allegedly unconstitutional act of Congress. Thus challenged, Congress might break the resulting impasse by repealing the act, amending it, or attempting to sustain it by an appeal to the states in the form of a proposed amendment to the Constitution specifically authorizing the power in question. In case the amendment carried, the nullifying state would be morally obligated to submit. The extraordinary shrewdness of Calhoun's formula lay in the fact that only one more than one fourth of the states might defeat the amendment, thereby sustaining the nullifying state. It was distinctly the device of a minority calculated to protect its interests within the Union.

[27] C. S. Boucher: Nullification Controversy in South Carolina, pp. 1–3.
[28] H. Adams: John Randolph, pp. 35, 36.

As a trial balloon the ordinance nullifying the Tariff Act of 1832 proved utterly disappointing to the South Carolinians who passed it. It failed also as a formula with which to promote Calhoun's presidential aspirations. Instead of a hoped-for general alignment of states with South Carolina, not one responded favorably — not even another cotton-planting state. The Georgia and Alabama planters had already been won over to Jackson by his policy of removing the Indians from the black belts. The troops Adams had sent to Georgia to protect the Indians' rights had been recalled by Jackson when the rush of miners into the Cherokee strip followed hard upon the discovery of gold there.

Jackson's counter-move against the Ordinance of Nullification was a proclamation so stern as to place the now isolated South Carolinians in a predicament from which they were eventually rescued, with some semblance of face-saving, only by consummate political legerdemain. The proclamation was more than a landmark in our constitutional history. It was in fact a master stroke of an artist in political leadership *en rapport* with the American masses. Warning fellow citizens of his native state that "the object of nullification is disunion and disunion by armed force is treason," he notified them that the laws of the United States must be executed and that their "First Magistrate cannot if he would avoid the performance of his duty." [29] While not so palatable to the Georgia cotton-planters, the proclamation stirred the inherent nationalism of yeoman and pioneer even if it was "too ultra and consolidating" for Henry Clay,[30] who worked out the compromise of the gradual reduction of the tariff. A generation later, when Lincoln made ready to prepare his inaugural address in the midst of the secession movement, he asked his partner, W. H. Herndon, to get him a copy of the Constitution and of Jackson's Proclamation against Nullification. Jackson had made Lincoln's role possible.

Year by year as Jackson dealt with these burning issues, the original heterogeneous aggregation of anti-Adams men

[29] J. D. Richardson, *Messages and Papers of the Presidents*, II, 640 ff.
[30] *Clay's Works* (C. Colton ed.), IV, 345.

was being purged of its less harmonious elements. Even the removal of the Indians to the West lost Jackson some adherents, such as the Quakers and missionary friends of the aborigines.[31] To the cotton-planters this policy was but the fulfillment of the understanding with which the Crawford men had shifted to Jackson's support in 1828. In any case Jackson's handling of the Indians was the execution of a legislative policy, the House of Representatives having by a vote of 99 to 89 tabled a bill designed to render effective Marshall's opinion that the Indians were wards of the nation and not subject to Georgia.[32] Whatever the outspoken President may have said about Marshall enforcing his own decision, the failure to carry it into effect seems to have been legislatively determined as well as sanctioned by the preponderance of prevailing public opinion. More grateful even than the planters were the settlers on the wheat lands of the old Northwest just vacated by the removal of the Indians.

When Andrew Jackson retired from the presidency he was the unchallenged chieftain of a compact militant party combination consisting of the residuum of faithful followers remaining after the successive defections of the lukewarm. Thousands who had at first supported him as the supposed champion of internal improvements were no doubt impelled by the Maysville veto to turn to Clay. When he designated Van Buren instead of Calhoun as the vice-presidential candidate for his second term, he lost the partisans of the discarded Southerner; and a Jacksonian leader, John Bell of Tennessee, also carried a group to the opposition when Van Buren was designated as the heir apparent. The state-rights Virginia planters under John Tyler now turned away from the nationalist President who had prepared to crush the nullificationists with military force and went over to the opposition, to be followed presently by the Crawford cotton-planters nurtured on the Virginia and Kentucky Resolutions. Prosperous Jacksonians had difficulty stomaching the bank veto, however much it elated the common man. Yet when accounts had

---

[31] Martin Van Buren, *Autobiography*, p. 284.
[32] *Worcester* v. *Georgia*, 6 Peters 515 ff.

been cast, with profits and losses carefully calculated, it was evident enough that the Jacksonian party was stronger than ever. The great political chieftain inspired the petty planters of the South, the yeomanry and frontiersmen of the West, the humble folk of the urban East — in short, the common man everywhere — with a new sense of membership in the body politic such as not even Thomas Jefferson had succeeded in doing.

The assumption that Jacksonian Democracy was merely a Western movement ignores the significant fact that for a generation before the Civil War Democrats everywhere were derided with the epithet Locofocos after a movement springing from the very sidewalks of New York. From the early decades of the century the elder Duane through his *Aurora* had conducted a crusade against banks, the judiciary, and the incorporation of the common law of England into American jurisprudence. A manifestation of the ferment of these ideas among the Eastern masses was the Workingmen's Party, originating in the late twenties. It represented a revolt against the Regency-dominated Tammany organization of New York City, and alarmed conservatives with its virulent attacks on bankers and especially their paper money, the ruinous depreciation to which it was subject proving particularly disastrous to wage-earners. When the new party astounded old politicians by polling 6,000 votes in a New York municipal election and then spread to other cities, anti-Regency, anti-Van-Buren, anti-Masonic, and other political factions began bidding for the now politically conscious labor vote. By 1832 the Workingmen's Party had spread so widely that a convention at Albany had delegates from every New England state except Vermont. The delegates discussed the effect of banks and monopolies on labor, the abolition of imprisonment for debt, the workingman's lien, factory conditions, and free public schools.

The Workingmen's Party proved transient, but popular discontent presently took the form of the Equal Rights Party in New York City, more commonly known as the Locofocos. When Jackson had diverted the deposit of Federal funds from the Bank of the United States to the selected state banks, called "pet" banks, a spree of "wildcat" banking set in. These banks were known to be profiting corruptly from the Federal deposits. Unchecked now by the great bank's salutary policy of presenting the state-bank notes promptly for redemption, uncontrolled issues of paper were put out which created a sharp inflation, and wages failed to keep pace with doubling commodity prices. This, along with a short wheat crop, provoked the New York City bread riots of 1836 and 1837.

When at irregular intervals, perhaps weeks or months apart, the poor laborer received his meager wages, paid in the unstable state-bank currency, he was unable to know to what various stages of depreciation the bills of the different banks had sunk or even which were counterfeit. Here was the setting for the birth of the Locofoco Party, with its demand for a return to hard money and the absolute separation of government funds from banking.

Nor was the Locofoco revolt against Tammany confined to laborers. "Small grocers and shop keepers who felt the pinch of wholesale prices," wrote the contemporary historian of the party, "together with mechanics who read books on Sunday were most numerous though there were some disgruntled office holders and at least a dozen physicians were important in their councils." [33] In the campaign of 1834 the new party's convictions, expressed in rhyme and set to a patriotic air, revealed the nature of the group combination as well as its class consciousness:

> Mechanics, Carters, Laborers
> Must form a close connection
> And show the rich Aristocrats
> Their powers at this election.
> Yankee Doodle, smoke 'em out
> The proud, the banking faction.
> None but such as Hartford Feds
> Oppose the poor and Jackson.[34]

---

[33] Fitzwilliam Byrdsall: *The History of the Loco Foco or Equal Rights Party* (New York, 1842).

[34] Quoted by D. R. Fox: *The Decline of Aristocracy in the Politics of New York*, p. 386.

In New York every bank charter was a special enactment obtained by corrupting the state legislature. Even the purchase of stock in a new bank was a special privilege granted by the State Bank Commission, customarily only to Regency Democrats. Quite naturally the Locofoco platform proclaimed hostility to "all monopolies by legislation because they violate the equal rights of the people." Voting with the Whigs, they carried the New York City elections in 1836 and 1837, and the next year the combination carried the state elections including those for the legislature, whereupon the "free banking" system displaced the vicious one just described. Thereafter any group of qualified persons might establish a bank under a general law instead of having to bribe legislators for a special act establishing a new bank.

Shortlived though the Locofoco Party was, its soul went marching on and profoundly affected Jacksonian Democracy, its influence spreading far and wide throughout the new West. These urban Jacksonians no less than their fellow partisans of the frontier based their demands for justice on the broad foundations of natural rights and the Declaration of Independence. This movement came just as the slavery element of the Democratic Party began its pressure to soft-pedal equalitarian doctrine. Slaveholders could not keep a plank reaffirming the Declaration of Independence out of the Democratic national platform of 1840 — Locofocoism was too strong for that — but four years later the Southerners had their way and it did not again appear in that party's platform until long after the Civil War.

Locofocoism proved especially acceptable to the Democracy of the Northwest. For example, the Locofoco faction in control of the Ohio legislature in the late thirties practically stopped the incorporation of new banks and checked the issue of bank notes of less than five dollars by laying a tax of twenty per cent on these smaller denominations, hoping thereby to keep specie circulating. By the middle of the century Locofocoism was still strong enough to fasten into the Ohio Constitution of 1851 the double liability of owners of bank stock so securely that it could not be repealed until 1935. For sev-

eral years in the forties the movement obtained legislation
that made banks practically impossible in Illinois, Wisconsin,
Iowa, and Missouri. The outstanding Western exponent of
the Locofoco idea of hard money was Thomas H. Benton of
Missouri, who bore the appropriate sobriquet of "Old Bul-
lion." Paper currency of the state banks had promoted the
hysterical land speculation that hampered the purposes of the
settler in search of a farm. Jackson's Specie Circular, an executive order issued in 1836 requiring payments for land in
gold or silver instead of bank paper money, ruined land
speculators and elated the small farmers at the same time
that it established a Locofoco policy.

So profound was the effect of Locofocoism on the Democratic Party that its long traditional adherence to hard money,
free trade, resistance to governmental interference and special
legislation has been attributed to the shortlived Equal Rights
or Locofoco Party. When the Locofocos disappeared within
the general body of the Democratic Party, "it was rather because they had drawn it to themselves than because it had
absorbed or defeated them." [35] Mid-century state constitutional conventions incorporated in their handiwork such Locofoco principles and prejudices as popular election of judges
for short terms, rigid limitation of state debts, and the severe
and detailed restrictions of legislatures that have cluttered up
state constitutions during the last century. When Jackson's
successor, Van Buren, resolutely resisted the pressure to rescind the Specie Circular and sponsored the Independent
Treasury as a depository for Federal funds, thereby divorc-
ing public finance from private banking, he was simply going
Locofoco or following the party trend of the movement that
originated in the metropolis of his own state. In his first annual
message to Congress Van Buren recommended so many of
the milder Locofoco proposals that henceforth the Whigs
throughout the nation, Lincoln among them, substituted the
word Locofoco for Democrat. The propaganda value of the
term to the Whigs was admitted by the *Democratic Review*

---

[35] Woodrow Wilson: *Division and Reunion*, p. 96.

of January 1838, in its statement that in the recent election "a use was made of the unfortunate word Loco-Foco . . . alone sufficient to frighten fifty thousand very worthy and honest people away from the ballot boxes."

The urban Equal Rights Party of New York City had its counterpart in the rural Barnburners, with whom it is fre‑ quently confused. These Barnburners derive significance from the fact that they challenged and then overthrew the powerful New York Regency with repercussions that deter‑ mined presidential elections. This Regency had originated in the partyless period after the War of 1812, and by the time under consideration it consisted of a group of extraordinarily expert Democratic politicians who, through caucuses and newspapers, ruled as long as they could maintain party unity by appeasing dissident Democratic minorities. One of their number, Van Buren, gave an inkling as to their methods when he said: "They had sense to know that, when they were in power, they could be served better in places of trust by their friends than by their enemies . . . and they acted accord‑ ingly." [36] Another member of the Regency, W. L. Marcy, ex‑ pressed the same idea more bluntly in the pithy slogan: "To the victors belong the spoils."

The Barnburner movement was a revolt against enterpris‑ ing promoters, among both politicians and contractors, who sought to satisfy the persistent demand of remote communi‑ ties for lateral canals to the Erie, regardless of mounting state indebtedness. When a bill halting canal extensions and sub‑ stituting taxing for borrowing was enacted, it split the New York Democratic Party, wrecked the Regency, and pitted the radicals or Barnburners against the conservatives or Hunkers. The basis of the division is another illustration of the moti‑ vation of party politics. Election maps [37] reveal that the Hunk‑ ers, who might in this case be called the canal party, drew their strength from the regions of projected lateral canals as well as from prospective contractors, pick-and-shovel labor‑ ers (mostly Irish) who expected to do the excavating, and

[36] W. A. Butler: *Martin Van Buren*, pp. 28–9.
[37] See H. D. A. Donavan: *The Barnburners*, p. 20.

politicians scenting votes and canal patronage. This last element accounts for the term "Hunker"; they "hunkered" after
office. Many of them had profited corruptly by the connection
between the state-chartered "pet" banks and Jackson's Federal funds deposited in them. They were horrified at President Van Buren's measure to take these funds out of all banks
and their Congressmen prevented establishment of the Van
Buren Independent Treasury until almost the end of his administration. "Respectability," as a whole, characterized the
Hunkers, with bankers an influential element among them.
On a national scale Democratic solidarity and loyalty impelled
them to co-operate with the slaveholding wing of the party
and support the expansionist urge of the South.

The Barnburners, like the Locofocos, were party dissenters
on much more than canal expansion, and represented, in fact,
a reform movement that culminated in the liberal New York
Constitution of 1846. Their deadly earnestness is revealed in
the designation their enemies gave them, "Barnburners." This
term may have been due to the contemporary incendiarism
of the defeated Dorrites in Rhode Island, although the popular explanation is that of a Dutchman who burned down his
barn to get rid of the rats. Election maps show Barnburners
strongest in the outlying districts and resentful of taxes laid
to benefit canal-favored regions. President Van Buren's courageous anti-bank policy appealed powerfully to them and he
became their national hero. No fonder of Southern slaveholders than of Northern Hunkers, they will be found opposing
the annexation of Texas, the war against Mexico, the expansion of slavery into the territories, and the Southern domination of the Democratic Party. These "Methodists of Democracy," as one of their leaders called them, initiated, in fact,
"one of the most democratic movements ever staged on the
American continent. Appealing to the first principles of the
Declaration of Independence and the Bible they strove to
overthrow privilege and make America truly democratic." [38]
Intense moral convictions inspired these crusaders against

---

[38] Avery Craven: *Democracy in American Life,* pp. 91–2.

slavery as Barnburners evolved through Liberty men, Free-Soilers, and Free Democrats into Republicans and then Union soldiers singing as they marched,

I have read a fiery gospel writ in burnished rows of steel,
As ye deal with my contemners so with you my grace shall deal.

In 1836 Van Buren had been carried into the presidency on the momentum of the Jacksonian movement in the face of a Whig opposition divided among three candidates who had hoped merely to throw the election into the House of Representatives. Four years later he became the first of the Presidents to be punished at the polls for a depression during his administration. When seeking re-election, Van Buren was confronted by a united opposition supporting William Henry Harrison, who proved to be a sufficiently convincing imitation of "Old Hickory." [39] The Whigs managed to turn the social forces that had elected Andrew Jackson against his successor. Van Buren's followers were confident they needed only to wait four years for vindication, but in 1844 the slavocracy was demanding the annexation of the independent Republic of Texas, which Van Buren, true to his devoted Barnburner constituency, would not sanction. Consequently the compact planter minority in the Democratic National Convention, through the rule they had succeeded in getting established, prevented Van Buren's clear majority among the delegates from reaching the two-thirds vote required for a nomination.

As to Texas, the planters entertained a not altogether baseless fear that it might become an English possession. This threatened the mouth of the Mississippi at the same time that it would give the English a source of cotton supply outside the customs union of the United States. Worse still, since English soil meant free men, Texas would provide a sanctuary for fugitive slaves far more dangerous than Canada, since it would be separated from the slave states only by an imagi-

---

[39] The significance of Tyler's administration in American party history is dealt with in the chapter on the Whig Party, which was responsible for his occupancy of the presidential office.

nary line instead of the buffer of such intermediary states as
Ohio and Indiana. Moreover, gigantic Texas dangled before
the eager slavocrats the prospect of division into several
states, each to strengthen their "peculiar institution" in the
Senate, and the electoral college. This very possibility, however, alarmed an important element of the Northern Democracy and created a problem in conciliation for Democratic
party leaders.

Robert J. Walker of Mississippi, a genius in party management, was at hand to devise the party strategy. A native of
Pennsylvania and connected with its powerful political families by marriage, he was known as a land speculator and advocate of free homesteads and western expansion, a demand
for which the long depression since 1837 had revived. The
most unifying sentiment of Jacksonian Democracy was still
a bitter antipathy for England. Farmers of New York, Ohio,
and Michigan blamed England for the fact that their crops
had remained unharvested for seven years and they were organizing leagues to protest against the Corn Laws that shut
their grain out of England.

Utilizing the intense anti-English feeling prevalent throughout the Mississippi Valley, Walker would cement the Northern and Southern wings of Western Democracy with the
inspiring slogan: "The re-annexation of Texas and the re-
occupation of Oregon," the prefix "re" being used to camou-
flage an implicit belligerency. The Oregon issue concerned a
pending dispute with England over the boundary between
the territory of England and the United States in the far
Northwest. Representing upper Mississippi Valley Democrats, eager to push the Oregon boundary claim hundreds of
miles to the north, Senator "Foghorn" William Allen of Ohio
supplemented Walker's slogan with his "Fifty-four Forty or
Fight." Not yet satisfied that the anti-English prejudice had
been thoroughly exploited, Senator E. A. Hannegan of Indiana, proposed completing the slogan with "or *delenda est
Britannia.*" [40] Walker managed to have the convention nomi-

---

[40] D. W. Howe: "The Mississippi Valley in the Movement for Fifty-
four Forty or Fight," Mississippi Valley Historical Association *Report*, V, 103.

nate James K. Polk, a low-tariff man from Tennessee, for President and George M. Dallas, a Pennsylvania protectionist, as his running mate.

The easy success of Walker's dynamic formula in uniting the party and electing Polk fascinated the slavocrats and gave them a fatuous obsession as to their own invincibility. Between Polk's election and his inauguration the planters had already obtained their share of the campaign pledge of the "re-annexation of Texas." Whether by design or accident, Polk's Mexican War was soon to give them hundreds of thousands of square miles more in the Southwest, practically all of which would ultimately make slave states if the Missouri Compromise line were extended to the Pacific. In striking contrast with this overflowing reward of Southern Democrats was Polk's handling of the "re-occupation of Oregon." No matter how much prudence may have dictated his retreat from "Fifty-four Forty" without a "Fight" and his acceptance of forty-nine degrees instead as the northern boundary of the Oregon territory, it was "truckling" to England and basely sacrificing the promises held forth to Northern Democrats. In exasperation they retaliated with the Wilmot Proviso, designed to shut slavery out of any territory that might be acquired from Mexico, thereby opening a party breach presaging the split of Democracy in the fifties and of the nation itself in the sixties.

During Polk's administration the conviction became firmly planted in the minds of hundreds of thousands of Northern Democrats that the slavocracy was a dog in the manger persistently preventing the satisfaction of the interests of the Northern wing. The Walker tariff was a free-trade, cotton-planter's measure, rather than a grain-grower's, although it should be noted that the conciliatory Walker believed the repeal of the English Corn Laws would follow the lowering of the tariff, especially since Ireland was in the agony of the potato famine. Of a like color was Polk's veto of the bill to improve Western rivers and lake harbors — it was the hand of the slavocrats. Polk's Secretary of War, W. L. Marcy, was the leader of the New York Hunkers and he dealt out Federal patronage in accordance with his well-known maxim: "To the victors belong the spoils," making certain that none but Hunkers were appointed. The Van Buren men, as we shall see presently, were already headed for the Free-Soil Party, through which they were, for the most part, to pass into the yet-to-be new Republican Party.

With clairvoyant prescience the Elder Statesman Calhoun had disapproved of the War with Mexico, declaring in its first year: "Mexico is to us the forbidden fruit; the penalty of eating it would be to subject our institutions to political death." [41] He foresaw the agitation of the slavery issue that the acquisition of new slave territory would provoke and the possible creation of new free states to offset Texas. In 1848 the slavocrats met the party crisis produced by the Wilmot Proviso with a new strategy for controlling the presidency, the nomination of a "doughface." Their "Northern man with Southern principles," nominated in 1848, was Lewis Cass of Michigan. This shrewd politician had his own plan for restoring and preserving party unity by dodging the issue of slavery in the territory acquired from Mexico. He would employ the extremely acceptable dogma of popular sovereignty and let the settlers there vote slavery in or out as they chose. Even if the Whigs had nominated a less popular candidate than General Taylor, Cass could scarcely have overcome the handicaps piled up by the four years of slavocracy's frustration of Northern Democracy under Polk. In any case Cass was defeated by General Taylor, who died in office and was succeeded by Fillmore.

It was no mean achievement for the Whigs, after Fillmore's accession, to translate into statutes the ingenious formulas of the Compromise of 1850 for settling the immediate issues of slavery. This extraordinarily, though not universally, popular measure was backed by an imposing array of economic interests. Business men were reveling in a boom induced by California gold and an amazing outburst of railroad construction. In a few short years farmers saw the price of

---

[41] *Congressional Globe,* 29th Cong., 2nd Sess., App., p. 324.

wheat more than double, thanks to the gold inflation and England's new free-trade policy, and American shipping had never been busier. Laborers were paid high wages, manufacturers enjoyed a good Southern market, and the cotton-planters received good prices. Abolitionists became extremely unpopular, since their agitation imperiled the prevailing prosperity, and especially the Northern trade with the South.

Missing a grand opportunity to exploit their great achievement, the Compromise of 1850, by nominating Fillmore, who had exerted presidential pressure to ensure its passage,[42] the Whigs nominated instead the politically inept General Winfield Scott. The Democratic Convention, in order to satisfy the slaveholders, nominated the relatively unknown but typically doughface politician Franklin Pierce of New Hampshire. They endorsed the Compromise and swept the counties of the North and South with a thoroughness indicative of the immeasurable weariness of the people with the agitation of the slavery question. Slavery, now assumed to be limited with "finality" to a definite area both by a gentleman's agreement and by formal statutes, was henceforth to be taboo as a political issue. What scornful mirth would have greeted a prophet with the temerity to predict in 1852 that within two years the truce would be broken, with a consequent outburst of public indignation unparalleled in American political history and all but fatal to the party of Andrew Jackson!

---

[42] See a letter of Salmon P. Chase, *American Historical Association Report* (1902), II, 217.

CHAPTER VII

THE WHIGS

"THE WHIGS *were the party of property and talents. In the North under Daniel Webster they carried on the nationalist and paternal tradition of Alexander Hamilton. The manufacturing interests which wanted protection, the merchants and bankers who suffered from Jackson's financial vagaries, went Whig. The Anti-Masons, the nativists, and the anti-slavery followers of J. Q. Adams were also absorbed. A large number of Westerners were attracted by the personality of Henry Clay and the hope of getting something done about the public lands. In the South the Whigs were the party of gentility and property, owning over two thirds of all the slaves. Sugar planters of Louisiana who wanted protection against Cuba; big cotton planters who regretted the veto of the United States Bank, and who in state politics resisted the repudiating of their poor fellows; antique Republicans of Virginia and North Carolina, who disliked Jackson's aggressive nationalism and 'executive tyranny' — all went Whig. Nowhere but in America could a political party have been formed from such heterogeneous elements."* Adapted from S. E. MORISON and H. S. COMMAGER.*

I T is remarkable how tenaciously American citizens of the late twenties and the early thirties clung to the conviction that there could be but one political party — the Republican — and that all of them belonged to it. There might be factions, but Adams and Clay men no less than Jackson men insisted they were the true Jeffersonians. Gradually, in the late twenties, the former assumed the distinctive designation of National Republicans and the latter that of Democratic Republi-

---

* From *The Growth of the American Republic,* I, 450, 451. By permission of the Oxford University Press, publishers.

cans. Since Clay's "American System" and Adams's reduction of it to the practical blueprint of his messages had been strikingly nationalistic, the term applied to these Republicans was accurately descriptive.

As President Jackson's party in the early thirties lost, one by one, its less democratic elements — Western promoters of internal improvements, Southern state-rights planters, Eastern banking interests — the militant residuum took on more and more the character of a radical mass movement distinctly challenging to a nation-wide congeries of interests in American society. The problem of finding bases of agreement among these elements, too divergent in nature to coalesce at once, if ever, into a party, enlisted the political talents of the most notable galaxy of party leaders of any generation of Americans.

Nature apparently decreed that the Ohio Valley should produce the most eminent leader of the National Republicans. The importance of this valley in the history of the Whig Party justifies a brief survey of its vast extent. It is well to note that the Ohio River runs its southwesterly course rather through the northern part of the valley. The three states of Kentucky, Tennessee, and West Virginia lie almost entirely within the valley, as do also two thirds of Ohio and Indiana and a strip of eastern Illinois. Fringing the valley are a southwestern corner of New York, the western third of Pennsylvania, a portion of western Virginia, a broad strip along the entire border of North Carolina, the northern fringe of Georgia and Alabama, and the northeastern tip of Mississippi.

Here was a region with economic interests and lines of communication and trade that bound it to every other section of the Republic. Thus, with hostages in every direction, stern necessity prompted a prudent if not passionate devotion to the Union and required, as did no other region, the cultivation of the arts of conciliation and compromise. It was, then, no mere coincidence that the pre-eminent political leader of the Ohio Valley, Henry Clay, of whom the National Republicans and the Whigs were, at times, literally a personal following, has come down from his generation bearing the merited title of the "Great Pacificator."

Henry Clay, by crystallizing a nation-wide opinion in his American System, had produced the fundamental formula of the National Republicans, which Adams reduced to the blueprint of his earliest presidential addresses. Jackson's election in 1828, however, had cast some doubt on the vote-attracting power of Clay's formula, at the same time that Adams's defeat had transferred party leadership to Clay. When Jackson vetoed the Maysville Road in Clay's own state, he dramatically challenged the internal-improvement feature of the American System [1] and believed he was sharply defining party issues. Webster promptly wrote to Clay designating him the leader of the opposition.[2] Back in the Senate in 1831 Clay set to work unifying the anti-Jackson elements, but Jackson dealt his plans another blow by signing instead of vetoing the Tariff Act in 1832.

In 1832 Henry Clay neglected no issue that his fertile ingenuity could weave into a complex formula for balancing interests and recruiting the National Republican ranks. The accumulating Treasury surplus, the protective tariff, internal improvements, and the public land policy all found their place in the jig-saw puzzle. First of all, by not reducing the current price of $1.25 an acre for government land he would relieve the fear of the depression of land values in the older states as well as the alarm of land speculators at the prospect of the public domain being sold for a song or even given away to squatters and impecunious settlers. Moreover, maintaining this price would relieve Eastern industrialists, merchants, and real-estate owners anxious lest too many employees, customers, and tenants catch the "Western fever." Clay's Distribution Bills of 1832 and 1833 provided that the proceeds of public-land sales should be divided among the states in proportion to their respective presidential electoral quotas. The Treasury would thus be emptied, to the relief of protectionists, who otherwise feared reduction of tariffs, and of state-

---

[1] See *supra*, p. 176.

[2] *Writings and Speeches* (National edition), XVI, 197–9.

rights Southerners, alert to the danger of raids on the Treasury surplus in order to carry on internal improvements. The vast lump sums to be distributed would be especially acceptable to states teetering on the brink of bankruptcy that had been induced by reckless canal construction, and already clamoring for a second great assumption of state debts. Other states might be enabled to use these Federal funds on their own internal improvements without offense to the scruples of state-rights purists. Whether North, South, East, and West might ever have been rallied to the standard of Clay and his National Republicans by means of the distribution plan is doubtful. In any case Jackson chose to give Clay's Distribution Act of 1833 a pocket veto on the ground of unconstitutionality, as he later explained in his annual message to Congress of December 4, 1833.

It was Clay's misfortune to have made one of the major miscalculations of his career in 1832 by tying his presidential fortunes to the issue of rechartering the Bank of the United States. Jackson vetoed the measure and gained thereby more friends than he lost. It certainly did not strengthen Clay among Western farmers to have appeared before the Supreme Court as counsel for the bank in the bitterly contested Osborne case,[3] in which it was decided that Ohio could not tax the two branches located in the state. His defeat in 1832 was overwhelming. He carried not much more than scattered counties in his own Ohio Valley and fewer counties than Adams had in 1828 in the zone of New England settlements. He obtained majorities in a clump of counties bordering the Delaware and Potomac rivers and in the lower Louisiana parishes. Elsewhere Jackson made a clean sweep. The National Republicans had waged their last campaign for the presidency.

Clay had scarcely time to catch his breath after the campaign when the Nullification crisis brought the nation to the verge of civil war. With an astonishing resiliency the spokesman of the Ohio Valley, convinced that the Union must be

---

[3] *Supra,* p. 144.

preserved at almost any cost, broke the impasse between South Carolina and the administration with his famous Compromise Tariff of 1833. Thereby faces were saved and tensions eased through a gradual reduction of the tariff over a period of years. Two fortuitous developments enabled Clay to do this without sacrificing his prestige among his Ohio Valley constituents. His immediate neighborhood had failed to get established the factories they were counting on when he had devised his protective-tariff policy. Moreover, the valley had discovered an unexpected home market for its surpluses in their sale to the rapidly expanding, one-crop cotton plantations, and had consequently lost some interest in protection. In short, this section was ready for an *entente cordiale* with Calhoun and the state-rights planters, who constituted a group of customers very essential to their prosperity. Here was to be an economic bond of unity between the Northern and Southern wings of the yet-to-be Whig Party.

Clay had regarded his Distribution Bill with its maintenance of the price of government lands as an absolutely essential part of his Compromise of 1833 and he bitterly resented Jackson's veto of the former, by a pocket veto at that, thereby irreparably marring the symmetry of his formula and alienating his protectionist following. So great now was their "heritage of defeat" that the Nationalist Republicans absolutely abandoned their ill-fated name, and a realignment of groups in parties on an entirely new fundamental basis appeared imminent in 1833.

Clay's eclipse gave Webster his great opportunity. Having begun his congressional career two decades earlier as a champion of the anti-tariff shipping interests of New England, he had challenged Clay's American System upon its first presentation, not as an enemy of manufacturers, he averred, but as an opponent of rearing them in hothouses. However, as his wealthy constituents one by one shifted their capital from shipping to textiles, Webster learned to fraternize with the Lawrences and Lowells and the great mill-owners generally, even becoming in due time a heavy investor in wool-textile production. By 1832 the erstwhile chief challenger of Clay's

System had become pre-eminently the champion of protection, gaining personal adherents from among the disillusioned deserters of Clay, now the apostate "Compromiser."

The combination of interests that Webster represented also needed the Union, not just the Ohio Valley's loosely federated association of "sovereign" states, cherishing the tradition of the Virginia and Kentucky Resolutions, but a stalwart Union, functioning through a national government capable of collecting imposts, even by military force if necessary.

In his classic reply to Hayne the godlike Daniel has never been surpassed by any orator in capturing a developing national trend and utilizing it to rationalize a set of interests in terms of devotion to the nation and the flag. Here was a game of giants gambling for one of the greatest stakes in history, the political allegiance of the West. When Webster declared: "It is, Sir, the people's government, made for the people, made by the people and answerable to the people," the superb debater had maneuvered Hayne into a position where state rights seemed to be a denial of popular sovereignty, then the dominant political dogma of the Jacksonians and the whole Democratic West. Here was the spokesman of New England inviting the Democratic nationalists of the West to join the East in common cause, as well as the keen presidential aspirant in search of a majority-commanding formula for capturing the presidency, a prize fate seemed to be dangling even then before the great orator's eyes.

Such party confusion had the crisis of 1833 created that Senator Clay was compromising with Vice President Calhoun and the nullificationists at the same time that Senator Webster was fraternizing cordially with President Jackson in shaping a Force Act to crush resistance to Federal authority when collecting tariff duties in South Carolina. So fluid had the elements constituting parties now become that a Jackson-Webster party of Unionists in opposition to one of state rights seemed logical if not imminent. Webster made a trip to the West, feeling out sentiment, and was wildly welcomed everywhere by Jacksonians. The success of the developing alliance, however, depended upon Jackson's abandoning his war against the Bank of the United States, and when instead he compelled the cessation of government deposits in the bank, the new party movement suddenly collapsed. Since Congress, in the statute creating the bank, had specifically vested discretionary power over removal of Federal funds exclusively in the Secretary of the Treasury, and Jackson had exercised the President's power to remove his appointees in order to get a Secretary who would exercise his statutory discretion as to deposit exactly as Jackson desired, the opposition of every description raised the cry of "executive usurpation." This became the shibboleth of the now emerging Whigs.

Competing for position as a major party until merged with the National Republicans in order to produce the Whigs was a parallel political movement strikingly illustrative of the natural history of American parties. Farmers of the twelve western counties of New York, settled principally by New Englanders not of the Democratic affiliation, were accustomed to bring their grain to the Erie Canal at Buffalo, Lockport, or Rochester for shipment east to the "home market" they believed dependent upon Clay's American System.[4] Their religious prejudice against secret societies was suddenly intensified by the mysterious disappearance and alleged murder of one William Morgan, who had announced an intention to publish a revelation of the mysteries of Freemasonry. Immediately a strange new political party sprang into existence, known as the Anti-Masons.

Since the movement originated in counties that had supported Adams, who was not a Mason, while Jackson was, shrewd politicians such as Thurlow Weed promptly exploited the Anti-Masons in order to overthrow the Democratic Regency. The New York Democrats having opposed the Chenango Canal, designed to connect the interior lakes of New York with the Pennsylvania system, the Anti-Masons supported it as an outlet for their own section. Political leaders persuaded the Anti-Masons to favor exempting New York City banks from the burden of the safety-fund tax imposed

---

4 D. R. Fox: *Decline of Aristocracy in the Politics of New York*, p. 424

by the Locofoco Democrats under Van Buren's leadership. The Anti-Masons sought recruits in the Great Lakes region by condemning Jackson's veto of a harbor bill, and elsewhere by condemning his treatment of the Cherokee Indians. They advocated protective tariffs and internal improvements, and by 1832 had so completely abandoned their crusade against Masonry as to be scarcely distinguishable from National Republicans, who absorbed the Anti-Masons as soon as the latter had elected William H. Seward Governor of New York.

Anti-Masonry spread across the New York boundary into Pennsylvania, first into the northern tier of counties populated by New England stock, then among the Scotch Presbyterians and the numerous German pietistic sects that feared and hated oath-bound societies, with the result that here the party designation Anti-Masons became precisely descriptive. Many of these Pennsylvanians were geographically connected with the Baltimore market, and they accordingly opposed the state Democratic program for the expenditure of millions of dollars to connect Philadelphia with the West. In Massachusetts the Anti-Masonic movement was strengthened by rural orthodoxy and the prejudice against the aristocracy of Boston and other cities, who were tainted with the free-thought of Unitarianism as well as with Masonry. In New York and New England the temperance movement was associated with Anti-Masonry. The great-grandchildren of the Puritans were shocked by the wild tales of wine-drinking at Masonic festivals.[5] As a party, Anti-Masonry had a brief career and derives its historical importance chiefly from the fact that it "furnished the first solid basis for the Whig movement of the future."[6]

Early in Jackson's second term his anti-nullification policy had alienated most of the great planters. As state-rights men they could never affiliate with Republicans bearing the tabooed term "National," even if the National Republican

---

[5] John D. Hicks: "The Third Party Tradition in American Politics," *Mississippi Valley Historical Review*, XX, 3.

[6] C. McCarthy: "The Anti-Masonic Party," American Historical Association *Report* (1902), I, 391.

party had not been demoralized by defeat. So these state-righters were first to assume the name Whigs, aiming thereby to fasten the odious term Tory on the Jacksonians. The designation spread from South Carolina to the North until it was used by practically all anti-Jacksonians. It was these state-rights Southern planters, more than any other one group of adherents, that enabled the Whigs for nearly twenty years to contend with the Democrats on fairly even terms in the South as well as the North. Yet they were at first allied with, rather than incorporated in, the Whig Party. Still so inchoate was the party in 1836 that it merely permitted three regional candidates to run against Van Buren. These were Hugh White, a recently estranged Jacksonian Democrat in the South; William Henry Harrison in the West; and Daniel Webster in the East. There was a hope of preventing Van Buren from obtaining an electoral majority and of thereby compelling election by the House of Representatives. Democracy, however, had now turned sufficiently reactionary for many New England and Middle State manufacturers to prefer taking their chance with Van Buren to risking a House election. Even counties of the old South where Jackson had been most feared supported Van Buren.

By the late thirties the Whig movement had matured into a fairly well-integrated combination actually on the verge of capturing the presidency. Its largest single element consisted of the old Adams-Clay men, advocates of the American System and formerly known as National Republicans. Through the political craft of Thurlow Weed and William H. Seward the Anti-Masons had been easily maneuvered into the Whig Party, where they promptly lost their identity. Former Jacksonians, alienated for various reasons, came over to the Whigs. Among them were Hugh L. White and John Bell, outstanding Democratic leaders from Jackson's own state. The biggest single accession from the supporters of Jackson were the state-sovereignty men alienated by his proclamation against the nullifiers, such as John Tyler, a leader of the tidal tobacco-planters, and the old Crawford men among the cotton-planters. The death blow to the bank, administered through the removal of Duane from the Treasury and the appointment in his place of the subservient Taney in order to get the deposits removed, was too dictatorial for many Democrats. Then there was the group known as the "Conservatives" consisting of Democrats, led by N. P. Tallmage of New York and W. C. Rives of Virginia, state-bank men whose pressure could not compel Van Buren to rescind the Specie Circular.[7] Alarmed at the new President's Locofocoism, they affiliated themselves with the Whigs without sacrificing their own organization. Whigs ostentatiously used them as chairmen or speakers at their celebrations. Moderate anti-slavery Democrats, convinced that Van Buren was truckling to the South, turned Whig. Finally, there were many recruits hitherto indifferent to politics who were becoming alarmed at what they conceived to be executive autocracy and a threat to free institutions.

It was no mere coincidence that the Whigs developed into a nation-wide party at the moment when the industrial revolution in America was getting its first marked impetus. Nor is it astonishing that New Englanders, gladly accepting the American System, became more unified as Whigs than they ever had been as Federalists, since the latter could never have countenanced internal improvements farther back from the harbor than the fall-line. By 1830 agriculture was already so subordinate that the section was importing corn and flour in large quantities from the West. Economic, social and political power had shifted from mercantile shipowners to textile-manufacturers and their financial allies. "The purest intellect ever applied to business"[8] was at their command in Daniel Webster, the personally improvident recipient of their bounty, particularly when in debt, "virtually their pensioner,"[9] not to say, as Brooks Adams put it, "the jackal of the interests."[10]

Dependent upon Southern planters for their cotton, these

---

[7] *Supra,* p. 196.

[8] R. W. Emerson: *Journals,* VI, 341.

[9] A. C. Cole: "Daniel Webster," *Dictionary of American Biography,* XIX, 588.

[10] Henry Adams: *The Degradation of the Democratic Dogma,* p. 92.

masters of the textile mills developed so close a community of interests with their fellow Whigs of the South as to bear the designation of the "Cotton Whigs." The disposal of their textiles depended, in no small degree, upon the Southern plantation market, which came to be regarded the very basis of Northern prosperity. Since New England shippers stood to get the carrying trade on two hauls, another tie was made between the Northern and Southern wings of the Whig combination. "The slave power overshadowed all the great Boston interests," [11] and the financier on State Street paled at the thought of anything that would disrupt this Northern-Southern complex of interests and dry up the flow of profits from financing the gigantic traffic. Webster might sanctify the Union with the wizardry of words, but Emerson, the master of pungent phrase, revealing keen insight into social forces, knew the reason. "Cotton thread holds the union together; unites John C. Calhoun and Abbott Lawrence. Patriotism [is] for holidays and summer evenings with rockets but cotton thread is the union." [12]

In New England as elsewhere the Whigs were primarily the party of accumulated property, supported at the polls by their dependents, paradoxical though the expression sounds. In the more prosperous communities, whether urban or rural, these notables could count upon the allegiance of lawyers, clergy, and teachers, while shopkeepers, native laborers, and other urban elements also accepted their leadership. Except at Democratic Baptist Brown University, college professors were almost universally Whigs, as indeed were the literary Brahmins generally. Conservative Unitarians made up the backbone of the party instead of the orthodox sects. Constituting an interest in itself was the class of rising Whig professional politicians, skilled technicians in the art of social co-ordination, eager to negotiate the inter-group understandings that could command majorities and capture the chief magistracy of state and nation with the attendant patronage. Before textile-manufacturers turned to Irish labor, which

11 Henry Adams: *Education of Henry Adams,* p. 25.
12 *Journals,* VII, 201, 232.

voted Democratic, the native mill hands had voted for "jobs" and against the "pauper labor" of Europe and the free-trade "slave-drivers" of the South, with whom their employers, however, fraternized. Native New England labor resented so intensely the competition of the impoverished Irish that Whig politicians managed to divert their animosity from their employers to the aliens themselves, whom Democratic politicians were receiving with open arms. More and more the New England Whigs became identified with the nativist movement until the Know-Nothings absorbed the rank and file of them in the middle fifties.

In the farming communities of better land values the "squirearchy," as Charles Francis Adams called them, provided agrarian allies for the urban Whigs. When the competition of Western grain, brought in by the Erie Canal and the Western Railroad, drove the poorer farmers, mostly Jacksonians, to the wall, the new owners turned to dairying and sheep-raising, the latter industry culminating in the historic "sheep craze" of Vermont and western Massachusetts. These wool-growers were protectionists and their communities show up on election maps as Whig. Markets, such as that at Brighton, near Boston, bore evidence of the enterprise of truck gardeners, dairymen, and stock-raisers. Since such producers tend to take on the partisan color of their urban customers, New Englanders of this description also were Whigs. Indeed, as the party matured, New England became more and more closely integrated on the basis of the various Whig interests and principles.

Wherever the sons of New England settled in their western migration, the Whigs found ready recruits. Those who dwelt on the better soils or along transportation routes, as well as capitalists, bankers, merchants, and manufacturers, here too became Whigs. Jackson's patronage in making "pet" state banks depositories of Federal funds had created a group of Jacksonian bankers, but when his Specie Circular well-nigh ruined them along with influential speculators in Western land, Thurlow Weed and other leaders managed to maneuver both disgruntled groups into the Whig Party.

What Van Buren did for the Democrats, Thurlow Weed did for the Whigs of New York. Politics was a fascinating game for him, affording an infinite satisfaction in the expression of an inner urge for civic service. "Leaving principles to Seward and others he could trust," wrote Dixon Ryan Fox, "he specialized in finding votes for what he recommended, advising only as an expert on the likelihood of the popularity of any given measure. In his domain he was as close a student, as unselfish and as patriotic a man as they in theirs. . . . Struggling slowly up from cabin boy and printer's devil he had learned the hopes and fears of the great mass of men better than the scholarly Seward or the courtly Francis Granger." [13] When Lincoln sent Weed to England on a mission of goodwill during the Civil War, sophisticated young Henry Adams, secretary of the American Ambassador, found "his faculty of irresistibly conquering confidence" so compelling that the young man "followed him about not only obediently — but rather with sympathy and affection, much like a dog." [14]

Even more dependent on the cotton traffic than the Boston financiers, merchants, and shippers were those of New York. The direct trade between the South and England had been diverted into the "cotton triangle," with both the import and export streams flowing through New York, where a heavy toll was exacted for trans-shipment, insurance, and financing. Packet lines brought the cotton to New York and reloaded it to give the east-bound Atlantic vessels their cargo, while on the return voyage English goods destined for the South again enriched New Yorkers on their passage through the port. New York City Negroes voted Whig against the Democrats, the party of the alien laborer who resented the pick-and-shovel competition of the black man and hated the abolitionist who would depress wages by flooding the labor market with emancipated Negroes.

Let those who think of the Whigs as constituting an anti-labor party reflect on the fact that Horace Greeley, the greatest of the Whig journalists and editor of the most influential

[13] Op. cit., p. 366.
[14] *Education of Henry Adams,* p. 146.

newspaper of his day, was a passionate champion of labor. While employers were arguing for protection because wages were too high, he converted the argument into one for the laborer in order to improve his condition and meet the competition of the pauper labor of Europe. In contrast with abolitionists such as Garrison, who scorned to consider the privations of free factory labor, Greeley was too distressed by conditions near at hand to go crusading with them. In 1845 he astonished an anti-slavery convention at Cincinnati when he wrote to them: "If I am less troubled by the slavery prevalent in Charleston or New Orleans it is because I see so much slavery in New York. . . . Whenever opportunity to labor is obtained with difficulty and is so deficient that the employing class may virtually prescribe their own terms and pay the laborers only such share as they choose of the product there is a very strong tendency to slavery."[15] Conservative Whigs promptly denounced him for "attempting incessantly . . . to excite the prejudices of the poor against the rich" and even against the Whig Party.[16] The acceptability of Greeley's doctrines to his vast reading public is indicative of the fact that the Whig Party, while not just a cross-section of American society, was nevertheless, like every major party in our history, a broad multi-group combination.

Wherever the New England stock with its mingled strains of moral enthusiasm and practical common sense predominated in the old Northwest, which included the states north of the Ohio River, the Whigs carried the counties. These pioneers readily occupied the treeless prairies shunned by the migrants from the South. Though Southern stock predominated in the beginning, the New Englanders eventually subordinated it and stamped the Puritan tradition and culture permanently upon the Northwest. Yet the Southern heritage was by no means obliterated, and the ironic sequel to the amalgamation of these contending cultures is the fact that a son of the South became the most notable contribution of the Whig Party to American history. Abraham Lincoln, a native

---

15 *New York Tribune*, June 20, 1845, p. 7, col. 3.
16 Ibid., August 5, 1845, p. 7, col. 2.

of Kentucky, as the chieftain of a later party was to rally to
his standard the Western sons of the Puritans almost to a man.
The frontier had a powerful influence, its absence of an aristocracy democratizing the Whigs of the Northwest. When
Abraham Lincoln married a Springfield belle of proud Kentucky lineage, he did not enhance his political strength but,
to use his own words, was "put down here as the candidate of
pride, wealth, and aristocratic family distinction." [17]

In the Northwest of the forties the prosperous grain-grower
or sheep-, cattle-, or hog-raiser was generally a Whig. As contrasted with the typical Jacksonian Democrat, the vocation of
these Whigs was likely to be something more than a way of
life; in fact, a method of making money on capital invested.
Clay's American System captivated these venders of cash
farm commodities, but they could never have carried elections had they not been able to lure many a less prosperous
but hopeful farmer from the Jacksonians by the promise of
protection and internal improvements. Stock-buyers, usually
Whigs, drove their herds south to the plantations through
Whig sections, cultivating on the way the goodwill of Whig
bankers, who provided them the loans with which to pay the
farmers cash for their live stock purchased en route. When
drovers gave way to packers, Whigs again were the typical
enterprisers, one of whom in 1844 offered $2.50 per hundred
for pork if Clay should be elected President, but only $1.50
if Polk was victor.[18] The typical enterpriser of this bustling
West was more likely than not to be a Whig, interested in
land speculation, urban booms, canal and railroad construction, or mining and lumbering.

Even as early as the twenties, in every Southern state where
local parties had developed, "the well-to-do and aristocrati-
cally inclined had lined up against the illiterate and the un-
prosperous." [19] The former, consisting of the great cotton-,
tobacco-, and sugar-planters and owners of more than two
thirds of all the slaves, became the dominant element of the

---

[17] Quoted by A. J. Beveridge: *Abraham Lincoln*, II, 63.
[18] C. A. and Mary Beard: *Rise of American Civilization*, I, 573.
[19] U. B. Phillips: "The Southern Whigs," *Turner Essays*, p. 208.

Southern Whigs. The center of gravity among them lay in the cotton-planters of the black belts. Unlike their predecessors, the deistic contemporaries of Jefferson, these Whigs professed the Christian faith, assumed control of the congregations to which they belonged, and proceeded to dictate to the pulpit the promulgation of pro-slavery dogma. So distinctly were the Whigs the party of slavery that a map shaded to indicate the density of slave population in various localities would roughly approximate one designed to show the distribution of the Whig vote in the South. In the lowlands of central Georgia, the alluvial river belts and the limestone area of the Tennessee Valley in northern Alabama, and the alluvial lowlands of the Mississippi River with adjacent counties, were located the great Whig cotton plantations.

Even more generally than in the deep South were the prosperous planters of the Ohio Valley attached to the Whigs under the leadership of Clay. Election maps show Whig strength in such centers of tobacco culture as the rich limestone areas of middle Tennessee and the Kentucky bluegrass region. In Maryland and Virginia were followers of John Tyler and Henry A. Wise. Tyler's and Calhoun's coastal planters left the Democrats and went over to the Whigs after Jackson's denunciation of the nullifiers. By the summer of 1836 Jackson's policies had unintentionally built up an anti-Van-Buren organization in every Southern state so strong that Van Buren obtained only half the Southern electoral votes that year. In order to recognize and reward these state-rights allies the Whigs nominated and elected John Tyler as W. H. Harrison's running mate in 1840.

The votes of prosperous Whig planters alone could never have carried the counties. They managed a shrewd leadership over their immediate lesser neighbors. The prestige of the planters' success carried conviction and commanded the votes of neighboring farmers, merchants, and the dependent professions of law, theology, and teaching. These masters of the plantations were usually well educated, many having studied law in preparation for the public service. When they went to Congress they proved more than a match for the typical country lawyer or local politician sent to represent the Northern farmers.

More closely affiliated in national policy with the Northern Whigs than the cotton- and tobacco-planting Whigs were the masters of the great sugar plantations of Louisiana. These planters were also manufacturers and, feeling keenly the competition of Cuban sugar, they sought tariff protection. Requiring abundant capital, they were judges of good banks and appreciative of the New Orleans branch of the Bank of the United States that Jackson destroyed. The wool-growing Whigs of Missouri, too, were protectionists. And, strange to say, when cotton in the forties fell to five, four, and even three cents a pound and bankruptcy and ruin spread far and wide among the plantations, there was a reaction against the ill-fated anti-tariff radicalism of Calhoun. State-rights men became converts to a moderate protective tariff as a potential stabilizer of business, giving the Whigs a momentary approach to unity on this issue. Alexander H. Stephens and Robert Toombs, rising leaders of the Southern Whigs, committed themselves in Congress to this policy. Incidentally there was also a lurking fear of the potential competition of Indian and South American cotton.

Along the James and Potomac rivers, the Kanawha Canal, the Roanoke Valley and the Dismal Swamp Canal there were Whigs interested in internal improvements, as there were also fellow partisans in Tennessee demanding a national turnpike and a canal around Muscle Shoals, as election maps reveal.[20] Whig counties along the Ohio and Great Kanawha represented wool-growing and salt industries, and, foreseeing the development of manufactures, they wanted transportation, and access to interior mineral resources. An anomaly of Whig politics was the persistent party allegiance of the rough, illiterate, poor white mountaineers of western North Carolina and eastern Tennessee. Cherishing the ideals of early Jeffersonian Republicanism, they refused to view complacently the executive "usurpations" of Andrew Jackson. Un-

---

[20] See C. O. Paullin, op. cit., Plate 104.

able to forget the bloody civil war with the tidewater planters before the Revolution, they hated the coastal squires of North Carolina, who alone of all that class remained steadfast partisans of Jackson.

As the party of commerce and finance, the Whigs carried the cities of the South even when their opponents were sweeping the rural sections. The greatest of these, New Orleans, had plenty of reasons, since the arbitrary military rule it had experienced in 1815, to be anti-Jackson even if it had not been the commercial metropolis. Richmond, Raleigh, Louisville, Nashville, Savannah, and Augusta could be safely counted on by Whig leaders.

If Jacksonians were characterized by their antipathies, then the Whigs were distinguished by their phobias. Nor were the Southern Whigs haunted much more by the specter of slave revolt than the Northern Whigs by the actual hordes of foreign laborers, mainly Catholics, so that the shadow of the Papal power presumably threw its ominous threat athwart the American scene. Yet urban "mobocracy" was scarcely more sinister to Whigs than rural radicalism expressed in the Locofoco crusade against American enterprise. Webster, most notable of the Whigs, had acquired early this dismal social outlook, although prudence dictated a discreet reticence concerning it. Indelible marks had been made on his young mind by lugubrious tales of the then current Reign of Terror in Paris. Later he feared the time "when American blood shall be made to flow by American swords." Jefferson's election was "an earthquake of popular commotion" and he lamented that the Constitution left "a wide field for the exertion of democratic intrigue." [21] Southern planter, Northern capitalist, prosperous Western yeoman, all shared this fear of populism. The dogma that "one man is as good as another" threatened the very foundations of society and substituted impulse for deliberation in government. Van Buren's acceptance of Locofocoism, with its attacks on credit, banks, and corporations, spelled economic anarchy. Nor was this a mere

---

[21] *Writings and Speeches*, XVII, 79, 111, 112.

selfish concern for themselves. Prosperous Whigs believed that the collapse of ordered society was imminent, in which the masses no less than the classes would be ruined. Francis Parkman was but expressing the opinion of the Whig intelligentsia in his statement that democracy meant "organized ignorance, led by unscrupulous craft, and marching, amid the applause of fools, under the banner of equal rights." [22]

When John Randolph declared: "Northern gentlemen think to govern us by our black slaves, but let me tell them, we intend to govern them by their white slaves," [23] he touched upon one of the favorite phobias of the Northern Whig notables, the threat of labor, especially alien pick-and-shovel men, whom the Democrats, as Randolph implied, were to use to overwhelm the Whigs. "Thousands in the North," wrote Calhoun during his Whig years, "now look to the South, not only for protection against the usurpation of the executive, but also against the needy and corrupt in their sections. They begin to feel what I have long foreseen that they have more to fear from their own people than we from our slaves." [24] Calhoun wanted to ally the privileged groups of both sections for defense against labor whether black or white and he frankly maintained that the solution in the North was white slavery. Clear-visioned Emerson, looking out across the fields near Concord at the miserable Irish, laboring for a pittance on the new Western Railroad, directed his Olympian scorn at the most conspicuous of the Cotton Whigs. "Boston or Brattle Street Christianity," he wrote, "is a compound of force, or the best diagonal line that can be drawn between Jesus Christ and Abbott Lawrence [who] was fully possessed with that hatred of labor, which is the principle of progress in the human race," and so "like his Southern acquaintances, he bought slaves, the Irishmen who worked in his growing cotton mills." [25]

Since the Whig Party originated as an anti-Jackson coali-

[22] H. D. Sedgwick: *Francis Parkman*, p. 308.
[23] Van Wyck Brooks: *The Flowering of New England*, p. 395n.
[24] J. F. Jameson (ed.): Calhoun Correspondence, American Historical Association *Reports* (1899), II, 374–7.
[25] *Journals*, VI, 443; VII, 197, 300.

tion, resistance to executive autocracy became the common denominator of all the elements in it. When Daniel Webster, protesting against the removal of Federal deposits from the Bank of the United States, declared: "A Briareus sits at the center of our system and with his hundred hands, touches everything, moves everything, controls everything," [26] Whigs of every description could applaud without a trace of a mental reservation. And when he continued with the question: "I ask, Sir, is this republicanism?" he struck a universal, ideological keynote of the Whigs. They were the only true Republicans left in America. They alone were the heirs of the hallowed Jeffersonian tradition. Their patron saint had been elected in 1801 to restore the national legislature to its preeminent position, and there the Virginia dynasty had maintained it. John Locke had written the Bible of Whiggery in his *Treatises on Government* in order to vindicate the sovereignty of the legislature and settle for all time the issue of just such autocracy as Jackson was now imposing on the American people. Had not the statute establishing the Treasury Department made its Secretary answerable specifically to the "sovereign" organ of the people, Congress? Yet this did not deter Jackson when he chose to have the deposits removed from the Bank of the United States. "In one hand he holds the purse," shouted Henry Clay, "and in the other brandishes the sword of the country." [27] Here, the Whigs believed, was the very definition of tyranny. Yet the wail against tyranny and spoils ought to be taken with a grain of salt. Let it not be forgotten that when Jackson decided to democratize the civil service by ousting a permanent governing class of office holders, practically every removal meant the turning of a National Republican or Whig out of office. No wonder, then, that "in New England and the Middle States their dislike of executive encroachment was grounded chiefly on the fact that they were excluded from executive offices." [28]

Of all our major political parties the Whigs were least suc-

---

[26] *Writings and Speeches*, VIII, 137.
[27] *Life and Speeches* (1843), p. 277.
[28] D. R. Fox, op. cit., p. 420.

cessful in translating the pressures of their component interests into established national policies. In part this was due to
the confusion produced by the death in office of both their
elected Presidents, Harrison and Taylor. More fundamental,
however, was the absence of a distinct center of gravity in
the combination and the presence instead of three almost
equally balanced sectional interests — the capitalistic East,
the farming West, and the planting South. Yet each of these
desired a Federal government paternalistic enough to make
them prosperous. Nor was their party record altogether bar-
ren of achievement. It was no less fitting that a Whig administration should subsidize the merchant marine in 1845 than
that the policy should be terminated under Democratic President Buchanan in 1859. During the first Whig administration trade in the Far East was promoted by the opening of
diplomatic relations with China. President Fillmore used the
navy as an instrument of commercial policy when, in 1854,
he sent Commodore Matthew Perry to pry open hermetically
sealed Japan. During the same administration foreign nations
were solemnly warned away from our sphere in the Hawaiian
Islands and that archipelago was almost annexed.

The Whig Party found its noblest positive purpose expressed in the dogma of the preservation of the Union. For
this the party was born, lived, and even died. It is scarcely
an exaggeration to say that it perished a martyr to this great
purpose by producing the Compromise in 1850 in order to
defeat the mid-century secession movement. For the Whigs
the Compromise was a mortal success, but so persistently did
they cling to their purpose of saving the Union that a valiant
remnant led a forlorn hope as the Constitutional Union Party
as late as 1860. Nor can this devotion to the Union be said to
have been less sincere in the nullificationist John C. Calhoun,
as a Whig, than of ultra-nationalist Daniel Webster. Calhoun
had well-nigh exhausted human ingenuity in devising the
Nullification formula whereby, through the amending process of the Constitution,[29] the Union might be still rendered

---

[29] See *supra*, p. 138.

tolerable to a panic-stricken and almost intransigent sectional interest. Between these giants of the Whig affiliation stood Henry Clay, exponent of the sentiment of the Ohio Valley, where, of all sections, national disunity would be most disastrous, deploring alike the consolidating dogma of Webster and the lurking secession implicit in Calhoun's Nullification. More than any other major American party, the Whigs were compelled to cultivate the fine art of tolerance of the conflicting interests of a nation. The nation-wide extent of the combination — as strong in the South as in the North — forced the party to be the exponent of national as opposed to partisan policies. It was, then, no mere coincidence that when the Whig Party disintegrated, the supreme crisis of the Union itself was at hand.

In the South no less than in the North the Whigs were the party of the Bank of the United States. At the time of Jackson's veto one fourth of the bank's circulation was in the South Atlantic states, as indeed was one half of all the shares of its stock held by Americans. South Carolinians were second only to Pennsylvanians in ownership of this stock, and the former together with Marylanders owned one third of the shares in the United States. Jackson's bank veto and Van Buren's acceptance of the Locofoco program with its radical crusade against credits, banks, and monopolies simply strengthened the Northern-Southern Whig solidarity. The Locofoco platform looked like social explosives in the hands of a party of rampant populism. Jackson's cavalier vetoing of the statutory determinations of public policies by our deliberative assembly, Congress, was anti-republican, while the justification of the veto as "the people's tribunative voice speaking again through the executive" [30] was mere rabble-rousing. The Whig counter-move was Clay's vain attempt to amend the Constitution so that only a majority vote of both houses of Congress would be required to override a President's veto.

As the party grew in experience and wisdom, the Whigs learned "to moderate and enlighten rather than antagonize

---

[30] Levi Woodbury: *Writings*, I, 571.

the new democracy." [31] For example, when the anti-renters of eastern New York were revolting against the outmoded quit-rents of the lords of the Hudson, the Whigs, realizing that the insurrectionists controlled ten counties and eager to gather in their five thousand votes, refused to champion the land-lords' claims for the rents, and the Whig Governor even emp-tied the jails of the anti-renters. It has been said that the Whigs had no steady principle other than that "business should go on." Nor was this necessarily an unworthy motive. Doubtless they believed that it would bring benefits to all Americans as well as honor to the nation. As the party of the "outs" they became peculiarly the beneficiaries of depres-sions, making gains in or winning local and state elections during "hard times." While not the only factor in either case, it was not merely a coincidence that the Whigs won their two presidential elections in 1840 and 1848 during downward sweeps of business cycles.[32]

W. H. Harrison had done so well in the quadrangular presi-dential contest of 1836 that the Whigs nominated him as their one candidate in 1840. Excepting John Quincy Adams, prob-ably no other President has ever entered the White House with a longer — practically continuous — public service. More important to the West than his victory at Tippecanoe was the liberal land law he obtained in 1800 when a territorial delegate to Congress. Harrison became for forty years prac-tically the symbol of the West. The law had made the settler and the government joint venturers in an enterprise and for twenty years every farmer taking up land came under Harri-son's influence.

Carefully calculating the forces that had made Jackson President, Harrison concluded that they were now set to elect him. He thought the old soldiers and pioneers "might be will-ing again to give their support to another of the same class although of inferior pretensions, rather than to any one whose

[31] A. D. Morse: "Whig Party," Encyclopædia Britannica, eleventh edi-tion, XXVIII, 589.

[32] See chart of the Cleveland Trust Co., L. M. Hacker: United States: a Graphic History, p. 199.

pursuits and course of life had no resemblance to their own." [33]
Nor did Harrison overlook the depression: "We have also
many recruits in our ranks from the pressure of the times.
Most of them however will not be Whigs, but vote for me,
as they say, on the same grounds as they supported General
Jackson." [34]

That Whig leaders had acquired skill as political craftsmen
was revealed in many ways. To bind substantially the Southern alliance they nominated for Vice President John Tyler,
the most notable of the state-rights leaders, now that Calhoun had returned to the Democratic fold, and the gesture
of goodwill to the tidewater planters proved profitable on
election day. No opportunity was missed to promote the idea
that Whiggery had become a mass movement. The Whigs
attempted to fasten the odious term "Federalists" on the Democrats, maintaining that they themselves were the true Jeffersonians. The national meeting nominating Harrison was
even officially designated the "Democratic Whig Convention." Harrison's democracy was impressed upon the voters
by such symbols of the frontier as log cabins, cider barrels,
gourds, coonskins and latchstrings. Liquor-dealers labeled
their dispensaries Log-Cabin saloons. The Democrats consequently made a serious bid for the developing temperance
vote, solemnly drinking their own toasts in pure water and
averring that the Whigs' log cabins were mere groggeries and
that their hard cider was sometimes "diluted with whiskey." [35]
So many songs were sung by the Whigs that a contemporary
declared: "The campaign was set to music," [36] while disgusted
Democrats called the Whigs the "sing sing" party. The appetite of laborers was whetted by the slogan: "Harrison, two
dollars a day, and roast beef." Harrison captured the church
vote in a way Clay could not have done, and abolitionists

---

[33] Letter to J. R. Giddings, quoted by E. M. Carrol: *Origins of the Whig Party*, p. 164.
[34] Tallmadge Manuscripts in Wisconsin Historical Society Library, quoted by E. E. Robinson: *The Evolution of American Political Parties*, p. 116.
[35] D. R. Fox, op. cit., p. 414.
[36] George W. Julian: *Political Recollections, 1840–1872*, p. 17.

who could not have voted for Clay, the slaveholder, supported Harrison. Indicative of democratization was the participation of women in the rallies, a thing shocking to the sense of propriety of Southerners, including Clay. By fall "half the population" quit work to engage in campaign festivities.[37] Farmers with their families in primitive farm wagons bumped for days over unimproved Western roads to hear Harrison speak at a mass meeting of one hundred thousand at the frontier village of Dayton, Ohio. "We have been sung down, lied down, drunk down," wailed the *Wheeling Times* upon learning the outcome of the balloting.

Striking half blindly, a depression-harassed West had overwhelmed, as they believed, the moneyed East symbolized by Van Buren. Van Buren was now the victim of the same tactics he had viewed with complacency when he managed Jackson's election over the luckless Adams.[38] For twelve years the Whigs had dinned into the ears of the electorate their condemnation of radical experimentation — bank veto, Specie Circular, tariff reduction, internal-improvement vetoes, exclusion of abolition literature from the mails, congressional denial of the right of petition — the cumulative effect of all which was the conviction that this tendency, unless checked, meant tyranny. When Van Buren had courageously checked the movement of his partisans gathered along the Canadian border, ostensibly to aid Canadian patriots in their war for independence, but actually to seize and annex Canada, he no doubt influenced many Democrats to vote against him and for the candidate who had chastised the British at the Battle of the Thames.

So heterogeneous was the Whig aggregation which elected Harrison and Tyler in 1840 that disintegration set in almost at the moment of victory. Internal dissension, particularly between the Webster and Clay factions, confused the aged Harrison and no doubt contributed to his untimely death only a month after inauguration. Tyler's accession made glar-

---

[37] J. B. McMaster, *History of the American People*, VI, 584–5.
[38] See *supra*, p. 115.

ingly apparent the fact that his following were merely allies, and not Whigs themselves. Not having made a party platform in 1840, Clay presumed to supply the deficiency by a set of resolutions presented in the special session of Congress in 1841. This proved, however, to represent the Whiggery of the old National Republicans, and the attempt to realize it in legislation encountered the inevitable vetoes of the state-rights President, John Tyler, and the consequent formal ejection of him from the Whig Party.

Nominated in 1844 on a clear-cut platform of Whig tenets, Clay proceeded to throw away an opportunity for election almost certainly within his grasp. In deference to the developing Free-Soil sentiment he had agreed with Van Buren, who appeared to be the certain Democratic candidate, that both would oppose the pending annexation of Texas. Alarmed at the consequent dissatisfaction of Southern Whigs, Clay hedged on this position in an equivocal statement that weakened him both North and South. In any case, the air was electric with the sentiment of "manifest destiny," and the emotion-evoking Democratic slogans of "Re-annexation of Texas and Re-occupation of Oregon" and "Fifty-four Forty or Fight" could not be argued down. Moreover, millions in depreciated securities of the Republic of Texas had been acquired by influential Northern men, and their conviction that annexation meant fabulous profits created, in conjunction with Southern pro-slavery interests, irresistible pressures upon Congress.

The dominant interests of the party, whether Northern Cotton Whigs, industrialists, common carriers, financiers, or Ohio Valley farmers, all dependent more or less on the slave economy of the Southern plantation, to say nothing of the greater planters themselves, dreaded nothing more than agitation of the slavery issue. Whig party strategy accordingly dictated opposition to Polk's Mexican War, "unconstitutionally begun." These planters saw that their security lay in the undisturbed maintenance of the status quo rather than conquest, annexation, and rupture with the North over the issue of slavery in the new territory. What folly to acquire the disturbing territory anyhow, when it was not even suitable for slavery! The Wilmot Proviso came in time to confirm their predictions and vindicate the wisdom of the party position.

President Polk's extraordinary partiality to Southern interests and his frustration of Northern desires even in his own party set the stage for a Whig victory in 1848. When party managers showed a preference for the Mexican War hero, General Taylor, as a candidate, Clay expressed his exasperation with the remark: "I wish I could kill a Mexican." [39] The Southern Whigs, seeking insurance against the aftermath of the Mexican War, promoted the candidacy of this Louisiana planter, popular with the Northern masses as the victor of Buena Vista. Thurlow Weed, working with Southern Whigs, managed the nomination of Taylor, at the same time obtaining the vice-presidential nomination for a fellow New Yorker, Millard Fillmore, who was an old-line conservative Whig, a matter that was to have profound consequences. Since it was the Van Buren Democrats who were starting the sectional Free-Soil Party, while the Whigs were electing both a President and a Vice President committed to slavery, unquestionably the latter constituted the national party in the middle of the century.

Presently the planters discovered they had elected to the presidency no special agent of their interest. When Taylor advised admitting California even with its free-state constitution, they were dumbfounded. These state-rights Whigs soon broke with Taylor, who then fell under the influence of Senator W. H. Seward of New York, with the strange result that presently he was practically a reversed doughface — that is to say, a Southern man with Northern principles. It was evident that Taylor had made up his mind to be a nationalist President after the tradition of Andrew Jackson. When a group of state-rights Whigs, erstwhile backers of his candidacy, confronted him with a hint of secession, he threatened to take the field and hang all those captured in rebellion "with

[39] Horace Montgomery, "The Crisis of 1850 and Its Effect on the Political Parties in Georgia," *Georgia Historical Quarterly*, XXIV, No. 4 (December 1940), p. 300n.

as little mercy as he had hanged deserters and spies in Mexico." [40]

Clay's solution of the clash of interests was his famous Compromise of 1850. He proposed that, in return for Southern consent to the admission of California with a free-state constitution, the rest of the territory acquired from Mexico be organized without mention of slavery. Texas was to be indemnified handsomely for consenting to the definition of her western boundary. Anti-slavery forces were to get abolition of the slave trade in the District of Columbia without abolition of slavery itself. The South was to have a new and strong fugitive-slave law. President Taylor's inflexible opposition to the Compromise held it up until his death elevated to the presidency Vice President Fillmore, an anti-Seward Cotton Whig. He recommended paying Texas $10,000,000 for giving up her flimsy boundary claim, whereupon Texas securities skyrocketed, and under the pressure of the security-holders' lobby opposition to the Compromise disintegrated. Nor should the stream of California gold pouring into the mints and inflating the medium of exchange be neglected as a potent force in stimulating business and creating a demand for the passage of the Compromise. After one of the leanest decades in American history, business seemed to be on the eve of an era of unprecedented prosperity and insisted upon cessation of the disruptive controversy.

Seldom has a more golden opportunity come to any political party than fortune flung at the Whigs in 1852. Theirs was the chance to exploit, as party achievements, both the prosperity and the Compromise. Elder statesmen of the party, Clay and Webster, had made the passage of the great statutes the crowning events of their long careers, while President Fillmore had promoted the program and signed the measures. Of course few Northern Whigs rejoiced over the vicious Fugitive Slave Act, but many believed, with Rufus Choate, that the return to slavery of fugitive slaves was an insignificant sacrifice on the altar of the Union as compared to the heca-

---

[40] H. A. Weed: *Life of Thurlow Weed*, II, 117.

tombs to be sacrificed through civil convulsions. So fed up with slavery agitation had the public become that even the Free-Soil vote fell off nearly one half in four years. The Whigs were now unquestionably the outstanding national party. Yet they failed signally in playing their cards in 1852. Although they approved the Compromise of 1850 in their platform, they failed to nominate some candidate such as Fillmore or Webster who would symbolize the party's achievements. Instead, they offered once more a military hero, General Winfield Scott, whose ineptitude as a campaigner marked a new low in candidates. When the returns were tabulated it was painfully evident that the combination which constituted peculiarly the party of the Union was disintegrating, presaging not only its own end but also a break in national unity itself.

The Whig Party had its genesis in the miscellaneous and heterogeneous elements stirred to self-defense against the policies of the Jackson administration. As Locofocoism, with its militant anti-capitalistic dogmas, came more and more to dominate Democratic party policies, the Whig Party's dominant element became emphatically that of the well-to-do. Unfortunately for the Whigs, however, the community of interest among the "haves" proved less cohesive than that of the "have nots" and consequently the Whig Party never attained the integration and robust vitality of Jacksonian Democracy. Originating as a party of the "cons," despite all its remarkable leadership it never quite managed to complete the transition into an effective party of the "pros." In fact there could be found no single great compelling purpose to unite Eastern capitalists, prosperous Western mixed farmers, and the great Southern planters. The one outstanding ideological Whig dogma, that of the "Union," did not develop its overwhelming emotional drive until the party had passed from the political scene.

CHAPTER VIII

THE BREAKUP OF THE MAJOR PARTIES

"PRACTICAL politicians, in order to win national elections, have been forced to reconcile rival interests and sections in their platforms. Their so-called cowardice in excluding popular issues such as slavery, religion, and prohibition has really been a form of wisdom, for once let an issue of that nature divide the parties from each other along sectional or class lines civil war or social violence is likely to happen." SAMUEL ELIOT MORISON.*

DURING the forties probably ninety per cent of the American electorate proudly professed either the Democratic or the Whig political faith, and the two-party system has never stood higher. Both parties had become well organized on the common pattern still prevalent today and their leaders had already developed a high degree of proficiency in the tactics and strategy of practical politics. If, as Max Ascoli has said, political parties project somewhat different images of the state and each plays in "true earnestness the game of being the state," [1] then it would seem that the Democratic Party was on the whole somewhat more successful than the Whig Party in "projecting an image of the state" in this era of the Rise of the Common Man.

The perennial problem of the politician of a major party is the placating of dissident elements within his own combination as well as attracting similar ones away from his opponents. Third parties are indicative of a failure of major-party

---

* From *An Hour of American History*, published by J. B. Lippincott Company. Copyright 1929, by Samuel Eliot Morison.
[1] Max Ascoli: "Political Parties," in Max Ascoli and Fritz Lehman (ed.): *Political and Economic Democracy*, p. 211.

politicians to perform this function. Minor parties might be said to condition and modify major parties somewhat as the habitat of an organism determines its characteristics. As the nineteenth century approached its meridian the early stages of a passionately felt controversy over slavery found expression in the Abolitionist, the Liberty, and the Free-Soil parties, presaging a realignment of the major-party combinations.

Early in the century slavery had been a debatable issue in the South. Southern Quakers, free white farmers, and students in some Southern colleges argued against the institution. Migrants from Pennsylvania, New York, and New England, having settled in the South in what came to be known as "Northern towns," spoke out against the peculiar institution. With the spectacular success of cotton-planting and the appearance of some servile unrest, the era of tolerance ended, and intellectuals, business men, and religious leaders who could not conform went North. While the great Whig planters deprecated any discussion of slavery, the elements in the Jacksonian combination became thoroughly aroused against the abolitionists. Even more agitated than the owner of only a few slaves was the slaveless poor white, who trembled at the thought of the loss of his peculiarly precious social superiority, which would be imperiled by Negro emancipation. Northern pick-and-shovel alien-born Jacksonians enthusiastically mobbed abolitionists who threatened to flood the labor market with competing black freedmen.

Utterly uncompromising in his attitude toward slavery was the radical abolitionist William Lloyd Garrison. At a single stroke and without compensation to slaveholders he would eradicate the "sin" of slavery. "Gradualism in theory," he declared, "is perpetuity in practice." [2] He encountered in his own New England contempt more bitter and apathy more frozen than among slaveholders themselves. One day in 1835 the mayor of Boston had to provide him sanctuary in the city jail after rescuing him from a mob. "It was," wrote a spectator, "a mob of people, dressed in black broadcloth; a mob

---

[2] Quoted by A. C. McLaughlin: *History of the American Nation*, p. 317.

of gentlemen-capitalists, merchants, bankers; a mob of the Stock Exchange and the first people of Boston. . . ." [3] Antislavery business men were, in fact, silenced by fear of the boycott or of being blackballed by élite clubs, while urban antislavery pastors lost their pulpits, teachers their schools, and lawyers their clients. Charles Sumner, Professor Henry W. Longfellow, and Ralph Waldo Emerson were hissed and hooted at by Harvard faculty and students for expressing antislavery sentiments.

Crusaders for abstract righteousness were these Garrisonians, theoretical anarchists, condemning alike Constitution, church, and political party. Political abolitionism, however, found its seed-bed in the depression of the late thirties, and its institutional expression in the Liberty Party. These Liberty men concluded that the depression of 1837 had been imposed by a "spendthrift, slave-holding South upon a frugal, industrious, and unsuspecting, free-labor North." [4] The South, financed by greedy Northern capitalists, had plunged too deeply into cotton-planting, but the marplot was the slave system. "Slavery must be destroyed," the party argued, "or the agricultural, mechanical, manufacturing and commercial interests of the country must perish." [5] This Liberty Party movement was unquestionably stimulated by the exasperation of free-state farmers, merchants, and manufacturers over the cotton-planters' practice of purchasing beyond their ability to pay, and their defaults in payment were attributed to the moral depravity resulting from slaveholding. In 1840 the Liberty men nominated for the presidency James G. Birney, a former Alabama slaveholder, who polled about one third of one per cent of the popular vote that year.

When the Liberty men met for their first national convention, delegates appeared from all the New England states and from New York, New Jersey, Pennsylvania, Ohio, and Indiana. Evidently this grandfather of the Republican Party was no ordinary, one-ideaed third party, but was already making

---

[3] T. L. Nichols: *Forty Years of American Life, 1821–1861*, p. 85.
[4] *Fourth Annual Report of the American Anti-Slavery Society*, pp. 50–1.
[5] *Seventh Annual Report of the American Anti-Slavery Society*, pp. 13–14.

appeals, characteristic of a major American party, to multiple interests. Thus the delegates were charging the slavery interests with enacting a protective tariff in 1816 for their own advantage and abandoning it later in order to check the manufacturing interests of the free states. Northern farmers knew that the slave power, in control in Washington, profited too much by the low prices of the glutted grain market to urge repeal of the British Corn Laws and thereby open that market also to Northern staples. In striking contrast with this, Salmon P. Chase was pointing out how these same Southern interests had induced England, France, Austria, and Russia to remove all onerous duties against their cotton and were endeavoring to obtain the same privileges for tobacco and rice. The antislavery movement had evidently been taken over by practical politicians who had discovered the key to the future and were already driving a wedge between the cotton- and the grain-growers. It was no political amateur who inserted in the Liberty Party platform of 1843 the provision: "That the practice of the general government, which prevails in the slave states, of employing slaves upon public works, instead of free laborers, and paying aristocratic masters with a view to secure or reward political services, is utterly indefensible and ought to be abandoned." [6]

Although Birney received more than sixty-two thousand votes in 1844, it was apparent that the Liberty Party had run its course. The party was charged with being responsible for the extension of slave territory in the annexation of Texas because its fifteen thousand votes in New York had divided the opposition to Polk and given him the electoral vote of that state and the presidency. The party's argument, that economic recovery could never come as long as slavery remained, had been disproved by returning prosperity. They had, however, discovered the true basis for the fight to overthrow the slave power in the dynamic motivation of the white man's interest rather than mere moral enthusiasm for abolitionism. These political pioneers had hit upon the social drives with

---

[6] E. Stanwood: *History of the Presidency*, p. 218.

which the Republicans were finally to break the hold of the slavocracy on the Federal government.

The Wilmot Proviso, "that neither slavery nor involuntary servitude" should ever exist in any territory that might be obtained from Mexico, provided the polarizing device for bringing about the Free-Soil party combination of 1848. When the Whig National Convention of that year voted down the Wilmot Proviso, Henry Wilson of Massachusetts announced the revolt of the "Conscience Whigs," who then became available for some new party combination. From the New York delegation in Congress the Wilmot Proviso had received the votes of the Whigs, the Van Buren men or Barnburners, and even the "soft" or antislavery Hunkers, and these same elements put a resolution favoring the Proviso through the New York legislature. President Polk visited the wrath of the administration on the Barnburners by diverting all the New York patronage to William L. Marcy, leader of the "hard" or pro-slavery Hunkers. Eventually, if not as a result, the Barnburners severed their affiliation with the Democratic Party and, as an independent faction, became another element available for a new party combination.

Lying about in the late forties were the potential elements of a new multi-interest party requiring only appropriate leadership to stress common interests and facilitate combination. Fortunately, competent leadership, schooled in the rough-and-tumble give-and-take of practical politics, was present in every one of these factions. In August 1848 the elements convened at Buffalo, the geographic center of the zone of New England settlements in which the new ideology was fermenting. Seventeen states were represented in this National Free-Soil Convention. Present were the Van Buren Barnburners, the Conscience Whigs, the Liberty men, and even "soft" Hunkers. Despite the undoubted moral enthusiasm present, these men at Buffalo were less exasperated with slavery than with the slavocracy that ran the nation in the interest of cotton and tobacco to the utter neglect of Northern interests. The common purpose uniting them was certainly not abolition, although abolitionists were among them. Edward Channing considered "repugnance to the presence of the Negro" as the essence of Free-Soilism.[7] The fact is that the Negro, whether free or slave, was not wanted in the territories by Free-Soilers. "Let the soil of our extensive domains," they put in their platform, "be kept free for the hardy pioneers of our own land and the oppressed and banished of other lands, seeking homes of comfort and enterprise in the new world." Their final platform plank contained the slogan "Free Soil, Free Speech, Free Labor, and Free Men." The men who shouted this in 1848 had only to add "Frémont," as they repeated it eight years later, all of which is indicative of the lineage of the Republican Party. The convention nominated Van Buren as the Free-Soil candidate for the presidency.

In terms of economic groups the Free-Soilers included the small farmer, the village merchant, the household and mill worker, and debtors who cherished the equalitarian dogmas of the Declaration of Independence, as well as moral enthusiasts — practically all dwellers in the area of New England culture. "Freedom" was a symbol and a watchword to them, contrasted with "slavery," which epitomized the South, the planting interest, that had shaped the Democratic Party into a sinister instrument for cheating them of their prosperity. One of the compromises of the Constitution, the three-fifths rule, had permanently loaded the dice to the planters' advantage in every congressional vote and presidential election. Nor were Northern resentments mollified by the magisterial manners of these planters as they sat in Senate or House or dominated congressional committees, presidential cabinets, or the Supreme Court, which they customarily did in the middle of the century. Free-Soilers preceded Republican orators in dilating with telling effect upon the "criminal usurpations of the slave power." On the election map for 1848 can be perceived faintly the geographical pattern of the future Republican Party in the vote for the Democratic Free-Soil candidate. Van Buren carried seven counties in New York, six in the northeast corner of Ohio, six in Wisconsin, and ten

[7] *History of the United States*, VI, 4.

in Illinois, all in the zone of New England colonization. Almost the entire Western Reserve of Ohio had gone Free-Soil. The phenomenon was contemporaneously attributed by an Ohio politician to the fact that this great maple-sugar region recognized in the Whig candidate, General Taylor, a Louisiana sugar-planter, the symbol of a competing commodity produced by slave labor.

Scarcely any factor played a greater part in the breakup of old party alignments in the fifties than the astonishing mid-century influx of aliens. As early as the thirties native laborers were becoming deeply concerned over the threat to their own living-standards due to the competition of this alien pauper labor. Sometimes they refused to work alongside the sons of Erin or they compelled employers to erect above the factory gate the legend: "No Irish Need Apply." "For the first time in our history," wrote the late General Francis A. Walker, "the people of the free states became divided into classes." [8] Since Democrats fraternized freely with the foreigners, the native workers forced Whig politicians into a nativist attitude. Harrison received scarcely a naturalized citizen's vote in New York in 1840 because Democratic politicians circulated the assertion that he opposed adopted citizens. Four years later the Hunkers regimented the hordes of Irish working on their canal contracts and marched them to the polls to cast their ballots for Polk and thus the Democrats obtained the great block of electoral votes of New York which decided the presidential election of 1844. In fact, Clay's defeat was widely attributed to the solid foreign vote for Polk, preceded by wholesale naturalizations in Eastern states.

With Democratic politicians completely committed to the aliens, and the Whig politicians from time to time tempted to bid for the foreign vote, uncompromising nativists quite naturally turned to the formation of a new party. In 1841 there originated in Louisiana what presently came to be known as the Native American Party. It was committed to the protection of American principles and the exclusion of

[8] "Immigration and Degradation," *Discussions in Economics and Statistics*, II, 426.

foreigners from office. Since Louisiana was more lax than New York in administering the standards for admission, New Orleans was almost swamped with new arrivals. Europe was unloading its almshouses, asylums, hospitals, and prisons in America. While the newcomers gradually dispersed upstream and throughout the Mississippi Valley, only the sturdiest ever reached the frontiers. The larger river cities "acted as a filter for the scum," who clogged city almshouses, jails, and hospitals and infested the streets with pickpockets, thieves, and beggars.[9] These were normally Whig cities, but not only were the Whigs, as the heavier taxpayers, burdened by supporting the immigrants, but they were about to be outvoted by the foreigners regimented under the management of the Democratic ward heelers. Similar problems exasperated the Atlantic seaboard Whigs. General Zachary Taylor's hesitancy in announcing his candidacy as a Whig in 1848 and his toying with the idea of a non-partisan candidacy were prompted by the anti-Whig attitude of these aliens. Under the circumstances the instinct of self-preservation prompted the Whigs to nativism and explains their almost wholesale conversion to Know-Nothingism in the middle fifties. As it was, the Native American Party of Louisiana spread to the North and elected a mayor of New York City and six members of Congress in 1844, but its poor showing in 1848 finished its career under that name, and both old parties began courting the favor of the incoming hordes of famine-stricken Irish.

The revival of the nativist movement centered in New York City, and this time it took the form of a secret society, the Supreme Order of the Star Spangled Banner, apparently absorbing half a dozen minor organizations. The abortive European Revolution of 1848 had contributed to the stream of immigration the "Red" republicans, as conservatives called them, political refugees, particularly the "Forty-eighters" from Germany who settled in Missouri and throughout the Northwest. California gold-mining was attracting the motliest concentration of migrating humanity ever seen. The conviction

---

[9] A. C. Cole: "Nativism in the Lower Mississippi Valley," *Mississippi Valley Historical Association Reports*, VI, 258.

grew that English and Irish authorities were shifting their own tax burdens to Americans by shipping the potato-famine victims to the United States. In 1851, at any rate, the number of immigrants reached the unprecedented peak of 600,000.

At this juncture the arrival of a Papal nuncio, sent here to settle an internal church controversy, was pounced upon as proof of a diabolical popish plot against America. To the economic, social, and political pressures against the foreign-born was now added that of intense sectarian prejudice. An apostate Barnabite monk initiated a campaign of street preaching which, taken up by others, became epidemic and stirred the masses to a frenzy against Catholics. Nativist gangs were organized to protect the street preachers, particularly against Irish mobs. The "finesse" of these gangs is implied in the names they assumed, such as the Black Snakes, Tigers, Rough Skins, Red Necks, Thunderbolts, Gladiators, Screw Boats, Stay Lates, Hard Times, Plug Uglies, Dips, and Blood Tubs. In Baltimore the Plug Uglies came to the polls with shoemaker's awls attached to their knees to intimidate voters without the password and "persuade" them to vote the American ticket. Since members of the secret society habitually professed ignorance of any matter pertaining to their organization, Horace Greeley gave them the name of the Know-Nothing Party. They were compelled to discard their secrecy when they discovered the utter incompatibility of a political party and a secret order. The old party archives in Worcester, Massachusetts, reveal it as a popular mass movement. Very many misspelled the names of their streets in signing the rolls, and the taxes they paid fell far below the average per capita of the community.

The nativist movement was stimulated in the North by the Compromise of 1850, particularly by the severe Fugitive Slave Act. Since both major parties endorsed the Compromise, its irreconcilable opponents gravitated to the growing Know-Nothing Party. When Pierce's election by a landslide in 1852 demoralized the Whigs, their bewildered membership, in search of a scapegoat to account for their disaster, found it in the vote of the foreign-born, and they began co-

operating with the Know-Nothings in order to wreak vengeance. As befitted the President elected by the "party of foreignism," Pierce sent foreign-born August Belmont and Pierre
Soulé on European missions and appointed a Catholic as
Postmaster General. The deaths of Clay and Webster at this
critical moment deprived the Whigs of national leadership
when it was most needed and the membership of the disintegrating party went over to the Know-Nothings, *en masse* in
many communities both in the North and in the South.

The polarization into permanent new party alignments
came in 1854 with startling suddenness and as an utterly un-
predictable consequence of the conflict of rival sections and
interests for the route of a Pacific railroad. Pierce's Secretary of War, Jefferson Davis, had well-matured plans for a
southern route. The Gadsden Purchase had been the last link
in a right of way through settled territory, free from hostile
Indians and sharp mountain gradients, with Memphis as the
eastern terminus and New Orleans as a beneficiary. In order
to save the faces of state-rights purists, Davis would have the
road constructed under the war powers of the Federal government on the convenient assumption that it was a national
defense measure. Yet Davis must have entertained no delu-
sions as to procuring the required legislation for this astonishingly feasible project from a Congress the majority of
whose members represented Northern constituencies. No
doubt it was to be a bargaining proposition in the inevitable
higgling of sections and interests. The leader of the Northern
Democrats was Senator Stephen A. Douglas of Illinois, who
was allied with railroad, business, and real-estate interests
of Chicago. He was consequently under powerful pressure
to obtain a northern route for the Pacific railroad, with Chicago as a terminal.

A visitor from Mars in 1854, unfamiliar with the dynamics
of American politics, would have been mystified at Douglas's
rejection of the convenient southern route for a central one
through the Platte country, uninhabited except by a few
squatters and Indian tribes utterly unable to provide the
freight and passenger traffic indispensable for a railroad.

Moreover, this route required the scaling of mountain passes by herculean engineering feats, problematic if at all feasible. Such, however, were the exigencies of American politics, and to the achievement of this purpose the indomitable Douglas devoted his superb talents for leadership.

First of all, Congress had to provide civil government for the Platte country. Presently the evolving measure provided for two territories; hence the Kansas-Nebraska Bill. Douglas thought to cancel out in advance the disruptive slavery controversy from the congressional debates by permitting the voters of each territory to settle for themselves that issue. By utilizing the extremely popular Western dogma of popular sovereignty, he believed he might, in time, bring about the peaceful settlement of the slavery question. Eventually he would encounter the St. Louis interests and the proponents of Davis's southern route, who might be satisfied with a *quid pro quo* understanding. The slave interests had been disappointed in the net gains of the Compromise of 1850 and were in desperate need of new slave states with their additional representation in Congress and the electoral college. They accordingly decided to drive a hard bargain with Douglas. Both proposed territories were in the "free" zone north of the Missouri Compromise line. It was not enough for slaveholders that popular sovereignty merely by implication obliterated that line; they demanded explicit repeal and got it.

In forcing the repeal of the Missouri Compromise the power-mad slavocracy achieved a fatal victory, for when the social forces that day set in motion had run their course the cotton kingdom lay prostrate at the conqueror's feet. Somehow the Missouri Compromise had become a cherished and sanctified Northern tradition, and its repeal, without adequate public warning, resulted in the most astounding outburst of mass indignation ever provoked by an act of Congress. Douglas regarded the fury against the Kansas-Nebraska Act as sheer madness manufactured by such Free-Soil conspirators as Chase, Sumner, and Seward. He did not perceive that these politicians, whether by chance or superior prescience, had accurately calculated the existing balance of potential and actual social forces. Despite his undoubted political acumen, the "Little Giant" had failed to perceive the extraordinary sensitiveness of an emerging set of Northern interests to this latest demand of the imperious planters.

These were the same interests that had backed the Wilmot Proviso and fought the Compromise of 1850 with success until Taylor's death and Fillmore's accession, together with the bustling prosperity of the mid-century years, had overwhelmed them. The crowning outrage of the Compromise had been the Fugitive Slave Act. To provide the Federal commissioner a fee of five dollars if he set the fugitive free, but ten if he returned the Negro to the claimant, was indefensible. Obligating citizens of free states — even abolitionists — to join in the chase after a poor fugitive whose only offense was a dash for freedom was under the circumstances sheer madness. *Uncle Tom's Cabin* was becoming the nation's best seller. Planter protests against its unfairness were nullified by the indisputable spectacle of the pursuit of black men through free states. Bloodhounds and blacksnake whips became symbols of the South, in the face of which reason and argument were sheer waste of effort. The Fugitive Slave Act proved to be "the greatest propagator of abolitionism which Machiavellian ingenuity could have devised." [10] Humiliating as the Compromise measures were to the antislavery agrarians, these men had hitherto been sustained by the consolation that there remained the vast, potential grain-growing West perpetually dedicated to freedom by the sacrosanct Missouri Compromise.

Scarcely had Douglas reported to the Senate the Kansas-Nebraska Bill as matured by the committee when there was published in the newspapers the most effective single piece of propaganda in American party history. Signed by Senators Chase and Sumner and four antislavery members of the lower House, it bore the title: "Appeal of the Independent Democrats in Congress to the People of the United States." The Independent Democrats were a small third party that had re-

---

[10] Carl Schurz: *Henry Clay*, II, 375.

sisted the "finality" of the Compromise of 1850 and they constituted the remnants of the now practically defunct Free-Soil Party. As the first number in the documentary history of the unborn Republican Party this Appeal stands as a sovereign corrective of the myth that Republicans were merely revived Whigs. The authors of the Appeal were keen students of public opinion, alert, as politicians must be, for opportunities to advance their personal fortunes by bidding for votes. They had caught Douglas off guard and, indeed, employed tactics not over-nice, even if ethically defensible. He was denounced as an unscrupulous politician "willing to barter away free-state interests for the presidency." The bill's purpose of facilitating the development of the great West was ignored. It was mercilessly condemned as "a gross violation of a sacred pledge; as a criminal betrayal of precious rights; as part and parcel of an atrocious plot to exclude from a vast unoccupied region immigrants from the Old World and free laborers from our States." An appeal was made to the people to save the West from being converted into "a dreary region of despotism, inhabited by masters and slaves." [11]

The effect of the Appeal was astounding. "Its inflammable sentences fell like sprays of oil upon the fires which *Uncle Tom's Cabin* had started in every northern community." [12] Spontaneously the people of the North gathered in community mass meetings, and night after night lights gleamed from country schoolhouse, village church, and town hall, where the bill was berated and action taken to meet its ominous threat. Congressmen who had supported the measure returned home to confront the candidates of the Anti-Nebraska men, the Republican Party in embryo. It is difficult to tabulate the results of the confused fall elections. Parties multiplied prolifically, no less than twenty-three of them presenting candidates in Connecticut in 1854 and 1855. Suffice it to say, the Democratic strength in the House of Representatives fell from 159 to 79 while the Anti-Nebraskans elected 117 members. The function of the Know-Nothing Party becomes ap-

[11] H. S. Commager: *Documents of American History*, p. 329.
[12] A. J. Beveridge: *Abraham Lincoln*, III, 186-7.

parent when one learns that a majority of these Anti-Nebraska Congressmen were members of the councils of Know-Nothing lodges. Fundamentally, the tidal wave of Anti-Nebraskans in Congress was a triumph of the New England zone and influence. This was especially the section of the family-sized grain-growing farm. The West, as the land of promise for the younger sons, must, at any cost, be kept free from the "curse of slavery." "Freedom" accordingly became the battle cry of the emerging Republican Party.

The crushing defeat of Scott in 1852 had demoralized the Whigs and sent them by hundreds of thousands into the American or Know-Nothing Party. The Northern "Conscience Whigs" joined it to fight the slavery-ridden Democracy. At the same time the Southern Whigs who had not gone over to the Democratic Party welcomed escape to the Americans. This shift was facilitated by the fact that isolated rural communities were suspicious of new and, especially, alien forces. The specter of Papal domination of America was then no less portentous than it was to be in 1928. Yet the Southern drift to Know-Nothingism had a much more rational motivation than religious fanaticism. Governor Smith of Virginia revealed its political basis in his complaint that the North already had fifty-five more representatives than the South and, despite a one-third greater natural increase of the South's population, "foreignism brings 500,000 who settle annually in the free states with instincts against slavery, making fifty representatives in ten years to swell the opposition to the South. . . . The effect of Know-Nothingism is to turn back the tide of immigration and our highest duty to the South is to discourage immigration." [13] "The mistake with us," snorted a slaveholder, "has been that it was not made a felony to bring in an Irishman when it was made piracy to bring in an African." [14] Election maps reveal the fact that the Know-Nothings literally swallowed up the Southern Whigs, carrying such of their old strongholds as the regions of rich limestone soils, the

---

[13] *New York Tribune*, March 14, 1855.
[14] Quoted by H. J. Desmond: *The Know Nothing Party*, p. 98.

black belts, and the flood plains of the Mississippi.[15] The poor upland Whigs of North Carolina turned Know-Nothing almost to a man.

In Massachusetts the Know-Nothings in 1854 elected the Governor, every state Senator, and a strong majority in the lower House, and as a consequence they sent Henry Wilson, a "Conscience Whig," to the United States Senate. Fusing with Whigs, they carried Pennsylvania. In the Thirty-fourth Congress, elected in 1854, the Southern Know-Nothings held the balance of power between the Democrats and the Anti-Nebraska men. While the Know-Nothings were not so strong in the Northwest, where foreigners were scarcer, in 1855 every one of the nine nominees on the Ohio Republican state ticket was Know-Nothing except Salmon P. Chase, the candidate for Governor.

The phenomenal growth of the Know-Nothings convinced them that they were destined to become the new party of the opposition to the Democracy, now rapidly degenerating into a sectional party of slavery under Pierce's doughface presidency. Their peculiar claims to non-partisanship appealed powerfully to a public heartsick with partisan dissension. Douglas Democrats as well as Northern Whigs welcomed escape to an organization that promised to stamp out corruption in high places. By ignoring the issue of slavery, sectional discord was to be allayed, while devotion to the Union would inspire harmony. In 1856, they believed, they would certainly elect the President. The *New York Herald* thought they could carry ten states with 140 electoral votes and possibly enough more to make the 149 required to elect, while Catholic newspapers feared that very result. But when the Know-Nothings assembled in their national convention in 1855, short-sighted Southern politicians mismanaged the delegates and with suicidal fatuity forced through pro-slavery resolutions, whereupon fifty Northern delegates "took a walk," and thereafter the Know-Nothings were merely a Southern party. The convention chose as standard-bearer, ex-President

---

[15] C. O. Paullin, op. cit., Plate 105.

Fillmore, a conservative Whig. He was endorsed by the Silver Grays, the indomitable "Old Guard" of the once proud Whig Party, but he received only eight electoral votes. Since Fillmore was poison to the antislavery Know-Nothings, they quite generally joined the motley aggregation shouting for Frémont.

Thirty-five years had elapsed since the almost solid alignments of North against South on the Missouri question had startled Jefferson "like a firebell in the night." Compromises in 1820 and 1850 had forestalled party and national disruption, but a third compromise proved impossible. Jefferson's fear of the coincidence "of a moral principle and a geographical line" [16] had now been justified. By the middle fifties the moral absolutes of the abolitionists' "sin of slavery" on the one hand and the slaveholders' conviction of its "divine sanction" on the other ended the careers of the old national statesmen and rendered impossible national parties and national unity. No longer could Southern Whigs reach an understanding with fellow partisans of the long Puritan zone of culture extending from Massachusetts Bay to the Missouri River. Economic as well as moral issues were impairing the time-honored Jacksonian entente between Southern planter and Western grain-grower. These farmers, not so dependent on the foreign market as the planters, were more susceptible to Eastern tariff arguments. Nor was the West any longer as intolerant of Eastern plutocrats as it had been when Jackson fought them to a standstill. Wildcat banking had taught its lesson, but now Locofocos could have "hard" money and good prices too, with California gold stimulating business. Economic forces were clearing the way for an alliance of East and West.

Perhaps no single factor had done more to integrate physically the economics of Jacksonian Democracy than the traffic of the Mississippi River system. Downstream had gone the Ohio Valley's wheat, pork, and other commodities, much of it destined for the plantations, while the steamers returned

---

[16] Quoted by U. B. Phillips: *The Course of the South to Secession*, p. 144.

with considerable plantation produce, such as sugar. No one in the mid-century would have dared predict that anything could ever disturb this magnificent system of river transportation. Yet it was due for a jolt from which it never recovered. A glance at two railroad maps of the old Northwest showing operating lines in 1850 and 1860, respectively, reveals a startling transformation in a single decade. At the beginning there were only a few short railways, but ten years later a fine network of lines appears, with four trunk systems from the Mississippi River across the map to the East.[17] These railways were overbuilt and depended for their salvation on rapid Western settlement. Planters were alarmed at this threat of new free states with their representation in Congress and the electoral college, and they fought it by voting down homestead legislation. Thus they aroused not only the railroads and the Free-Soilers but even their own land-hungry Northern fellow Democrats and strengthened the tie the railroads were making of East with West. Meanwhile the once haughty captains of Mississippi steamboats became obsequious in their search for cargo as traffic shifted to the railways.

Crowning the pyramid of Southern society in the fifties were some thousands of great planters, most of whom had been, if they were not still, Whigs. Though the masters of many slaves, they sought rather to avoid discussion of the "peculiar institution." They had opposed war with Mexico because they foresaw abolitionist agitation over the territory that might be acquired by conquest. Their security was less imperiled by economic pressures than that of the lesser planters. They enjoyed the economies of large-scale operations of slaves in gangs and of easier access to transportation and credit facilities. Consequently, when the crisis in cotton culture came in the fifties, the gentry were somewhat sheltered against its severity. They were not readily agitated by the fire-eating politician, ranting about Southern rights and secession. To the very end — even after Sumter — this ruling class with its enormous hostages to fate hoped against hope to stay the

---

[17] See maps in E. Channing, op. cit., VI, 380, 381.

evil day and effect an old-time compromise. In this they were defeated by the impetuosity of the hard-pressed little planters.

An inexorable fate seemed to be closing in on the little cotton-planters, usually Democrats, in the late fifties. For a dozen years or more, counting from the late thirties, there had been a reasonably satisfactory correlation between the general trend of cotton and slave prices. In the fifties, however, while the price of cotton was somewhat erratic but scarcely upward, the cost of slaves went skyrocketing.[18] As in the case of other commodities, slave prices reflected the general inflation induced by California gold pouring into the circulating medium. Even more important, however, were the flourishing new plantations of the Southwest, bidding the price of slaves to new heights. At this juncture the border "breeding states" reduced their export of slaves, retaining them instead because of a renewed tobacco-cultivation, large-scale construction of railroads, new iron works, and cotton textile plants. Farther south the use of slaves in extensive public works, in Appalachian coal and iron mines, and in tidewater production of lumber and turpentine cut down the normal flow of slave labor to the cotton plantations.

While the large plantation escaped much of the increased cost of slaves by raising its own, the little planter lacked the capital to tie up in that long-time process. Nor with his one slave or very few could he utilize the speed-up efficiency of the gang routine that stepped up per-capita production from two to four times that of the small farm. Handicapped by his poorer upland soils, by his remoteness from convenient river wharves, by difficulty in obtaining credit except at ruinous interest rates, the small planter would have been scarcely human had he not developed a pronounced persecution complex.

The unhappy lot of these half-desperate men provided a golden opportunity for emotional political exhorters of the William Lowndes Yancey type. Compared with the purpose

---

[18] See chart in U. B. Phillips: *Life and Labor in the Old South*, p. 177.

of the family-sized Northern farm, cotton-planting was rather less a way of life than a profit-making enterprise. If only the African slave-trade were reopened, argued the fire-eater, the South might be flooded with cheap slaves, within the reach of the poor planter so that every Southerner, rich or poor, city-dweller or hillbilly, might own at least one slave. Thus might the quasi-monopoly of the detested gentry be broken. The great planters perceived that this move would turn the North into an abolitionist madhouse, and opposed it as a policy feasible only in case of secession, a consummation repulsive to the great planter as a Whig, nurtured on the dogma of the Union.

The stranglehold of New York City on the cotton traffic with its alleged toll of forty cents on every dollar of Southern trade [19] was tightened when the panic of 1857 prostrated business. Sterling declined so sharply that presently New York banks refused it altogether and cotton purchases ceased in that metropolis. Planters consequently got ten cents in the glutted New Orleans market when cotton was selling in London for almost twice as much. Nearly a century earlier, Southern planters had achieved economic freedom from the thralldom of English agents through political independence. Might not their grandchildren now cut the Gordian knot and end their disastrous colonial subjection to Northern capital by secession? Such, at any rate, was the fire-eater's solution.

Quite naturally, then, the demand arose for direct "free trade" with England and the convenient exchange of American cotton for that country's cheaper manufactures. This would reduce Northern manufactures, and force factory hands back on the farms, which would glut the agricultural market, deflate the price of farm staples, and enable the one-crop planter to feed and clothe his human stock at less expense and thereby cut substantially the production cost of his own staple. English capital might then be more available, possibly with English branch banks functioning in the South.

It is a curious fact that, disregarding individual tempera-

---

[19] L. M. Hacker: *The Triumph of American Capitalism*, p. 241.

ments, the fewer the slaves a Southerner held, the more intensely he was likely to hate abolitionism. The first to tear limb from limb an abolitionist who might have ventured into the South would probably have been a crowd of poor whites, none of whom could ever have hoped to own a slave. Hemmed in on every side by prosperous planters and thus shut off from egress to new frontiers, these forgotten men of the Southland became the useless supernumeraries of cotton culture. Dimly sensing the cause of their degradation, they could have for the blacks none of that affection the great planters had for their human property. Yet these practically propertyless men clung tenaciously to their one precious stake in society — their social superiority to the better-housed and better-fed slaves. Immense satisfaction was derived from the fact that they "constituted the police patrol who could ride with the planters and now and then exercise unlimited force upon the recalcitrant or runaway slaves." [20] The suggestion of emancipation filled the soul of the poor white with something akin to terror. "Now suppose they was free," said one of them to Olmstead, "they'd all think themselves just as good as we." [21]

The intuitions of the poor white may have been essentially sound, for he envisaged the social anarchy imminent if hordes of suddenly emancipated Negroes were turned loose upon the South. So, when the time came, he proudly followed Lee, confident he was protecting his social heritage as a freeman. If he survived the war, he probably lived to see in the confusion of Reconstruction the fulfillment of his premonitions. The poor white's conduct has been consistently based on the resolute determination that, come what may, the South shall remain a white man's country. Poor white districts were predominantly Democratic and radical politicians were disposed to flatter this element by condemning the blacks.[22]

In the middle fifties the Democratic slavocracy was losing its influence over the Northern wing of the party, in conjunc-

---

[20] W. E. B. DuBois: *Black Reconstruction, 1860–1880,* p. 27.

[21] *The Cotton Kingdom,* I, 289.

[22] See political maps in A. C. Cole: *Whig Party in the South,* and U. B. Phillips: *State Rights in Georgia.*

tion with which it had so long ruled the nation. A Young American movement had arisen, jealous particularly for Western interests and representing a revival of the Jeffersonian tradition so long subdued in deference to the slaveholding planters. Something of the missionary spirit of the French Revolutionists animated these enthusiasts for democracy as they talked of annexing Ireland and Sicily. When the Hungarian war of independence failed in 1848, the legislatures of Indiana, Ohio, and New York demanded the severance of diplomatic relations with Austria. In time Stephen A. Douglas became the unchallenged leader of this movement and he sought to preserve the *entente cordiale* between planter and mixed farmer by utilizing popular sovereignty in order to cancel out the disruptive issue of slavery. It had a chance to succeed if only the slavocracy had been willing to play fair. But, as a keen contemporary politician observed, "A rebellion is preparing in the Democratic party and possibly Buchanan will be the gravestone of the country gentry as Fillmore is that of the Whigs." [23] When President Buchanan, under pressure of the imperious slavocrats, made the acceptance of that travesty of popular sovereignty, the Lecompton Constitution for Kansas, a test of party loyalty, the Little Giant made his nation-rocking break with the administration. Knowing well his large constituency of small farmers and mechanics, Douglas broke the planter hegemony over the Democracy of the Northwest. The audacity of the unprecedented challenge astounded the slave power and created a party breach that was never repaired.

The questions Lincoln propounded in the joint debate at Freeport in August 1858 were artfully designed to aggravate Douglas's difficulties. By the Kansas-Nebraska Act Congress had authorized territories to vote slavery out, but three years later in the Dred Scott decision the Supreme Court had held that Congress had no power whatever over slavery in the territories. Now Lincoln wanted to know whether Douglas stood by both the act and the decision. In replying to Lincoln's

---

[23] Carl Schurz to Friedrich Althaus, February 6, 1857.

questions Douglas admitted that, despite the Dred Scott decision, slavery did not automatically become established in a territory, since, under popular sovereignty, the territorial legislature might fail to enact a slave code, without which property in slaves could not exist. Two years later, when the Democratic National Convention assembled at Charleston, South Carolina, Douglas's Freeport doctrine became the focal point of controversy. Southern extremists demanded a platform declaration that neither Congress nor territorial legislature could exclude slavery or impair the right to slaves in the territories. Realizing that this would turn over the Northwest to the Republicans, the Douglas delegates sought to frame the type of non-committal plank with which party breaches had habitually been bridged. Since property rights are questions for the judiciary, they would have pledged the party to the faithful execution of the decisions of the Supreme Court and thereby have evaded the direct issue of slavery in the territories.

The slavocrats were obdurate. A Southern historian of the Democratic Party gives the significant reply made by a Mississippi delegate to a proposal of Douglas's manager for healing the breach in the party. "We are for principles," he retorted. "Damn the party." [24] Then rose Yancey, spokesman of the Southern extremists, and with the inflexible consistency of a Robespierre taunted the Douglas men for lack of courage. An exceptionally competent eyewitness reports that Yancey "charged the defeats of Democracy were to be traced to the pandering by the party in the free states to antislavery sentiments; they had not come up to the high ground that must be taken on the subject in order to defend the South, namely that slavery was right." [25] To this Senator Pugh of Ohio, leader of the Douglas delegates, replied: "Gentlemen of the South, you mistake us — you mistake us — we will not do it." [26]

---

[24] Henry Minor: *The Story of the Democratic Party*, p. 267.
[25] Murat Halstead: *A History of the National Political Conventions of the Current Presidential Campaign* (1860), p. 49.
[26] Ibid., pp. 49–50.

By this time Douglas Democrats at Charleston had almost forgotten the Black Republicans in their bitterness toward the Southern delegates. The brilliant young journalist whose report has just been quoted commented: "I have never heard Abolitionists talk more rancorously of the people of the South than the Douglas men here. Our northwestern friends use language about the South, her institutions, and particularly her politicians, that is not fit for publication, and my scruples in that respect are not particularly tender. A good many of them will eventually become the most intolerant Republican partisans." [27] "Whom the gods would destroy they first make mad" is said to have been on the lips of many who witnessed the Charleston Convention.[28]

When the convention voted down the Southern plank, the extremists bolted and the convention eventually adjourned without making any nominations. A later convention at Baltimore, boycotted by the bolting extremists, nominated Douglas on the proposition that the Supreme Court was to be the final arbiter of the question of slavery in the territories. Then the Southern extremists had a convention of their own and nominated Vice President John C. Breckenridge of Kentucky to head their ticket and Joseph Lane of Oregon as his running mate. They countered Douglas's fundamental position with a declaration that neither Congress nor the territorial legislature could impair the right of property in a territory and that the Federal government was obligated positively to protect this right. Meanwhile Republicans were insisting that Congress could and should exclude slavery from the territories.

The reluctance of the great planters as erstwhile Whigs to affiliate with the Southern Democrats, dominated by radicals, is strikingly evident in the election returns of 1860. Reappearing as the Constitutional Union Party, the Whigs nominated John Bell of Tennessee for President and Edward Everett of Massachusetts for Vice President, and appealed to the voters with the slogan: "The Constitution of the Coun-

[27] Ibid., p. 87.
[28] Henry Minor, op. cit., p. 263.

try, the Union of the States and the Enforcement of the Laws."
The delegates to its national convention were usually older
men, veteran disciples of Clay and Webster, and the old
Southern opponents of Nullification. Nor did the Constitutional Unionists cut an insignificant figure in the election of
1860. If Missouri is excepted, the contest south of the Mason
and Dixon line was between Breckenridge and Bell, with
Douglas receiving a light or insignificant vote. Breckenridge's
pluralities were wide or comfortable only in the deep South,
and scarcely that in Louisiana. Shifts of a few more than three
hundred votes in Missouri and a few more than seven hundred in Maryland would have given Bell those two states,
with a total electoral vote of fifty-six for Bell and fifty-two for
Breckenridge.[29]

In the face of Lincoln's strength, the strategy of the field
against him became that of preventing a majority in the electoral college, thus throwing the election into the House of
Representatives. In that contingency the Constitutional Unionists, as heirs of the historical party of compromise, believed
they occupied the strategic middle ground, both ideologically
and geographically, with which to break the impasse that
might occur in the electoral college and the House of Representatives. A people distracted with factional strife might
then welcome the happy solution of an election of Bell and
Everett. When a comparison is made of the county election
maps of 1852, when the last Whig presidential candidate had
run, with those of 1860, the historical background of the Constitutional Union Party becomes apparent.[30] It might be noted
that the Constitutional Unionists constituted a party of the
tobacco-planters to a greater extent than had the Southern
Whigs. With the outbreak of the Civil War the Constitutional
Union Party disappeared, its border-state members becoming largely Republicans. And one of the historians of the Republican Party, W. S. Myers, points out that "their platform
in fact became the bedrock of Lincoln's plan of action after

    [29] See tabulation of the vote in E. Stanwood, *History of the Presidency*,
p. 297.
    [30] C. O. Paullin, op. cit., Plate 105.

the South had attempted secession and the Civil War had begun." [31]

With consummate courage Douglas carried his campaign into the deepest South. Exponent of the indomitable unionism of the upper Mississippi Valley, he asked a Southern audience: "Do you think that a citizen of Illinois will ever consent to pay duties at the custom house when he ships his corn down the Mississippi to supply the people there? Never on Earth! We shall say to the custom house gate keeper that we furnish the water that makes the great river, and that we will follow it throughout its whole course to the ocean, no matter who or what may stand before us." [32] Three years later blue-clad boys of the upper Mississippi Valley literally fulfilled Douglas's prophecy by investing Vicksburg until it fell and permitted the Mississippi once more to flow "unvexed to the sea."

Douglas left no one in doubt when he replied to a campaign question at Norfolk, Virginia, as to what should be done in case of secession. "I answer emphatically," said he, "that it is the duty of the President of the United States and of all others in authority under him, to enforce the laws of the United States, passed by Congress and as the Courts expound them; and I, as in duty bound by my oath of fidelity to the Constitution, would do all in my power to aid the government of the United States in maintaining the supremacy of the laws against all resistance to them, come from whatever quarter it might." [33] Paradoxical as it may sound, here was expressed a concept of national unity scarcely less disruptive of the Democratic Party than of the Union itself.

---

[31] *The Republican Party*, p. 105.
[32] Newbern (N. C.) *Daily Progress*, September 5, 1860.
[33] Quoted in Allen Johnson: *Stephen A. Douglas*, p. 433.

CHAPTER IX

THE BIRTH OF THE REPUBLICAN PARTY

"WE are now to witness the merging of associated groups into what finally became a militant array, limited to the North — a combination of moral and economic forces, of ancient partisanship and racial prejudice, of industrial philosophy and religious exaltation. A new political party is arising, sectional in membership, national in policies." ALBERT J. BEVERIDGE.*

INEVITABLY a new party must constitute an opposition. So every one of our major parties began as a party of the antis. The antis to the government of the Confederation became the Federalists; the Anti-Federalists became the Jeffersonian Republicans; the anti-Adams men, the Jacksonian Democrats; the anti-Jacksonians, the Whigs; and now we are to find the Anti-Nebraska men about to become the new Republican Party. Our problem is to ascertain how this aggregation of Free-Soilers, Independent Democrats, Conscience Whigs, Know-Nothings, Barnburners, abolitionists, teetotalers, Germans, and others combined into a well-integrated party, developed a positive program interpreted in terms of the national welfare, and pushed it to triumphant reality with the conviction of militant crusaders.

The tidal wave that swept a majority of Anti-Nebraskans into the House of Representatives in 1854 confounded the Democrats and paralyzed the decrepit Whig Party. "What will now become the party of the opposition to the Pierce administration?" became the question of the hour. Since most Anti-Nebraskans were affiliated with the Know-Nothings, that

* *Abraham Lincoln*, III, 218–19. By permission of Houghton Mifflin Company, publishers.

party was confident it had been cast for the new role. Douglas, in a pardonable rationalization of the election result, declared it had been a Know-Nothing instead of an Anti-Nebraska victory. Indeed, the Know-Nothings scored a signal victory when the new House elected one of their members, Nathaniel Banks, to the Speakership, an office then more influential in determining public policies than the presidency itself. Not until a quarter of a century had elapsed did the Democrats again elect a Speaker of the House.

Many a Republican has made his pilgrimage and stood in devout reverence on the spot pointed out to him as the birthplace of his party. Not all of them, however, have stood at the same place, and the number of these shrines is confusing until one understands that the movement began as a leaderless and spontaneous uprising, appearing simultaneously in many communities and even accompanied by considerable confusion at first. Four months before the Kansas-Nebraska Bill became a law, a gathering of Whigs, Democrats, and Free-Soilers, aroused by the pending measure, met at Ripon, Wisconsin, and resolved, if the bill passed, "to throw old party organizations to the winds and organize a new party on the sole basis of the non-extension of slavery." [1] Five months later a similar event occurred in Michigan, and in both cases the name "Republican" was adopted. These were state parties, and in other states the Anti-Nebraskans organized "fusion tickets" under various names. Out of these spontaneous local movements was to be formed eventually the Republican Party, but that could not then be foreseen, and the betting odds in 1855 were in favor of the Know-Nothings as the coming major party of the opposition.

The Republican Party is a unique phenomenon of our political history in that it originated spontaneously without the aid of an outstanding leader, such as Washington was of the Federalists, Jefferson of the first Republicans, Jackson of the Democrats, or Clay of the Whigs. Senator Chase of Ohio, whose "Address of the Independent Democrats" had set off

---

[1] J. A. Woodburn: *Political Parties and Party Problems*, p. 97.

the almost explosive movement, probably possessed the greatest prestige of any leader at first, but it was difficult for Anti-Nebraska Whigs to forget him as an old political opponent. Senator Seward of New York stood better with ex-Whigs, but his long and consistent courting of the naturalized citizens and the Catholic vote made him unacceptable to the Know-Nothings, who constituted practically the entire Anti-Nebraska strength in many a community, especially in New England. Not only was Abraham Lincoln as yet merely a local leader, but this conservative Whig had such a pronounced aversion to the radical abolitionist element then dominant among Illinois Anti-Nebraskans that he clung tenaciously to the name and remnant of his own dissolving party. As he put it, the nomination of the abolitionist Owen Lovejoy for Congress by the Illinois Anti-Nebraskans "turned me blind." He went through the campaign of 1856 as a presidential elector and speaker for Frémont, scrupulously avoiding reference to himself and fellow partisans as Republicans. Lincoln, then, played no part in the founding of the Republican Party. "Its members came together by a magic attraction," wrote John R. Commons, "as crystals appear in a chilled solution. Not one man or one set of men formed the party, though there were many claimants for the honor of first suggesting the name or calling the first meeting that used the name. The fluid solution was there and when the chill came the crystals formed." [2]

Wherever the census had indicated a preponderance of New England stock, the Republicans carried the counties. Persistent in establishing free schools in their communities, along with literary societies, lyceums, and libraries, these Yankees were mainly responsible for that high degree of literacy that long distinguished Republican counties. Greeley's *Tribune* provided the political resources with which Republicans out-argued their opponents in the country churchyard, the village store, and the rural literary society. No doubt the slaveholder's acute awareness of this Yankee-Puritan pre-

[2] "Horace Greeley and Working Class Origins of the Republican Party," *Political Science Quarterly*, XXIV, 469.

ponderance in the Republican Party sharpened his animosity against it. Moreover, this was a region of competing isms — transcendentalism, abolitionism, nativism, Fourierism, spiritualism, vegetarianism, feminism, to mention only a few, but they all had one common factor, "reform." The Republican party was unquestionably then a party of reform. Perhaps the term "crusading" has been more often applied to the young Republican than to any other major American party. The contrast between the Republicans and the Whigs becomes striking when one recalls that the latter were never charged with "reform." "No new reform ever emanated from the party," wrote A. C. Cole concerning the Whigs, "to save it from withering decay under its proud record for aristocratic conservatism." [3] In its earliest years the Republican Party was plagued with the tendency of the nativist and temperance elements of its combination to subordinate its fundamental purpose of restricting slavery to the slave states.

In the old New England states themselves it was the rural and not the urban precincts that cast the Anti-Nebraska votes. Senator Charles Sumner, the outstanding leader of the revolt in this section, was despised in the cities and sustained by the rural towns. No wonder he wrote that the pro-slavery sentiments of Northern cities almost justified Jefferson's denunciation of them as "sores of the body politic." [4] Had not Boston fired a hundred-gun salute to express its joy over the passage of the Fugitive Slave Act? But if this emerging Republican Party did not capture the business interests, the literati were with them. "Whittier wrote its campaign songs, Lowell translated its doctrines into poetry, while Emerson, Bryant, Longfellow, Holmes and Motley were some of the names high in American Literature counted on its membership rolls." [5]

Know-Nothingism in New England hampered politicians in effecting the adherence of other varieties of Anti-Nebraskans to the Republican Party. Native urban laborers had been

---

[3] *Era of the Civil War,* p. 111.
[4] Sumner: *Works,* V, 234.
[5] A. M. Simons: *Social Forces in American History,* p. 234.

resisting the incoming Irish for almost a generation, and by the middle fifties orthodox New England agrarians could scarcely sleep for fear of Papal conspiracies in America. So Know-Nothingism swept New England, and late in the decade the phobia culminated in the amendment to the Massachusetts Constitution denying the privileges of voting or officeholding to all naturalized citizens until two years after naturalization, which Midwestern Germans claimed put the Negro above the naturalized white and created an inferior rank of American citizenship. This specimen of ultra-nativism was to create a major problem for Republican leaders like Lincoln when the time came to integrate the multi-group combination into a winning party.

Second only to nativism as a disintegrating factor in the Republican Party was the temperance movement, then sweeping the North. Here was a crusade congenial to the Puritan, with his deep concern for the morals of the community, but the South escaped its effect because of the aversion to sumptuary laws in that section. Extremists in the party proclaimed temperance the paramount issue even above slavery. These enemies of the "demon rum" demanded search, seizure, confiscation, and destruction of all liquor kept for sale, and wanted to deal with the rum-seller as a criminal. This was the element, retained in the Republican Party, that gave it the anti-saloon reputation it long enjoyed. But these teetotalers baffled Republican leaders, who needed all the votes they could capture of Germans who had brought to America a tradition of joyous living and who shocked the sanctimonious sons of the Puritans with their dance halls and beer gardens, open even on the "Lord's day."

It was a shrewd observation of Woodrow Wilson that the Republican Party got "its radical and aggressive spirit from the Abolitionists, whom it received without liking." [6] They certainly constituted no dominant element in the combination. Practical politicians like Lincoln took pains to disclaim the term "abolitionist," and he felt more tolerant toward

---

[6] *Division and Reunion*, p. 188.

slaveholders than toward these radicals. To the very day of his assassination this radical element in the party was to confront him with pressing problems of factional conciliation. The earnest antislavery Republicans constituted a salutary counterbalance to the Know-Nothings, whom they con-demned at first for affiliating with the slaveholders and even after the separation from them still condemned them for concentrating attention on the alien question when slavery was the paramount issue.

No element of the Republican combination was more sub-stantial than that of labor, not as a proletarian class-conscious group but as wage-earners, proud to be considered productive members of society, sincerely motivated by the Puritan conviction of the dignity of labor and the saving virtue of diligence. "A new Republican party," wrote A. C. Cole, "was being launched under the ægis of Horace Greeley and other prophets, a party intended in many ways to be an American labor party." [7] Because his career in politics closed with a crushing defeat for the presidency in 1872 on a ticket endorsed by the Democratic Party, Greeley's work as an architect of the Republican Party was long neglected.

The panic of 1819 having reduced Greeley's father from a farmer to a day laborer, eleven-year-old Horace was apprenticed to a printer. Some years later as a journeyman printer he arrived in New York City in the midst of the fermenting Workingmen's Party movement and at once became acutely aware of the pressing problems of labor. As a struggling editor, almost bankrupted by the panic of 1837, "the poverty of the wage earners about him impressed him more than his own." The social anarchy it represented turned him toward utopian socialism. We have already seen him transforming the employers' argument for protective tariffs to compensate for the higher wages here into one to protect the laborer against the pauper wages of Europe. [8] This national legislation Greeley would supplement with state legislation

---

[7] "If Lincoln Were Living Today," *Cleveland Plain Dealer*, February 13, 1938.

[8] *Supra*, p. 165.

for the benefit of labor. Even though this feature may never have fulfilled its early promise completely, nevertheless Republican states have been the leaders in labor legislation.

In vain did abolitionists endeavor to divert Greeley's attention from Northern labor to Southern slavery. Garrison ignored the patent facts pointed out to him by labor leaders that Massachusetts cotton-mill hands worked longer hours than plantation slaves for miserable pay and without the slave's security against sickness and old age. Garrison retorted with bitter condemnation of the Workingmen's Party and in the first issue of the *Liberator* denounced editorially labor agitators for their efforts to "inflame the minds of our working classes against the more opulent and to persuade them that they are contemned and oppressed by a wealthy aristocracy." [9] Meanwhile, as we have seen, Greeley was telling a convention of abolitionists that he was too conscious of wage slavery in New York to be concerned over black slavery in the South.[10]

Greeley's *Tribune*, particularly the weekly edition, was eagerly read throughout the New England zone of settlement and it became pre-eminently the journalistic organ of the emerging Republican Party. The labor-class bent of the *Tribune* was evident in the column on Utopian Socialism contributed each week by Albert Brisbane, the Fourierite, and *Tribune*-readers first knew Karl Marx as that paper's chief European correspondent. There are Republicans today who might be shocked by the source of some of the intellectual pabulum on which pioneer Republicans were nourished. By the middle fifties Greeley had passed through an experience with social problems that enabled him to combine the transcendentalism of New England with the working-class movement. "In 1854 the Republican party built both into a platform." [11] The Republican Party had appropriated the equalitarian doctrines of the Locofocos and the Barnburners in its fight against the slave power.

---

9 Quoted by W. E. Woodward: *A New American History*, p. 415.
10 *Supra*, p. 165.
11 J. R. Commons, op. cit., p. 474.

When Ralph Waldo Emerson placed Horace Greeley first in a list of eminent public servants [12] he gave a just estimate of his journalistic service. Americans recall him chiefly for his advice: "Young man, go West." This passionate enthusiasm was prompted by an intelligent understanding of that section, based on accurate, first-hand information. The West was an element in his plan for ameliorating labor conditions by granting all "equal share of the earth." He probably derived his homestead idea from the Workingmen's Party, where the ferment was already active in the thirties. No matter how completely recent research may have exploded the myth that many laborers became homesteaders, the historian is concerned with the power of the homestead idea in forming the Republican Party. So potent was it, in fact, that the party was even more a homestead than an antislavery party, and, as Commons put it, "Only because slavery could not live on one-hundred-and-sixty-acre farms did the Republican party come into conflict with slavery." [13] Let those who puzzle over the problem of how an antislavery party has so long outlived the institution of slavery reflect on the fact that the slavery issue was merely incidental to the party's fundamental purpose of ensuring the West to free laborers and farmers.

Economic factors in the fifties were forcing a decision on the old conflict of Southern planter versus Northern graingrower over the question of free homesteads. Wheat rose from 93 cents a bushel in 1851 to $2.50 a bushel in 1855 at the New York market, and a thousand miles of new railroads a year were extending a network into the prairies.[14] At this unprecedented price there was being created an irresistible demand for new wheat land, and against this pressure the Southern planters pitted their power in vain. They voted down homestead bills as long as they could, and when the Republicans had captured control of Congress and enacted such a measure they persuaded President Buchanan to veto it. Thus did they unwittingly cement the farmer-labor alliance of the Re-

---

12 *Journals*, IX, 519.
13 Op. cit., p. 488.
14 See Morison and Commager, op. cit., I, 514–15.

publican Party more securely and even reinforce it by thousands of their own Democratic yeomanry.

While this farmer-labor combination was employing the lure of free prairie homesteads to separate planter and yeoman, it was making no headway in its attempt to break the bonds that united cotton capitalism with the business capitalism of the Northeast. As a sectional party that might provoke disruption of the Union, the Republicans alarmed the banker who financed the intersectional trade, as well as the manufacturer who produced for it, the merchant who handled it, and the common carrier who transported it. Moreover, these powerful vested interests could not view with equanimity a new party whose very *raison d'être* was to give away the prairies. Eastern manufacturers feared dispersion of their labor force and consequent high wages, while merchants and real-estate interests foresaw urban growth checked, with reduced profits and declining property values ensuing. The moral enthusiasm of the early Republicans left these hardheaded business interests unmoved. Those who are familiar with the historic timidity of capital can picture the grim determination with which this capitalistic phalanx shifted to the conservative Democrats and fought the upstart party. "The Democratic party," wrote Cole, "had now outdone its dying Whig rival as the champion of vested property interests." [15]

No matter how "Red" the Republicans looked to conservative Whigs who had joined the slaveholding Democrats, the new Republican combination was fundamentally a middle-class movement, a party of small enterprisers. Quite naturally the little-capitalist way of thought had taken possession of the upper Mississippi Valley employers, wage-earners, and farmers alike, providing a common pattern of Republican thought and feeling from the very beginning. Here was the passionate desire of the American bourgeois mind, the unlimited opportunity to rise — a favorite theme of Lincoln — and one certainly to be improved by free prairie farms. No

---

[15] "If Lincoln Were Living Today," *Cleveland Plain Dealer*, February 13, 1938.

wonder A. N. Holcombe pronounced the Homestead Act "the crowning achievement of middle-class agrarianism in national politics."[16]

The myth that the Republican Party was merely the rejuvenated Whigs dies hard. Examination of the first Republican national platform reveals that the party took over the program of the Free-Soilers, whose central group had consisted of the old Barnburner seceders from the Democratic Party. Leaders came to the Republicans in about equal numbers from both the old major parties, but the Whig rank and file came in greater numbers because after 1856 there was no other opposition party, while the less adventurous Democrat could stick to his own party. Even if Holcombe's estimate that the Republicans drew four Whigs to one Democrat[17] is accepted, these ex-Democrats played a part out of all proportion to their numbers because they constituted a balance whose goodwill had to be courted assiduously by the new party combination. Among them was a distinct group of border-state Democrats, known as the "Heirs of Jackson." They constituted a faction, first alienated by Polk, and they came into the Republican Party under the old Jacksonian leader Francis P. Blair, who was made permanent chairman of the first Republican National Convention in 1856. We shall find President Lincoln holding this group to the party with infinite patience in the face of the intolerant Radical Republicans. Moreover it was Jackson's Proclamation against nullification that was to provide Lincoln the formulas for meeting secession in 1861.

The name of Thomas Jefferson provided a stimulating symbol for the early Republicans. Once the inspiration of Democracy, the very mention of the author of the Declaration of Independence had been suppressed by Democrats after the slaveholders had captured party control in 1844. Not until 1892 did a Democratic platform again reaffirm that old allegiance, and William Jennings Bryan was particularly active in reviving the Jeffersonian tradition in his party. To the Re-

[16] *The Middle Classes in American Politics*, p. 192.
[17] *Political Parties Today*, p. 172.

publicans of the fifties Jefferson at once became a patron saint, his name and Washington's appearing in their first platform. Jefferson was considered the original "free-soiler," since his formula for restricting slavery by excluding it from the territories had been incorporated in the Northwest ordinance. The anniversary of the passing of the ordinance, July 13, became an annual festal day of the Republicans. "The principles of Jefferson are the definitions and axioms of free society," [18] declared Lincoln in 1859. When it is recalled that both the Democratic and the Whig parties evolved out of factions of the Jeffersonian Republicans, the universality of the appeal of the great name is more easily understood. Jefferson has thus been the patron saint of every one of our major parties except the Federalist.

Time and again the new movement was saved from collapse by the imprudence of Southerners. When "Border Ruffians" from Missouri crossed into Kansas merely to stuff the ballot boxes on election day, the Republicans could not have fabricated any better news for propaganda purposes. The ensuing Border Warfare provided the new party with its incomparable symbol of "Bleeding Kansas." Just at the right time Congressman Preston Brooks caned Senator Sumner into insensibility in revenge for a savage speech attacking South Carolina and Brooks's uncle, Senator Butler. Now the party had a Republican "martyr" almost as useful as the slogan "Bleeding Kansas." The contention of Southerners that Sumner was merely shamming injury carried no weight, since this explanation came from the group that applauded Brooks no less fervently than they had the outrages of the "Border Ruffians." In the opinion of a Buchanan Democrat, the Brooks affair induced thousands of wavering Democrats to desert their party and vote for Frémont in 1856.[19] Events were producing among Republicans an intense antipathy for the South, its customs, its industry, its way of life, and its economic and social philosophy. Even the long-pent-up Northern resentment of the Southern control of Federal appointments

[18] J. G. Nicolay and John Hay: *Abraham Lincoln: A History*, II, 87.
[19] A. K. McClure: *Recollections*, p. 394.

contributed to the origin and growth of the Republican Party. Growing ever more intense was the conviction that, through its hegemony in the Democratic Party, the slavocracy was the dog in the manger to a number of Northern interests.

Having sprung into being spontaneously without the aid of an outstanding national leader, the Republicans gathered in their first national convention in 1856 without a "logical candidate" clearly indicated. Lincoln, whom tradition was erroneously to canonize as the founder of the party, had only that year relucantly consented to work with the Republicans. There were strong objections to both Chase and Seward for reasons already given,[20] and Speaker Nathaniel P. Banks was too tainted with Know-Nothingism to satisfy the numerous German delegates. "It will never do," declared Mace of Indiana, "to go into this contest and be called upon to defend the acts and speeches of old stagers. We must have a position that will enable us to be the challenging party. Frémont is the man."[21]

John C. Frémont, the "Pathfinder of the Rockies," had fired the imagination of youth as a figure of romance and adventure. The Know-Nothings almost worshipped him, and yet, paradoxically, he had a grip on the German vote. Many of the "Forty-eighters" were interested in science, and Frémont's association, as a topographer, with German scientists had won him the sobriquet "the American Humboldt." He became a son-in-law of Thomas H. Benton as the result of an elopement with the vivacious Jessie, and his political affiliations were with the "Heirs of Jackson," whom Benton had strongly supported. Who could better assimilate these somewhat uncertain groups with the more essential elements constituting the Republican Party proper? So his availability rather than his ability decided the nomination of Frémont. Josiah Royce, after sparing no effort even as a personal acquaintance to solve the riddle of his elusive personality, concluded "that General Frémont possessed all the qualities of genius except

20 *Supra,* p. 208.
21 J. F. Rhodes: *History of the United States,* II, 178.

ability." [22] No matter how tarnished his name may have become by later disclosures, there still remained in the opening decades of the twentieth century tens of thousands of aging men who cherished the treasured memory of their earliest political enthusiasm and who were wont to say with sparkling eye and tremulous voice: "I cast my first vote for Frémont."

The idealists of the party challenged the slavocracy-ridden Democratic Party with a platform pledge of the "maintenance of the principles promulgated in the Declaration of Independence." Yet the platform reflected also material interests and condemned not so much slavery as an institution as the slavocracy's control of the government against the interest of the little enterpriser, whether farmer, worker, or merchant. Congress's "sovereign power over Territories of the United States" to prohibit slavery was asserted. Planks favoring a Pacific railroad and river and harbor improvements indicated the preponderance of Western interests, as did also omission of any mention of a tariff. Whoever is puzzled as to why the homestead party did not once mention homesteads in its first platform can find a clue in the fact that the party could not spare the votes of its Know-Nothing element, who, incidentally, feared that free farms would flood the West with aliens. [23]

Republican campaign orators in 1856 kept red-hot the burning issue of "Bleeding Kansas." The party organized relief for free-state Kansas settlers in practically every Northern neighborhood. So active in the campaign were the women and Protestant clergymen, excepting Episcopalian, that the strongest aids of the Black Republicans were declared by sneering Democrats to be "Pulpit and Petticoats." The rallies exceeded in both numbers and enthusiasm those of the Log-Cabin campaign sixteen years earlier. It was with a touch of historic propriety that this revolutionary party, crusading in the Jeffersonian tradition, should appropriate the air of the

---

[22] "Frémont," *Atlantic Monthly*, LXVI (1890), p. 548.
[23] For the platform see E. Stanwood, op. cit., pp. 271–3.

Marseillaise and, at exciting moments of their rallies, rise *en masse* and make the Western welkin ring as they sang:

> Arise, arise, ye brave,
> And let your war-cry be
> Free speech, free press, free soil, free men,
> Frémont and victory.[24]

Campaign devices reflected the labor complexion of the Republican Party. Over a million wage-earners were already employed in manufacturing and as many more in mining, transportation, and trade, so that there were already more dependent wage-earners than independent farmers.[25] Buchanan, the Democratic candidate, was reported as having said that ten cents a day was enough for the workingman. Floats in Republican parades represented underfed laborers toiling at various trades beneath a tattered legend: "Buchanan's Work Shop: Ten Cents a Day." [26] Republicans profited immensely from a new apologia for slavery published by George Fitzhugh, a Virginia lawyer. Utilizing the same shocking data as Karl Marx in preparing *Das Kapital*, Fitzhugh, too, prepared an indictment of the capitalistic system. In contrast with Marx's proposal of the revolt of the "wage slaves," Fitzhugh instead serenely suggested reducing them to genuine slavery. It was concerning the "free society as well in Europe as in America" that he was to commit to writing the following irretrievable *faux pas*: "The association of labor properly carried out under a common head or ruler, would render labor more efficient, relieve the laborer of many of the cares of household affairs, and protect and support him in sickness and old age, besides preventing the too great reduction of wages by redundancy of labor and free competition. Slavery attains all these results. What else will? " [27] It is not surprising that such responsible Southern opinion should lead to a Republican campaign pamphlet entitled: *The New Democratic Doctrine: Slavery not to be confined to the Negro*

24 See A. W. Crandall: *Early History of the Republican Party*, p. 205.
25 *Statistical Abstract of United States* (1931), p. 813.
26 A. J. Beveridge, op. cit., IV, 77.
27 *Sociology for the South* (1854), p. 27.

*race, but to be made the universal condition of the laboring
classes of society. The supporters of this doctrine vote for
Buchanan.*

In contrast with Fitzhugh's restrained comments on free
society were the editorials of fire-eating Southern newspaper
editors, whose wild effusions were gleefully clipped by Republican editors and campaigners. One can imagine the dramatic effectiveness with which the following Southern editorial was used by Lincoln, who pasted it in his campaign
book: "Free society! We sicken of the name! What is it but
a conglomeration of greasy mechanics, filthy operatives, small-
fisted farmers, and moon-struck theorists? All the northern
and especially the New England states are devoid of society
fitted for well bred gentlemen. The prevailing class one meets
is that of mechanics struggling to be genteel, and small farmers who do their own drudgery; and yet are hardly fit for association with a southern gentleman's body servant. This is
your free society which the northern hordes are endeavoring
to extend to Kansas." [28]

Little sentimentality over the Negro's lot was spilled by Republican speakers. Senator John P. Hale of New Hampshire,
campaigning in Illinois, spoke not for the black man but for
the "fair-haired, ruddy-cheeked Saxon — to plead the cause
of the laboring class," threatened by slavery.[29] Likewise, Lincoln in the Douglas debates would restrict slavery in order to
keep the territories for white men, not only natives, but for
"Hans, and Baptiste and Patrick to find new homes and better
their condition in life." [30] In his acceptance speech Frémont
denounced the Kansas-Nebraska Bill for enabling slave-
owners to monopolize the Middle West and force free laborers to work on the same footing as slaves. The Republicans'
purpose is strikingly underscored by the fact that when they
obtained control of Kansas, they excluded free Negroes as
well as slaves.

When the ballots had been counted and the returns tabu-

---

[28] A. J. Beveridge, op. cit., IV, 78.
[29] *Chicago Daily Democratic Press,* October 27, 1856.
[30] A. J. Beveridge, op. cit., p. 332.

lated in the fall of 1856, it was evident that Frémont had carried practically every county where New England stock predominated, and scarcely any others. Here was a region bound together by the ties of blood kinship as well as by lake, canal, and railway traffic. But as one approached the southern fringe of this region, Frémont's support shaded off into the positive opposition of the Ohio basin, where the voters were oriented, by blood and trade, to the South. For a new party, not even foreseen thirty months before this election, to have polled forty-two per cent of the major party vote was astounding, but that was not enough, and the politicians who live to wrestle with such problems knew it. Fundamentally, the vote was an achievement of farmers, native laborers, and little enterprisers. The economic royalists of the old Whigs, the captains of finance, industry, transportation, and commerce, by and large, had backed Buchanan.

The Republican Party might have disintegrated rapidly following the defeat of Frémont had not fortune chosen to smile upon it again and again during the following year. Two days after Buchanan's inauguration came its first lucky break in the Dred Scott decision. Chief Justice Roger B. Taney, speaking for a majority of the Court, gave the opinion that the due-process clause in the fifth amendment to the Constitution invalidated the already repealed Missouri Compromise as a discrimination against a single kind of property, slaves. Here was a challenge to the Republican Party, a challenge to the death, for if the opinion became a precedent, Congress had no control of slavery in the territories and the party's very reason for existence ceased. It is a curious fact that, under the circumstances, in Congress the Republicans, as true Jeffersonians, rejected the authority of the Court and turned to the Virginia and Kentucky Resolutions, with the strange result that this extreme doctrine of state rights was, for a season, a fundamental of the Republican faith, though Lincoln did not accept it as such.

It fell to Lincoln to invent the soundest ideological device for resolving the Republican dilemma. "We do not propose," said he, "that when Dred Scott has been decided a slave by the court we, as a mob, will decide him to be free . . . but we nevertheless do oppose that decision as a political rule, which shall be binding on the voter to vote for no one who thinks it wrong, which shall be binding on the member of Congress or the President to favor no measure that does not actually concur with the principles of the decision. . . . We propose so resisting it as to have it reversed if we can, and a new judicial rule established upon this subject." [31]

The second stroke of fortune for the Republicans was the publication of Hinton Rowan Helper's *Present Crisis in the South*, a book that angered slaveholders more than had *Uncle Tom's Cabin*. Using statistics from the Census Reports of 1790 and 1850, Helper compared the growth of North and South and attributed the very evident economic backwardness of the latter section to the impoverishment of free labor by the institution of slavery. His book was a plea for redress of the grievances of the non-slaveholders, to whom he calculated the slaveholders owed seven billion dollars in damages, which he threatened to collect by inciting an uprising of the slaves. The slaveholders were still purring serenely over Fitzhugh's soul-satisfying contrast of the idyllic Southern slave economy with the tragic anarchy of Northern free labor. Fitzhugh had derived peculiar satisfaction from revealing the misery of the New England mill towns. Now it was positively maddening to have a fellow Southerner, fortified by imposing data, yank from its closet slavocracy's skeleton — the miserable poor white — and rattle it, to the infinite glee of the Black Republicans. Helper took refuge in New York City, while in the South copies of his book were publicly burned, those who bought or possessed it were jailed, and Helperites lost their jobs and privileges. Republicans, jubilant over such damning testimony out of the mouth of a Southern witness, printed 100,000 copies of Helper's book, which proved to be the most potent campaign document of 1860 if not of our entire political history.

Then came the Panic of 1857, with business failures, unem-

---

[31] Nicolay and Hay (ed.): *Complete Works*, I, 464.

ployment, and hard times all accruing to the advantage of the "outs." The depression, together with the low tariff of 1857, hit the wool-growers of Ohio and the ironmasters of Pennsylvania hard in their competition with the British. Thousands of Pennsylvania Democrats went over to the Republicans and in 1858 every Democratic Congressman from that state was turned out. Never had there been such pressure on the government to do something about a depression. The Northwest had not forgotten Pierce's veto of five rivers and harbors bills, one for Chicago among them.[32] Captains, engineers, and deck hands of both lake and Mississippi River boats, as well as longshoremen, were embittered, and farmers and shippers condemned the Buchanan administration. Even soldiers of the War of 1812 were adding to the clamor for benefits, all to the advantage of the Republicans.

Republican luck in 1857 was climaxed by the savage feud that broke out between Senator Douglas and the Buchanan administration. Though free-state men had captured control of Kansas, a pro-slavery convention had framed what was known as the Lecompton Constitution. This was being submitted to the voters with no possibility of rejecting the Constitution as a whole, but only the opportunity to accept it with or accept it without slavery. Douglas instantly denounced this travesty on popular sovereignty. Under Southern influence Buchanan not only championed the Lecompton Constitution but made support of it a test of loyalty to the administration. Every administration resource of prestige and patronage was employed to crush the recalcitrant Senator, and every Douglas appointee was ousted. Douglas sought reelection in 1858, and the Illinois Republicans challenged his candidacy with the nomination of Lincoln, taking every advantage of the Democratic feud. The ensuing Lincoln-Douglas debates are a landmark in the history of the Republican Party because they brought to national attention a leader with an unparalleled skill in clarifying public issues through discussion.

[32] J. D. Richardson, op. cit., V, 386–8.

Lincoln's aptitude for politics had appeared early. It was concerning the twenty-three-year-old candidate's earliest appeal to the electorate that his politician-biographer, Beveridge, wrote: ". . . we see in the vagueness and dexterity of his first public utterance the characteristics of the natural politician, a type of which he was to become, excepting only Jefferson, the supreme example." [33] Though defeated this time, his almost unanimous election on a second attempt was long afterward attributed by his law partner, W. H. Herndon, to his advocating a canal from the Sangamon River to serve his constituents.[34] The outstanding achievement of his first four years in the legislature was, by bargaining, to get Springfield, in his own district, made the state capital instead of Vandalia. At twenty-seven he was the floor leader of the Whigs in the House. When the State Bank of Illinois, so completely owned by Whigs as to be considered a Whig concern, was under fire, Lincoln opposed a legislative investigation and thereby won the confidence of finance and business, as befitted a Whig leader. He was outspoken in his opposition to the Locofocos and Locofocoism.

Presently Lincoln found the typical frontier leader's calling in the law, with politics as an avocation. Before long he became the most persistent follower of the court on the circuit of the Eighth Judicial District of Illinois, a practice continued until within a few weeks of his nomination to the presidency. Here the ambitious politician learned how to deal shrewdly with men in achieving the purposes of the state. As President he was eventually able to apply the cunning of the Illinois circuit to the business of managing Congressmen.

In the late forties Lincoln's circuit-riding was interrupted by two years in Congress, during which he made warm friends of the group of young Southern Whigs who were to back the candidacy of General Taylor. Accepting the strategy of the Whig caucus in criticizing Polk's Mexican War policy, he lost favor with his ardently pro-war constituency back

---

[33] Op. cit., I, 118.
[34] See letter of Herndon to W. H. Lamon, February 25, 1870, in E. Hertz: The Hidden Lincoln, p. 64.

home. After his single term in Congress, Lincoln resumed his riding the circuit, chastened by the coolness of many former friends. He had committed treason — had even been called Benedict Arnold. He had defied the Sovereign — the People — in that spot on this earth where that potentate was more jealous of his prerogatives than anywhere else on the planet.

Did Lincoln ever again challenge that sovereign? Let his most competent political biographer answer that question as he comments on Lincoln's refusal to join the movement in the early fifties for repeal of the Fugitive Slave Act. "As he afterward declared," wrote Beveridge, "he was against the abrogation of that tempest-arousing statute. This indeed was the prevailing view of central and southern Illinois at that time; and as we have seen, Lincoln almost perfectly reflected public opinion. His only misinterpretation of sentiment at home was his attitude toward the Mexican War while in Congress and he was in that but supporting the national party program; but not again did he fail to express dominant popular thought and feeling. He neither led nor retarded mass movements but accurately registered them. In short Lincoln was the spokesman of the people. So it came about that he was 'available' when at a critical hour a new party sought for a presidential candidate." [35]

Four years of comparative aloofness from party affairs suddenly ended when the Kansas-Nebraska controversy plunged Lincoln once again into the thick of politics. In 1856 came the golden opportunity to demonstrate his political maturity in a supreme effort before his own state convention of Anti-Nebraska men at Bloomington, Illinois, where Lincoln is said practically to have created a new state party. Facing delegates representing an incongruous aggregation of groups — the raw material of a possible party — the artist-politician met the challenge with his famous "Lost Speech." Compelled to stir their passions, he yet held them within bounds. Doubting Whig conservatives had to be satisfied without alienating neu-

[35] Op. cit., III, 143. Cf. Jesse Macy: *Political Parties in the United States, 1846–1861*, pp. 248, 252, 253.

rotic abolitionist radicals. Germans must be won over, but touchy Know-Nothings not meanwhile lost. Not a single group could be spared. Bygones and grievances simply had to be forgotten by everybody. "With the politician's eye for vote-getting and for uniting incongruous elements of his party, he avoided the language of the antislavery crusade and narrowed the issue to the clear-cut doctrine of freedom in the territories." [36] As the inspired orator, speaking extemporaneously, warmed to his theme and purpose, veteran reporters, among them John L. Scripps, editor of the *Chicago Press*, fell under the spell and forgot their notes, with the consequence that the world will never know just what Lincoln said. "Never," wrote Scripps, "was an audience more completely electrified by human eloquence. . . . It fused the mass of hitherto incongruous elements into perfect homogeneity." [37] Influential men in the convention at once concluded that Lincoln was a presidential possibility, and as he left the hall that historic day someone told him so. He said nothing, but from that hour it is suspected he cherished the great ambition. That the convention marked the founding of the Republican Party Lincoln himself indicated in his Freeport debate with Douglas twenty-seven months later.[38]

Calculating developing forces in 1858, Lincoln concluded that a sinister inter-sectional alliance was imminent between the capitalism of cotton and the capitalism of industry, finance, and commerce for the purpose of subjecting the toiling masses, Northern whites as well as Southern blacks. Unless prompt action were taken, the late John C. Calhoun's cold-blooded recommendation for enslavement of all labor might be attempted. The practiced eye of this inveterate newspaper-reader and frontier politician, with an expanding vision now sweeping the broad national horizon, saw the strategy whereby to circumvent this conspiracy against the aspirations of the common man. Fortunately for Lincoln's purpose, labor-

---

[36] J. G. Randall: "Abraham Lincoln," *Dictionary of American Biography*, XI, 248.

[37] Quoted by H. C. Whitney: *Life of Lincoln*, p. 77.

[38] *Complete Works*, III. 272.

ers were becoming aware that Northern capitalists, who exploited them, were allied with the slavocrats, who called them "hirelings" and "mudsills." Lincoln had but to appropriate for his ideological weapon the equalitarian idealism of Jefferson's Declaration of Independence, the "white man's charter of freedom," as he was accustomed to call it.[39] Had not the Cotton Whig, Rufus Choate, a spokesman of the Northern plutocracy, sneeringly called the Declaration's inspiring phrases "glittering and high sounding generalities of natural right," [40] which slur Lincoln would not let his campaign audiences forget? At his Galesburg debate with Douglas a banner bore the legend: "Small Fisted Farmers, Mud-sills of Society, Greasy Mechanics, For A. Lincoln." [41] Earlier in the year Senator Zachariah Chandler of Michigan, destined to become the most forcible of the Civil War Senators, in his maiden speech in the Senate, paid a tribute to the workingmen that turned out to be one of the most effective pamphlets of the congressional campaign of 1858.

Lincoln's political skill may have saved the Republican Party from disintegration in the two years between the Douglas debates and the presidential election. His constant purpose, he avowed in a letter to Schuyler Colfax, was "to hedge against divisions in the Republican ranks generally and particularly for the contest of 1860." Condemning the Massachusetts alien-disfranchisement amendment, he wrote: "Massachusetts Republicans should have looked beyond their noses, and then they could not have failed to see that tilting against foreigners would ruin us in the whole Northwest. New Hampshire and Ohio should forebear tilting against the Fugitive Slave law in such a way as to utterly overwhelm us in Illinois with the charges of enmity to the Constitution itself. Kansas, in her confidence that she can be saved to freedom on 'squatter sovereignty,' ought not to forget that to prevent the spread and nationalization of slavery is a national concern and must

---

[39] J. G. Nicolay and John Hay: *Abraham Lincoln: A History*, II, 247–8.

[40] M. C. Tyler: "The Declaration of Independence in the Light of Modern Criticism," *Harper's Encyclopedia of United States History*, III, 40.

[41] A. J. Beveridge, op. cit., IV, 317.

be attended to by the nation." These issues, he thought, would explode a national convention.[42]

In the midst of Lincoln's strenuous labors there came like a bomb the news of John Brown's raid at Harpers Ferry. The episode let loose on the Republican Party a torrent of abuse, even in the North, that threatened, for the moment, to overwhelm it. The extraordinary alarm produced among Southerners by the raid was due to their unshakable conviction that this was merely preliminary to other and greater raids. Presently, however, this very hysteria worked to the advantage of the Republicans when hundreds of native Northerners living in the South came trekking north after having been harried out of their homes by "vigilance committees." Before long there was scarcely a Northern community that did not have one or more of these outraged refugees, in no wise disposed to temper the tale of his banishment in the telling. So in the local newspaper, in public addresses, as well as in private conversations, the worst possible impressions of Southern society seemed to be confirmed by the testimony of these victims of intolerance. Republican leaders, without exception, condemned the raid, and Lincoln, in his Cooper Union speech, challenged the Southerners to implicate a single Republican in the affair.

Meanwhile Senator Seward, who looked to many Republicans like the logical presidential candidate for 1860, hesitated to seize party leadership boldly. Paled by the furor over Brown's raid, the erstwhile courageous Seward of the "irrepressible conflict" disappointed the moral enthusiasts with a conservative speech in the Senate. Brown and his men had "committed an act of sedition and tyranny" for which they were "justly hung." Seward was evidently bidding for the votes of the ultra-conservatives of the southern counties of New Jersey, Pennsylvania, Ohio, Indiana, and Illinois, and hoping to lure the rich merchants of the North away from their Democratic affiliations.[43] Seward's past dogged him, however, and the ex-Governor who had once procured finan-

---

[42] Nicolay and Hay (ed.): *Complete Works of Lincoln*, V, 136.
[43] E. D. Fite: *The Presidential Campaign of 1860*, pp. 120–1.

cial aid for Catholic parochial schools was handicapped in New England, Pennsylvania, and Indiana, where the Republican Party was saturated with Know-Nothingism.

"The Republican standard is too high. We want something practical," said Horace Greeley to Lincoln's law partner, W. H. Herndon, in 1858.[44] Frémont's defeat in 1856 and Lincoln's failure to win against Douglas two years later convinced Republican leaders that the idealism of the Declaration of Independence provided insufficient motivation for the winning of elections. Lincoln attributed his defeat for Senator to the fact that "nearly all the old exclusive, silk-stocking Whiggery is against us. I don't mean nearly all the old Whig party but nearly all the nice, exclusive sort." [45] The promoters of Lincoln's candidacy consequently decided to subordinate idealism and present Lincoln as a conservative, "a Henry Clay Whig." The Cooper Union speech, prepared after Lincoln had saturated his mind with Elliott's *Debates,* was in accordance with this new departure. It was so conservative, indeed, that Lincoln said the people of the West did not care for it and he did not blame them. However, it proved to be a shrewder bid for the conservatives than Seward's. It was indeed a decided "hit" and made Lincoln a national figure.

In the Republican National Convention at Chicago in 1860 the idealists, fighting for a reaffirmation of faith in the Declaration of Independence, were almost shouted down by the "practical" politicians. The field, combining against the leading candidate with the slogan: "Success rather than Seward," concentrated on Lincoln. His managers demonstrated that, in the employment of current party practices for managing delegates and crowds, the politicians of the old Northwest were more than a match for the most cunning leaders of the sophisticated East, as indeed befitted a party whose center of gravity was destined to be in the corn belt.

The platform, framed at Chicago, was a masterpiece of

---

44 Letter of Herndon to Lincoln, March 24, 1858, quoted in A. J. Beveridge, op. cit., IV, 189.

45 Gilbert A. Tracy (ed.): *Uncollected Letters of Abraham Lincoln,* p. 95.

the politician's multi-group appeal. In the homestead plank, native and alien alike were promised trans-Mississippi prairie farms for the asking, an idea presently to be translated into the telling campaign slogan: "Vote yourself a farm." However few recent research may have proved the actual settlers resulting from this policy to have been, the Homestead Act as a symbol of party generosity held the prairie states willing captives of the Republican Party for many a decade. It was not the first or even the last historic revolution consummated by means of the distribution of land tenure. In the successful bid for Pennsylvania's electoral vote is revealed the crowning achievement of political craftsmanship, a revival of Clay's almost forgotten American System, skillfully phrased in an omnibus appeal: ". . . we commend that policy of national exchanges which secures to the workingman liberal wages, to agriculture remunerative prices, to mechanics and manufacturers an adequate reward for their skill, labor and enterprise and to the nation commercial prosperity and independence." [46]

Republicans were well aware of the Democratic hope that even if they could not elect, they might still prevent any candidate from obtaining a majority in the electoral college and thereby throw the election into the House. Because of this possibility the congressional contest of 1858 had been intense, and while the Republicans had won a majority of the seats, they had failed to capture control of enough state congressional delegations to ensure the election of a Republican President. The Democrats hoped that, in case no compromise candidate could be agreed upon, the Senate might then elect Breckenridge's running mate, Joseph Lane, as Vice President, who would then step into the presidential vacancy. During the campaign the Republicans consequently hammered away with the slogan: "It's Lincoln or Lane," a warning shouted from almost every platform.

The successful drive to capture the labor vote was the key to Lincoln's election. With telling effect Republican stump speakers persisted in raising the question: "How can the free laboring man ever get two dollars a day when a black slave costs his master only ten cents a day? " [47] In confirmation the laborer might read such *New York Tribune* stories as that of the South Carolina mechanic who was tarred and feathered for protesting against the competition of skilled slaves hired out by their masters, or of the North Carolina law taxing mechanics' tools twenty times as heavily as slave property. In March 1859 Senator Henry Wilson of Massachusetts, the "Natick Cobbler" as this former laborer was called, made a notable speech in reply to Senator James H. Hammond's notorious characterization of laborers as the "mudsills of society." Wilson's printed speech made an effective Republican campaign pamphlet.

Lincoln had told the striking shoe workers of New Haven, Connecticut: "I am glad to see that a system of labor exists in New England under which laborers can strike when they want to, where they are not obliged to work under all circumstances, and are not tied down and obliged to work whether you pay them or not. I like a system that lets a man quit when he wants to, and wish it might prevail everywhere. One of the reasons why I am opposed to slavery is just here." And then, with the ambidexterity of the politician who suddenly recalls that not all voters are laborers, he continued: "I don't believe in a law to prevent a man from getting rich; it would do more harm than good. So while we do not propose to war upon capital, we do wish to allow the humblest man an equal chance to get rich with everybody else. When one starts poor, as most do, in the race of life, free society is such that he knows he can better his condition; he knows that there is no fixed condition of labor for his whole life." [48]

So alert were German politicians that they had forty-two delegates at the Chicago Convention, and they were able to drive some sharp bargains with the platform committee on the assumption that they represented a balance of voting power in the coming election. This ethnic group feared the Know-Nothingism rampant among Eastern Republicans and

[47] Morison and Commager, op. cit., I, 533.
[48] *Complete Works,* V, 360.

they forced upon the no doubt somewhat reluctant Republican leaders the platform plank pledging protection to "naturalized" no less than "native" citizens. The more recent arrivals among the Germans, particularly the "Forty-eighters," hated slavery and, even more, the slave power that had persistently blocked homestead acts. They forced a homestead plank into the Republican platform despite the Know-Nothing Republicans, who still feared filling up the prairies with aliens. However, the older and more conservative Germans not only outnumbered in the population this newer kind two to one, but also looked upon them as dangerous infidels and radicals. This attitude was no less true of the Catholic than of the very numerous and extraordinarily conservative Missouri Synod Lutherans, whose patriarch, C. F. W. Walther, had approved slavery on Biblical authority. A posthumously published study of the late Joseph Schafer casts considerable doubt on, if it does not conclusively disprove, the traditional belief that the Germans elected Lincoln. Using the factual data of the Wisconsin Domesday Book project, "a superior 'Gallup Poll' covering the time in question," he concluded that five sixths of the Wisconsin Germans supported Douglas, the Catholics almost unanimously, because of the Know-Nothing nativism the Republicans had absorbed, and the Lutherans overwhelmingly. He suspected that factual studies of other Northwestern states would upset the long-accepted speculative conclusions there also and "that Lincoln was elected through an upsurge of moral enthusiasm and determination on the part of the distinctly American folk." [49]

Least of all did the "capitalists" elect Lincoln, for, in the main, they were busy in the other camps. Of course, after the combination mainly of farmers and laborers had elected their President, we shall find these captains of finance, and trade, and even industry belatedly lifting a flap, crawling under the Republican tent, and gravely claiming the show as their very own. While there were industrialists, such as the ironmasters of Pennsylvania and New Jersey, who demanded protection in the platform, got it, and contributed to

---

[49] "Who Elected Lincoln," *American Historical Review*, XLVII, 51 ff.

carrying those states for Lincoln, there were many others whose products were largely manufactured for the Southern market and who feared the sectional party that might ruin them by provoking secession. For this very reason Connecticut manufacturers condemned the Republicans, and unemployment there increased as Southern orders fell off during the 1860 campaign. New York and Newark manufacturers urged their employees to vote the anti-Lincoln, fusion tickets. Let no one, then, assume that industrialists hailed the Republican tariff with unanimous acclaim. The so-called free-trade tariff of 1857 had angered the farmers, particularly the wool-growers, and not merely the manufacturers. This induced Representative John Sherman of Ohio to say in 1860: "The tariff of 1857 is the manufacturers' bill " and since then "the manufacturers have asked over and over to be let alone." [50] Years later Justin Smith Morrill, whose name the first Republican tariff act in 1861 bore, was to say that his "act was not asked for, and but coldly welcomed by manufacturers, who always and justly fear instability." [51]

So desperate, indeed, had many conservatives become in their effort to throw the election into the House that politicians among the die-hard Whigs (alias the Constitutional Unionists), the Douglas Democrats, and the Breckenridge Democrats all made common cause in a last-ditch effort to stem the Republican tide through fusion tickets of presidential electors in New Jersey, New York, Rhode Island, Pennsylvania, and Connecticut. The great merchants of the North were in a panic over the possibility that Lincoln's election would provoke secession, which threatened them in that contingency with the loss of their trade and of $200,000,000 due them from Southern customers, and they accordingly contributed heavily to the support of the fusion tickets in New York. William B. Astor alone is reputed to have contributed the then fabulous total of one million dollars to defeat the Republican electoral ticket in New York.[52] So vigorously did

---

50 *Congressional Globe*, 1859–60, p. 2053.
51 Ibid., 1869–70, p. 3295.
52 A. M. Schlesinger: *New Viewpoints in American History*, p. 271.

finance capitalism fight Lincoln that Greeley likened the "commercial furor" against the Republican Party to the hysteria over the bank controversy in Jackson's time.

Maps representing the results of the election of 1860 by counties reveal the fact that Lincoln made a cleaner sweep of the zone of New England culture than had Frémont, and, moreover, he had pushed the southern boundary of practically solid Republican counties to the Mason and Dixon line except in Illinois and Indiana, and had reached the Ohio River at two points in the latter state. Douglas counties in the Northwest were mostly south of the divide that separated the streams tributary to the Ohio from those that flow to the Lakes. This was, of course, the region where Southern cultural traditions persisted in the children of migrants from the South. In terms of economic interests, farmers and native laborers, whatever they may have thought of slavery as a moral issue, voted to keep that institution out of the territories. In carrying Pennsylvania against the fusion ticket, the Republicans demonstrated the practicability of grain-growers and mixed farmers allying themselves with industrialists and their employees. Most Democrats who became Republicans had made the transition before 1860, but in this campaign the hitherto hesitant rural Whigs voted for Lincoln.

There persists an almost ineradicable delusion that Lincoln slipped into office because the Democratic vote was split. Holcombe has pointed out what the election returns clearly show — that Lincoln, in carrying the free states, won a decisive victory in the electoral college, a result that would not have been changed if the votes of his three competitors had gone to a single candidate, which in effect they did through the anti-Lincoln fusion tickets in every Northern state where there seemed to be a reasonable chance.[53] The maneuvering of the field to throw the election into the House of Representatives had been defeated by a clear-cut, perfectly constitutional victory for Lincoln in the electoral college.

[53] A. N. Holcombe, op. cit., p. 176; see table of popular vote by states in E. Stanwood, op. cit., p. 297.

CHAPTER X

THE PARTY OF THE UNION

"It *was fully demonstrated by the state and Congressional elections of 1862 that without uniting the War Democrats to the Republicans the conquest of the South was practically out of the question. This indispensable combination could hardly be hoped for, in any effective form, save through the frank abandonment by the Republicans of their distinctive party character. . . . The process which went on was not a temporary fusion of two parties, but that of the creation of a new party, with a purpose and a policy distinct from what had been characteristic of any party heretofore.*" W. A. DUNNING.

No sooner was Lincoln's election assured by the returns than South Carolina took steps preparatory to her Ordinance of Secession, and the great cotton-planting states, one by one, followed in her footsteps. Extraordinary efforts were at once undertaken to appease the malcontents through compromises, the most notable of which were the resolutions introduced in Congress by John J. Crittenden on December 18, 1860. Whether their adoption might have averted the Civil War no one can tell. Republican Congressmen opposed them on the insistence of Lincoln, who centered his objection on the proposal to re-establish the Missouri Compromise line. On this proposition the President-elect was adamant and his intransigence may have made the Civil War inevitable, though he could not have foreseen that. As a party chieftain, bearing the mandate of a following of 1,866,452 voters, he apparently had concluded that here he must take his stand and could not do otherwise.

Lincoln had expressed the theory before his election "that

the pressure of the campaign was an external force coercing the party into unity." [1] That "external force" ceased to function on election day and then nothing remained that could hold together the already disintegrating Republican combination but firm adherence to its one ideological common denominator: restriction of slavery within its present boundaries. "Prevent as far as possible," Lincoln wrote to a Republican Congressman, "any of our friends from demoralizing themselves and our cause by entertaining propositions for compromise on slavery extension. There is no possible compromise upon it but which puts us under again and leaves all our work to do over again . . . on that point hold firm, as with a chain of steel." [2]

Lincoln arrived in Washington the week before his inauguration in the midst of the greatest confusion of tongues on a critical issue that has ever afflicted that sovereign of public opinion, the American people. This statesman who was "never the apostle of a cause," but who "was to become the perfect interpreter of public opinion and so the instrument of events," [3] was baffled by the incoherence of the oracle. In the absence of agreement, he marked time on public policies while he sought to strengthen his administration's party support through the construction of his cabinet. His young secretaries saw him attempting to "combine the experience of Seward, the integrity of Chase, the popularity of Cameron; to hold the West with Bates, attract New England with Wells, please the Whigs through Smith and convince the Democrats through Blair." [4]

Standing firm on the one issue on which they could not hedge without sacrificing the very reason for the existence of their party, Republican Congressmen and the administration avoided disruptive issues and more than respected the slaveholder's legal rights. All reference to the slavery issue

[1] Leonard Swett to W. H. Herndon, July 17, 1866, in E. Hertz: *The Hidden Lincoln*, p. 297.
[2] G. H. Putnam and A. B. Lapsby (editors): *Complete Works of Abraham Lincoln*, V, 196.
[3] A. J. Beveridge, op. cit., I, 107.
[4] Carl Sandburg: *Lincoln: The War Years*, I, 153.

had been omitted from the bills organizing the territories of Colorado, Dakota, and Nevada passed by a Republican Congress. Lincoln had consistently admitted the Southerner's right to the Fugitive Slave Law, and he took prompt measures as President to enforce it more vigorously than even Buchanan had done. He endeavored to give Southerners the representation to which they were entitled in Federal appointments and even a place in the cabinet.

But how should the paramount issue of secession itself be dealt with? Opinion ranged from the hysterical joy of abolitionists at the final separation from the slaveholders to the grim determination of a not so vocal minority to crush the movement with military force. If anyone wonders why Lincoln did not at once abandon his policy of restricting slavery and proclaim national unity as the fundamental Republican doctrine, let him be reminded that that would have been proclaiming a falsehood instead of a fact in March, 1861. Many a radical Republican rejoiced that the secession of the cotton states had relieved the nation of just that much responsibility for the "curse of slavery." Greeley, the "Republican oracle," no doubt expressed a pretty widespread Republican sentiment when in a *Tribune* editorial he declared: "If the cotton states shall decide that they can do better out of the Union than in it we insist on letting them go in peace."[5]

Latent in the public mind, however, and only awaiting the event to release its dynamic potentiality was this concept of the Union based on mingled sentiment and economic advantage. The recent four-cornered presidential contest bore testimony to its universally recognized propaganda value. "The Union must be preserved," said Douglas, while Lincoln was proclaiming: "the inviolability of the Constitution and perpetual Union." John Bell's Constitutional Union Party had revealed its fundamental function in its very name, while even Breckenridge, the candidate of the fire-eaters and the slavocrats, had declared: "The Constitution and the equality of the states are symbols of everlasting Union."[6] Nor should

[5] November 9, 1860.
[6] Henry Minor: *Story of the Democratic Party*, p. 272.

it be overlooked that, in the midst of the Civil War, the despised Copperheads never ceased to shout their slogan: "The Constitution as it is and the Union as it was." Alexander H. Stephens, who knew Lincoln well long afterward, characterized his attitude with the statement: "The Union with him, in sentiment, rose to the sublimity of religious mysticism." [7]

For thirty years the vibrant measures of Webster's peroration on "Liberty and Union" had been pulsating through the minds of Lincoln and his compatriots. Printed in practically every series of school readers and recited again and again by youthful speakers on thousands of pioneer "literary" programs, the time came when Webster's phrases were to fall from the lips of common men and women with the familiar ease of the Lord's Prayer. Gradually the majestic periods accumulated the compelling power of words of holy writ. Civilian and soldier alike were to respond to the inspiring imagery "of the gorgeous ensign of the republic now known and honored through the Earth, its arms and trophies streaming in their original luster, not a stripe erased or polluted nor a single star obscured." Then came Sumter and the North rose *en masse.* The fire from the crescent of hostile batteries around Charleston harbor had been directed at that "gorgeous ensign," symbol of the Union. Instantaneously the South Carolinians had converted the confusion of Northern opinion into emphatic agreement. Forgotten now was the fundamental Republican objective of restricting slavery, and in its stead Lincoln had thrust into his hands the broader group appeal of the public mandate to preserve the Union.

Fortified by the new unity of public opinion, Lincoln proceeded promptly to prepare for the employment of force to restore Federal authority in the disaffected sections of the Union. At once politics was adjourned, to use a later expression. Practically spontaneous mass meetings, without regard to party, assembled in almost every Northern community to declare allegiance to the administration. Everywhere were heard the words of the last speech of the lamented Stephen

---

[7] Quoted by C. Sandburg, op. cit., I, 213.

A. Douglas: "Whoever is not prepared to sacrifice party organizations and platforms on the altar of his country does not deserve the support or countenance of honest people." [8] Many of Douglas's supporters now affiliated themselves with Republicans in a sort of non-partisan coalition known as the "Union men." Nor was this merely a fusion, but instead the creation of a new party distinguished in its purpose and personnel from the Republican or any other previous party.[9] Those Democrats who still clung to their own party became the political opposition to the administration and the emerging Union Party. Regular Democrats endeavored to check further desertions to the Unionists by designating the latter "Black Republicans," despite the fact that Lincoln's supporters had now completely discarded the term "Republican." These Democrats, proclaiming their devotion to the Union, felt outraged at seeing erstwhile Republicans, some of whom had been anything but ardent Unionists, now monopolizing the term and implying that their political opponents were disunionists. Former Democrats within the Union Party resented Lincoln's suspension of the writ of habeas corpus, but were placated by his summary revocation of General Frémont's abortive proclamation of emancipation within his military district.

It is a curious fact that the Lincoln who had belatedly affiliated himself with the Republican Party in 1856, without personally accepting the designation Republican,[10] was scarcely more than settled in the White House when the Republican Party was absorbed in the Union combination and dropped its very name. Lincoln perceived that the exigencies of the crisis made this necessary. Patronage at once began to be dispensed to Unionists, not simply to Republicans. After distributing the post offices to importunate partisans, the President turned to the creation of captaincies, colonelcies, and brigadier-generalships galore in order to cement the new Union

---

[8] Quoted by G. H. Porter: *Ohio Politics during the Civil War*, p. 87.

[9] See W. A. Dunning: "The Second Birth of the Republican Party," *American Historical Review*, XVI, 57.

[10] *Supra*, p. 208.

Party and achieve the salvation of a democratic nation. His friend Whitney said he even made colonels and brigadiers out of politicians, in some cases, to keep them out of the opposition. Illinois newspapers complained that forty out of seventy Illinois regiments had Democratic colonels, and other Republican organs protested that there was only one Republican among six major generals appointed by Lincoln and that he had appointed eighty Democrats among a total of one hundred and ten brigadier generals.[11] If he seemed ungrateful to his friends in distributing patronage it was, as his friend Leonard Swett shrewdly observed, "because he never had anything to spare, and in the close calculation of attaching the factions to him he counted upon the abstract attraction of his friends as an element to be offset against some gift with which he might appease his enemies."[12]

The "little woman who caused the big war" perceived intuitively even then what has since become the judgment of history. "Lincoln's strength is of a peculiar kind," wrote Harriet Beecher Stowe. "It is not aggressive so much as passive and among passive things it is like the strength not so much of a stone buttress as of a wire cable. It is strength swaying to every influence, yielding on this side and on that to popular needs, yet tenaciously and inflexibly bound to carry its great end; and probably by no other kind of strength could our national ship have been drawn safely thus far during the tossings and tempests which beset her way. Surrounded by all sorts of conflicting claims, by traitors, by half-hearted timid men, by Border State men and free State men, by radical Abolitionists and Conservatives, he has listened to all, weighed the words of all, waited, observed, yielded now here and now there, but in the main kept one inflexible, honest purpose, and drawn the national ship through."[13]

Though the radical abolitionists irked Lincoln, slavery itself was so repulsive to him that he once said: "I bite my lips

---

[11] See C. Sandburg, op. cit., I, 334.
[12] Letter to W. H. Herndon, in E. Hertz, op. cit., p. 299.
[13] *Watchman and Reflector*, January, 1864.

and keep quiet." [14] While he could not justify it, yet he resisted all attempts to introduce it as a moral issue in politics since as such it would disrupt his party combination. Slaveholders were not wicked, but rather the victims of circumstances. "They are just as we would be in their situation." [15] He saw it as a "prudential question to be dealt with according to the accident of the times." [16] Here we have the pattern of Lincoln's diplomatic handling of the faction of his party combination known as the Radicals, Jacobins, or Vindictives. Many of them as ex-Whigs were dogmatists on congressional supremacy to whom Lincoln's profound sense of direct responsibility to the people was rank political heresy. The President's revocation of Frémont's proclamation of emancipation was unpardonable to them even though Kentucky troops were throwing down their arms rather than fight to free "niggers." The President knew that emancipation would cause desertions by the thousands among troops from the regiments recruited in southern Ohio, Indiana, and Illinois — that is to say, where the fear of an influx of emancipated blacks dominated opinion.

Yet the consummate politician who habitually "managed his campaigns by ignoring men and by ignoring all small causes but by closely calculating the tendencies of events and the great forces which were producing logical results" was to say to his friend Swett: "I can see emancipation coming; whoever can wait for it will see it; whoever stands in its way will be run over." [17]

So the time was to come when Lincoln, after calculating his balance of profits and losses, would conclude that the hour had struck for emancipation. Though the proclamation was designed to silence radical abolitionists at home and reinforce liberal support of the Union abroad, the sharp pioneer lawyer so phrased the document as to apply to no region

---

[14] A. C. Cole: "If Lincoln Were Living Today," *Cleveland Plain Dealer*, February 13, 1938.
[15] Nicolay and Hay (ed.): *Complete Works*, II, 186.
[16] Jesse Macy: *Political Parties in the United States, 1846–1861*, p. 280.
[17] E. Hertz, op. cit., p. 298.

where Federal authority was effective, and consequently not a single border-state slave-owner lost a slave. This was the region dominated by the old Whigs or Constitutional Unionists, whom Lincoln was resolved to retain in the Union Party along with the Radicals. In the elections that followed the preliminary proclamation it was these border states that elected Union Party Congressmen to compensate for the seats lost to the Democrats in the North, since the latter profited by the strong anti-emancipation sentiment there. In his next annual message to Congress Lincoln was to idealize the proclamation in the glowing phrases: "In giving freedom to the *slave* we *assure* freedom to the *free*. We shall nobly save or meanly lose the last best hope of earth." [18]

No wonder veteran abolitionists barely escaped apoplexy when this tardy politician came to be canonized as the Great Emancipator. "Lincoln was an emancipator by compulsion," wrote indignant James Redpath. ". . . Lincoln was made a saint and liberator in spite of himself. He was cuffed into the calendar; he was kicked into glory; he did not voluntarily rise up, he was floated upon the restless will of the people to the height he now occupies." [19] Nor would Lincoln have denied the allegation, but might have remarked as he did almost in the shadow of the assassin: "I claim not to have controlled events but confess plainly that events have controlled me." [20]

We have seen that the captains of finance, of business, and even some of industry fought Lincoln to a finish in 1860 and lost. But as the Federal armies grew in size the meat-packers and distillers of the Ohio Valley found the government contracting for what the planters no longer purchased. Manufacturers of boots and shoes, as well as of cotton and wool cloth, found the Union Party providing through the requirements of the army a gigantic market the Republicans could never have hoped to offer. Bankers found more than consolation for the loss of cotton-financing in the investment in war bonds

---

[18] J. D. Richardson, op. cit., VI, 142.
[19] Boston *Commonwealth,* quoted by Columbus (Ohio) *Crisis,* January 24, 1866.
[20] E. Hertz, op. cit., p. 265.

purchased at bargain discounts and bearing high interest rates. Economic royalists who had detested the Republicans found their place in the Union Party combination, and even Lincoln no longer looked so radical as his homely figure began to take on the features of an economic savior. Patriotism was fine, but patriotism along with fabulous profits was even better. Northwestern grain-growers benefited from army requirements as well as from European crop failures. The agrarian conviction of triumph found confident expression in the refrain of a popular song:

> Old King Cotton's dead and buried;
> Brave Young Corn is King.

Meanwhile railways hummed with unprecedented traffic, and the depression of the late fifties had become history.

It fell to the Union Party to execute the pledges of the Republican platform of 1860, and the result was the neatest "translation of social pressures into public policies " [21] in all American history. The rank and file of the original Republican Party were assured of their Homestead Act from the moment the Southern Congressmen had walked out. This act made available 160-acre tracts of the public domain, free of charge, to those who complied with the conditions set forth. This satisfied the land-conscious agrarians, and so indifferent were they toward a measure to establish an agricultural bureau or department that Senator Hale thought their attitude was accurately expressed in the cry: "For God's sake let us alone." [22] The Pacific railroad appealed scarcely more to the farmers than to land speculators, construction contractors and merchants, interested in the Chinese trade. Either because or in spite of his experience as a poverty-stricken prairie youth Lincoln manifested no enthusiasm for agrarian legislation, but as an old-time Clay Whig he enthusiastically promoted the government-subsidized Pacific railroad. From his early

---

[21] The expression is from P. H. Odegard and E. A. Helms: *American Politics*, p. 1.

[22] E. D. Ross, "The Civil War's Agricultural New Deal," *Social Forces*, XV, 97.

days in the legislature the promotion of railroads had been such a passion with Lincoln that he had once aspired to become the "Illinois DeWitt Clinton." [23] His most lucrative legal practice had been as a railroad attorney, and he had collected one fee of five thousand dollars. The signing of no other one measure afforded him greater pleasure than that of the Pacific Railroad Act.

The assumption that Northern capitalists deliberately forged the Republican Party into their own peculiar instrument with which to crush cotton capitalism betokens a naïve misconception of social forces. It would ascribe to a set of economic interests a prescience none has yet revealed in human history. Northern capitalists as a whole did not cast in their lot with Lincoln's party with the clairvoyant prevision of seers, but belatedly and with the inveterate opportunism of their kind. Of course, the industrialists seeking protective tariffs were pre-Sumter Republicans, but not those supplying the Southern markets. After consorting with cotton capitalists until secession put a stop to that practice, the Northern captains of transportation, trade, and finance began taking advantage of the unexpected opportunities — the heavy railway traffic in troops and supplies, the enormous army contracts, and the bond sales. When heavy internal taxes had been laid on domestic producers in order to raise revenues for war expenditures, it seemed only fair to burden the foreigner with a corresponding heavy import tax. Under the pretext of equalization and the pressures of industrial interests duties were raised to 47.06 per cent in the act of 1864. So extreme was the measure, indeed, that Lincoln said he signed it only on condition it would be repealed at the close of the war. Since these measures were due to the exigencies of war it was not at the time generally assumed that they represented a fixed and permanent policy. Having once tasted the sweets of protection, however, its beneficiaries clung to it with a tenacity that frustrated every post-war effort at readjustment, and as a debtor nation the "unfavorable" balance

---

[23] Ibid., p. 99.

of trade facilitated the checking of imports through tariffs. So even the manufacturers who had supplied the Southern market came to welcome protection.

Unquestionably the Civil War upset a balance of economic forces in American politics. The cotton-planters had been the most articulate agrarian group in our history, and the planter-farmer combination had exercised a check on Northern capitalism. When the Southern Senators and Representatives walked out in 1861, the agrarian combination was broken and capitalism was no longer adequately counterbalanced in the councils of the nation. Kate Chase Sprague's keen observation that most of the brains of the Democratic Party had departed with the secessionists was emphasized by the death of Douglas June 3, 1861, which left Northern Democracy to flounder for years practically leaderless. The Union Party's membership in Congress was thus faced by a disorganized, sniping opposition. Under the circumstances no adequate public opinion developed as to a proper program of taxation, and so consumption taxes were piled on the common man.

Lincoln never forgot the vast following of laboring men who were the decisive factor in his first election. So he was to say that "the existing rebellion means more than the perpetuation of African slavery — that it is, in fact, a war upon the rights of working men." [24] The closing paragraphs of his first annual message to Congress contain the familiar passage: "Labor is prior to and independent of capital. Capital is only the fruit of labor, and could never have existed if labor had not first existed. Labor is the superior of capital and deserves much the higher consideration." The economic pattern of thought here is not so astonishing in one who "ate up, digested and assimilated Wayland's little work on political economy and Mill, Carey and McCullough in that field." [25] However, Lincoln entertained no conception of a class-conscious laboring group, but followed his comment with the

[24] Nicolay and Hay (ed.): *Complete Works of Lincoln,* II, 501, 502.
[25] Letter of Herndon to Weik, January 1, 1886, in E. Hertz, op. cit., p. 117.

conventional American idea of a fluid society in which "the prudent penniless beginner in the world labors for wages a while, saves a surplus with which to buy land and tools for himself, then labors on his own account another while, and at length hires another new beginner to help him." [26]

The war forced upon the working men perplexing problems with respect to their interests as a group. Native laborers, Republicans to a large extent, could resist the geographical extension of slavery since it poisoned the atmosphere for free labor wherever it prevailed. Emancipation, however, was another matter, for it raised the specter of millions of freedmen as potential wage competitors. Although there were exceptions, native labor quite generally supported the Lincoln administration, and even the class-conscious European laborers, organized as the International Workingmen's Association, in December 1862 sent a resolution of sympathy for the Union cause to Lincoln at the instigation of Karl Marx, the *New York Tribune* correspondent. Owing to lack of organization, labor probably paid a higher price for the preservation of national integrity than any other Northern interest. In addition to sacrifices in the military service, exemption from which could scarcely be purchased at the three hundred dollars required, laborers generally were victims of a paper inflation that sky-rocketed prices while wages rose only slowly. Nor were they in a position to prevent the enactment of a "contract labor" statute by Congress in response to Lincoln's request for the encouragement of immigration in order to meet an acute labor shortage. The act legalized contracts "whereby emigrants shall pledge their wages for a term of years . . . to repay the expenses of their emigration." [27] Thus were Eastern employers compensated for and reconciled to the Homestead Act as an expected depleter of their labor supply. After the war, as labor became better organized, they forced planks condemning contract labor into one Republican platform after another until the obnoxious statute was repealed.

---

[26] J. D. Richardson, op. cit., pp. 57–8.

[27] The statute is printed in part in H. S. Commager: *Documents of American History*, I, 436.

Lincoln's skill in finding his way through the welter of factional strife in the Union Party to the common ground where all might confidently take their stand was fortified by his mastery of those traditional patterns of thought by which Americans habitually interpreted their political experience. Wherever Lincoln had dwelt in the Northwest, a public agreement once reached on a political issue was universally regarded as having settled that question. This principle would have been doubted there no sooner than the law of gravitation. It would be putting it mildly to say that Lincoln had a profound respect for public opinion. When the time came at Gettysburg to utter the phrases: "government of the people, by the people, for the people," we have the testimony of one who heard him that he placed the emphasis not, as is ordinarily done today, upon the prepositions "of," "by," and "for," but each time upon "the people" and with an increasing stress upon each repetition.[28] Whoever would sound the depths of feeling and the fervor of conviction that the great war President put into these words must delve into the records of Indiana and Illinois society of a century ago and recapture its democratic spirit. Noah Brooks noticed that while President Lincoln casually touched his hat in return to an officer's salute, he uncovered his head to the men in the ranks.[29] The common soldier reciprocated with a devotion little short of worship.

By 1864 Lincoln's keeping in touch with the masses had given him a devoted following of the rank and file of the Union Party at the very moment when its politicians had deserted him. Some of them, in search of another candidate, concentrated on the impossible Frémont and nominated him in the abortive mass convention at Cleveland. Although the convention that renominated Lincoln was, almost of necessity, called by the National Committee that had been selected by the Republican Convention of 1860, it was neither spoken of nor thought of by its delegates as a Republican convention. In his "keynote speech," the temporary chairman made that

---

[28] See Christian Gauss (ed.): *Democracy Today*, Appendix, p. 29.
[29] C. Sandburg, op. cit., II, 88.

clear. "I see before me," said he, "not only primitive Republicans and primitive abolitionists, but I see also primitive Democrats, primitive Americans and primitive Whigs. . . . As a Union party I will follow you to the ends of the earth and to the gates of death; but as an Abolitionist party, as a Republican party, as a Whig party, as a Democratic party, as an American party I will not follow you one foot." [30] At a Lincoln rally in Washington a few days later a transparency displayed the name of the late Stephen A. Douglas along with others bearing the names of Lincoln, Johnson, and Grant. Of these four only Lincoln had ever voted for a Republican candidate for President. Somewhat later an editorial in *Harper's Weekly* revealed that "the party of the Administration is composed of men as different as the late Edward Everett, General Butler, John A. Griswold, Thurlow Weed and Charles Sumner who were respectively leaders of the Bell-Everett, the Breckenridge, the Douglas parties and both wings of the Republican party before the war. We are at the end of parties." [31]

In the gloomy summer and early autumn of 1864 the Union cause almost collapsed under the reverses of Grant's costly Wilderness campaign. Greenbacks became almost a barometer of the Union prospects, and one critical day they fell to thirty-nine cents on the dollar in terms of gold. The Union Party leaders of the Senate and House respectively, in the sensational Wade-Davis Manifesto, made a devastating attack on the President — that is to say, their party candidate — in the very midst of the campaign. A contemporaneous entry in the diary of grouchy Count Gurowski bears unwilling testimony to Lincoln's popular strength then: "The masses are taken in by Lincoln's *apparent* simplicity and good naturedness, by his awkwardness, by his vulgar jokes and, in the people's belief, the great shifter is earnest and honest." [32] The autumn victories of Sherman, Sheridan, and Farragut no

---

[30] W. A. Dunning: "The Second Birth of the Republican Party," *American Historical Review*, XVI, 57.
[31] February 25, 1865.
[32] Quoted by C. Sandburg, op. cit., II, 564.

doubt helped, but the wide margin of 400,000 plurality for Lincoln arouses the suspicion that the politicians had been in the dark all the time. Edward Channing concluded that "at no time in the year 1864 was the re-election of Abraham Lincoln within the realm of doubt." [33]

Just as the Republican Party had lost its identity by absorption into the Union Party almost at the moment it came into power, so now the very *raison d'être* of the Union Party ended with the surrender of Lee. No longer would Radical and Conservative wings be held together by the menace of a common enemy active in the field, but inherent centrifugal party forces would now be released. In the midst of the rejoicing of the populace over the triumph of the Union cause, the assassin removed Lincoln, the Conservative leader, who had thwarted the purpose of many a Radical conspiracy to seize the reins of the administration. Curiously enough, these very Radicals who were eventually to provide the nucleus of the reincarnated Republican Party regarded Lincoln's death and Johnson's accession "a god-send to the country." [34] As the spokesman of the Radicals, Senator Benjamin F. Wade reassured the new President with the declaration: "Johnson, we have faith in you. By the gods, there will be no trouble now in running the government." [35]

Expecting "to get rid of the last vestige of Lincolnism," [36] the Radicals were bitterly disappointed at Johnson's retention of Lincoln's cabinet, mostly Conservatives, and his uninterrupted continuation of Lincoln's conciliatory Reconstruction policy of recognizing the new governments formed by conventions in the late Confederate States. These had repealed their ordinances of secession, abolished slavery, and, with one exception, repudiated their war debts. They had elected Senators and Representatives who came to Washington in December expecting to take their seats in Congress.

---

[33] *History of the United States*, VI, 605.
[34] MS. Diary of J. W. Julian, April 15, 1865; quoted by C. Bowers: *The Tragic Era*, p. 6.
[35] Ibid., pp. 6–7.
[36] Ibid., p. 6.

Their appearance there created a major crisis in the history of American political parties. On the issue of seating them depended the future of Radical control of the government and even the renaissance of the Republican Party. Unless heroic measures were promptly adopted, the Radicals perceived that their war-time political opponents, the Northern Democrats, would absorb on the one hand these Southern Congressmen and on the other the Conservative wing of the Union Party, leaving the Radicals an impotent minority. Worse yet, the thirteenth amendment had annulled the three-fifths rule and now five fifths of the prolific blacks would count in apportioning representatives and would even accelerate the growth of Southern strength in Congress and the electoral college. To the vanquished belong the spoils, or so it seemed to the Radicals.

History records no instance of a militant group, flushed with victory, as these Radicals were, who complacently submitted to self-effacement. The Radicals accordingly managed to block the seating of the Southern Congressmen-elect, and whoever is astonished at the vigor with which the instinct of self-preservation asserted itself betrays an unfamiliarity with the dynamics of political society. Then the Radicals got Congress to establish a Joint Committee on Reconstruction, captured control of it, and turned it into an engine of aggression against the President and his conciliatory Reconstruction policy. "By the political dexterity of the Radicals," wrote Congressman James G. Blaine, "no opportunity was afforded the Conservatives to get together and support the President though Congress was in a frame of mind at that time to do so." [37]

The strategy and propaganda of the Radicals first divided the Conservatives and then attracted tens of thousands of them away from the President and into the Radical congressional camp. The Conservatives who clung to the President presently attracted the regular or War Democrats, the Peace Democrats, often called Copperheads, and the Southern Dem-

---

[37] *Twenty Years in Congress*, II, 80.

ocrats or ex-Confederates. This, then, became the group con\ bination supporting Johnson and foreshadowed the make-up of the post-war Democratic Party. This was evident in the congressional elections of 1866, which were to settle the question: "Shall the President or Congress reconstruct?" The Radicals were aware of the serious handicap under which they would labor unless they could prevent the threatened augmentation of the opposition in Congress and the electoral college. Enfranchisement of the freedmen coupled with disfranchisement of ex-Confederates might convert the Southern states into Radical strongholds. Northern opinion, however, could not yet stomach the imposing of Negro suffrage on the Southern states. So the next attempt was to confront the Southern states, through the fourteenth amendment, with the alternative of Negro enfranchisement by the states themselves under penalty of automatic reduction of representation in Congress and the elec*oral college.

These Radicals were no less sensitive than the ante-bellum Republicans to the charge of being a sectional party, and necessity compelled them consequently to make Negro suffrage the most essential party dogma. Strange to say, they were somewhat fortified on this issue by the reply of John Stuart Mill to an inquiry of an Ohio judge. The eminent English liberal thought it would not be right to allow the Southern states to be restored as they were and reduce the Negroes to practical slavery; he proposed "a new community in which the population who have been corrupted by vicious institutions will be neutralized by black citizens and white immigrants from the North." [38] The fear of alienating Conservatives, however, induced the Radicals to subordinate the issue of Negro suffrage in the congressional campaign of 1866, but in championing the cause of the persecuted Southern loyalists they had a nationalizing issue with a powerful appeal to Northern sentiment and they made the most of it.

Since Andrew Johnson had become the titular head of the Union Party and, as the leader of the Conservatives, a per-

---

[38] *Cincinnati Commercial,* September 20, 1865.

sonal issue in the congressional campaign, his background ought to be examined. As an illiterate tailor lad he had migrated from North Carolina to Tennessee, where he later married a woman who taught him to write. Since not even the poor whites "hired out," that is, worked for wages, Johnson belonged to the socially ostracized wage-earners — in Southern parlance, "the hirelings" — and consequently he spoke as a member of a persecuted class. "If Johnson were a snake," said a well-to-do Tennesseean, "he would lie in the grass and bite the heels of rich men's children." [39] Living in the east Tennessee highlands, where whites outnumbered the blacks 27 to 1, Johnson became a champion of Jacksonian Democracy. No less than Hinton Helper did he believe his people to be victimized by the slaveholding aristocrats. In 1864 he would be found speaking for abolition "because in the emancipation of slaves we break down an odious and dangerous aristocracy. I think we are freeing more whites than blacks in Tennessee. . . . Their great plantations must be broken up and sold to honest, industrious men." [40] Quite understandable, then, is President Johnson's excepting from the general amnesty of May 1865 all ex-Confederates with taxable property in excess of $20,000, whom he required to apply individually to him for pardon. [41]

As a Jacksonian Democrat Johnson had risen to local leadership and had served successively as alderman, mayor, member of the lower house of the legislature, state Senator, elective Governor and then Military Governor of Tennessee, and Vice President of the United States. It was the free yeomanry and laborers of east Tennessee for whom Johnson spoke, not the blacks, who, whether slaves or freedmen, were their dangerous competitors. Negro suffrage was unthinkable to him and his people, a matter that rendered him impossible as a leader of the Radicals. What could the bondholders think of a President who now warned "that an aristocracy in the South based on $3,000,000,000 in Negroes who were a productive

---

[39] C. R. Johnson: *Andrew Johnson, Military Governor of Tennessee*, p. 22.
[40] John Savage: *Life of Andrew Johnson*, p. 293.
[41] J. D. Richardson, op. cit., VI, 311–12.

class has disappeared and their place in political control of the country is assumed by an aristocracy based on nearly $3,000,000,000 of national debt"? Other interests would be alarmed at Johnson's observation: "The manufacturers and men of capital in the eastern states and the states along the Atlantic seaboard . . . these are in favor of high protective and, in fact, prohibitive tariffs and also favor contraction of the currency." [42] It was the crowning tragedy of this radical agrarian and pioneer champion of the homesteaders that, as titular head of the Union Party — the party of bankers, bondholders, industrialists, farmers, and laborers — he could not use those personal convictions that had animated the early Republicans and to which the independent liberals of the upper Mississippi Valley might have gladly responded, if he only could have presented the issue squarely to them. Thus might he have broken the sectional alignment and restored an inter-sectional one of the ante-bellum, national type of party.

The President's supporters as National Unionists held a midsummer convention at Philadelphia, where they made the President's Reconstruction policy the issue of the impending congressional campaign Some of the delegates gave the Radicals an excuse for calling it a gathering of "rebels" and "near rebels" to endorse the policies of Andrew Johnson. The *New York Tribune* averred that ninety-nine out of one hundred of the delegates were men who in 1864 had voted for McClellan or Jefferson Davis.[43] Only too late were the malodorous "Copperheads" Fernando Wood and Clement L. Vallandigham persuaded, under pressure, to withdraw from the convention. Thus the National Unionists had got off to a bad start. When the delegates returned to their homes they found the local Radical politicians in charge of the old Union Party machinery, the Democratic politicians controlling the other party machinery, and themselves without any party organization. Wherever Democratic politicians sought to mend their party's damaged reputation by adopting the Conservative cause, they

---

[42] Quoted by L. M. Hacker: *Triumph of American Capitalism*, p. 375.
[43] July 27, 1866.

only succeeded in ruining the opportunity of the President's party for success. For example, in Maine, where the elections were held in September and were even then considered a barometer, Johnson's cause was championed by a Copperhead candidate for Governor who had been identified with draft riots, and the Radicals overwhelmed their opponents with a majority of 26,843.[44]

Radical strategy degenerated into a campaign to "smear" Johnson's party as a combination of Copperheads and rebels bent on undoing the results of the Civil War. Unquestionably the concealed pressures of powerful Eastern interests urged on this disreputable propaganda of the politicians in order to divert the attention of Western agrarians from their growing concern over tariffs, banks, bonds, and other economic issues. Every Northwestern community had a score or more of Union veterans, daily reminders of the sacrifices made to preserve national unity. In 1865 these communities approved Johnson's mild Reconstruction policy. The Democratic Party was out of favor, and to desert the Negro and the Southern Unionists was to relinquish the gains of the war. By the spring of 1866, however, their attitude toward Johnson had become a doubtful hope. In July they were disturbed by the dubious elements in the National Union Convention, and Radical propaganda had won over most Unionists in the West to the support of the congressional party by election day.

The fourteenth amendment served the Radicals as practically a party platform in the congressional elections. In its passage through Congress it had, after the fashion of a party platform, taken on more and more the character of an omnibus appeal. It was designed to ensure the Negroes citizenship; to protect against punitive state measures "persons" — that is to say, both Negroes and investors of capital in Southern states; to penalize states with reduced congressional representation unless they enfranchised Negroes; to disqualify ex-Confederates from holding office; to guard against repudiation of the debt of the United States while requiring the

---

[44] See H. K. Beale: *The Critical Year*, pp. 382–7.

repudiating of the Confederate debts. To most Unionists these were all perfectly reasonable provisions and when every Southern state rejected the fourteenth amendment, moreover upon the advice of President Johnson,[45] the Radicals were provided with an irresistible campaign argument.

Behind the Radical platform, as promulgated in the fourteenth amendment, and constituting the grand stake in the congressional elections of 1866, was the entire economic program the Union Party had placed upon the statute books during the Civil War. Powerful interests now saw these measures threatened with repeal if Johnson's National Unionists won a majority of the seats. It was, then, an offensive-defensive drive that the Radicals were waging. New England cotton-textile magnates, who had disdained increased protection in 1861 because it stimulated ruinous competition, now had Congressmen Blaine and Stevens not only working strenuously for protection but even proposing a constitutional amendment to repeal the export-tax prohibition in order to keep raw cotton in the country, all of which led editor Horace White of the *Chicago Tribune* to voice Western protest in the question: "Have we killed King Cotton and set up King Sheeting?"[46] The Radicals won over the powerful wool-growing and wool-manufacturing interests by letting their lobby write their own schedule into the tariff act of 1866.

Railroad promoters and contractors were almost in a panic at the threat of cessation of the gigantic government land grants to new ventures that was implicit in Radical defeat. Johnson, champion of the homesteaders, was steadily insisting that the public domain should go to actual settlers instead of railroad corporations. Big land speculators who had circumvented the Homestead Act and acquired vast holdings of the best land recognized Johnson as their deadly foe and accordingly became ardent Radicals. Northern enterprisers, eager to invest capital in business in the South, were depending upon the Radicals' pending fourteenth amend-

---

[45] S. P. Chase correspondence, American Historical Association *Report* (1902), p. 516.
[46] H. K. Beale, op. cit., pp. 290–1.

ment to throw the protecting arm of Federal authority around
their dubious ventures. The new national banks, only
recently established throughout the country, saw in the National Union Party, including Southern and Western agrarians, a resurrection of the old Jacksonian anti-bank combination.

That Johnson's election meant rejection of the fourteenth
amendment, the repudiation of the national debt, and the
assumption of the Confederate debt was dinned into the voters' ears. "Do you want to give up your interests once more
to this alliance with two-fifths added to the old slave power?"
asked the campaign orator Roscoe Conkling. ". . . What
would become of the pension rolls of widows and orphans?
. . . of the public debt and public credit? What would greenbacks and five twenties and seven thirties be worth? . . .
Are you ready to put your rights, your property and the honor
of the nation, to be raffled by the murderers of your children
and the betrayers of your country?" [47] Meanwhile Congressman Bingham of Ohio was declaring: "I do not wish to sit
side by side with men whose garments smell of the blood of
my kindred." [48]

While Roscoe Conkling was waving the bloody shirt in
order to get the minds of agrarians off the current deflation,
induced by the retirement of greenbacks, Thaddeus Stevens
came to the rescue of the farmers and helped hold them to the
Radicals. He thought agrarians and non-agrarians should
share alike in party benefits and, to the consternation of Eastern financiers, he prevented further retirement of greenbacks
and, even in the shadow of the grave, was to sustain farm
prices by preventing the resumption of specie payments for
greenbacks. One curious Radical scheme for resolving this
conflict of interests was the encouragement of the freest opportunity to exploit mineral resources, especially of gold and
silver. They calculated that half a million dollars' worth of
the precious metals poured annually into the market would
reduce the speculative value of gold, head off a greenback

[47] A. R. Conkling: *Life and Letters of Roscoe Conkling*, pp. 276–7.
[48] J. A. Woodburn: *Thaddeus Stevens*, p. 401.

craze by sustaining farm prices, and incidentally enrich the mine promoters, who would constitute a powerful Radical interest.

The temperance forces were intensely bitter against Johnson, who was represented to them as little better than a common drunkard. Protestant churches, in the tradition of the antislavery crusade, become a powerful Radical group, especially the Methodist Episcopal church, whose ministers were Radicals with scarcely an exception. In Michigan, which was probably a typical Northern state in this respect, the Congregational, Baptist, Methodist Episcopal, Wesleyan, and Quaker congregations were Radicals. Perhaps pastoral partisanship found its most extravagant expression in what might be called the miracle theory of the origin of the Republican Party, that it was "created by no man or set of men but brought into being by Almighty God himself." [49]

The Radicals even broke the Democratic near monopoly of the Irish vote by making an English sympathizer out of Johnson because he had dealt rather vigorously with the Fenian conspiracy to invade Canada. They capitalized on the false impression created by General Grant's silence concerning his breaking off relations with the President after a close friendship. The Grand Army of the Republic, as a secret order of Union veterans dominated by Radical leaders, became practically an auxiliary of that party's organization.

Since in most congressional districts the Unionist voter had to choose between a Radical Unionist or a Copperhead Democrat, the Radicals succeeded in obtaining the two-thirds margin of seats in Congress that would render the President's vetoes innocuous. Hundreds of thousands of Conservatives having now entered the Radical ranks, that name began to sound absurd if not offensive to the new recruits. Moreover, now that Unionist Democrats were gravitating in considerable numbers back to the Democratic Party, the term "Republican" was coming back into use and appeared in the new gather-all designation, National Union Republican Party.

---

[49] Quoted by L. P. Stryker: *Andrew Johnson, A Study in Courage*, p. 332.

Quite naturally the incorporation of the Conservatives in the Radical organization tempered its tendency to extremes and by 1868 even defeated the Radicals' attempt to convict the impeached President.

The Tenure of Office Act, about which the impeachment trial revolved, had been enacted to prevent President Johnson from removing hundreds of thousands of Lincoln appointees and then packing the civil service with personal followers who might be lax in enforcing the Radical Reconstruction statutes. Moreover, the patronage-seeking politicians were no less a dynamic element in the Radical combination than they have been in our other multi-interest parties. Johnson was but following the precedent of Lincoln and his predecessors in making removals and appointments in order to strengthen his administration. Representative George S. Boutwell, as one of the committee of prosecutors of Johnson in the impeachment trial, rather let the cat out of the bag when he enumerated the offices and the millions of dollars in patronage at the President's disposal.[50]

Viewed in the retrospect of not much less than a century it is now evident that the Radicals overplayed their hand and finally alarmed their most powerful economic allies in attempting to seize the government and make the super-Radical Benjamin F. Wade President. This Midwestern extremist had alarmed conservatives like Hamilton Fish, Jay Cooke, and other capitalists by such proposals as free distribution of land to Negroes and by his championing the farmers and workingmen against the capitalists, not even hesitating at woman suffrage. It is not without significance that among the legal counsel defending the President on the impeachment charges was William Evarts, the foremost corporation lawyer of that day.

Conservative Eastern interests had been astonished at the intense Radical partisanship of the West in 1866, which was to culminate in the hysterical demand for impeachment and conviction of the President. Yet this vindictiveness declined

---

[50] *Congressional Globe*, XL, supplement, p. 269.

rapidly after the trial. Radical reverses in the elections of 1867 reconciled doubting Westerners to the necessity of Negro suffrage in order that those who had saved the nation might continue to rule it. The West was losing interest in Reconstruction and becoming engrossed in immediate, pressing economic problems of its own. Politicians who puzzled over social pressures they could not comprehend managed to hold the Western wing of the reborn Republican Party by passionate appeals to patriotism, which they were soon to make synonymous with Republicanism in the minds of millions of Americans.

In Ulysses S. Grant the Radicals or re-emerging Republicans had, made to order, a presidential candidate to rescue them from the impending disaster forecast by the reverses of 1867. Grant had been a supporter of Johnson until alienated by a misunderstanding with the President. For a while it looked as if he might be the Democratic candidate for President in 1868. The Radicals, however, had attached to their service this simple-hearted soldier and, as he related it, had set him to work lobbying Senators during the trial of the President. If he could persuade enough wavering Senators to vote for conviction, the Radicals would make him their presidential candidate, provided that he would agree, when elected, to continue intact the cabinet Benjamin F. Wade had slated for appointment as soon as he should succeed Johnson. At the head of this group as Secretary of State was to sit the notorious Benjamin F. Butler, who the utterly unvindictive Lincoln had said was "as full of poison gas as a dead dog." The elevation to these proud eminences of an extremist as President and a charlatan as Secretary of State was a consummation that gave pause to the Conservatives now within the fold of the re-emerging Republican Party. The economic interests that had used the Radicals so effectively for their purposes now put on the brakes and prevented by a single vote a major blunder of the party.

CHAPTER XI

CONFUSION OF THE DEMOCRATIC PARTY

"THROUGHOUT *the darkest hours of the Civil War, Democrats of the North were willing to endure much suffering on account of their sympathy with their brethren in arms in support of the 'lost cause.' Does anyone suppose that such an achievement as the re-uniting of the disrupted Republic could have been possible had it not been for the tie between the sections furnished by unbroken continuity of the Democratic party? After the surrender of Lee, those Confederates who had been Democrats before the War were Democrats still. Their brethren at the North were ready to extend the right hand of fellowship."* JESSE MACY.*

T HE DEATH of Stephen A. Douglas six weeks after the fall of Sumter may have been the most disastrous loss of leadership ever sustained by a major American party. Until Douglas had challenged and fought out his battle with the cotton-planters, they had provided most of the leaders who determined national Democratic policies. "When the South seceded the brains of the party went with it," as Kate Chase sagely observed,[1] and then, in a few weeks, Douglas too was gone. His departure left his devoted following leaderless in the most critical hour in the history of the party and of the Republic.

No man of Douglas's generation, excepting Lincoln, had been more resourceful in discovering or inventing the formulas that enable vast aggregations of voters to rationalize divergent interests by means of a common pattern of thought.

---

* From *Political Parties in the United States*, pp. 75–6. By permission of The Macmillan Company, publishers.

[1] A. M. Schlesinger: *Political and Social Growth of the United States*, p. 21.

The "popular sovereignty" device of the Kansas-Nebraska Bill is no exception and it deserved a better fate. It was intended to enable Southern Congressmen to save their faces with their constituents at the very moment when they had no shadow of a hope of planting slavery in Northern territory — in short, squatter sovereignty would scarcely have spread slavery north of the Missouri Compromise line, which was looked upon as a boundary nature itself had decreed. For all the feverish pro-slavery activity, the census of 1860 showed the utter failure to get slavery planted in Kansas. Douglas was just as confident as Lincoln that he had the formula for easing slavery out of existence. "I am not pro-slavery," he declared. "I think it is a curse beyond computation to both black and white." [2] Nor can anyone be certain today that squatter sovereignty might not have doomed slavery without secession and civil war.

Once committed to popular sovereignty, Douglas maintained his position with consummate skill, indefatigable energy, and inflexible courage in the face of threats such as had made Clay falter and hedge, as for example on the annexation of Texas. Douglas's consistency was astonishing despite such myths as that Lincoln covered him with confusion by his Freeport questions. [3] Not for a long generation, until the rise of William Jennings Bryan in the nineties, were the Democrats again to have such a dynamic leader, and even Bryan lacked the versatility and broad tolerance that enabled Douglas to combine in a single following big business, farmers, and workers.

After Sumter, Douglas Democrats almost *en masse* and even many Northern Breckenridge Democrats rushed to the support of the Lincoln administration and the Union cause. "The mass of the Democracy were even more furious than the Republicans," wrote Alexander Johnson. [4] When the Thirty-seventh Congress organized in July 1861, the Demo-

---

[2] G. F. Milton: *The Eve of Conflict: Stephen A. Douglas and the Needless War,* p. 150.
[3] See A. J. Beveridge, op. cit., IV, 302.
[4] *American Politics,* p. 198.

cratic members held no caucus and nominated no candidate for Speaker, but joined the Republicans in passing war legislation. Under these circumstances Democracy as a party was disappearing from American politics. At this point the Republicans, in deference to the Democrats, abandoned their party name and as Unionists invited all supporters of the administration to joint their ostensibly non-partisan organization.

Upon sober second thought there were those Democrats who wondered what would now become of the party with the hallowed Jacksonian tradition. Calculating politicians with a vested interest in their peculiar skills as social co-ordinators and by no means forgetful of the stakes of power for which they lived to play their game — these all sought to rally the dispersing forces. Then, too, if the two-party system was to be maintained, there must be an opposition, and the losers of the election of 1860 would logically constitute it.

The Democratic Party was revived by Lincoln's breathtaking assumption of extra-constitutional and even unconstitutional powers, particularly his suspension of the writ of habeas corpus, without the congressional authorization the Constitution seemed to require. Henceforth the opposition to the administration was assumed to be a Democratic Party function. Insisting that they were the true unionists, the Democrats refused to accord that term exclusively to Lincoln's supporters, but sought to deter further defections of Democrats in that direction by fastening upon the Lincoln men the opprobrious epithet of "Black Republicans."

Indicative of the confused political scene is the difficulty of classifying the War Democrats, who, of course, favored a vigorous prosecution of the war in order to restore Federal authority throughout the Union. Many of them co-operated with, or even lost their identity as Democrats within, the Union Party. We shall find them eventually contributing a galaxy of notable leaders to the reborn Republican Party of the late sixties. Most of the War Democrats did not sever their connection with their old party but, by remaining in it along with the Peace Democrats, gave it two discordant wings. Consequently there was an internal clash and confusion that confounded every effort to find a compelling common party purpose, especially in the absence of such a genius at that game as the late lamented Douglas had been.

Especially convinced that Democracy should not disperse were those who had shouted least in the hysterical demonstrations that followed the fall of Sumter. These were the Democrats who had opposed coercion of seceders and who consequently could not be quite reconciled to the gigantic military preparation projected for that very purpose. They constituted the Peace Democrats, whom the Republicans, within the Unionist combination, were soon to brand as Copperheads. Nothing would shake their convictions that the South could never be conquered by force and that the abolitionists were responsible for secession.

Two leaders of the Peace Democrats stood out above the others: Fernando Wood, mayor of New York, and Clement L. Vallandigham, who represented a southwestern Ohio district in Congress when the war began. Wood's constituency of urban followers suggests the economic ties of the metropolis with the cotton trade. Elected as a Tammany mayor of New York in the middle fifties, he enjoyed the support of many reputable bankers and merchants. Friendly at first with President Buchanan, he suddenly turned to Douglas in 1858 and made him a heavy loan with which to finance his senatorial campaign when Lincoln was his opponent. Ousted from Tammany after a clash with its leaders, Wood organized a personal following of business men, mechanics, immigrants, and stevedores and in defiance of Tammany returned to the mayor's office in 1859. Two years later, just as the Southern states, one by one, were seceding, he made, in an official address to the municipal council, the startling proposal for which the Unionists never could forgive him. "With our aggrieved brethren of the slave states," he reported, "we have friendly relations and a common sympathy." Then after protesting against up-state New Yorkers "unfortunately imbued with the fanatical spirit which actuates a portion of the people of New England," he wanted to know whether "if part of the states form new combinations and

governments . . . why should not New York City, instead
of supporting, by her contributions in revenue, two-thirds of
the expenses of the United States, become equally independent? . . . When disunion has become a fixed and certain
fact, why may not New York disrupt the bonds which bind
her to a venal and corrupt master? " [5] No doubt this should
be interpreted in the light of the $169,000,000 due New York
merchants from Southern customers.

Far more typical of the Peace Democrats, and in truth
their outstanding leader, was the chief of the Copperheads,
Clement L. Vallandigham. Two generations after his death
historians have scarcely yet managed to clear away the mountains of obloquy under which his contemporary enemies
buried his reputation. His career was long misinterpreted because his intemperate oratory obscured his deep and unquestionably sincere desire for national unity. He believed himself to be a better unionist than Abraham Lincoln himself.
Late in 1862 he introduced a series of resolutions in the House
the central idea of which was that anyone advising the acceptance of peace on any other basis than the integrity of
the Union should be guilty of high crime against the Constitution and the Union. [6]

Those who dispose of this extraordinarily earnest man
with the easy formula of the devil theory of politics ignore
the sectional and economic interests rationalized by his dogmas. Sectionally he was neither pro-Southern nor pro-North-
ern, but rather pro-Western. As one reads Vallandigham's
speeches one detects once more the agrarian pattern of
thought of John Taylor of Caroline. [7] "The great dividing
line," said Vallandigham in 1861, "was always between capital and labor — between the few who had money and wanted
to use the government to increase and 'protect' it, as the
phrase goes, and the many who had little but wanted to keep
it and who only asked the government to let them alone." [8]

[5] *Harper's Encyclopedia of United States History*, X, 436–7.
[6] *Congressional Globe*, 37th Congress, 3rd Session, p. 15.
[7] *Supra*, pp. 64, 65.
[8] Quoted by C. A. and Mary Beard: *Rise of American Civilization*, II,
677.

Though Wall Street was yet to become the hobgoblin of Western farmers, Vallandigham was, in a real sense, a John the Baptist, a herald of post-Civil War populism and the Bryan crusade. Here, indeed, is one of the secrets of the vast following of this utterly fearless friend of the small farmer and mechanic.

Secession confronted with imminent disaster the dwellers of the Ohio Valley, where Vallandigham and the Peace Democrats were very numerous. As C. R. Fish has pointed out, "No section, except New England, had its livelihood so closely bound up in the preservation of the Union." [9] Here is an explanation of the extraordinarily large number of Ohio Valley counties carried by Bell and Everett of the Constitutional Unionists in 1860. Their party slogan: "The Constitution, the Union and the enforcement of the laws," slightly paraphrased becomes "The Constitution as it is and the Union as it was" of the Vallandigham Peace Democrats. Wheat, flour, beef, pork, lard, whisky, and manufactured products, particularly from Cincinnati, the Wabash and Illinois valleys, had passed down the Mississippi River and were, in no small degree, paid for by the counter traffic in molasses, sugar, and cotton. The loss of their bacon market alone in the South because of the war was estimated at $6,000,000.[10] Only a few days before Lincoln's inauguration the *Cincinnati Enquirer* was insisting that the prosperity of this entire lower West depended on the Southern trade and the continued culture of cotton in the South through slave labor.[11]

With the opening of the Civil War innumerable owners of hotels and summer resorts in the Ohio Valley lost the lucrative patronage of Louisiana, Alabama, and Mississippi planters. River-boat owners and their employees as well as trainmen of the Cincinnati and Charleston Railroad faced ruin. Moreover, southern Ohio had hundreds of large tobacco

---

9 "The Decision of the Ohio Valley," *American Historical Association Report* (1910), p. 162.

10 E. J. Benton: *The Movement for Peace without Victory during the Civil War*, p. 16.

11 See H. C. Hubbert: "Pro Southern Influences in the Free West," *Mississippi Valley Historical Review*, XX, 50.

farms, some containing from 500 to 1,000 acres, dependent on the labor of Virginia and Kentucky slaves hired out by their masters to these free-state tobacco-raisers. Scarcely second to these economic bonds was the fact that the old migration of Southerners northward had populated almost the entire Ohio Valley, with the consequence that the ties of blood, marriage, and a common culture made abhorrent to them the idea of permanent separation of North and South.

When the war-time depression hit the Ohio Valley these Peace Democrats wanted nothing so much as the restoration of their lost Southern market. Their slogan, "The Union as it was," meant the old union of South and West through compromise, characterized by a weak nationalism with an emphasis on state rights. The absurdity of the old idea that the Peace Democrats desired the triumph of the Confederacy strikes one in the face when one recalls the persistent and inflexible resolution of the Ohio Valley that no foreign power should ever be permitted to command the mouth of the Mississippi. They prayed for the triumph of neither Federal nor Confederate armies, but a stalemate, and "peace without victory." Southern independence would be scarcely less disastrous to the Ohio Valley than a prostrate and impoverished South, conquered by Federal troops. Morgan's raiders were to discover that the Copperheads were not pro-secession when they rallied to the call of the defending Ohio militia instead of to that of the invaders.

Because of a "disloyal" speech delivered by Vallandigham at Mt. Vernon, Ohio, May 1, 1863, the orator was arrested, tried by a military court, and sentenced to close confinement during the continuance of the war. Anxious to avoid creating a Copperhead martyr, Lincoln commuted the sentence to transfer to the Confederate lines. Jefferson Davis would not have consented to Lee's invasion of Pennsylvania and the Gettysburg campaign had he heeded the refugee Vallandigham's personal protest to him that it would weaken the influence of the Peace Democrats. Vallandigham was quite naturally unwelcome in the Confederacy and he presently ran the blockade and fled to Canada. While he was there the

Ohio Democrats nominated him for Governor. The Unionists nominated against him John Brough, who defeated Vallandigham by the then overwhelming majority of 101,000 at the end of a campaign so crucial that it gripped the attention of the loyal states, the Confederacy, and even the English people.

The old National Road from Wheeling to Indianapolis has been considered a Mason and Dixon line of the Old Northwest since it marked roughly the northern limit of migration from the South. Aversion to slavery had largely impelled this movement, but during the Civil War these migrants feared, above all else, emancipation and the swarming of hordes of free Negroes into the Northwest. Their *bête noire* was the abolitionist, whom they hated as the provoker of secession, the destroyer of their Southern market, and the cause of the hard times of the early sixties. Lincoln as the Emancipator was the prince of abolitionists, and Vallandigham's vicious attacks on the war President were music to their ears. Democratic editors never let them forget the black peril for which "Black" Republicans were responsible. Resolutions of the Butler County (Ohio) Democrats expressed the prevalent fear in 1862 in their condemnation of emancipation "as calculated to overrun the free states with a brutalized and worthless race and to beget a ruinous competition with and degrade free labor." [12]

It was Negrophobia that bound rural and urban Peace Democrats securely together. "Why," asked the *New York Daily News,* "should a worker leave his family destitute while he goes out to war to free a Negro who will then compete with him for a job?" Negroes had exasperated the Irish during the war by invading the pick-and-shovel field, long monopolized by the sons of Erin. When New York employers were guilty of importing "contrabands" to break a strike of stevedores, the stage was set for a "massacre" of Negroes in the Draft Riots of 1863. The Draft Act not only had been abominably framed so as to permit the legal purchase of exemption, but was apparently maladministered so as to bear

[12] G. H. Porter: *Ohio Politics during the Civil War,* p. 139.

unduly on Democratic wards in New York. The rioters were principally Irish, the Germans as opponents of slavery not participating. However great the provocation, the Draft Riots irreparably damaged the cause of the Peace Democrats.

Widely scattered throughout the North was a variety of elements held to the Peace Democrats by an intense resentment against the arbitrary conduct of the Lincoln administration. If Lincoln's serene disregard for certain constitutional prescriptions puzzles some of his best-informed admirers today, what could be expected of bitter political opponents, dead set against this chief of the Black Republicans even before he reached the presidential chair? His disregard of the constitutional provision that Congress has the power "to raise and support armies" when he substantially increased the standing army [13] prompted his fellow Republican, Senator John Sherman, to protest: "I have never met anyone who claimed that the President could, by proclamation, increase the regular army." [14] No more constitutional was Lincoln's ordering without the required legislation the construction of naval vessels. In utter disregard of the Constitution's empowering Congress "to make rules for the governing of the land and naval forces," Lincoln issued an elaborate code of laws covering the matter. Despite the constitutional provision that "no money shall be drawn from the treasury but in consequence of appropriations made by law," Lincoln directed the Secretary of the Treasury to advance $2,000,000 of money, without appropriation or security, to three private citizens to be expended for military purposes.[15] Two days after issuing the Emancipation Proclamation in what Dunning considered "a perfect platform for despotism," [16] the President declared "all persons discouraging enlistments, resisting militia drafts or guilty of any disloyal practice affording aid and comfort to the rebels against the authority of the United

---

[13] J. D. Richardson, VI, 15, 16, 18, 19.

[14] Letter to *Cincinnati Gazette,* quoted by Randall: *Constitutional Problems under Lincoln,* p. 38.

[15] J. D. Richardson, op. cit., VI, 79.

[16] "The Constitution in the Civil War," *Political Science Quarterly,* I, 188.

States shall be subject to martial law and liable to trial and punishment by court martial or military commission," and with respect to these the writ of habeas corpus was suspended.[17]

Whoever is curious as to the counter-blasts of the Democrats against such conduct on the part of the Lincoln administration will find them conveniently summarized in the list of toasts of the Jackson Day banquet at Columbus, Ohio, in 1863: "Civil Liberty and its Greatest Bulwark, the Writ of Habeas Corpus"; "Executive Proclamations"; "Freedom of Speech and the Press"; "The Lincoln Bastile"; and finally epitomizing the paramount objective of the Peace Democrats: "The Constitution as it is, the Union as it was and the Negroes where they are." [18]

If, as Edward Channing concluded, Lincoln and the Union Party were handicapped by the lack of an opposition in the summer of 1864, the Democrats came to their aid with their platform in August. Convened in the Wigwam at Chicago were "Peace Democrats, War Democrats, Whigs, Know-Nothings, Conservatives, State Rights extremists who indorsed the doctrine of secession, millionaires in broadcloth, run-down politicians in paper collars, men who had braved the wrath of violent communities and suffered for the right of free speech and a free press, and a remnant of Confederate loyalists who necessarily could not be open in their efforts." [19] In retrospect, the most significant fact of the convention was the presence of Vallandigham along with enough Peace Democrats to dictate the platform. This refugee, sufficiently disguised, had slipped back into the United States from Windsor, Canada, in June 1864, and Lincoln chose to pretend he did not believe the reports of his return. "As long as he does not raise any disturbance," remarked the President, "he will be as completely disguised as the man who went to a masquerade party with a clean face." [20] This marplot was not

---

[17] J. D. Richardson, op. cit., VI, 98–9.
[18] *Ohio Statesman*, January 9, 1863; *Crisis*, January 14, 1863.
[19] C. Sandburg, op. cit., III, 226.
[20] Ibid., III, 109.

content until he had got inserted into the Democratic platform the plank: "That this convention does explicitly declare, as the sense of the American people, that after four years of failure to restore the Union by the experiment of war . . . justice, humanity, liberty, and public welfare demand that immediate efforts be made for a cessation of hostilities, with a view to an ultimate convention of the States, or other peaceable means, to the end that, at the earliest, practicable moment, peace may be restored on the basis of the federal union of the States." [21] It should be noted that this did not signify what the Union Party distorted into "Peace at Any Price," but instead an armistice and that great objective of the Peace Democrats, a stalemate and the restoration of the old Union.

In a bid for the soldier vote the convention nominated for President General George B. McClellan, whose soldiers had been extraordinarily devoted to him and who was known to be out of sympathy with the administration on its emancipation policy. In his letter of acceptance he sought to counteract the effect of the peace plank by declaring: "I could not look into the face of my gallant comrades of the army and navy who have survived so many bloody battles and tell them that their labors and the sacrifice of so many of our slain and wounded brethren had been in vain; that we have abandoned the Union for which we have so often periled our lives." [22] McClellan's repudiation confused the party position, and Vallandigham not only canceled his speaking engagements but withdrew from the canvass for a while. When the facts are squarely faced, it is evident enough that McClellan differed from Vallandigham in little else than that he had no faith in the latter's formula of an armistice as the preliminary step to a restoration of the Union. On this point Lincoln and McClellan saw eye to eye. The most striking political difference in the fall of 1864 was rather that between Lincoln and the Radicals within his own party as revealed by the sensational Wade-Davis Manifesto, which warned the President that

[21] E. Stanwood, op. cit., p. 304.
[22] Ibid., p. 306.

"the authority of Congress is paramount . . ." and "his executive duties to obey and execute not to make the laws."

While Vallandigham and his agrarian Peace Democrats wrote the platform, powerful economic leaders who had cultivated McClellan for three years were responsible for his nomination for the presidency in 1864. Among them were such giants of finance, transportation, and industry as August Belmont of the New York branch of the house of Rothschild; Dean Richmond, railroad millionaire; William H. Aspinwall, Panama Railroad and steamship-line multimillionaire; and Cyrus H. McCormick, the pious Chicago manufacturer. Wealth and respectability were represented by Governor Horatio Seymour of New York and others, while the aristocratic intelligentsia appeared in the person of such a notable as Robert Winthrop of Massachusetts, one-time Whig Speaker of the National House of Representatives, the immediate successor of Senator Daniel Webster, but by the middle fifties a Buchanan Democrat and now a leader who unblushingly gloried in being called a Copperhead. Strange as it may seem, the name Copperhead, first applied by enemies who attributed to Peace Democrats the treachery of the reptile of that designation, was transfigured by these Democrats into a symbol of liberty through the copper head or image of Liberty on the copper cent which they made into a badge proudly worn on the breast. Lincoln's electoral vote of 212 to McClellan's 21 obscured the impressive Democratic strength. With all its handicaps the party polled forty-five per cent of the major-party strength. To do this without the Southern Democrats and on a platform rejecting every Democratic issue that had ever proved successful for one that doomed it to failure indicated that the party was not dead beyond the hope of resurrection.

The collapse of the Confederacy utterly discredited the Democratic Party that had staked its future on the "War is a failure" platform. Robert C. Winthrop, campaigning for McClellan, had warned that Lincoln's re-election meant that the South would fight on for thirty years,[23] and now it had folded

---

[23] C. Sandburg, op. cit., III, 253.

up in less than that many weeks. In the summer of 1865 it was a plausible prediction that the Democratic Party had become only a historic memory. No other major party in our history has ever recovered from such overwhelming damage to its prestige. During the war it had lost to the Union Party beyond recovery a galaxy of notables destined to become energetic leaders of a reborn Republican Party. Among them were Secretary of War E. M. Stanton and Generals U. S. Grant, John A. Logan, B. F. Butler, D. E. Sickles, and John A. Dix.

In the summer of 1865 came the first glimmer of an opportunity to repair the party's damaged fortunes. Its hope of recovery centered in the person and developing policies of President Johnson. No one can say what Lincoln would have done had he survived, but it is incontrovertible that Johnson adopted Lincoln's Reconstruction policy, whereupon the Radicals in Congress continued against him the bitter feud they had conducted against Lincoln. They constituted the nucleus of the group we have already seen evolving into the new Republican Party.[24] Around the President there rallied not only the Conservative Unionists, but also what was left of the old Northern and Southern wings of the Democratic Party.

When Congress convened in December 1865, the Radicals, as we have seen, prevented the seating of the Southern Congressmen elected from the presidentially reconstructed states, and wrested from the President control of Reconstruction. The forty Democratic Congressmen, though elected on the peace platform of 1864, were none the less Unionists, and preparatory to the next congressional campaign they issued an address to the people in which they proclaimed their acceptance of the results of the war and asserted mild state-rights doctrines. In the summer of 1866 was held the National Union Convention [25] planned by W. H. Seward and Thurlow Weed and called by Henry J. Raymond, the National Chairman of the Union Party, who later played a very prominent part in

---

24 *Supra*, p. 257.
25 *Supra*, p. 253.

the convention. The dynamic word "Union" in the party designation was now surcharged with patriotic sentiment. Its use seemed to imply that their antagonists, the Radicals, were neither nationalists nor unionists but, instead, sectionalists, and the subtle implication stung hard.

Despite the fact that the chief promoters of the gathering — Seward, Weed, and Raymond — had been founders of the Republican Party, in retrospect it is now clear that the National Union Convention of 1866 was a landmark in the rehabilitation of the post-war Democratic Party, and the Convention's endorsement of Johnson's Reconstruction program made its platform practically Democratic. The delegates included many of the War Democrats who, like Johnson, had joined the Union Party. There were a few Republicans and some former Whigs, especially from the border states. Since the purpose was to abate sectionalism, many moderate Southerners were delegates and, indeed, this was the first genuinely national convention in half a dozen years. The apparently sincere professions of acceptance of the results of the war by ex-Confederates and the recognition of these delegates by the Unionists presaged the restoration of the old Jacksonian alliance of sections. In fact the Democrats, now becoming incorporated in this Union Party combination behind Johnson, were performing their historic function in reuniting the sections on a basis of equality, a consummation difficult to imagine had not the Democratic Party survived the vicissitudes of war-time politics. John Sharp Williams of Mississippi was to express the opinion in 1928 that if it had not been for the encouragement and support of Northern Democrats, especially in Indiana, New Jersey, and New York City, the Southern Democrats might have given up their fight and the cotton states have been subjected to the fate of Haiti and Santo Domingo.[26]

The presence of the Peace Democrats in the Johnson gathering confronted the movement with a portentous problem. Here was a discredited element, eager to repair its damaged

---

[26] Letter of J. S. Williams to Henry Minor. See Henry Minor, op. cit., p. 296.

reputation by identifying itself with a political movement promising now to develop an impressive prestige. The conspicuous Copperheads Wood and Vallandigham were present until, too late, they were persuaded to leave. The Radicals missed no opportunity to smear the convention with the charges of rebellion and Copperheadism, and called Johnson's supporters "Copper-Johnsons." Unfortunately, the President had no personal following of consequence in either the North or the South. The congressional elections resulted in a tidal wave which gave Johnson's enemies the two-thirds majority that rendered him henceforth helpless.

The *Buffalo Advertiser*, which had supported Johnson's congressional candidates, admitted after the election: "The Democratic party as it existed during the war [had] become so odious that it [was] hopeless to seek to perpetuate and keep it alive." [27] One Johnson man said: "The mere apprehension that the Democratic party might be brought into power . . . and the unfounded allegation that Mr. Johnson and others had joined the party, so excited the nerves of the patriotic masses as to make them blind to every other consideration." [28]

A reorientation of the Democratic Party in preparation for the presidential campaign of 1868 seemed necessary if the party was ever to live down its war reputation, and circumstances offered an opportunity. The post-war recession of business had arrived, accompanied by the usual agrarian demand for inflation, particularly in the Northwest. The opportunity to exploit this break was too great to be passed by, though there was something paradoxical in the party of Andrew Jackson, Locofocoism, and hard money championing the cause of greenback issues and resisting the resumption of specie redemption. George H. Pendleton, an erstwhile Peace Democrat, became the exponent of this so-called "Ohio Idea," epitomized in the slogan: "The same currency for the bondholder and the plough-holder." This was a formula peculiarly appealing to the Peace Democrats, who certainly wanted to avoid paying in gold a debt incurred in greenback values —

27 Quoted in H. K. Beale, op. cit., p 383.
28 Ibid., p. 382.

that is to say, at a ruinous discount, with high interest rates, and moreover, as many believed, to finance a needless war. So popular did the greenback idea prove that Western Republican leaders, the financier-statesman John Sherman among them, bent before the inflationist breeze. The editor of the *Cleveland Leader* on February 20, 1868, wrote: "I will say confidently that in the cry being raised by the Copperhead Demagogues of 'Gold for Bondholders and Greenbacks for laborers' I see the defeat of the Union party next fall which even the military prestige of Grant cannot prevent."

Pendleton, apparently the logical Democratic candidate, arrived at the convention held in Tammany Hall, New York, with his dynamic "Ohio Idea" and the expectation of the presidential nomination. Chief Justice Chase was more than a receptive candidate, with his capable daughter Kate on the scene to look after his interests. Also promoting his candidacy were two notable southern-Ohio Peace Democrats, Alexander Long and Clement Vallandigham. In the pull and tug of factions it turned out that the Easterners nominated Horatio Seymour, a "sound money" man, for President, while the Westerners were permitted to write the "Ohio Idea" into the platform with the proposal to pay the bondholders in "legal money" — that is to say, greenbacks — except where otherwise specifically stipulated in the bonds. It sounded reasonable enough to declare that there should be "one currency for the government and the people, the laborer and the office holder, the pensioner and the soldier, the producer and the bondholder," [29] but here was a golden opportunity for the remorseless Republican campaigners to raise the specter of repudiation and induce sinking spells in those patriots who had put their savings into war bonds. The situation was now as paradoxical as in 1864 when the War Democrat McClellan was nominated on a "war failure" platform; and to make the parallel complete, Seymour, like McClellan, repudiated the outstanding plank of his platform.

Certain elements in the personnel of the delegations caught

---

[29] E. Stanwood, *op. cit.*, p. 322.

the eyes of the newspaper reporters, and presently readers of Republican papers knew that the Confederate generals Forrest, Wade Hampton, and Garland were there and, worse still, that arch-conspirator and chief secessionist Robert Barnwell Rhett. These ex-Confederates, with the blindness that had afflicted the old slavocracy, returned home satisfied with their achievement of getting inserted in the platform a plank roundly condemning Negro suffrage, oblivious of the fact that they were thereby inviting the Republicans to overwhelm them with an extra amount of waving of the bloody shirt.

As it turned out, however, the most disastrous single act of the convention was the nomination for Vice President of General Francis P. Blair, Jr. He was one of Sherman's generals, a one-time Congressman whom Lincoln in 1864 had hoped might be elected Speaker and in the interest of the administration wrest control from the Radicals. No sooner had the Democrats nominated Blair than the Republicans unearthed and gave the widest possible publicity to a letter of his in which he did not stop at condemning the entire Reconstruction setup but proposed drastic direct action to overthrow it. "There is but one way to restore the Government and the Constitution," he had written, "and that is for the President-elect to declare these acts null and void, compel the army to undo its usurpations at the South, disperse the carpetbag State governments, allow the white people to reorganize their own governments and elect Senators and Representatives." [30] Since Seymour refrained from campaign activity, under the circumstances Blair was so much in evidence that he attracted the concentrated fire of the Republicans. "Americans! if you want another civil war vote the Blair ticket," warned the *New York Tribune*. Blair had enabled the Republicans to convince a majority of the voters that his proposal was a real and not an imaginary danger. Yet in spite of all this, together with the fact that the Republicans profited from the disqualifications of ex-Confederates and the enfranchisement of Negroes and most of all from the mighty prestige of General Grant,

---

[30] W. E. Smith, *The Francis Preston Blair Family in Politics*, II, 406.

considered by many as the savior of the Union, the Democrats polled forty-seven per cent of the popular vote. Moreover this was achieved without a ballot from the unreconstructed states of Virginia, Florida, Mississippi, and Texas.

By 1868 it was becoming crystal clear that keeping alive the Civil War issues was simply damning the Democratic Party. Vice-presidential candidate Blair's blunders had demonstrated that fact. One by one the party had fought the three great war amendments now securely planted in the Constitution. While Democrats had been ruining party prospects by fighting for lost causes, serious economic problems were crying for solution and offering issues for party leaders shrewd enough to utilize them. What a commentary upon the poverty of post-war Democratic leadership that it remained for the Copperhead Vallandigham himself to perceive the exigencies of the party situation and, in 1871, prepare to make the necessary shift of issues as he proclaimed it in his "New Departure"! This consisted of a set of resolutions he got the Montgomery County (Ohio) Democratic Convention to adopt, and later his state Democratic Convention. Commenting on these resolutions the *Dayton Journal* of May 19, 1871 declared: "The Resolutions of '68, States' Rights, Negro suffrage, greenbacks for public debts, our Southern brethren, justice to the South and everything else which Democracy had held destructive as opposed to Black Republicanism, was turned into the hopper to be seen no more in the original." It signified in substance an acceptance of the results of the war and a turning to the future with its emerging and pressing new problems. Ideologically, at least, the Democratic Party had turned a corner.

CHAPTER XII

THE REBORN REPUBLICAN PARTY

"THE *factory on the one side and on the other the husbandry of pasture, cornfield and prairie wheatland joined in an alliance which was the more tenacious because the cold bargains it involved were overspread by sentiment."* A. W. MACMAHON.

THE NOMINATION of Ulysses S. Grant in 1868 by the Republican Party is itself indicative that this was not quite the ante-bellum party of that name. Those Republicans who were shocked in 1940 at the nomination of Wendell Willkie, whom relatively few of them knew and who according to the issue of *Who's Who* current during the months when his candidacy was maturing was a confessed Democrat, ought to be reminded that Grant, the only Republican President ever to serve two full terms, had never voted the Republican ticket in a presidential election until he was himself the candidate of that party. In 1856 he had voted for Buchanan because, as he explained, he "knew Frémont." [1] He is believed not to have voted in 1860 and to have voted the Union ticket of Lincoln and Johnson in 1864. Under the circumstances there was nothing inconsistent, then, in the Democrats considering him their logical candidate for 1868. This event was prevented, however, by his break with Johnson and the foresight of the Radicals in practically pre-empting him as a candidate of the re-emerging Republican Party. [2]

Leadership of the revived Republican Party revealed striking changes since Lincoln's first election. Edwin M. Stanton, the great War Secretary and only recently the storm center

---

[1] L. A. Coolidge: *The Life of U. S. Grant,* p. 270.
[2] *Supra,* p. 259.

of the impeachment trial, had been brought into Lincoln's cabinet as a War Democrat. Benjamin F. Butler, chief of the impeachment prosecutors and soon to be practically a lieutenant of Grant in the lower House, had been an ardent Breckenridge Democrat in 1860, active in the Charleston convention. John A. Logan, who made the speech nominating Grant in the Republican Convention, hailed from "darkest Egypt" of southern Illinois and had been an energetic Douglas Democrat before the war. Generals Daniel E. Sickles and John A. Dix had both been ante-bellum Democrats. The diligent research of one scholar reveals the interesting fact that of thirty-four outstanding Republican members of the two houses of Congress in the late sixties, nineteen had at some time or other made the transition from the Democratic Party, while only fifteen were former Whigs.[3]

Far more significant than the former party affiliation of these Republicans were their new sponsors, the captains of finance, industry, and commerce. Never had a President entered the White House so mortgaged to wealth by campaign contributions as was Grant, though he was unaware of it. Whether such knowledge would have embarrassed him is doubtful. The capitalists could not have imagined how completely they had captivated the imagination of this honest, simple-hearted soldier. As one whom military service had rescued from a grinding poverty, Grant was wont to measure a man by the millions he had amassed, with little curiosity about the method by which he acquired them. Naïve indeed was the President who could serenely appear along with the millionaire Jim Fisk in that unprincipled speculator's theater, which incidentally provided the owner simultaneously with an investment and a harem.

So far as Grant's deference to wealth is concerned, it is doubtful whether another man could have been elected more representative of the common man's views. William Allen White in *A Certain Rich Man* has captured and portrayed in bold relief the adoration of wealth that cursed that genera-

---

[3] L. K. Bowersox: *Reconstruction of the Republican Party, 1865–1870,* unpublished doctoral dissertation. Ohio State University, p. 22.

tion. John Barclay, a genius in devising artistic refinements
of the then prevalent skulduggery of business practices, builds
a fortune on defrauded farmers, corrupted officials, wrecked
romances, ruined homes, and bleeding hearts generally, only
to receive the wild plaudits of his proud fellow citizens. It is
significant that when President Grant argued that Santo Domingo ought to have been annexed because in that case "the
soil would have soon fallen into the hands of the United States
capitalists," [4] there is no record of a public outburst of resentment at the suggestion.

It is to be doubted whether a generation that is now the
heir of half a century's gradual development of the social concept of conservation of national resources has any right to pass
stern moral judgment upon grandparents who were obsessed
with a mania for the exploitation of those resources. In any
case, it is the function of the social scientist at this point to
endeavor to understand rather than to condemn what then
amounted to an irresistible social force in American politics.
The evidence is clear that when the Republican Party was
"reborn" in the late sixties, the "American Dream" of a land
of opportunity was seeking fulfillment in the unrestrained
exploitation of a continent fabulously rich in natural resources. To this purpose, for better or for worse, the new
Republican Party was dedicated. From the head of the party
in the White House down through the network of national,
state, county, and precinct leaders to the very rank and file,
the Republican Party was in substantial agreement on this
great objective until Theodore Roosevelt began the crusade
for conservation that presaged the great Progressive schism.

So the exploiting interests both great and small attacked
the continent's natural wealth with the reckless abandon of
the earlier tobacco- and cotton-planters. In the midst of a
nature so prodigal, a pinch-penny economy was hooted at.
Much of the forest, mineral, grazing, and farming resources
lay in the public domain. Why should not the government
be generous in dispensing them to capitalists who could de-

---

⁴ J. D. Richardson, op. cit., VII, 412.

velop them, thereby supplying the nation's needs while "giving" work at good wages to laborers? The idea that these
resources might ever be considered social wealth seemed preposterous in this era of extremely "rugged individualism."
Mining "rights" as well as practically every other claim to
natural resources were the individual "rights" of the first person to "stake the claim." What if there were sharp practices
in acquisition and extreme waste in development when the
supply seemed inexhaustible? What if public officials took
toll of whatever passed through their hands? This seemed
only the inevitable concomitant of administering natural
wealth that was only a little less abundant than air and water
and hence akin to what the economists considered "free
goods." Improper perhaps in a technical sense, but under
the circumstances surely not to be confused with embezzle-
ment or larceny. C. C. Arbuthnot expressed perfectly the
conception of this matter held by the post-war generation
when he wrote: "The officers were like men passing through
a dripping orchard. To pluck and eat was to follow a natural
impulse easily yielded to when everybody was receiving according to their [sic] needs." [5] The spirit of the age was to
"live and let live" and to apply the classic proverb: "*De mini-
mis prætor non curat.*"

No one need assume that any loftier ethical standards qualified the party of the "outs" to act as censors of the exploiting
Republicans. It was, indeed, a patron saint of the Democratic
Party, Samuel J. Tilden, who, years before his martyrdom,
perpetrated one of the earliest riggings of the stock market
and thereby gave the "lambs" a thorough fleecing. Later, as
befitted the competent enterpriser that he was, he resorted to
one of the corrupt New York courts and obtained an order
confiscating the entire edition of the historian James Parton's
Manual for the Instruction of "Rings," Railroad and Political,
written to expose Tilden's practices in high finance. Horatio
Seymour, the Democratic candidate in 1868, no doubt knew
whereof he wrote when he penned the sentence in a letter

[5] "Economic Interpretation of Present Politics," *Popular Science Monthly,*
LXXXI (1912), p. 188.

to his fellow financier Tilden: "Our people want men in office who will not steal but who will not interfere with those who do." [6] Mark Twain, in collaboration with Charles Dudley Warner, gave us the extraordinarily frank novel *The Gilded Age*, in which every blot was blackened and the politician played the major role of the star villain. Long afterward Parrington was to take the great satirist to task in his comment: "Mark Twain hated graft — the word had not been coined but the ugly thing was there — and with the innocence of his generation he damned the agent and overlooked the principal." [7] It is doubtful whether Parrington himself had probed deeply enough, down even beneath the sinister interests themselves to the bed rock of the sovereign people, fascinated as they were by "successful" men who never missed the "main chance." It is evident enough now that the American people had not yet recovered from the psychosis produced by civil strife. Complaints against the corrupt alliance between "business and politics" were scarcely audible, since the common man deferred to the captains of industry who had demonstrated their worth by making the most of their opportunities. The circumstances seem to call for the indictment, not so much of the politician and the party, as of the American people themselves. Be that as it may, the election returns indicate that the Republican Party mirrored the mores of the Gilded Age somewhat more convincingly than its opponents did. The "picture of the state" reflected by the party seems to have been a pretty faithful one.

So the stock-raisers appropriated the prairies, the lumber kings the forests, and the gold, silver, iron, copper, coal, and petroleum barons the mineral sites, with scarce a thought in anybody's mind of a "special privilege." Indeed, so firmly did the concept of individual property then become established as part of the American tradition that to this very day the common man grasps with difficulty the idea that even a public-utility franchise constitutes a special privilege. So

---

[6] Quoted by De A. S. Alexander: *A Political History of the State of New York*, III, 311.

[7] *Main Currents of American Thought*, III, 94.

keenly was the need of capital for development purposes felt that the public angrily resented legal restrictions of every kind. Usury laws, limiting interest to six per cent, promptly became a dead letter nor was the West concerned over the "soundness" of investments. The capitalist was a public benefactor who "developed" the community, "gave" work to laborers, was a "big taxpayer," and contributed liberally to charities, for all of which he was entitled to whatever millions he could get, with no questions asked. Let the youth of the land emulate his enterprise.

The completion of the Union Pacific Railroad captured the imagination of Americans as has no other peace-time achievement in our history. Colossal grants of national domain and credit were made to the promoters, secured only by second-mortgage bonds. When, after this unprecedented generosity, the "builders," as the Union Pacific corporation, contracted with themselves under the alias of the spurious Crédit Mobilier corporation which constructed the road and in a single year paid dividends of 348 per cent, incidentally corrupting Congressmen and ruining the career of the Vice President of the United States, the public was not greatly disturbed. Americans were entranced with the physical fact of the prompt execution of the grand project. Never before had a people been so exhilarated as with the sheer sense of triumph over vast spaces and stubborn nature represented in this fulfillment of Lincoln's dream. Moreover, to most Americans it seemed to be a Republican achievement. Grant the warrior had conquered at Appomattox; Grant the man of peace could not be quite separated from this greatest engineering triumph in human history even if the road was practically completed when he was inaugurated.

Election maps reveal that the post-war Republicans, like the ante-bellum Republicans, could depend on the counties of the New England zone of culture only a little less confidently than the Democrats eventually commanded the vote of the solid South. The spirit of the Northern Know-Nothings, whom the early Republicans had absorbed bodily, survived in a persistent nativist tendency of the party even to our own day. Democracy still promptly absorbed the arriving immigrants, and the laborers of the older stocks consequently adhered to the Republican Party. When employed in industries with brisk foreign competition, laborers generally were likely to be fellow Republicans along with their employers in ardent support of protective tariffs.

The old Northwest, which the slavocracy had exasperated by persistently blocking its demands for internal improvements, now reaped the rewards of party loyalty in ever increasing river and harbor appropriations allocated as party interests dictated. Wisconsin, for example, was no doubt influenced in its support of Grant in 1868 by the Federal appropriations for ship canals for lumbering, river and harbor improvements for farmers and merchants, as well as by land grants for rail- and wagon-roads. Miss Helen M. Jenson found this significant confession in a Wisconsin Republican newspaper of that year: ". . . the American people owe a debt of gratitude to the Republican party for constructing a highway to the Pacific, for giving homesteads to the helpless, and freedom to the slave. And the people of this congressional district are especially indebted to a Republican Congress for liberal appropriations and for the improvement of their harbors. . . ." [8] Everywhere conflicting interests within the party responded to the powerful solvent of patriotism symbolized by the omnipresent blue-clad Union veteran, whose loyalty received its due reward ultimately in pensions of unprecedented generosity.

The corn belt, lying south of the Great Lakes and extending into the trans-Mississippi prairies, was the key to Republican strategy. It included the three pivotal states of Ohio, Indiana, and Illinois, where the party found its winning presidential candidates: Lincoln, Grant, Hayes, Garfield, Benjamin Harrison, McKinley, Taft, and Harding. Every Republican who became President through election lived in the corn belt. Theodore Roosevelt and Calvin Coolidge having first entered the White House through the vice-presi-

---

[8] Unpublished essay, quoted by L. M. Hacker, op. cit., p. 384.

dency, it can be said that every Republican originally designated for President by the electorate came from the corn belt until Herbert Hoover, whose early life in the corn belt was no mean consideration in his nomination. Here is a persistent phenomenon due to no mere succession of coincidences. The farmers of this section held a conscious balance of power in the party and compelled the politicians to court their favor. "In national politics," wrote Holcombe, "the reign of King Corn was as well recognized as that of King Cotton had been and with much better justification." [9]

Powerful Western interests attached to the Republican Party became its particular beneficiaries. Among them were the cattle barons, the lumber kings, the mineral exploiters, the land speculators, and the humble homesteaders, all of whom at least obtained, if they did not boldly appropriate, portions of the public domain. The European, and particularly the English, demand for American foodstuffs then seemed simply insatiable. The prairies were becoming the world's bread basket, to say nothing of the demand for American beef now coming to be processed in gigantic packing houses. The factory farm, the limits of which were lost to the eye in the hazy horizon, operated with gang plows and giant combines, and unnumbered family-size farms were pouring a deluge of wheat into the markets of the world. Here, among other products of the Western soil, was an export commodity constituting an essential element in the gigantic mechanism of foreign trade.

The Civil War had produced a crop of self-confident millionaires eager to finance the accelerating industrial and agricultural revolutions. Their accumulations of capital stimulated ventures in mining and manufacturing of every sort. True to the dictum of John Taylor, these captains of finance, industry, and transportation, with some notable exceptions, gravitated to the party of power and prestige. Thanks to a deep-seated American ideology of individual enterprise, even the small farmers generally remained faithful to the party

---

[9] *Political Parties of Today*, p. 204.

they had helped to initiate in the fifties. They too were entrepreneurs, after a fashion, seeking profits through capital invested in a plant, employing apparatus and credit. The typical Republican farmer looked forward to the day when he might retire to dwell in the neighboring village in his declining days, supported by the income of a landlord. Here was a common denominator that made fellow Republicans of farmers and urban capitalists and that, at the same time, obscured an incompatibility of interest between the two groups.

Nor were American millionaires and lesser investors able to appease the voracious appetite of American enterprise for capital to develop the country's resources and its industrial system and to fling the gigantic network of railways across the face of the continent. Foreign investments here mounted year by year and before the end of the century totaled more than three billions. The interest alone, to say nothing of amortization, of these obligations, amounted to hundreds of millions of dollars annually, and these payments gave us what economists still designate, in terms of an outmoded economic theory, a favorable balance of trade — that is, an excess of exports over imports. Of course the payments were not usually made in monetary metals, but, through the mechanism of foreign exchange, mainly in commodity exports. Here, then, was a set of circumstances favorable for exporters, and the farmers found a ready foreign market for their surplus products. This accounts for the madness with which wheat culture expanded after the Civil War. However, the dice were loaded against the agrarians in this game. They sold in a world market at uncontrolled prices and bought of American industrialists who sold mainly in a domestic market at prices controlled by protective tariffs and by combinations with monopolistic tendencies. Worse still, farmers purchased and developed their mortgaged farms with Eastern credit, obtained at interest rates that remained inflexibly high when depression rendered their crops unsalable. Thus was the Western wing of the Republican Party made tributary to the Eastern capitalists and their satellite interests.

Somewhat doubtfully, Western agrarians followed the party in its protectionist policy. For two long generations Republican ideology, as represented in its theory of foreign trade based on the economics of a borrowing nation and the resulting favorable balance of trade, rationalized protective tariffs that were at least workable and productive of large revenues. Unfortunately for the party, the dogma of a high protective tariff which functioned with facility in a debtor nation petrified in the thinking of the typical Republican before the First World War. When, in the 1920's, we had become a creditor nation, Republicans generally lacked the philosophic flexibility to shift to the necessary new pattern of thought of a creditor nation that could not penalize imports and at the same time receive enormous payments on foreign loans, either public or private. Such was the magic potency persistently assigned to protection that in 1930, when the Great Depression was deepening, the Republican floor leader of the Senate, James E. Watson, in a radio address announcing to the nation the passage of the Hawley-Smoot tariff, predicted that within thirty days smoke would again be pouring from factory stacks.

In recording the history of the Reconstruction era those publicists who have avoided grays, light or dark, and confined themselves exclusively to jet blacks in depicting the Republican regime in the South thereby discredit their own testimony. Even Margaret Mitchell, nurtured in the Confederate traditions of a Georgian, avoids this folly in her *Gone with the Wind*, where the good is distinguished from the evil in the Reconstruction government. Military rule was welcomed in some sections of the South as security against otherwise imminent anarchy. With no mention of Republican Reconstruction and apparently no thought of passing judgment on it, the research of E. P. Cubberly reveals that, while the state school systems of the North all antedate the Civil War, "the establishment of state educational systems in the South were in reality the work of the period following the Civil War." [10]

---

[10] *Public Education in the United States*, p. 251.

He ascertained that the dates of "the real beginning of a state school system" in the several Southern states were: Virginia, 1870; North Carolina, 1868; South Carolina, 1868; Georgia, 1870; Tennessee, 1870; Louisiana, 1877; Mississippi, 1868; Alabama, 1875; Arkansas, 1867; Florida, 1869; Texas, 1866. These dates are significant since practically all of them fall within the period when the carpetbagger and the scalawag dominated the Southern state governments.

The planting aristocracy that ruled the South before the war had then maintained its local policy only by constant vigilance in the face of persistent popular discontent. In vain had the Southern white yeomanry pressed the planting aristocrats in state legislature and constitutional convention for universal white manhood suffrage, prison reforms, tax-supported free schools, and representation in the state legislature based upon white population alone. When the fourteenth amendment disqualified the planting class from officeholding, the time was at hand for an accumulation of needed reforms to be carried out by the Reconstruction governments. The Southern Republicans came to consist of the scalawags, the carpetbaggers, and the freedmen. The first of these were the Southern Unionists, especially mountaineers, who had vehemently opposed secession and consequently were scalawags to the Confederates even before they had become Republicans. Many were formerly Whigs, but others, like Andrew Johnson and his following, had been Jacksonians. One and all they had hated the planting aristocrats who were now delivered into their hands. The carpetbaggers, in addition to unprincipled adventurers, Union veterans, Federal Treasury officials and Freedmen Bureau agents, included social workers inspired by a sincere if impractical idealism, and small capitalists looking for business opportunities.

Inasmuch as this scalawag-carpetbagger coalition required Negro votes, it was not unwilling to write Negro suffrage into the new state constitutions it framed. Consequently the election maps of the seventies reveal Republican districts in the South with geographic patterns suggestive of the strongholds of the Whigs in the forties, the Know-Nothing support-

ers of Fillmore in 1856, or the Constitutional Unionists of
1860. Such, for example, were the famous black belts, especially conspicuous in the alluvial plains.[11] Here, then, was
the tripartite coalition with a common set of interests sufficient to sweep from the Southern state constitutions the last
vestiges of aristocracy and give them a new orientation toward social progress. Thus there was incorporated in these
new constitutions the provisions for free schools, already
noted, the guaranteeing of property rights of women, the democratizing of local government, the popular election of the
local judiciary, the establishment of reformed systems of
taxation more nearly adjusted to the ability to pay, the abolition of imprisonment for debt, and the creation of state char-
itable institutions. Nor were these monuments of carpetbag
rule swept aside when President Hayes withdrew the Federal troops and Southern rule was rc-established. Even the
enormous state debts were, in no small degree, due to the
sale of bonds at ruinous discounts in the Northern money
markets. Physical reconstruction of the war-torn South was
bound, in any case, to be very costly.

James S. Pike has given us his unforgettable picture of the
South Carolina legislature, where "the Speaker is black, the
Clerk is black, the door-keepers are black, the chairman of
the Ways and Means is black, and the chaplain is coal
black. . . ."[12] When his whole miserable story is told, however, there arises the question: Is there not the possibility
that Pike's picture ignores substantial and worth-while work
going on behind this disheartening façade? Has not many a
citizen of our own day, after his first visit to the gallery of
Congress or of his own state legislature during which he
looked down with utterly incredulous eyes upon the scene
of confusion, indifference, or horseplay on the floor, returned
home to report confidently that the depth of legislative degradation has at last been reached and that democracy is certainly doomed. Pike and the present-day citizen reported on
vastly different scenes, but there is one thing in common in

[11] See C. O. Paullin, op. cit., Plates 105, 106.
[12] *The Prostrate State*, p. 15.

the two cases — the work of the legislative committees passes unobserved.

"It is impossible," wrote W. E. B. Du Bois, "to be convinced that the people who gave South Carolina so excellent a constitution, who founded good social legislation, a new system of public schools, and who were orderly and earnest in their general demeanor, could at the same time in all cases be stealing, carousing, and breaking every law of decency." [13] And elsewhere Du Bois points out the incontrovertible facts that "there stands on the statute books of the South today law after law, passed between 1868 and 1876, which has been found wise and worthy to preserve. Paint the carpetbag government and the Negro rule as black as may be, the fact remains that the essence of the revolution which the overthrowing of the Negro governments made was to put these black men and their friends out of power. Outside the curtailing of the expenses and the stoppage of extravagance, not only did their successors make few changes in the work these legislatures and conventions had done but they largely carried out their plan." [14]

Enormous as the corruption unquestionably was, that was an accidental and certainly not the essential feature of Reconstruction. Whatever the motives that prompted them, the fundamental achievement of the Republican combination of carpetbaggers, scalawags, and Negroes had been a social revolution in the interest of the underprivileged which the subsequent restoration of Southern home rule certainly did not completely undo. The opinion of a Southern white historian on this point is worth noting. Says Francis B. Simkins: "A reinterpretation of the tax policies of the Radical regimes suggests a new explanation of the odious reputations possessed by these governments. . . . It seems that the worst crime of which they have been adjudged guilty was the violation of the American caste system." [15]

---

[13] *Black Reconstruction in the South, 1860–1880*, pp. 419–20.

[14] "Reconstruction and Its Benefits," *American Historical Review*, XV, 799.

[15] "New Views of Southern Reconstruction," *Journal of Southern History*, V, 49–61.

The sequel, at any rate, was the enthronement of Bourbon Democracy and a reversal of the trend toward social reforms that had been in the interest of the yeoman, the poor white, and the Negro. The progressive features of the Reconstruction constitutions may have been odious to the reactionaries, but, while they could not quite turn back the hands of the clock, they could stop it so far as social legislation was concerned, and that is precisely what they did for more than a generation. The counter-revolution that overthrew the Southern Republicans was no doubt inevitable, under the circumstances, but it unquestionably left high and dry certain elements in Southern society that have ever since sadly needed effective spokesmen in the state legislatures and in Congress. Bourbon Democracy came to represent the merchants, bankers, railroad interests, manufacturers, and the dependent professions. From such a setting emerged a climate of opinion that found its appropriate expression in stringent lien legislation and the rest of the efficient devices of a creditor class. Almost as politically impotent as in the days of the cotton kingdom, innumerable lesser Southern folk were thereby fastened to the soil about as securely as medieval serfs, while cumulative poll taxes reduced tens of thousands of them to civic ciphers.

The devices that emerging Bourbon Democracy employed to consummate this counter-revolution by breaking up the coalition of carpetbaggers, poor whites, and Negroes were not particularly nicer than those of the carpetbaggers themselves. Apart from the violence of the hooded night riders, John G. Randall has described some of the less violent methods employed. Organized as rifle clubs and ". . . armed with pistols they would invade Republican political meetings, heckle the speakers, and insist on their own speakers being heard. In the course of the meeting, they would move about in the crowd, persuading Negroes and White Radicals that the healthy course would be to vote Democratic. If forced to disband they would reorganize as missionary societies and dancing clubs and carry on as before. . . ." By such means Negroes in large numbers, and a great many white Republicans as well, were induced usually without actual violence, to "cross Jordan" (that is, shift to the Democratic party).[16]

How was this nation-wide aggregation of groups that the Radicals had managed to attract into the new Republican combination to be knit into a permanent party? This was work calling for the expert political skill of a Jefferson, a Clay, or a Lincoln, and no such leader was at hand. Instead, the party was dependent upon a titular chief utterly devoid of political experience, aptitude, or even a comprehension of the nature of government and party. The contrast of Grant with Lincoln underscores the principle that a competent President must be a politician. Lincoln appeared positively to enjoy the challenge presented to him by factional clashes within the Republican or Union party combinations. His expert skill apparently defied the appearance of a factional problem for which he could not invent a solution. Thus he held intact the Republican Party on the issue of preventing the spread of slavery until secession afforded him the broader integrating principle that held together the party of the Union. His cabinet was always a party council in which factions were represented and party solidarity was assiduously cultivated. So utterly impersonal was Lincoln's method of choice as to evoke the remark that he had not a single personal friend in the cabinet of 1861.[17]

Not a trace of party consideration could be found in Grant's cabinet, and patronage was dispensed from personal rather than party considerations. He saw in the presidency only a merited personal award bestowed by a grateful nation upon its savior. No man since Washington had such an opportunity to be a great President. The masses looked to him "with an almost superstitious hope." [18] "To doubt Grant is to doubt Christ," is the way someone sought to phrase this faith.[19] James Russell Lowell in 1869 expressed a well-nigh univer-

---

[16] John G. Randall: *The Civil War and Reconstruction*, p. 866. Quoted by permission of D. C. Heath and Company, publishers.

[17] See C. Sandburg: *Lincoln: The War Years*, I, 153.

[18] George F. Hoar: *Autobiography*, I, 264.

[19] Elizabeth N. Barr: "The Populist Uprising," *A Standard History of Kansas and the Kansans* (Chicago, 1918), II, 1115–95.

sal expectation in the belief that the extremists in the Republican Party would be disappointed in the new President.[20] "No one," wrote a contemporary observer of the Washington scene, "could fail to see the mingled feelings of alarm and defiance with which Senators and politicians waited the President's first move. Nor was it they alone, but almost the entire public, that expected to see him at once grasp with a firm hand the helm of government and give the vessel a steady and determined course." [21]

The disillusionment came with sickening suddenness when the announcement of Grant's cabinet nominations was made. The President who, above all others who have held that office, needed political advice in making these selections had admitted no one to his confidence — not even his wife. Neither Pennsylvania Senator had ever heard of the Pennsylvanian, Adolph E. Borie, nominated Secretary of the Navy. The Radicals were startled at the nomination of Alexander T. Stewart, a multimillionaire New York merchant prince, as Secretary of the Treasury, a strategically dangerous post for an importer who might oppose protective tariffs, but they were relieved to find a statute disqualifying one engaged in mercantile trade from that office. While there were a few able men in it, the cabinet was packed with personal friends of the President. The Radicals drew a long breath of relief and promptly grasped the opportunity offered by the inexperience of their party chief. Soon they had imposed upon him a sort of kitchen cabinet, a clique of Radical politicians such as Butler of Massachusetts, Conkling of New York, Patterson of South Carolina, and Morton of Indiana, the representatives of personal party machines rather than of genuine elements of the party membership.

This was not the way to integrate the party, and the predictable result was described at the close of Grant's first year as President by Donn Piatt: ". . . I am forced to say that there is no more cohesion, beyond mere office holding and

---

[20] *Letters*, II, 7.
[21] H. Adams: "The Session," *North American Review*, CXI, 31, 33.

public plunder, in the Republican party than there is in a rope of sand . . . the Republicans are of one party only in name — and each leader is the representative of a faction in deadly hostility to some other faction inside the organization. . . . The Republican party in Congress is composed of factions in such deadly antagonism to each other that the hate among them is more intense than that given the Democrats." [22]

Yet the Republican Party did possess inherent elements of strength that somehow compensated for Grant's lack of leadership and for the appalling instances of maladministration among the subordinates he was not competent to manage. Even these glaring delinquencies were obscured when they were not eclipsed by the more conspicuous if not monumental corruption of Democratic Tammany and the Tweed Ring. No other party in American history has been blessed with such dynamic emotional resources as were possessed by the post-war Republicans. They were indeed sustained and motivated by the most inspiring myth ever to take possession of a political party. It found its epigrammatic expression in the campaign slogan: "The party that saved the nation must rule it." The Democratic Party was assumed to have forfeited all right to that high trust by its dubious war record. While it was not claimed that every Democrat was a rebel, no Republican doubted that every rebel was a Democrat, an assumption rendered plausible by the fact that not a single vote, either electoral or popular, had been cast for Lincoln in any of the states that were to secede. Of course the "bloody shirt" was waved often, vigorously and effectively, and if the conscience of the waver ever twitched over the propriety of the practice, it was promptly soothed with the comfortable conviction that a noble end justified the employment of the doubtful means. Certainly it struck Democracy in its most vulnerable spot — in a veritable Achilles' heel — while at the same time it served to obscure Republican Party division, utilized patriotic fervor, and stirred the faithful to action against the enemies of

---

[22] *Cincinnati Commercial,* June 9, 1870.

the Republic. Political parties that have been restrained by a nicer sense of propriety in comparable circumstances might appropriately cast the first stone.

When a Republican saw the flag — his flag — being carried at the head of a Democratic parade, his thoughts were prone to turn in bitterness to the memory of Copperheads, slave-drivers, South Carolina, secession, and the whole catalogue of Democratic "crimes." If he heard that Lincoln's picture had been used to decorate the walls of an auditorium where Democrats convened, his sense of propriety was outraged at the profanation of the sainted savior of the Union. It is scarcely possible to overestimate the dynamic resource the Republicans possessed in the tradition of Lincoln, the reputed founder of the party. Whether the tradition was historically sound is as much beside the point as the question whether or not the post-war Republicans deserved him. Significant indeed is the fact that year after year Republican campaign orators managed to extract the last ounce of inspirational drive from the great name. The prestige attaching to the Emancipator for two generations bound whites and blacks together in the compelling conviction of a common purpose and enthusiasm. Indeed many a Republican veteran who, upon receipt of the news of the Emancipation Proclamation, had flung down his musket and resolved never to fight to free "niggers" lived to sit among his comrades each autumn upon the platform, beaming with pride as the campaign orator pointed to those "battle-scarred heroes" who had "struck the shackles from four million slaves." There was just enough historical basis to make it difficult to argue the point.

It would be difficult to find elsewhere in the history of political parties anything comparable to the morale of the post Civil War Republicans. When one of them went to the polls to vote or when he merely looked serenely across the American landscape it was with a profound pride in his nation as well as with a sense of responsibility for the greatest obligation ever entrusted to a human organization. The nation was more than safe in the hands of his party, and for it all he felt a peculiar personal as well as collective responsibility. His was "a generation in whose ears state rights had become hateful, owing to its perversion in the interest of Negro slavery, and in whose eyes the comfortable doctrine of unlimited national sovereignty shone with the glory of a moral principle sanctified by the blood of innumerable martyrs." [23]

Let him who is disposed to marvel at the faith and fervor of these Republicans remember, as has been said, that error believed is in effect truth. Yet the Republican Party was certainly not based on sheer delusion. There must have been something essentially sound in a tradition that for most of the time during two full generations held a majority of Americans of every degree of education and well-being — literally a cross-section of our society — bound together in common purposes they deemed good and worthy. It is an absurd oversimplification to brush the party aside as the plaything of the capitalists. It is Schlesinger's conclusion that the success "cannot be accounted for solely by the new economic affiliations of the party. The party had won a deep and abiding hold on the affections of the North because, as it seemed to many, it had been the instrument of Providence in saving the nation in time of trial and stress." [24]

"Grantism" had set in motion centrifugal forces inherent in the Republican combination almost as soon as the President's glaring political ineptitude became apparent. The original Republican Party had been, as we have seen, an agrarian-labor alliance, but the adoption of the new Republican Party by powerful Eastern capitalistic interests had given it incongruous economic-sectional wings. Grant was dazzled by millionaires, and party managers then as now attached an absurdly magnified importance to heavy contributions to the party war chest. Suffice it to say that Grant and his party adherents came near repeating Hamilton's blunder of wrecking his party by neglecting the agrarian interests. The directorate of the Republican Party was failing signally in the seventies to implement the hopes and aspirations of the very

---

[23] H. Adams: *John Randolph*, p. 38.
[24] *New View Points in American History*, p. 273.

elements that had founded the original Republican Party and was thereby inviting revolt.

Fundamentally the Liberal Republican movement repre‐ sented a resurgence of the moral enthusiasm that had given the early Republicans the spiritual motivation of crusaders. Consequently many old Free-Soilers and other founders of the original Republican Party became insurgents in the early seventies. Surviving members of Lincoln's cabinet were among them as well as three out of the four still living Repub‐ licans who had refused to vote for the conviction of President Johnson.[25] Included also were Republican leaders who had been trying to temper the severity of Reconstruction. Thus it was largely the most genuine Lincoln men, the Conserva‐ tives of the sixties, who constituted these independents. Among them were some of the ablest Republican leaders, men who were presently to go over permanently to the Demo‐ crats, whom they were to aid in the coming renaissance of that party. Particularly conspicuous in the uprising was a galaxy of notable newspaper editors such as Murat Halstead of the *Cincinnati Commercial,* Horace White of the *Chicago Tribune,* Henry Watterson of the *Louisville Courier-Journal,* Samuel Bowles of the *Springfield Republican* and Whitelaw Reid of the *New York Tribune.* Unfortunately, innumerable petty politicians, disgruntled over Grant's distribution of pa‐ tronage, joined the reformers and embarrassed if they did not almost wreck the movement. They were out of place in a combination seeking to reform the civil service, which Grant conducted on the spoils basis. Civil-service reform as an issue, however, proved weak because of public indifference and the fact that Federal offices were packed with Eastern‐ ers whom Westerners were not eager to fasten there perma‐ nently.

The philosophic focus of the Liberal Republicans was a growing concern over the extraordinary centralizing effect of the war amendments. These had indeed wrought a consti‐ tutional revolution and were an expression of the Radical

---

[25] E. D. Ross: *The Liberal Republican Movement,* p. 61.

Republican purposes, particularly those of the capitalistic elements whose objectives called for unhampered national sovereignty facilitating protective tariffs, princely land grants to railroads, large appropriations for rivers and harbors, and wholesale exploitation of the natural resources of the public domain. The Liberals, on the contrary, while not state-righters, nevertheless foresaw the doom of the Federal system if the reserved powers of the states were to be swallowd up by an unrestrained national police power such as that of the Force Bill, enacted to suppress the Ku-Klux Klan. Here was a point at which they found common ground for a combination with the Democrats in 1872. The Liberal Republicans wanted to turn their backs on the war issues, let bygones be bygones, and come to grips with current issues. One of these was the tariff question, since the protection of the war years was being converted into a permanent policy and farmers were beginning to demand lower tariffs if not free trade.

The high hopes of the Liberal Republicans were dashed by the machinations of the petty politicians who packed the Cincinnati convention of 1872 and upset the well-laid plans of the leaders by nominating Horace Greeley for the presidency. Fortunately the platform had been framed with a view to capturing Democratic support, a hope fulfilled by the later adoption by that party of both the platform and the candidates. General Sherman pointed out the obvious paradox in the two major candidacies of 1872 in a letter to his brother John: "Grant who never was a Republican is your Candidate and Greeley who never was a Democrat, but quite the reverse, is the Democratic candidate." [26] Thus free-traders were supporting a protectionist so extreme as to have said: "If I had my way, if I were king of this country, I would put a duty of $100 a ton on pig iron and a proportionate duty on everything else in this country." [27] Greeley's having signed the bail bond of Jefferson Davis had touched, as nothing else could have done, the hearts of Southern Democrats and he stood

---

[26] Quoted by H. Minor, op. cit., p. 308.
[27] Speech of James A. Garfield, *Congressional Record*, Appendix, 45th Cong., 2nd Session, p. 293.

pledged to the restoration of Southern home rule, but this merely provoked some extra waving of the bloody shirt by regular Republicans. While Greeley's idiosyncrasies made him extraordinarily vulnerable in a campaign, a competent scholar has pronounced him "in his sympathetic understanding of the sections North and South, East and West, the most truly national of the candidates heretofore presented for the presidency of the nation." [28]

The Liberal Republicans and Democrats were handicapped by the fact that the American people were experiencing a post-war boom in 1872, with business activity exceeding even that of the dizzy war years. Greeley in his time had taken up many fads, even utopian socialism, and he had a reputation for instability, while Grant was "sound" and personally intimate with the mighty captains of Wall Street, including ex-Senator E. D. Morgan of the financial family of Morgans, who was made the Republican National Chairman. Though Greeley had been an outstanding champion of labor and the underprivileged, he was handicapped by the fact that, in times of steady employment, laborers vote for permanent jobs and are almost as timid as capitalists where threats to business are suspected. Republicans pointed to Grant's running mate, Senator Henry Wilson of Massachusetts, the "Natick Cobbler," as evidence of the party's friendship for labor. Strange to say, Wilson's having been an outstanding Know-Nothing did not prevent Republicans from making inroads on the Irish vote. Greeley had contributed heavily to Irish relief during the potato famine and had courageously denounced Know-Nothingism, but then he was a teetotaler and that was too much for the Irish. Moreover, Grant had commanded thousands of Irish when they had fought the Confederates with a conviction that the latter were allied with the English. Union veterans quite generally were loyal to Grant and the party of generous pensions, while the Liberals were affiliated with Democrats who might abolish Union veterans' pensions if they did not go so far as even to pension

[28] E. D. Ross: "Horace Greeley and the West," *Mississippi Valley Historical Review,* XX, 74.

"rebels." It was Greeley's misfortune to have received the endorsement of that supereminent corruptionist Boss Tweed during the campaign. On election day the Liberal Republicans carried scarcely one of the counties of the long New England zone where Greeley's *Tribune* had planted the fundamental doctrines of the early Republicans. Grant carried practically the same Northern counties as Lincoln had in 1860 and in addition scores of Southern counties.[29] The President was re-elected with a vote of 286 to 62 in the electoral college, while he received fifty-six per cent of the popular vote.

[29] See C. O. Paullin, op. cit., Plates 105, 106.

CHAPTER XIII
THE REVIVAL OF THE DEMOCRATIC PARTY

*"THE period exhibited a tremendous popular faith in an ever ex-
panding America and in the achievement of the general good
through the agency of enlightened self-interest. Grover Cleveland
epitomized this philosophy. The citizens, he said, should support
the government instead of the government supporting the citizens."* CORTEZ A. M. EWING.*

J ACKSONIAN DEMOCRACY reached its historic nadir in the
campaign of 1872, when the party nominated no national
ticket but accepted instead both the nominees and the platform of the Liberal Republicans. The utter failure of this strategy shrouded the party's future in gloom and uncertainty.
Since 1860 it had experienced one misfortune after another.
Inasmuch as none of the Northern Copperheads had been
Republicans, the Democratic Party did not easily establish a
reputation for patriotism. The universal opposition of Democrats to the three great war amendments put them in the
wrong in the eyes of the millions to whom the Union soldier
had been a crusader in a holy cause. No matter how extenu-
ating the circumstances may have been, the stern determination of Southerners to employ whatever means they deemed
necessary, not excluding violences, to prevent the Negro from
exercising his then unquestionably legal right to vote served
to intensify old prejudices against Southerners and Democrats
generally. Protestations, such as that of the Democratic platform of 1876, of "devotion to the Constitution of the United
States *with its amendments universally accepted* " [1] carried
slight conviction coming from those who chose to nullify

---
* From C. A. M. Ewing: *Presidential Elections,* published by University
of Oklahoma Press.
[1] E. Stanwood, op. cit., p. 375. Italics mine.

the purpose of the fifteenth amendment by the violence of the Ku-Klux Klan and similar sinister organizations.

While Democrats floundered, the Republican Party led a charmed life and seemed to enjoy a magic if unmerited immunity. No matter how great the maladministration of the Grant regime, the widely accepted reputation, if not character, of the Democratic Party discredited its members as critics of the administration and impaired its legitimate function as an opposition. Moreover, the dizzy post-war prosperity in almost every line so engrossed the public in the North that they were not interested in carping criticism while the boundless economic possibilities of the American continent and its enterprising people were unfolding.

The magic spell that gave the Republican Party its protective immunity broke suddenly under the impact of the disastrous depression following the panic of 1873. The economic exploiters had over-expanded and thereby dealt a blow to the party of the exploiters both great and small. Excessive development of agriculture, mining, manufacturing, and, above all, railroad construction culminated in the inevitable reaction. The collapse of the gigantic house of cards began with the failure of the mighty firm of Jay Cooke and Company, whose members were intimate friends of Grant. Jay Cooke had been successful in attracting the savings of preachers, teachers, and members of the professions generally, whose unbounded confidence he had enjoyed. Now the critics of Grantism could get an audience of eager listeners, and the Democratic Party could begin to perform its proper function as an effective opposition. The exasperated electorate sought a scapegoat to punish for its economic woes and as usual discovered it in the party in power. The result was the "tidal wave" in the congressional elections of 1874. The Democrats, who for fourteen long years had not controlled the presidency or either house of Congress, overthrew the Republican two-thirds majority and elected 169 Representatives to the Republicans' 109. At last the "bloody shirt" had been waved in vain, betokening a decline in the potency of the war issues. The "Salary Grab" Act by which Congressmen had voted themselves a retroactive salary increase irritated the electorate more than the revelations of administrative corruption. The floors of the two houses in the next Congress were to be sprinkled liberally with "rebel brigadiers" and civil officials of the late Southern Confederacy.

Quite naturally the "tidal wave" galvanized despondent Democracy with new vitality and the party approached the presidential election of 1876 with confidence of success. Fortunately for the faithful, Samuel J. Tilden, then Governor of New York, was developing the strongest nation-wide hold upon the Democratic Party of any leader since Andrew Jackson. He had been instrumental in crushing the Tweed gang in New York City and the State Canal ring. His availability was consequently due to his reputation as a reformer, and "reform" became the focal point of agreement of the aggregation marshaling its forces against Grantism. It was indeed by no means certain that Grant himself would not be a candidate for a third term, but the persistent cry of Cæsarism by Democrats joined in by Half Breeds and Independent Republicans, prevented another nomination. "Reform" became a Democratic war cry and ten planks of the party platform on which Tilden ran began with that dynamic word.

Samuel J. Tilden had been an old Van Buren Barnburner, but had adhered faithfully to the Democratic Party when that anti-slavery faction passed through the Free-Soilers into the Republican Party. His war record was sufficiently debatable to subject him to the charge of Copperheadism.[2] This invited frantic waving of the bloody shirt again by the panic-stricken Republicans. A plausible charge that he had failed to report considerable of his income for taxation in 1863 was, of course, thoroughly aired. Since Tilden as a practical politician had fraternized with Tammany and even with Boss Tweed, he was charged with being an "eleventh-hour reformer." This Democratic leader had accumulated one of the great fortunes in America as a railroad corporation attorney for such promoters, manipulators, and wreckers as Jay Gould,

---

[2] See *Harper's Weekly*, XX, 590, 730, 750, 826.

Jim Fisk, William Tweed, and others, from which activities he won the title of the "Great Forecloser." [3] Ten years before his presidential campaign there had been published the already cited [4] work of James Parton detailing Tilden's railroad-reorganization manipulations. So damaging were the allegations as to the manner in which Tilden's fortune had been accumulated that, as was said before, he obtained from a pliant New York court an order suppressing the publication of the book. In 1876, however, one of the very few copies that escaped destruction fell into the hands of the Illinois Republican State Committee, which printed ten thousand copies of the "classic."

Considerable wind was taken out of Tilden's sails when the Republicans managed to nominate Governor Rutherford B. Hayes of Ohio for President. Hayes was himself a reformer in no wise tainted with Grantism, but, thrice elected Governor of Ohio, a resolute practitioner of the merit system in the civil service. The Democrats were unable to turn up anything in the career of Hayes to put him on the defensive. Moreover, Hayes was a sound-money man who had defeated for Governor of Ohio that redoubtable Midwestern inflationist Senator William Allen. The strongly inflationist Western wing of the Democratic Party had forced the nomination of Thomas A. Hendricks of Indiana, a notorious inflationist, as candidate for Vice President. Under these circumstances Tilden's chronic poor health became an important factor in the presidential election.[5] What if Tilden, though himself a sound-money man, should attain the presidency and then die, thereby making way for the succession of Hendricks to his place? Hayes, no doubt, won many a conservative vote because of this dread possibility. In the South the old plantation aristocracy, as the new Bourbon Democracy, was now taking possession of the state governments and writing "finis" to the social revolution effected by the carpetbaggers and their allies. There was more than a touch of historical irony in the

---

[3] Matthew Josephson: *The Politicos*, p. 216.
[4] *Supra*, p. 281.
[5] H. Minor, op. cit., p. 315.

unanimity with which these former slaveholders threw their support to the old Barnburner, Tilden. The great urban Democratic machines in the North of which Tammany was the most conspicuous, though they had protested against Tilden's nomination, were ready to manipulate the hordes of laborers of recent immigrant stock for the good of the party cause. Nor did the Republicans then or ever monopolize the capitalistic element. Tilden himself was a multimillionaire, deeply involved in finance capitalism. That particular type of capitalism, of which August Belmont was a notable example, inclined rather to the Democratic Party. So also did the great free-trade importing merchants. Coastal ironmasters such, for example, as Abram Hewitt, Tilden's campaign manager, were Democrats, longing for duty-free coal and iron that would enable them to meet the pressing competition of the Pittsburgh foundries.

When the election of 1876 had become history and complete statistics of the balloting were available, it became evident that the backbone of Hayes's strength had been the faithful Republican counties of the New Englanders and their settlements westward into the prairies. For twenty years the practically solid block of Republican counties had been expanding farther and farther southward into the region where Southerners had settled in the old Northwest. In 1876 the Republicans lost practically all of these gains. One is struck by the remarkable similarity of the two patterns made on election maps by the Northern counties carried by Frémont in 1856 and by Hayes in 1876.[6] In fact, Frémont did better than Hayes in this area by carrying two states lost by the latter. While Frémont had made almost a clean sweep of the Connecticut counties, Tilden carried the western half of the state and obtained its electoral votes. The New England stock of up-state New York was overwhelmed in 1876 by the growing masses of the metropolis under the regimentation of Tammany, and Tilden obtained the Empire State's great block of electoral votes. A comparison of the Southern Grant counties in 1872 with the Republican counties of that

---

6 See C. O. Paullin, op. cit., Plates 105, 107.

section four years later reveals the suppression of the Negro vote — by extra-legal means, of course, since legal devices for that purpose had not yet been introduced.

Even in the election year the Democratic House had confidently voted the admission of Colorado upon the expectation that it would be safely Democratic. As it turned out, this miscalculation defeated Tilden. In a preliminary state election Colorado had proved to be overwhelmingly Republican. Nor should this have astonished anyone, since new states, created by national authority, usually manifest a nationalistic bias, and the Democratic Party was the champion of the state-rights "heresy" and so assumed to be tainted with secession. It is significant that Tilden lost the six Western states, their support of the Hayes ticket being, no doubt, an expression of the gratitude of the cattle, sheep, grain, and mining interests to the party of nationalism, generous land policy, and internal improvements, especially the Pacific railroad.

While never denying that Tilden had obtained a popular majority in the returns, the Republican organization promptly and persistently claimed that Hayes had 185 electoral votes and was elected. The details of the disputed election need not be recounted here. Suffice it to say that after months of bitter controversy Congress broke the impasse only by creating an Electoral Commission to determine which of the conflicting returns of several states were to be counted. When the commission had completed its work, Hayes was declared elected by a majority of a single electoral vote. It so turned out that eight of the fifteen members of the Electoral Commission were Republicans while seven were Democrats, and every crucial decision was made by a strict party vote of eight to seven. Much has been made of the fact that Hayes became President by the partisan votes of these eight Republicans. It should be noted that the seven Democrats were fully as partisan as the Republicans. It is a curious if not significant fact that the American people elected one of the Republican members of the commission to the presidency four years later.

"By both sides, frauds were probably committed," wrote

the Beards, "or at least irregularities so glaring that long afterwards a student of the affair who combined wit with research came to the dispassionate conclusion that the Democrats stole the election in the first place and then the Republicans stole it back." [7] We are indebted to the exhaustive research of Haworth for authoritative information as to just what happened. It was the conclusion of this diligent scholar that in a free election Hayes would have won. Many thousands of Southern Negroes were denied their then incontrovertible legal right to vote. Those who challenge Hayes's sense of propriety in accepting the presidency under the circumstances are confronted with the alternative problem as to how much more ethical it might have been for Tilden to have been made President by the particular thirty-three Southern electoral votes that were based on Negro population and obtained for Tilden by the illegal suppression of the black vote. "All things considered," concluded Haworth, "it appears, both legally and ethically, the decision was a proper one." [8]

The Democrats had no choice but to accept the result since the Electoral Commission had been their own child. James A. Garfield, the leader of the House Republicans, for example, reflected a rather general party view in opposing the creation of such an extra-constitutional agency although he accepted the act and even served on the commission. Probably the most important factor in breaking the jam was the fact that Southern Democrats wanted the restoration of home rule even more than a Tilden victory. They took advantage of Hayes's well-known conciliatory attitude toward the South in order to strike a bargain and obtain a gentleman's understanding that military rule in the South would end if Hayes was elected. Though not a party to the negotiations, Hayes eventually, as President, carried out the understanding. Southerners were keenly aware that only a Republican President could order the troops out of the South without provoking hysterical outbursts of super-patriots in the North. Tilden, as President,

---

[7] C. A. and Mary Beard: *The Rise of American Civilization*, II, 314.

[8] P. L. Haworth: *The Hayes-Tilden Disputed Presidential Election of 1876*, p. 341.

would scarcely have dared to end military rule in the South. If, as Democrats universally believed, they had won a moral victory, they failed signally to exploit its possibilities and so delayed party recovery. For one thing, their persistent reiteration of the charge of "fraud" began to tire people now becoming engrossed in the new prosperity that was taking them out of the valley of the great depression of the seventies. Then, too, the maladministration that had cursed the Grant regime had suddenly ended and, by contrast, there were no scandals to be aired under Hayes. The most direct cause of the party's failure to recover, however, was the pathetic incompetence of the now aging Tilden as a party leader, despite the partisan devotion his "martyrdom" had inspired. "I visited him at his home in Gramercy Park," wrote Colonel A. K. McClure, "when the [disputed election] contest was at white heat, and was amazed to find his table covered with legal briefs, as though his election depended upon the law that would govern before a competent and impartial tribunal. . . . He seemed to be utterly bewildered and the man who had organized his nomination and election with consummate skill shriveled up into pitiable indecision and inaction when he had the power to cast the die for or against himself." [9]

Under the circumstances it was the Republicans rather than the leaderless Democrats who profited by the subsequent congressional airing given the disputed election of 1876. For example, the collection of Democratic Western Union cipher telegrams that fell into the hands of the Potter investigating committee of the House of Representatives revealed, when decoded, that the returning boards of South Carolina and Florida had been ready to throw the election to Tilden if adequately recompensed. Some of these cipher telegrams were traced to Tilden's home address and to his nephew Colonel Pelton, living in the candidate's own home. When Tilden, at his own request, appeared before the committee, he answered clearly every question that helped his case, but to

[9] *Our Presidents and How We Make Them*, p. 266.

others he gave such evasive replies as "I presume I did," "I do not remember," "I guess not," "I may have done so," "I do not think I did, so far as I remember," "I think not," "I may have seen it." [10] This sensational episode shook the confidence even of many of Tilden's followers. The destiny of the Democratic Party was, for the time being, in the hands of an aging chieftain too ill to lead and the party had no choice but to flounder on.

In the absence of competent leadership the Democratic majority of the House of Representatives frittered away their opportunity in a petulant guerrilla warfare against President Hayes. Their strategy was to dominate executive policy by persistently attaching "riders" to important appropriation bills. They resorted to English precedents to support their course, claiming they were only insisting upon the ancient parliamentary practice of redress of grievance before the granting of supply. Under the minority leadership of James A. Garfield this attempt to coerce the Executive was denounced as revolutionary. Hayes did not hesitate to veto one rider-laden appropriation bill after another and, as a Harvard student who had learned his constitutional law at the feet of Joseph Story himself, he exposed the Democratic misapplication of English parliamentary precedents to a check and balance system.[11] There is abundant contemporary evidence that in this contest public opinion sustained the President.

With Garfield's victory in 1880 by a plurality of 10,464 in a major-party popular vote of 8,899,368, begins an era of the closest balance of party strength in American history. The war feelings persisted despite the disappearance of the war issues after the troops had been withdrawn from the South. Clear-cut differences on national policies were avoided. *Laissez faire* dominated the thought of a people not yet aware of the perplexing problems produced by the industrial revolution. Groups dissatisfied with the colorless platforms of the major parties organized such third parties as the Greenbackers, Prohibitionists, Anti-Monopolists, and Populists. The is-

10 H. T. Peck: *Twenty Years of the Republic*, pp. 117–18.
11 See J. D. Richardson, op. cit., VII, 531.

sueless major parties had become ends in themselves, with the politicians constituting the dynamic social force in each.

Business was sliding down into the trough of a minor depression when the Blaine-Cleveland election was held in 1884, and the electorate was inclined to penalize the Republicans for it. In the absence of issues the election turned on the public careers of the candidates. In this competition victory went to Grover Cleveland, the "veto" mayor of Buffalo and later Governor of New York who had captured the public confidence. It indicated a desire for a fresh start when the Democratic Party nominated a presidential candidate who but once in his life had seen the national capital.

Among the party leaders of the United States Grover Cleveland is distinctly *sui generis*. When his name is set down in the great succession with Jefferson, Jackson, Clay, Lincoln, or the two Roosevelts he, least of any, could be denominated a weather-vane. If it is the function of an American statesman to search for the integrating ideas that make party combinations tolerable, then Cleveland does not answer the description. One does not find him, like Lincoln, searching with superb intelligence to discover the point of equilibrium among the conflicting social forces of the nation and tolerant of all sorts and conditions of men. Cleveland thought Henry Watterson, the most notable of Democratic journalists, "a dirty little scoundrel," and once told him to "go to hell." Even as Governor of New York he had been a "bull in a china shop." [12]

Democrats found Cleveland to be incorrigibly individualistic. What he personally considered "right," not the party or popular opinion, determined the administration's policies. When, for example, his first term was drawing to a close, he decided to devote an entire annual message to urging tariff reduction as a remedy for the Treasury surplus. A year later, when defeat for re-election made the message, viewed in retrospect, look like a *faux pas*, he unburdened his somewhat troubled soul to one William B. Hornblower: "They told me it would hurt the party; that without it I was sure to be re-elected, but that if I sent in that message to Congress it would,

---

[12] W. A. White: *Masks in a Pageant*, pp. 139–40.

in all probability, defeat me; that I could wait until after election and then raise the tariff question. The situation as it existed was, to my mind, intolerable, and immediate action was necessary. Besides, I did not wish to be re-elected without having the people understand just where I stood on the tariff question and then spring the question on them after my re-election. Perhaps I made a mistake from the party standpoint; but damn it, it was right. I had at least that satisfaction." [13]

May not such cocksureness as to moral absolutes defeat its own purpose? At any rate the public reaction to the tariff message of 1887 was a Republican Congress that gave the nation the ill-fated McKinley tariff of 1890. When in his second term Cleveland finally got his tariff revision, it was a measure so mutilated in the Senate by high rates that he denounced it as representing "party perfidy and party dishonor" in a letter which he had read to the House by an administration spokesman, and which served no other purpose than to relieve the President's outraged feelings. The kind of tariff revision Cleveland asked for in 1887 had to wait twenty-seven years to be effected then by the adroit leadership of Woodrow Wilson.

For good and sufficient reasons Cleveland had hired a substitute during the Civil War. This episode should have rendered him discreet in the face of the super-patriots of the opposition. Nevertheless, he committed the blunders of illegally ordering the return to the Southern states of the captured Confederate flags and of going fishing on Decoration Day. No reasonable person can criticize his vetoes of outrageous private pension bills. When, however, he advised Congress that pensions should be handled by a general law and the House Pensions Committee in accordance with this recommendation drew up and had passed such a measure, Cleveland, nevertheless, vetoed it. "Such a fiasco," wrote the late Henry Jones Ford, "amounted to a demonstration of the lack of intelligent leadership. If the President and his party

---

[13] Quoted by Frank Kent: *The Democratic Party*, p. 302.

were cooperating for the furtherance of the same objects, as they both averred, it was discreditable all around that there should have been such a complete misunderstanding." [14]

Grover Cleveland experienced a radical change in his social outlook in the interregnum between his two terms as President. He had begun his political career as distinctly a man of the people as any party leader had ever been. According to Dennis Tilden Lynch, he had carried on his canvasses for sheriff and mayor "in saloons with beer barrels and tables for his rostrum. There wasn't a saloon kept by a Democrat, boasting a fair-sized back room, that he did not enter and harangue the thirst-slaking citizens after sharing a drink with them." [15] He left the White House in 1889 and began the practice of corporation law in New York City where he came to know intimately the Wall Street firm of Bangs, Stetson, Tracy and McVeagh. He became a crony of Stetson, who was a legal adviser of the house of Morgan. His close associates were William C. Whitney, E. C. Benedict, Thomas Fortune Ryan, Oliver H. Payne, James R. Keene, Oscar Strauss, and other leaders of finance. Speculating in stocks, he was becoming moderately wealthy. The supermen of New York resolved to put Cleveland in the White House again in 1892 and did so.

Four years in the peculiar climate of opinion of the mighty men of the metropolis had given Cleveland a more pronounced capitalistic ideology than any Republican President from the corn belt except Grant. "Of his company he was very choosey," wrote Ike Hoover, head usher of the White House, "and he seemed to prefer moneyed people. Looking over the list one might term it 'a millionaire's crowd.'" What a strange leader of the historic party of the agrarians and urban masses just when the ferment of populism was turning the South and West into a madhouse of radical agitation. Cleveland was doubtless as conscientious as ever, but Democracy had just elected a President unfitted to comprehend the social forces events had unloosed.

It is not surprising, then, that Cleveland appointed as his

[14] *The Cleveland Era*, p. 91.
[15] Quoted by W. E. Woodward: *New American History*, p. 658.

Attorney General Richard Olney, a corporation lawyer who had distinguished himself by riddling the new Sherman Anti-Trust Law before the lower courts. Thus the chief prosecutor of the trusts was to be one who had made sport of the law he was now sworn to enforce. No wonder the American Sugar Refining Company, controlling ninety-eight per cent of the country's output of sugar, won its case in the first "prosecution" under the Sherman Act to reach the Supreme Court, since, as the Court pointed out, Olney *had failed to submit any evidence that the law was violated.*[16] Olney had advised against the request of a railroad magnate that he urge repeal of the Interstate Commerce Act: "It satisfies the popular clamor for a government supervision of railroads at the same time that supervision is almost entirely nominal." [17] Yet the same Olney who let the sugar trust escape unscathed used the Sherman Anti-Trust Law so vigorously against the striking Chicago railwaymen in 1894 that Henry Demarest Lloyd promptly called it the Anti-Trade Union Law. This conspiring, former railway attorney, keeping the President in the dark as to the merits of the strikers' contention, got Federal troops sent into Chicago "to break the strike," as the brusque military officer in charge put it.[18] That Cleveland's action in the Pullman Strike was warranted neither by circumstances nor by law now seems to be the verdict of history.[19]

In 1890 the Senators from the silver-producing states held up the passage of the McKinley tariff until they had forced an agreement to an act requiring the Secretary of the Treasury to purchase monthly 4,500,000 ounces of silver to be paid for by a special kind of Treasury note. This extraordinary new demand for silver would enrich the silver-mine owners by the enhanced value of their product at the same time that the

---

[16] See 156 U. S., pp. 1–46; W. H. Taft: *The Supreme Court and the Sherman Act*, p. 59; Allan Nevins: "Richard Olney," *Encyclopedia of the Social Sciences*, XI, p. 466.

[17] Olney Papers, Library of Congress; quoted by Matthew Josephson: *The Politicos*, p. 526.

[18] See C. A. Beard: "Emerging Issues in America," *Current History*, November 1934, p. 203.

[19] See H. S. Commager: *Documents of American History*, p. 159.

inflationary effect of the circulating Treasury notes would make the agrarians the natural allies of the silver interest. These Treasury notes, however, were made payable "in coin," which came to be widely understood as necessarily meaning in gold, and the panic of 1893 was consequently accompanied by such a run on the special gold reserve of the Treasury designated for redeeming paper currency that immediately after his second inauguration in 1893 Cleveland called Congress into special session for the purpose of obtaining repeal of the Silver Purchasing Act. This purpose he accomplished only by executive pressure through patronage and otherwise, but his victory left the agrarians of his party in an extremely ugly mood. Thus at the beginning of his second term Cleveland lost the support of the rank and file of his party.

The social panic that accompanied the depression of the middle nineties is almost incomprehensible to this generation. "Rifles clashed and cavalry charged into mobs all over the Mississippi Valley," writes one who vividly recalls those hectic years.[20] Farmers and laborers were prepared for an onslaught upon accumulated wealth, and Cleveland and his coterie knew it. The famous gold contract the President had negotiated with his Wall Street friend J. P. Morgan, whereby at a fancy price gold was purchased in order to maintain the legal Treasury redemption fund, angered the agrarians even more than had the enforced repeal of the Silver Purchasing Act. It so happened then that a boundary dispute between England and Venezuela gave the agrarians an opportunity to charge Cleveland with failure to enforce the Monroe Doctrine and with subserviency to Democracy's traditional enemy, England, a nation somehow associated with the gold standard and second only to Wall Street as a phobia of the farmers. Letters began pouring in from Democratic politicians demanding drastic diplomatic action. A particularly striking one from Congressman Thomas Paschal of Texas to Richard Olney, now Secretary of State, has recently been

---

[20] W. A. White, op. cit., p. 139.

unearthed. "You are right, now go ahead," wrote Paschal. "Turn this Venezuela question up or down, North, South, East or West, and it is a 'winner' — pardon the slang — morally, legally, politically, or financially: your attitude at *this* juncture is the trump card. It is, however, when you come to diagnose the country's internal ills that the possibilities of 'blood and iron' loom up immediately. Why, Mr. Secretary, just think of how angry the Anarchistic, socialistic and populistic boil appears on our political surface, and who knows how deep its roots extend or ramify? One cannon shot across the bow of a British boat in defense of this principle will knock more pus out of it than would suffice to inoculate and corrupt our people for the next two centuries." [21] Whether or not this letter prompted the President, he presently sent an appropriately belligerent message to Congress which constitutes one of the major curiosities of our diplomatic history, and the electrified nation for the moment forgot its political and economic woes in a mad orgy of patriotism.

The price of wheat affords a tolerably accurate barometer of agrarian discontent, the social pressures moving inversely to the trends of the price of the cereal. When wheat fell from $1.50 a bushel, just after the Civil War, to 67 cents three years later, the Grange was founded. After climbing back above a dollar it had fallen to 87 cents by 1874 when the Anti-Monopoly, Independent, and Reform parties appeared in eleven states and the National Greenback Party was launched. When the price of wheat rose to $1.05 in 1877 the Granger movement had practically run its course. Then a fall of 25 cents in a single year produced the Grand Alliance, forerunner of the Farmers' Alliance, and the basis of the later People's Party. Three thousand Alliance lodges existed by 1887, when wheat averaged only 68 cents. Though the price climbed again, it was in the midst of a precipitous fall from 85 cents in 1891 to 49 cents three years later that the National People's Party nominated a presidential candidate who polled over a million votes. It is significant that Bryan's silver

[21] Olney Papers, Library of Congress; quoted by C. A. Beard: *The Open Door at Home*, p. 101.

316 AMERICAN POLITICAL PARTIES

crusade was undertaken and defeated in the midst of a sharp
upward sweep of 31 cents within three years, accompanied
by a good harvest as the presidential campaign of 1896 pro-
gressed.[22]

By the early nineties the long agricultural depression had
made Southern and Western farmers acutely aware of their
colonial relationship to the East, symbolized, in their minds,
by Wall Street. In better days bustling agents of Eastern
finance had negotiated tens of thousands of farm mortgages.
With the advent of 8-cent corn, 10-cent oats, 2-cent beef,
and no sale at all for butter and eggs, came wholesale foreclosures. It then began to dawn upon the American farmer
that his cherished dogma of *laissez faire* enabled the capitalists to play their game with loaded dice. The government
under the Republicans had given capital a protected market,
the world's greatest network of railroads, cheap immigrant
labor, and a sound currency and relieved it of Federal taxes
by confining taxes to imposts and excises, which, however,
burdened the farmers. The upshot of all this was an agrarian
movement for government intervention in order to equalize
the opportunity for the little fellow, and out of this emerged
the People's Party, or the Populists.

As described in a contemporary account of the first national convention of the Populists in 1892, "the great stage,
brilliant and vivid with national colors, was filled with the
leaders of the Alliance, the Knights of Labor, the single tax
people, the Prohibitionists, the Anti-Monopolists, the Peo-
ples party, the Reform party and the Womans Alliance." [23]
The platform was a catalogue of specific remedies for the
ills of agriculture. Deflation would be relieved by a circulating medium of fifty dollars per capita to be assured by the
free and unlimited coinage of silver and gold at the ratio of
sixteen to one. Wealth would be compelled to share revenue
burdens by a graduated income tax. Postal savings banks
would provide depositories that would be secure against fail-

---

[22] See graph in L. B. Shippee: *Recent American History*, p. 154; see also
pp. 28–30.
[23] *National Economist*, V, 394 (March 5, 1892).

ure in a depression. Railroads, whose arbitrary and excessive rates had harassed farmers, would be compelled to give back their unused land grants and be taken over by the government along with telegraphs and telephones.

Southern Populism was more than simply an agrarian movement. It was indeed an attempted resumption of the social revolt of the lower-income groups, rendered politically inarticulate by the overthrow of the carpetbag governments. The movement seriously threatened to absorb Southern Democracy, and old Democratic politicians stopped at nothing to prevent party extinction. Known Populists were arbitrarily denied voting rights, and ballots were counted as election boards chose. In Augusta, Georgia, Tom Watson's home, twice as many ballots were cast as there were legal voters in the precincts. Watson charged that wagonloads of Negroes were hauled from South Carolina into some Georgia precincts to save the Democratic Party, so that Populists claimed they were the only white man's party in the South.[24] To forestall future uprisings of the white masses, Bourbon Democracy next initiated its program of systematic disfranchisement through "understanding" clauses and cumulative poll taxes that today leave several Southern states with the lowest percentage of the population actually voting of any states in the Union. To combat wholesale ballot-box stuffing with the then privately printed ballots, the Populist platform had demanded the Australian ballot.

It was the historic function of the Populist Party to transform into governmental interventionists the party of the Locofoco tradition, the Democrats with whom they fused in 1896. Cleveland had been elected in 1892 on an old-fashioned, *laissez-faire* platform at the moment the prairies were on fire with radicalism. Nor did Cleveland give this conservative platform merely a perfunctory application. During four depression years the United States was a magnificent police state utterly oblivious of distress either rural or urban. Thus Cleveland Democracy unwittingly stimulated Populism and

---

[24] See J. D. Hicks: *The Populist Revolt*, pp. 253–4.

prepared the way for the advent of William Jennings Bryan. When the Democratic National Convention met in 1896, the Cleveland wing found itself outnumbered and outargued. Their rout was complete when Bryan in his "Cross of Gold" speech struck the vibrant chord that integrated the confused radical elements into an army of mad crusaders ready to follow their new chieftain to the ends of the earth on the issue of free silver. Three years earlier young Congressman Bryan had led the losing fight against the repeal of the Silver Purchasing Act. Later he became the outstanding critic of the Cleveland-Morgan gold-purchasing contract. "Cleveland might be honest," said Bryan, "but so were the mothers who threw their children in the Ganges." [25] The President's subsequent arrangements with the Nebraska Democratic boss by which Bryan was manipulated out of a renomination at the Congressional Convention of 1894 [26] boomeranged two years later when the "martyr" snatched national control of the Democratic Party from the Cleveland men.

As a youth Bryan's consuming passion had been to go to Congress and he deliberately prepared himself for it. So he became in college an inveterate contender for oratorical prizes. Somehow he missed getting that insight into human society that ought to be derived from contact with the courses that transmit the intellectual heritage of the human race. William Allen White, in looking over the books on sociology and economics in the library of the mature Bryan, found nothing but works of propaganda. "They were written by partisans of a theory rather than well-known social scientists seeking the truth." [27] Yet this limitation may have been an element of strength, for it must have intensified his paramount phobia against the money power, by means of which he cemented his heterogeneous following. It was of the Cleveland-Belmont Gold Contract that he was speaking when he said: "I am trying to save the American people from that

---

[25] E. P. Oberholtzer: *A History of the United States since the Civil War*. V, 199.
[26] See Paxton Hibben: *The Peerless Leader*, pp. 154–5.
[27] *Masks in a Pageant*, p. 252.

disaster — which will mean the enslavement of the farmers, merchants, manufacturers and laboring classes to the most merciless and unscrupulous gang of speculators on earth — the money power." [28]

Sensitive as Bryan was to popular movements, he was not so successful as Theodore Roosevelt in finding the dominant ones and so he missed the presidency. He was, in fact, rather more of a group champion than a combiner of divergent interests. Nevertheless he made a heroic effort to discover a common denominator in his "Cross of Gold" speech when he broadened the definition of a "business man." Thus he made the term include the wage-earner, the attorney in the country town, the merchant at the crossroads, the miner, and even the "farmer who goes forth in the morning and toils all day — who begins in the spring and toils all summer and who by the application of brains and muscle to the natural resources of the country creates wealth." He "is as much a business man as the man who goes upon the board of trade and bets upon the price of grain." [29]

As year by year Republicans stole his issues and enacted them into statutes, the Peerless Leader was wont to declare, good-naturedly, that he could rule the nation by losing the presidency. His imperturbable good humor, along with his sincere faith in democracy and his inexhaustible inventive ingenuity, all aided him in promoting combinations. His flair for the dramatic enabled him at critical moments to produce almost miraculous results. Since his appeals were to the feelings rather than to the intellect, it might be said of him as it was of Rousseau that his arguments constituted "a plausible imitation of logical force." [30]

In 1896, then, the Democratic Party made its about-face

[28] A. Kitson: "William Jennings Bryan," *Fortnightly Review,* October 1914.

[29] *The First Battle,* p. 200.

[30] The expression is W. A. Dunning's in *Political Theories from Rousseau to Spencer,* p. 1. On Bryan's leadership, see C. E. Merriam: *Four Political Leaders,* pp. 63 ff. I have found useful the unpublished doctoral dissertation of Marietta Stevenson: *William Jennings Bryan as a Political Leader,* University of Chicago.

from *laissez faire* to governmental intervention. In order to preserve Democracy's very existence in the South, Populism had to be embraced there and this meant more than merely free silver. The platform pledged the party to the restraint of the great economic powers in the interest of the common man, the farmer, and the laborer. Fusion with the Populists gave the Democrats the solid West for the first time, but the deal by which they got it lost them the East. When the ballots were all counted, it was strikingly evident that labor had defeated Bryan and free silver. For the first time since 1860 a Democratic candidate had lost every county in New England. Never has the South been so solidly Democratic as New England had become Republican. Industrial workers, unsympathetic with the agrarians, had voted for their jobs, which they believed to be threatened by free trade and free silver. Already the "Democratic" depression of the nineties had planted firmly and for a generation the conviction that a Democratic victory meant famine, starvation, and soup kitchens. Nor did workers relish prospective payment of wages in the inflated medium of exchange free silver meant to them. They knew how stubbornly custom anchors wage rates even while commodity prices soar. The Eastern farmers, dairy, truck, and fruit producers who supplied the urban workers, feared the effects of Bryanism on their section. Professional and religious leaders quite generally persuaded themselves that free silver was viciously dishonest.

CHAPTER XIV

THE REGIME OF THE CONSERVATIVE REPUBLICANS

"Mr. McKinley brought to the problem of American government a solution . . . which seemed to be at least practical and American. He undertook to pool interests in a general trust into which every interest should be taken, more or less at its own valuation, and whose mass should, under his management, create efficiency. He achieved very remarkable results. How much they cost was another matter: if the public is ever driven to its last resources and the usual remedies of chaos, the result will probably cost more." HENRY ADAMS.

WHATEVER strength President Hayes gave the Republican Party must have been due to his character rather than to his political leadership. Though his *Diary* reveals ceaseless vigilance as to trends of public opinion, so indifferent was he to group pressures that the Cincinnati editor Murat Halstead wrote: "He seems to have no feeling whatever for the popular thing." [1] His great handicap was the lack of a powerful personal following and, unlike Lincoln,[2] he resolutely refused to use patronage to cement the party combination. Almost without exception, party leaders were contemptuous of the Puritan President and they boycotted his wineless White House functions.

It was a matter of pride to Hayes that no effusion of blood resulted from the use of Federal troops during the railroad strikes of the late seventies. At a moment when even liberal Republicans were talking of strengthening the regular army

---

[1] Thomas Beer: *Hanna*, p. 87.
[2] *Supra*, p. 236.

in order to suppress a repetition here of the French Commune,[3] the President was setting down in his *Diary* [4] the question: "Can't something be done by education . . . of the strikers, by judicious control of capitalists, by wise general policy to end or diminish the evil? The railroad strikers, as a rule, are good men, sober, intelligent and industrious." Here is a note rare in the seventies, but prophetic of the humane labor views of Hanna and McKinley at the turn of the century. Hayes became deeply concerned over the concurrent growth of extreme wealth alongside the most degrading poverty, and by 1886, when the conservatives of New York City were in a panic over the nomination for mayor of Henry George by the United Labor Party, ex-President Hayes was sympathetic with the radical candidate.

James G. Blaine was undoubtedly the most notable Republican leader between Lincoln and McKinley. Had only his twenty years in Congress been as irreproachable as McKinley's he might have proved to be an invincible candidate. As it turned out, Blaine's nomination in 1884 made possible the first election of a Democratic President in twenty-eight years. If Blaine's reputation had been untarnished, it might have counterbalanced the other adverse factors that, in any case, ought not to determine presidential elections. Among these were the facts that in 1884 the Republican candidates were from safely Republican states in contrast with Democratic nominees from the important pivotal states of New York and Indiana; the defection of Mugwumps, "drys" and the Irish that lost Blaine the prize bloc of New York electoral votes by a hair's breadth; and, finally, the heavy rains in normally strong Republican counties on election day.[5]

Blaine's defeat in 1884 confronted the Republicans with a crisis. How might they avoid becoming as persistently a party of the opposition as the Democrats had been for most

---

[3] M. Josephson, op. cit., p. 255.

[4] III, 452.

[5] Roy V. Peel: "James G. Blaine: A Study in Political Leadership," *Abstracts of Doctoral Dissertations,* University of Chicago, Humanistic Studies, V, 215.

of a generation? It had become even more difficult to elect Republican Congresses than Republican Presidents, now that the apportionments, augmented by abolition of slavery and the three-fifths rule, gave the Solid South the largest Congressional delegation of any section. Since Negro suffrage had failed them, the Republicans now sought compensation in some formula that would win Eastern industry without alienating Western agrarians. That formula turned out to be a revival of Clay's American System, stressed by Blaine in 1884. Four years later Cleveland's obstinate disregard of his party's interest in urging tariff revision at an inopportune moment enabled the Republicans to present their new issue to the electorate with such telling effect as to capture at once the House, the Senate, and the presidency. Thus Blaine, the strategist of the new Republican policy, dropped the bloody shirt in order to twist the British lion's tail — Britishers being wicked free-traders and so inimical to American interests. However, there was the portentous fact that the vanquished Cleveland had obtained a plurality of the popular vote little short of one hundred thousand.

The substantial nation-wide strength of the Democratic Party is revealed in a contemporary analysis of the election statistics of 1888 made by Franklin H. Giddings: "The Democratic plurality of 98,017 included pluralities in all the southern states; in the northern commercial ports of Boston, New York, Brooklyn, and San Francisco; in the eastern industrial states of Connecticut and New Jersey and in twenty-five mining and farming counties of the strongly Republican state of Pennsylvania, not to mention counties of most unlike industries, qualities and densities of population scattered through the other northern commonwealths. The division of the total vote by percentages shows still more strongly the fact that a modern political party is created by the concurrence of minds of every type, of every degree of intelligence and power and motivated by every possible interest." [6] It was evident enough that the Republican Party was now confronted

---

[6] *Democracy and Empire,* pp. 185–6.

with a Democratic Party possessing an astonishing vitality. In complete control of the Federal government in 1889, the victorious Republicans applied their own peculiar solution of the issue of the Treasury surplus that Cleveland had raised. The McKinley Bill lifted the general tariff levels approximately from 38 to 50 per cent, but so extraordinarily sharp were the increases on textile and metal products as practically to deprive the Treasury of any revenue whatever from them. Fifty million dollars of the surplus were disposed of by putting sugar on the free list, and ten million dollars more by a bounty granted to domestic producers of sugar. Still more were accounted for by reducing internal-revenue rates. Moreover the Silver Senators held up the passage of the bill until McKinley, not unwillingly, consented to the monthly purchase of 4,500,000 ounces of silver. Then followed a general pension bill and the generous administration of it, and other pension legislation increased the annual expenditures for that purpose from $81,000,000 to $139,000,000 during Harrison's four years. Incidentally every item in the entire program gratified some interest — industry, agriculture, mining, veterans, or consumers. Thus was the surplus that had perplexed Cleveland during his first term converted into the deficit that appalled him when he came back to the White House in 1893.

This first Republican experiment with the tariff as a party formula proved disastrous. With the McKinley Bill as the dominant issue, the congressional elections of 1890, immediately following its passage, turned into a tidal wave sweeping 235 Democrats into Congress and only 88 Republicans, the smallest representation in the Republican Party's history. The party was shattered even in the zone of New England culture. However, the Republicans did carry the six Western states recently admitted in the expectation that they would add six Representatives, a dozen Senators, and eighteen electoral votes to the Republican strength, and this compensated somewhat for the loss of the Southern Negro vote.[7] Since the

---

[7] See map in L. B. Shippee, op. cit., p. 184.

strategy for capturing the East with protective tariffs had failed, there now arose a demand for a program attractive to the more promising West. Then came Bryan and free silver, throwing all party plans into utter confusion.

It was President Harrison's misfortune, as his campaign for re-election was opening, to be sending Federal troops against strikers in the Idaho and Tennessee mine fields and into the railway yards at Buffalo and elsewhere. If he was correct later in assuming that the strikes defeated him, there was a touch of poetic justice in the punishment. This protectionist and notorious anti-labor statesman had not been content, as a railway attorney in 1877, merely to prosecute strikers but had organized a military company armed to act against them. In 1892 the bloody Homestead strike injured him most. Battling armed Pinkerton detectives in order to prevent a lockout after a sharp reduction of wages, the strikers were eventually overwhelmed by militia, had their union crushed, and learned what "protection of American labor" meant in a tariff-protected industry. Carnegie's "gratitude" to the faithful Harrison appeared in his directing a contribution to the Republican campaign fund in 1888 only one fifth as great as four years earlier and in his confidential expression of satisfaction with Cleveland's candidacy, which was generally supported by the capitalists with heavy contributions.

The Republican Party appeared to be bankrupt of national leadership. Negro suffrage had failed to hold the South, and even the tariff did not capture the East. Then sheer luck brought the issue with which to trade the West for the East. But the opportunity would almost certainly have failed to be exploited had there not been at hand then the most harmonious pair of American politicians that ever teamed up for a common party purpose.

William McKinley inherited the business man's outlook from two ironmasters, his father and his grandfather. After creditable service as a Union soldier and officer, young McKinley prepared for and began the practice of law at Canton, Ohio. In 1876 when the coal-mining firm of Rhodes and Company in the Massillon district imported some laborers from

Cleveland to break a strike, rioting began and many miners were lodged in the Canton jail. In the inflamed state of public opinion no lawyer dared imperil his professional career by defending the strikers — none but young McKinley, who would not be dissuaded by the pleadings of his friends. His success was phenomenal. Of the thirty-three strikers indicted he obtained acquittal of all but one, and that one served only a short penitentiary sentence.[8] Here was an attitude strikingly in contrast with the contemporary one taken by Harrison in Indiana, and it paid McKinley lifelong dividends. Long afterward Samuel Gompers, president of the American Federation of Labor, whose White House experiences had been quite varied, wrote of President McKinley: "He would frequently ask me to the White House to see him and sometimes I would ask for the privilege. At no time was I disappointed."[9]

In 1877 McKinley entered Congress only to find the mighty men of the Republican Party persistently snubbing President Hayes. Not so the young Ohio Congressman, who made the White House a rendezvous, occupied as it was by the colonel of his old Union regiment, who now advised him to specialize on the tariff issue. By diligent application the ambitious politician accumulated an imposing fund of information concerning American industry. During fourteen years in the House, mostly on the Ways and Means Committee, McKinley had an unexcelled opportunity to develop the art of integrating conflicting interests, notably in the framing of tariff schedules. "Every tariff is a diagram of opposing forces," according to Harold W. Stokes.[10] Yet the process is not merely one of compromise, but rather the progressive satisfaction of the interests concerned by incorporating in the tariff bill the desires of each. This, of course, is "logrolling," a practice

---

[8] F. P. Weisenburger: "The Time of Mark Hanna's First Acquaintance with McKinley," *Mississippi Valley Historical Review*, XXL, 78.

[9] *Seventy Years*, I, 522–3.

[10] "The Paradox of Representative Government," *Essays in Political Science*, p. 82.

obnoxious to the academicians, but "when we have reduced the legislative process to the play of group interests, then log rolling, or give and take, appears as the very nature of the process."[11] In practicing this essential mode of American government, Congressman McKinley developed the skill of an artist.

In keeping with the American tradition, persistent since the construction of the very earliest tariff schedules, there were specific satisfactions for every articulate group. Employers and employees welcomed protection of their particular products. Low rates or none at all on non-competing imports were pointed out as benefiting consumers. The revenues collected satisfied taxpayers. McKinley was adept at presenting the advantages of a protective tariff in a manner astonishingly plausible, if not too critically examined. In the history of political parties the power of the idea is of course more significant than its economic soundness. Yet it may be asked whether McKinley's theory that the foreigner pays the tariff was one whit more erroneous than that of the wiseacre who assumes that the consumer always pays all of it. Until the law of demand and supply is repealed, the importer will sell for no more than the public consents to pay, and the foreigner consequently sometimes assumes part of the tariff or even may bear the full burden of it. Beard wrote concerning protection: "Perhaps, in fact, it has added more to the riches of the country by the stimulation of production than it has actually collected from the farmer and planter in subsidies, bounties and higher prices under protective duties. 'The foreigner pays the tariff' may have an element of truth in it."[12] The art McKinley mastered required patience and keenness rather than intellectual power. He was, indeed, acutely aware of his "ignorance of the subject," as he confided to William F. Burdell, who found him, as Governor of Ohio, studying an economic text on the tariff.[13] He continued to learn in the

---

[11] A. F. Bentley: *The Process of Government*, p. 371.
[12] *The American Party Battle*, pp. 136–7.
[13] *William McKinley*, pp. 11–12.

field of his specialty until his statesmanlike last address, in which he foresaw the end of economic isolation and the modification of the dogma of protection.

It is indicative of a keen insight into the functioning of the representative process in America that McKinley considered Garfield's determination to decide each question on its merits without regard to party a perilous experiment.[14] In this McKinley was Lincolnian, as he was also when he sought the sense of the multitude, persistently inquiring: "What do people up your way think of it?"[15] Unlike Lincoln, who ascertained the equilibrium of social forces by diligent and accurate calculation, the far less intellectual McKinley seems to have perceived that equilibrium almost intuitively. When the late Thomas Parker Moon, as indicated below, parenthetically annotated the well-known confession of McKinley as to how he arrived at the decision to retain the Philippines, may not the scholar have unintentionally paid a high tribute to the President's almost psychic sensing of the social forces that dictated the policy?

After wrestling with the problem of the Philippines in prayer, the President said: "And one night late it came to me this way — I don't know how it was, but it came! (1) That we could not give them back to Spain — that would be cowardly and dishonorable [national honor theme]; (2) That we could not turn them over to France or Germany — our commercial rivals in the Orient — that would be bad business and discreditable [economic nationalism]; (3) That we could not leave them to themselves — they were unfit for self government — and they would have anarchy and misrule worse than Spain's war [racial superiority]; (4) That there was nothing left f⌐   to do but take them all, and to educate the Fili-
⌐·   uplift and civilize and christianize them as our
        ʹor whom Christ also died [Altruism, the 'white
        ʹ and missionary zeal . . .]."[16] Thus when Mc-
        ⌐ he was consulting his conscience he appears

Record, 49th Cong., 1 Sess., p. 764.
op. cit., pp. 12–13.
ʹperialism and World Politics, pp. 394, 395.

to have been, by the implications of his confession, cataloguing precisely the ideas and interests that made the Philippine Islands an American dependency. Thus he became the instrument through whom the forces of American society functioned.

"Mr. McKinley," thought Herbert Croly, "represented, on the whole, a group of ideas and interests as nearly national as could any political leader of his generation." [17] Sophisticated Henry Adams believed "Mr. McKinley brought to the problem of American government a solution . . . which seemed to be at least practical and American. He undertook to pool interests in a general trust into which every interest should be taken, more or less at its own valuation, and whose mass should, under his management, create efficiency. He achieved very remarkable results." [18]

Lincoln had held the rank and file of his party while losing the politicians. Cleveland's obstinate independence alienated, in the end, both those elements in the Democratic Party. It was McKinley's unique achievement to have captivated both, and the affectionate devotion to him of countless thousands of followers in every walk of life from millionaire to day laborer is as astounding as it is significant in the recovery of the Republican Party and its long lease of power. Prosperity and other factors provided the opportunity, but the personality of the party leader is necessary to take advantage of them. Scarcely anyone well acquainted with McKinley rated him a weakling. "We who know him regard him as a man of extraordinary ability, integrity and force of character," wrote his intimate friend John Hay, who had been Lincoln's private secretary, and two weeks before McKinley's first election Hay added: "there are idiots who think Mark Hanna will run him." [19] Elihu Root, Jules Cambon, and other strong men bear like testimony. President Hayes thought Garfield vacillating, but his *Diary* reveals a quite different opinion of the dependable former captain in his regiment. It was

---

[17] *Marcus Alonzo Hanna*, p. 187.
[18] *Education of Henry Adams*, pp. 373–4.
[19] Quotations by Tyler Dennet: *John Hay*, pp. 175, 178.

no weakling that chose single handed to defend the Massillon strikers in the face of bitter class prejudice.

Curiously enough it was Marcus A. Hanna's own firm of Rhodes and Company whose management McKinley denounced when he defended the strikers that had destroyed its property. Under the circumstances one might have expected Hanna to curse McKinley, but he had just blasphemously damned militia generally because a striker had been shot.[20] Hanna already knew the young attorney, but when the latter "defended the miners and assailed the management of the mines" it was "the first time that he ever felt the full appreciation of the possibilities of McKinley." [21] Long afterward Hanna confessed he was then "strangely attracted to the quiet and methodical lawyer." [22]

Hanna had inherited the pioneer conception of a paternalistic government that showered favors on agriculture, industry, railroads, the lumber and the mining promoters. "To him it was the government's business to support business prosperity because he believed that prosperity made a better community. The party, to him, was an engine of government, and the party leaders were responsible for insuring prosperity, and it was the duty of prosperous business to support the party with generous campaign contributions." [23] If this operated to the advantage of capitalists, let it be remembered, as John D. Hicks has reminded us, that "in the last analysis, big business controls . . . because it has public opinion on its side and not merely party bosses." [24] At the turn of the century the various Republican interests, constituting a cross-section of American society, heartily accepted this philosophy.

The ublican Party had been under Lincoln's leaderparty in a sense, and the success of the McKinley-

cit., pp. 78–9.

Grosvenor: *Marcus A. Hanna, A Memorial Address Dete and House of Representatives* (Washington, 1904),

ine, XV (1902), p. 405.

The American Mind in Action, pp. 233–4.

olt, p. 422.

Hanna leadership was, in a high degree, due to the party's recapture of the industrial laborers whose ballots overwhelmed Bryan in the East. The labor philosophy of Hanna no less than that of McKinley assumes great importance since it was widely known by laboring men. Even in the seventies Hanna had preferred dealing with organized workers through contractual agreements and may be said to have been the originator of the practice. Once when a Philadelphia banker referred to laborers as the "lower classes" Hanna promptly inquired: "Do you mean working men? Or do you mean criminals and that kind of people? Those are the lower classes." [25] In 1894 Hanna had created a scene in the Cleveland Union Club, cursing Pullman in unprintable English for provoking the Chicago strike by refusing to arbitrate.[26] When someone suggested that Pullman had done much for his workers with his model town, Hanna exploded again: "Oh, hell! Model ——! Go and live in Pullman and find out how much Pullman gets sellin' city water and gas ten per cent higher to those poor fools! . . . A man who won't meet his men half way is a God-damn fool." [27] Sentiments like these made it extraordinarily difficult for Bryan to pry industrial labor votes away from the Republicans, especially when enforced by the promise and fulfillment of the "full dinner pail." Prosperity was a factor of enormous potency in Hanna's successful leadership.

Hanna's hobby during his last years was the Civic Federation founded to foster amicable relations between employers and employees. When Jacob Riis argued with him that the capitalists in the Federation would overawe the labor representatives, Hanna replied: "But the union men aren't fools, young man!" Hanna's contempt for the coal barons, especially George F. Baer, for their refusal to arbitrate the anthracite strike of 1902 was extremely bitter. When he heard that President Roosevelt, at his wits' end for a solution contem-

---

[25] T. Beer, op. cit., p. 215.
[26] J. T. Flynn: "Mark Hanna," *Scribner's Magazine*, XCIV (1933), p. 87.
[27] T. Beer, op. cit., pp. 132–3.

plated using the army to take the mines out of the operators' hands, he exclaimed: "Serve 'em right if Roosevelt seizes the mines. Go tell Baer I said so." [28] The insinuation of the operators that Hanna was only cultivating labor in order to promote his own candidacy for the presidency was countered with the proposition that if they would only arbitrate he would make affidavit not to be a candidate or to accept an election.[29]

Contrary to accepted American mythology, Hanna was not the idol of the capitalists. His cordial relations with labor savored of treachery in the eyes of many of them. Personally he distrusted Eastern financiers for their patronizing airs toward a democratic Midwesterner and this distrust was distinctly mutual. When Roosevelt's sensational suit that prevented the combination of the Hill-Morgan and Harriman systems brought excited railway representatives to him, Hanna said: "I warned Hill that McKinley might have to act against his damn company, last year. Mr. Roosevelt's done it. I'm sorry for Hill, but just what do you gentlemen think that I can do?" [30] What could capitalists think of a politician from their own ranks who wanted to know why the government should not run power plants? [31] Here was an idea that overshot by far the mark of the later Bull Moose. On one point Hanna's biographers are particularly insistent: his ideology was so flexible that he was by no manner of means a "standpatter," that term having been wrested from the context of an impromptu campaign speech and given an absurdly different meaning from that conveyed by the remarks.

Hanna was immune against the hysteria and the phobias induced by the Populist revolt. "There won't be any revolution," he told some of the panic-stricken habitués of the Cleveland Union Club. "You're just a lot of damn fools." Meanwhile Goldwin Smith was advising adequate military

---

[28] Ibid., p. 217.
[29] See R. M. Easley: "Senator Hanna and the Labor Problem," *Independent*, March 3, 1904, p. 486.
[30] T. Beer, op. cit., p. 246.
[31] Ibid., pp. 246–7.

forces in order to protect society against the social revolutionists.[32] Bryan had scared some of the gold bugs so stiff that Hanna couldn't get any campaign contributions out of them. "Many of my friends," wrote John Hay, "are saving money for the purchase of suitable residences in Paris." [33] The essential sanity of Hanna is strikingly revealed in Philander C. Knox's reply to an inquiry whether he had ever seen a row between Hanna and Roosevelt. "I did," said Knox. "Hanna got into an argument about the old Granger movement with Roosevelt. Roosevelt thought the Grangers were a lot of maniacs and Hanna thought they were useful citizens." [34]

Tolerance indeed placed Hanna in the great succession of politician-statesmen. His biographer Herbert Croly perceived the secret of his success in that "he was bound by the instinctive consistency of his nature to represent in politics, not merely his other dominant interest, but the essential harmony between the interests of business and that of the whole community." [35]

The extraordinary craftsmanship of this manager of men appears in his handling of the famous gold plank in the platform of 1896. McKinley's record was that of a bimetallist more than friendly to free silver. Hanna saw no need of deliberately alienating the Silver Republicans and would have made the most of McKinley's good standing among them. Moreover, he was a consummate actor. His assumed indifference to the money plank alarmed the gold-bug leaders among the delegates from the East. His problem was to conciliate the East while endeavoring to retain the West. He knew there had to be a declaration for the gold standard; a mere stand for sound currency would not suffice. So with surpassing skill he let the East force the gold plank upon him. So successful were his tactics that to the day of his death each of half a dozen Republican leaders believed that he personally had

---

[32] T. Beer, op. cit., p. 134; G. Smith: "The Brewing of the Storm," *Forum*, XXII, pp. 436 ff.
[33] T. Beer, op. cit., p. 157.
[34] Ibid., p. 245.
[35] Quoted by C. A. Beard, *Contemporary American History*, p. 245.

forced the plank upon Hanna.[36] Lincoln himself could hardly have done it more neatly, and he especially excelled in such management of men and issues for party purposes.

Republican politicians were alarmed when the National Chairman decided in 1900 to take the stump in person in Bryan's own country, the habitat of the desperate Populists, who might assassinate the wicked old capitalist. President McKinley's personal messenger sent to headquarters to warn Hanna against the peril received the curt injunction: "Return to Washington and tell the President that God hates a coward." [37] "By heaven, he has sand," exclaimed Hanna's old political antagonist, Tom Johnson.[38] Everywhere he spoke, the chairman's engaging frankness captivated crowds, far surpassing those that had greeted McKinley during the post Spanish War fervor or even the colorful vice-presidential candidate, Colonel Theodore Roosevelt. "What about the trusts?" shouted a heckling farmer boy, raising the touchiest issue of farmer-business relations. "Well, what about 'em?" inquired the amateur campaigner. "All you boys have got foolish reading the papers. You'll see that big combinations of capital end up by forcing down prices. Why's one wagon company sell your dad his wagon ten dollars cheaper than the next one? That's what comes of these big combinations in the long run. . . . Any old Grangers in the crowd, here? . . . Good morning. . . . I ask you this. Didn't the Grangers combine to run prices up, so's your families could live comfortably, and didn't you fight the railroads like — like Sam Hill, to get rates regulated? Of course you did! It was sound business and good practice. Anybody abusin' you people now? All right, combine and smash 'em! " [39] Three years earlier the Senator had disarmed an Ohio rural audience with the remark: "Mr. Bryan said just one thing in his big [Cross of Gold] speech at Chicago last year that strikes me as true. He said that farmers and workingmen are business men just

[36] T. Beer, op. cit., pp. 143, 144.
[37] H. Croly: op. cit., p. 333.
[38] T. Beer, op. cit., p. 230.
[39] Ibid., p. 231.

as much as bankers or lawyers. Well, that's true. I like that. . . ." [40] These examples will be mere claptrap to the closet academician as well as to the fomenter of class conflict. In any case Hanna's speeches constitute data in the case history of a remarkable political leader who believed wholeheartedly in the essential integrity of American economic society at the turn of the century. With clairvoyant insight he had hit upon common patterns of thought among such conflicting ideologies as those of farmers, laborers, and professional and business men and presented them with effective plausibility so far as those groups were concerned.

Hanna was, of course, a practical politician and not a reformer of party methods. Whatever the prevailing practices, he used them. It may be faint praise to say that he did not debase them. Certainly he does not at all belong with the spoilsmen who had disgraced the party in the previous generation. Since an inefficient administration could not serve the interests of business, the public service was not packed with incompetent appointees. For the first time in party history campaign accounts were audited and contributors knew Hanna would not waste funds. Enormous sums were spent on pamphlets and speakers, and Hanna considered it perfectly proper to pay a farmer or laborer for time he lost getting to and from the polls. A new day seemed to be dawning when Hanna had a ten-thousand-dollar check returned to a firm of Wall Street bankers because a definite service was by implication demanded in return for the contribution.[41] Of course factory-owners warned employees that Bryan's election meant closed plants, but something besides intimidation accounts for McKinley's carrying every county in New England in 1896 and doing almost as well in New York and New Jersey. Laborers do not have to be coerced into voting against an inflated circulating medium.

Ideologically McKinley's election in 1896 had signified a triumph over the Populistic dogma of governmental inter-

---

40 Ibid., p. 186.
41 H. Croly, op. cit., p. 326.

ference in behalf of distressed agrarians, particularly through inflationary free silver. The Republicans had appealed to the historic experience of the American people and won. The capitalistic system had been vindicated by the electorate, or, to express their verdict in the words of Henry Adams: ". . . Nothing could surpass the nonsensity of trying to run so concentrated a machine by Southern and Western farmers in grotesque alliance with city day laborers." [42] In the next four years the party reaped the benefit of the upward sweep of the business cycle. Moreover, it was a "Khaki" election in 1900, with the "Hero of San Juan Hill" as vice-presidential candidate rousing the traditionally expansionist West to such a frenzy of enthusiasm that Bryan was repudiated in the very cradle of Populism. Andrew Jackson alone of all the predecessors of McKinley had been re-elected by the free votes of the entire nation in the face of a strong opposition party.[43] So impressed was McKinley that he said: "I can no longer be called the President of a party. I am the President of the whole people." [44]

Since Hanna, the logical successor, was not to live until the next presidential election, the accession of Theodore Roosevelt to McKinley's office was to prove a stroke of fortune for the Republican Party as the nation entered an era of transition. Pledging himself to continue the McKinley policies, he was to give an extended lease to the regime of the conservative Republicans. The American people were becoming dimly aware of the inadequacy of pioneer ideologies to deal with emerging problems of trusts, tariffs, and the exploitation of natural resources. Roosevelt's successful leadership as measured by his immense following was due not only to his colorful personality but to an acute sensitiveness to the new currents of public opinion stirring in the body politic.

Theodore Roosevelt himself was, indeed, experiencing a remarkable personal conversion. Curiously enough, his social philosophy in more than one respect had long lagged behind that of Hanna and McKinley. Even a decade after the Hanna of the seventies had inaugurated the earliest labor-union contracts and McKinley had defended the Massillon strik- ers,[45] the legislator Theodore Roosevelt was branding the twelve-hour limit for street-car motormen as socialistic, un- American, and due to the spread of communistic ideas. Mean- while he was voting to retain the vicious New York contract prison-labor system and opposing pensions for teachers. Hanna was blistering Pullman in 1894 for not arbitrating, while Roosevelt was commending Cleveland for sending troops to suppress the strikers. When Roosevelt explained his anti-labor votes with the dogma that the law of supply and demand could no more be repealed than the law of gravita- tion, he was only applying the economics lessons he had learned in the Harvard classes of Professor J. L. Laughlin who had taken the inhuman economics of John Stuart Mill and made it still more inhuman.

Laughlin's dicta suddenly lost their validity when Presi- dent Roosevelt came face to face with the intransigent oper- ators in the anthracite coal strike of 1902. In a hectic White House conference between the parties involved, the President reported that "the operators assumed a fairly hopeless atti- tude." The chief among them was George F. Baer, whose solution was simply starving the miners into submission with the aid of Federal troops, even if the East meanwhile froze to death. So insolent was this shortsighted employer toward all who opposed him, not excepting the President, that Roose- velt afterward declared: "If it wasn't for the high office I hold I would have taken him by the seat of his breeches and the nape of the neck and chucked him out the window." [46] The composure of the head of the miners under Baer's insults won the President's admiration and he testified that none "appeared to such advantage as Mitchell whom most of them denounced with such violence and rancor . . . that . . . he did very well to keep his temper." "There was only one man in the conference who behaved like a gentleman and that

45 *Supra*, p. 326.
46 F. S. Wood: *Roosevelt As We Knew Him*, pp. 108–9.

was not I" was the President's astounding confession. The coal-consumers of the East, regardless of social philosophy, were solidified behind the President by the autumnal chill, the portent of approaching winter, and this enabled the President to threaten coercion of the operators and obtain arbitration. Thus Roosevelt reversed the role Cleveland played in the Pullman strike by exerting pressure upon employers instead of employees.

The upshot of Theodore Roosevelt's experience with the coal strike was that he caught up on labor policies with Senator Hanna, who had just collaborated with him in breaking the impasse. So it came to pass that Samuel Gompers, head of the American Federation of Labor, called at the White House even oftener than he had during McKinley's incumbency. Sometimes Roosevelt would invite him and would read parts of a message to him, and once he made changes as a consequence. One such conference lasted from noon until midnight. Gompers, Mitchell, and Duncan were even guests of the President and his family at Oyster Bay.

Judged by the wide range of elements in his following, Theodore Roosevelt stands pre-eminent among American artists in group diplomacy. No other political leader has ever managed to marshal beneath his banner such a complete cross-section of American society. Here was a wizard who could "organize the unorganizable," [47] and who, at least momentarily, integrated such incongruous and hostile elements as employers, employees, farmers, and the professions into an all-class combination captivated by the emotion-charged slogan of the Square Deal. Equally at home among boisterous cowboys or ward politicians or in the parlors of the intelligentsia, he fascinated them all with his infectious and convincing friendship. Realistic enough in his public utterances, he confessed "he knew there was not much in them except a certain sincerity and kind of commonplace morality which put him *en rapport* with the people. . . ." [48] His essentially middle-class outlook prepared him for his historic role and

---

[47] C. E. Merriam: *Four American Political Leaders*, p. 92.
[48] John Hay: *Diaries*, V, June 21, 1904.

he successively attracted and repelled elements to the right and the left. Thus he could declare in his first message to Congress: "We are neither for the rich man as such nor the poor man as such; we are for the upright man rich or poor." The inimitable Mr. Dooley heavily underscored Roosevelt's incomparable ambidexterity when he had him say: "The thrusts are heijious monsthers built up by the inlightened intherprise ov th' men that have done so much to advance progress in our beloved counthry. On wan hand I wud stamp thim undher fut; on th' other hand, not so fast. What I want more thin th' bustin' iv th' thrusts is to see me fellow counthrymen happy an' continted. I wudden't have thim hate th' thrusts. Th' haggard face, th' droopin' eye, th' pallid complexion that marks th' inimy iv thrusts is not to me taste. Lave us be merry about it an' jovial an' affectionate. Lave us laugh an' sing th' octopus out iv ixistence." [49]

The same Theodore Roosevelt who had blistered the Populists in the nineties with vitriolic denunciations of their proposals climaxed his political career by appropriating their platform plank by plank. As a catalytic agent his preaching activated an already stirring public conscience. John Barclay, the Midwestern robber baron of William A. White's *A Certain Rich Man,* suddenly found himself, in the first decade of the new century, no longer welcomed home to the plaudits of admiring fellow citizens, but instead old neighbors crossed the street in order to avoid meeting him. Here was a new popular attitude toward captains of industry that enabled the President to obtain passage of the Hepburn Act which removed the fear that the railroads were immune against all statutory control. The Meat Inspection, the Pure Food and Drug Acts served consumer interests. Railroad employees benefited by the Employers Liability Act, and the public domain was being vigilantly safeguarded against the avarice of the great land-grabbing exploiters when Theodore Roosevelt turned the presidential office over to William Howard Taft.

---

[49] Quoted by Morison and Commager, op. cit., II, 39.

Few Presidents have at inauguration enjoyed a greater prestige than William Howard Taft. The faithful lieutenant was being confidently counted on to carry to completion the captain's progressive program. Yet Theodore Roosevelt had scarcely reached the wilds of Africa when it became apparent that he had left behind him a party utterly bankrupt as to competent national leadership. Within ninety days of his departure the combination articulated by the brilliant group diplomacy of McKinley, Hanna, and himself into the most efficient political party in American history had begun to disintegrate. In deference to Western agrarians the Republican platform of 1908 had promised a revision of the tariff, and for that purpose President Taft promptly called Congress into special session. Presently, however, the new President was fraternizing with the senatorial majority leader, Nelson W. Aldrich, and the "Czar" of the House, Speaker Joseph G. Cannon, notorious standpatters in key positions, able to dictate the terms of a new tariff to suit the East. When this very design became apparent, it aroused to strenuous opposition a galaxy of resolute Midwestern Republican Senators: Albert J. Beveridge of Indiana, Joseph L. Bristow of Kansas, Albert J. Cummins and John P. Dolliver of Iowa, Robert M. LaFollette, Sr., of Wisconsin, Moses E. Clapp and Knute Nelson of Minnesota. In one of the historic debates of the Senate they attacked the measure in the interest primarily of the grain-growers of the upper Mississippi Valley. They sought to obtain lower rates on clothing, farm equipment, and supplies. Their efforts were in vain, however, against a combination representing the manufacturers of the East and the extreme West along with Pacific producers of citrus fruit and lumber and the grazing interests of the Rocky Mountain states, eager for protection on hides and wool. Though the confused President, breathing threats of a veto, had urged the insurgent Senators to "criticise the bill, amend, cut down duties — go after it hard," [50] the evidence is abundant that his inveterate vacillation lost him the confidence of both sides and marks

---

[50] R. M. LaFollette: *Autobiography*, p. 440.

him as the very antithesis of a competent party leader.[51] Though the public quite generally regarded the measure enacted a betrayal of the platform pledge, the President, in his ill-fated Winona speech, pronounced it "the best tariff bill the Republican party had ever passed." [52] The new administration was off to a bad start with a handicap it never overcame.

To the progressive-minded public, Speaker Joseph G. Cannon had now become the very incarnation of reaction. He had begun the special session by withholding the committee chairmanships to which, according to seniority, House insurgents George W. Norris and Victor Murdock would have been entitled. This power to appoint committees was the very basis of the Speaker's dictatorship. Twelve months later, catching the Speaker at a moment when the House had just voted down a particularly arbitrary change of the rules, Norris suddenly sprang a prepared resolution he had long held in reserve. It was no less than a proposal that the House elect the extremely important Committee on Rules. For thirty hours Speaker Cannon and his organization writhed in a vain effort to extricate themselves and defeat the resolution. Its passage ended the autocracy of the Speaker and a Democratic-Insurgent bloc dominated the House. Though the luckless Taft almost loathed Cannon and fretted over being photographed with him, the public had so linked the two that the President's prestige suffered from this severest rebuke ever administered to a Speaker of the national House of Representatives.

No master of dramatic technique could have invented a more appropriate episode with which to signalize the imminent disintegration of the power-proud Republican Party than the Ballinger-Pinchot controversy. Fate here decreed that the party historically dedicated to the appropriation of the natural wealth of the public domain through homestead and other legislation should split on the antithesis of this policy — the issue of the conservation of natural resources.

---

51 See C. Bowers: *Beveridge and the Progressive Era*, pp. 348–51.
52 *New York World*, September 18, 1909.

Theodore Roosevelt had been the first President to popularize the issue. With characteristic energy he had gathered a resolute group of conservationists in the Department of the Interior, formerly a compliant agency of the spoilsmen of the natural resources. At the head of the Department was the vigilant Secretary, James R. Garfield, and with him the Chief of the Forest Service, Gifford Pinchot, bent upon "bringing the Kingdom of God on Earth" and assuring a society consisting of small landowners instead of greedy monopolists. Straining every point of existing law to the limit, they withdrew from entry millions of acres of the public domain. Thus were vast tracts of coal, forest, and mineral land and water-power sites snatched from designing conspirators.

Roosevelt thought he had obtained Taft's assurance that Garfield would be continued in this crucial position, but the new President appointed instead Richard A. Ballinger. Presently this meticulous legalist had restored to entry most of the millions of acres recently withdrawn, though Taft, under Pinchot's pressure, directed him to reverse this order. Then twenty-five-year-old Louis R. Glavis, Chief of the Field Division of the Department of the Interior, discovered a conspiracy to induce Ballinger to turn over what he believed to be fabulously valuable coal and power sites to the Morgan-Guggenheim Alaska Syndicates. In the comedy of errors that ensued, both Pinchot and Glavis were dismissed for insubordination.

By this time the "scandal" was being thoroughly aired in the muckraking magazines, *Hampton's*, *McClure's*, and *Collier's*. The remorseless prying of Louis D. Brandeis, representing the conservationists before an embarrassed congressional investigating committee, turned up the fact that President Taft and Attorney General Wickersham, had antedated the written report explaining the dismissal of Glavis and Pinchot. The fact was technical and defensible and, in any case, had nothing to do with the guilt or innocence of Ballinger. But the upshot of the whole affair was that the Taft administration got the undeserved reputation of wanting to turn back to the marauding interests the natural resources Roosevelt had sought to protect by withdrawing them from entry.

Just as the uproar of the Ballinger-Pinchot controversy was becoming deafening came the mid-term congressional elections. For fourteen years the party of McKinley, Hanna, and Roosevelt had held uninterrupted control of the Senate, House, and presidency. Now the Payne-Aldrich tariff gave the Democrats an old battlefield with the terrain of which they were perfectly familiar and they made the most of their advantage. The burden of protection was dinned into the ears of consumers already keenly aware of the mounting cost of living. The flame of agrarian discontent was fanned by harping on the schedules protecting farm machinery. Nor were the Democratic tactics in vain, for when the ballots were counted it was evident that the Republicans had lost the close urban districts of New England and the close rural districts of the central states and on a national scale had been overwhelmed by a gigantic tidal wave. Thus at the end of twenty months the Taft administration stood decisively rebuked by an adverse popular verdict.

If Taft had assumed thus far that the defection of the insurgents could be ignored, the congressional elections must have disillusioned him. At any rate he now resorted to the formula of McKinley's last will and testament as promulgated in the Buffalo address, and negotiated a reciprocity treaty with Canada. Thus, he must have thought, might the party damage done by the Payne-Aldrich tariff be repaired and Eastern manufacturer and wage-earner reunited with Western grain-grower. But the ill fortune that dogged the President's every move persisted. Not in the least placated, the insurgents discovered that the treaty even more than the Payne-Aldrich tariff was weighted in favor of the Eastern manufacturer and against the Western farmer. The manufacturer had the Canadian market opened to his products while the farmer would face the unhampered influx of competing Canadian agricultural products. The farmers found powerful allies in the lumber and fishing interests. Losing ratification in the "lame duck" session, and insistent, "even if it cost his party the farmer vote," [53] the President called a special session of the new Congress and sought Democratic aid. The Democratic Southern planters and farmers, unaffected by Canadian competition, gleefully joined their Northern urban fellow partisans and the Eastern Republicans in passing the treaty, thereby incidentally and designedly helping the inept President to widen the rift in Republican ranks. Democratic strategy went even farther by passing the Farmers Free List Bill on agricultural implements and supplies, thus forcing the luckless Taft further to damage his prestige among farmers by vetoing the relief they might thus have obtained. And then, as if the President's cup of woe were not already overflowing, the Canadian Parliament rejected the treaty.

After the fiasco of the reciprocity treaty Republican wiseacres began advising the unhappy President to make another bid for insurgent reconciliation by a vigorous drive against the trusts. Presently Attorney General Wickersham startled Wall Street with a newspaper interview forecasting precisely such a new policy. The prosecutions that followed broke the record even of Theodore Roosevelt, the champion trustbuster. Stocks and bonds dived and the President's most faithful friends were thrown into despair. Even this new venture proved a forlorn hope and failed to win over the insurgents. To the party's loss of such traditional elements as the grain-growers and industrial laborers was now added an astonishing defection of some of the mighty men of Wall Street, whom we shall presently see financing the Roosevelt Progressives.

Fatalists who assume that the disintegration of the Republican Party in the second decade of the twentieth century was unavoidable miss the mark widely. The party was caught in the 1910–11 crisis without one of the specialists in group diplomacy such as Jefferson, Jackson, Clay, Lincoln, McKinley, Hanna, or the Roosevelts. Taft had a confessed distaste for party politics. Not one of the leaders just mentioned would

53 Mark Sullivan: *Our Times*, IV, 398.

have ignored the interests of the grain-growers, without whom no party since the disappearance of the Federalists has remained in power. Spurned by their party chief, the insurgents revolted and set out to make Senator Robert M. LaFollette the Republican nominee in 1912. Farmers, trade-unionists, socialists, the American Federation of Labor, progressives, the Scripps newspaper chain, and the liberal weeklies joined the movement. Under the indefatigable leader — erroneously denominated a radical — insurgency soon gathered the momentum that alarmed such magnates as George W. Perkins of United States Steel and International Harvester and Frank W. Munsey, who was a large stockholder in United States Steel, and induced them to back the ex-President in order to head off the LaFollette crusade. So Roosevelt reaped where the tireless LaFollette had sown and, failing to obtain the Republican nomination, accepted that of the Progressive Party, which had been made to order for his candidacy.

The strategists of the Progressive Party were at once confronted with a dilemma. The central core of the party consisted of the Northern grain-growers and dairymen. Should they attempt a new agrarian combination with the small farmers of the border and the South or attempt a revival of the Lincolnian combination of Western agrarians with Eastern labor? The latter was decided upon, since Wilson, the opposing Democratic candidate, and his party platform appealed less to laborers than to Southern farmers and planters. Standpattism was out of favor and the ferment of social and industrial democracy was at work among these normally Republican industrial laborers. So social justice became the Progressive keynote as Roosevelt utilized, in behalf of the employees, the very phrases Lincoln had coined to defend free labor against the slave power: "Labor is prior to and independent of capital. Capital is the fruit of labor, and could never have existed if labor had not first existed. Labor is the superior of capital and deserves much the higher consideration." [54]

---

[54] See *supra*, p. 245.

Roosevelt's Progressive Party program, designated "the New Nationalism," was a popularization of Herbert Croly's *Promise of American Life,* a copy of which the ex-President had carried into the African wilderness. This philosopher proposed a Hamiltonian centralization of power in a government to be devoted to "a new national democracy." Croly would "recognize the existing corporate organization" — fortunately, now that it was necessary for Progressives to rationalize fraternizing with magnates of such "good trusts" as United States Steel and International Harvester. Thus, in the old Rooseveltian manner, were men of the farm, the factory, and even the luxurious offices of Wall Street to be made brothers all in a great fraternity dedicated to human welfare.

Veteran newspaper men had never seen anything like the enthusiasm of the Progressives, not in the gatherings of the Populists or even those of the original Republicans. The sons of the Puritans were again on the march, passionate crusaders in a cause deemed holy. This time they sang no paraphrase of the *Marseillaise* as in 1856,[55] but instead the hymn of the church militant, "Onward Christian Soldiers, Marching as to War." At thousands of conventions and rallies it was chorused by men and women of the new political faith, but this was not enough. While Roosevelt proved strong among the dairymen and grain-growers, particularly those near the Canadian border, where the reciprocity treaty was resented, and among the Pennsylvania and West Virginia coal-miners, the fatal Progressive failure was in not having captured the expected and absolutely essential industrial labor vote. As Merriam, one of the leaders of the Progressive Party, put it, "Roosevelt for the first time lost the business group in the campaign of 1912 without capturing the solid labor or middle class." [56]

In the half a century that has elapsed since Theodore Roosevelt set forth on his big-game hunt in the wilds of Africa, the Republican Party has not had one single national leader expert in the art of integrating the group combinations that

---

[55] *Supra,* p. 219.
[56] *Four American Party Leaders,* p. 34.

constitute major political parties, while several of its titular chieftains have been positive disintegrators. Charles Evans Hughes, the candidate in 1916, was cut out for the Supreme Court, from which it was a mistake for him to have resigned. He did not measure up to Taft's stature in a national canvass, since the latter's long administrative service and familiarity with public affairs enabled him to discuss national issues with exceptional ease. On the contrary, Hughes's six years seclusion on the Supreme Court had so handicapped him in this respect that his friends sought, in vain, to keep him off the stump. On his 1916 swing around the circle he was hard put to it for subject matter for his speeches, and standpatters so manipulated the politically inexpert candidate as not to permit a Progressive near him despite the absolute necessity of conciliating that faction.[57] One cannot imagine Lincoln, McKinley, or Theodore Roosevelt, in Hughes's place, permitting himself to be photographed on top of the *San Francisco Times* building ostentatiously surrounded by notorious standpatters in the strongly Progressive state of California. The Democratic Committee saw to the wholesale distribution of the fatal picture. Nor would an experienced leader have permitted himself to be so mismanaged as to fail to meet, while within the same hotel, Senator Hiram Johnson, the idol and erstwhile vice-presidential candidate of the Progressives. Johnson's devoted followers remembered the gratuitous insult of Hughes's managers with a vengeance on election day, when he lost California and the presidency. We shall see later how Hughes's maladroit attacks on the Adamson Law alienated railway labor and lost him Ohio's electoral vote, which might have made him President. Far from being an integrator of social groups, Hughes's inexpertness made him rather an outstanding disintegrator of the potential elements in a Republican combination. His undoubted abilities lay in other directions.

In 1920 the country was in an anti-Wilson and an anti-Democratic mood bordering on hysteria, and the Republicans

---

[57] See Drew Pearson and R. S. Allen: *More Merry-Go-Round*, p. 73.

swept the country for lack of an opposition of any consequence. A deadlock of the followers of Leonard Wood, Frank O. Lowden, and Hiram Johnson in the Republican National Convention had provided the opportunity for a cabal of Senators to manipulate the nomination of Warren G. Harding of Ohio, who, as one of the Senators put it, "would, when elected, sign whatever bill the Senate sent him and not send bills for the Senate to pass." [58] Thus had the Senators seized the opportunity to rescue the Senate from its long subordination to such masterful executives as Theodore Roosevelt and Woodrow Wilson. So evident, indeed, had the senatorial hand become in party politics that Governor Beeckman of Rhode Island asked a group of newspaper men "whether this was a Republican Convention or just a Senatorial caucus." [59] Most of the leaders in the conspiracy to nominate Harding "wore unwittingly the collar of some commodity unit: steel, coal, oil, textile, banking, copper," [60] a fact prophetic of the advent of a new regime if not portentous of the debacle of the Republican Party a dozen years later. Such are the turns of the wheel of fortune that at the Republican Convention four years later the imperious Lodge and the resolute Colonel Harvey, who had dominated the cabal, were to be seen almost neglected as they wandered about the corridors of Cleveland hotels anxiously inquiring for scraps of news.[61] *Sic transit gloria mundi.*

"No one," wrote the Beards concerning Warren G. Harding, "loved the common people more sincerely or understood them better or had less of Wilson's penchant for the moral overstrain." [62] The candidate's plea for a return to "normalcy" caught the nostalgic fancy of every income stratum. Yet in retrospect it can now be seen that the Republican Party in 1920 mortgaged the future beyond reason and necessity to

---

[58] N. M. Butler: *Across the Busy Years;* quoted by W. A. White: *Puritan in Babylon,* p. 207n.

[59] C. W. Thompson: *Presidents I've Known;* quoted by W. A. White: *Puritan in Babylon,* p. 208.

[60] W. A. White: *Puritan in Babylon,* p. 208.

[61] Ibid., p. 200n.

[62] *Rise of American Civilization,* II, 676.

win a cheap victory. So ill-equipped did Harding prove to be that he became a problem for the capable ghost-writers, Richard Washburn Childs and Colonel George Harvey, whom the Republican National Committee provided in order to create a safe synthetic campaigner. To what depths had the party of Lincoln, McKinley, and Roosevelt fallen when its standard-bearer, making a campaign speech, could, after two stumbling attempts at reading a puzzling sentence, look up from the manuscript and with breath-taking frankness confess: "Well, I never saw this before. I didn't write this speech and I don't believe what I just read"! [63] Moreover, the directorate of the Republican Party, without any sense of history, could not comprehend the fact that the presidency had undergone such a transformation — had indeed become so decisively the focal point of a major party's strength — that in emasculating the great office they were seriously damaging if not dooming their party. In his unnecessary zeal to gather votes Harding promised to restore "party government as distinguished from personal government, individual, dictatorial, autocratic or what not." Here was a premature abdication of essential party leadership to which Congress rigorously held President Harding a shackled captive after his inauguration.

Once again there was historic propriety in the fact that the major scandal growing out of the Harding administration hinged on a resumption of the exploitation of the public domain, which had once been almost the *raison d'être* of the Republican Party. Only with difficulty could the dominant interests in the party, during the twenties, adjust themselves to the complete about-face required by the policy of conservation. Harding's blunder in appointing Albert B. Fall as Secretary of the Interior in charge of the public lands represented something immeasurably worse than Taft's appointment of Ballinger, who was, after all, a kind of left-handed conservationist. Fall, on the contrary, was a throwback to the Gilded Age of the seventies — an anti-conservation corruptionist, operating at a time when the rank and file of both parties were

---

[63] S. H. Adams: *The Incredible Era*, p. 172.

becoming conservation-conscious. Fall's effrontery consisted in persuading President Harding to sign what the Supreme Court later decided was an illegal executive order, transferring charge of vast naval oil reserves in the public domain from the complaisant Secretary of the Navy Denby to Fall's own department, whereupon, for a handsome personal consideration, he bartered them away in leases to oil magnates. This, however, was but one of several astounding instances of maladministration that marked the brief Harding incumbency.

Fate intervened and saved the Republican Party from the follies of a careless President by the death of Harding and the succession of the impeccable Vice President, Calvin Coolidge, who instantly caught the popular fancy as the veritable incarnation of the American middle-class virtues of homely thrift and civic worth. Thus Harding's blunders were scarcely an issue in the campaign of 1924. Coolidge was elected with a majority that looked so impressive in the three-cornered battle with Davis and LaFollette as to make the Democratic Party appear to be on the way out. Calvin Coolidge was by no means a political amateur, running for office having become, in his case, a veritable vocation. In his own peculiar way he was a political artist, meeting perfectly the specifications of a role to be played in the placid twenties. Speaking in November 1932 to Judson Welliver of some matter on which he had once been urged to take a position, he said: "I wouldn't take it. The situation had not developed. Theodore Roosevelt was always getting himself in hot water before he had to commit himself upon issues not well-defined. It seems to me public administrators would get along better if they would restrain the impulse to butt in or be dragged into trouble. They should remain silent until an issue is reduced to its lowest terms, until it boils down into something like a moral issue." [64]

The new President proved more acceptable to Eastern capital than Harding, who had some of the Midwesterner's indif-

---

[64] W. A. White: *Puritan in Babylon*, p. 433.

ference to, if not contempt for, New York finance, distrusting any business that was bigger than Ohio business.[65] What music it was to the ears of the high and mighty to hear that the man in the White House had once said: "We justify the greater and greater accumulations of capital because we be-lieve that therefrom flows the support of all science, art, learn-ing and the charities which minister to the humanities of life, all carrying their beneficent effects to the people as a whole"![66] While Coolidge had been elected with fewer commitments than any President since Theodore Roosevelt, such was the pattern of thought of the man who could say: "America's business is business" that he registered accurately the prevail-ing capitalistic climate of opinion. Though they had no strings attached to him, "he was the natural ally of organized capital, those vast amalgamations of wealth which controlled the banks and so suzerainty over major commodities of the land." [67]

Coolidge accepted as wholeheartedly as Hanna, but some-what less critically, the current philosophy of the "free" cap-italistic system. His economic naïveté is underscored by the fact that he opposed unemployment insurance on the ground that laborers would receive pay they did not "earn," a squeam-ishness he never felt about the "earnings" of stock-market speculators. It can now be seen that the Coolidge economic formulas were already outmoded for a system undergoing a radical transformation, if it had not even entered its twi-light zone. Historians may yet conclude that the Republican Party suffered immeasurably more from the social lag of party ideology in the heyday of its adulation of Calvin Cool-idge than from the maladministration of the Harding years in the White House. At any rate the economic legacy of the Coolidge prosperity to the Hoover administration was the stock-market crash of 1929, following which the Republican Party won no presidential election in twenty-three years.

By the middle twenties the Republican Party, at the pin-

---

[65] See W. A. White: *Masks in a Pageant*, pp. 427–8.
[66] *Boston Herald*, November 28, 1920.
[67] W. A. White: *Puritan in Babylon*, p. 309.

nacle of its prestige and pride, was growing flabby for lack of a stiff opposition. Coolidge's Democratic opponent, John W. Davis, had received a pitiful 28.7 per cent of the popular vote in 1924. In 1928 another rather easy victory was won by Herbert Hoover, who proclaimed a New Era in which, under free capitalistic enterprise, "poverty will be banished from this nation," as he fondly expressed the hope. Unfortunately, no President since the inauguration of General Grant had been so lacking in party experience as this "novice in politics." [68] In contrast with Coolidge, the inveterate candidate, Hoover made his very first appeal for votes as a presidential candidate. Even such a free lance as Senator George W. Norris had opposed Hoover's nomination on the ground that he had no right to seek it as a Republican. Inaugurated amid messianic expectations of miracles, his relations with Congress soon went from bad to worse until by 1931 the Republican Senators to a man sat silent for a solid week while the Democrats mercilessly flayed the President, and eight months later a Washington correspondent who had begun as an admirer of the new President was reporting: "Mr. Hoover is most poisonously unpopular in Washington. Never have I seen the time when there was meaner talk about an occupant of the White House than there is today." [69] Evidently the Republican Party had found no social co-ordinator, no specialist in group diplomacy, in Herbert Hoover.

Indubitably business — especially big business — was in the saddle in the twenties and easily translated its pressures into Republican policies. Andrew Mellon earned the title, bestowed by Coolidge, of the "greatest Secretary of the Treasury since Alexander Hamilton." Why not, when Congress readily accepted as gospel the theory propounded in his *Taxation, the People's Business*, published in 1924? If income and inheritance taxes in the higher brackets were drastically reduced, he argued, the money hitherto paid in taxes would

---

[68] F. A. Ogg and P. O. Ray: *Introduction to American Government,* p. 286.

[69] T. R. B.: "Washington Notes," *New Republic,* October 14, 1931, p. 219.

then be diverted from the Treasury to productive industry and provide ample employment and bustling prosperity. Instead, much of it served to stimulate a bull market and contributed to the stock-market crash of 1929, which left the Republicans a minority party for an indefinite period. Transportation and excess-profits taxes were repealed, but Harding's recommendation of the sales tax as a substitute called forth William Jennings Bryan's pertinent comment that this was a proposal to take the tax off the profiteer and put it on his victim.

No matter how diligently one examines the congressional legislation of the twenties, one searches in vain for a single great statute regulating business comparable to those that mark like monuments the course of the administrations of Woodrow Wilson before and Franklin D. Roosevelt after this period. Nor does it suffice to say that the Republicans left unrepealed the Clayton, the Federal Reserve, and the Federal Trade Acts. Conservative Republicans might as well have paraphrased an ancient saw and said: "We care not what laws Democrats enact so long as we can administer them." A product of Wilson's New Freedom had been the Federal Trade Commission set up to scrutinize business practices, warn violators of anti-trust laws, and, if necessary, recommend prosecution of the heedless. Five original members of the commission, appointed by Wilson, functioned in perfect harmony with its fundamental purpose of stamping out unfair and monopolistic practices. But as terms expired or vacancies occurred and were filled, the time eventually arrived when the original members were in the minority. This turning-point came with the appointment of the irrepressible William E. Humphrey, who at once became the spokesman of the Humphrey, Van Fleet, and Hunt majority triumvirate. Without delay he made known that the commission was no longer to be used as a "publicity bureau to spread socialistic propaganda." The "vocal and beatific fringe, the pink edges that border both the old parties," would not turn the new commission from its determination to "help business to help itself." In harmony with conservative Republican dogmas, Humphrey condemned the old commission because it "harassed and annoyed business instead of assisting it." The new commission even sought legal opinions of the Attorney General that would have narrowed their own powers. Businesses under fire were invited to appear before the commission, even in cases of fraud and misrepresentation, thus surrendering the government's powerful weapon of "pitiless publicity." [70] No wonder Senator Norris thought that "if the Commission is to function, if it is to continue the work that the law designed it to perform, its personnel must be men who believe in that kind of a law." [71] "The effect of Humphrey's appointment," declared Herring, "was more far-reaching than any decision of the Supreme Court." [72] No wonder Franklin D. Roosevelt felt impelled summarily to remove from the commission, after he had refused to resign, this man who was in a position to sabotage the legislation of the New Deal as he had that of the Wilson administration.

The expansive Humphrey by no means confined himself to his own commission in the twenties but assumed to speak for the forces dominant in Republican administrations. "The Interstate Commerce Commission has become the bulwark instead of the oppressor of the railways," he said. Then directing his fire at things wicked and Wilsonian, he continued: "Instead of passing obstructive laws for political purposes, Congress now satisfies its demagogic tendencies by ordering all sorts of investigations — which come to nothing. The President, instead of scoffing at big business, does not hesitate to say that he purposes to protect the American investor wherever he may rightfully be. The Secretary of Commerce, far from appealing to Congress for legislation regulatory of business, allies himself with the great trade associations and the powerful corporations — not to benefit them as such but to benefit the people through them. . . ." [73] Here is an au-

---

[70] E. P. Herring: *Public Administration and the Public Interest*, pp. 125–8.

[71] *Congressional Record*, March 20, 1926, p. 5962.

[72] Ibid., p. 126.

[73] Morison and Commager, op. cit., II, 534–5.

thoritative statement of the Republican credo of the twenties.

The dominant business interests of the East would have ignored the Western agrarian Republicans had the latter only remained decorously quiescent. Widespread distress in agriculture, however, impelled Midwestern Republican Senators and Representatives to combine with Southern Democrats in the Farm Bloc, an intersectional entente of corn and wheat with cotton and tobacco that grew out of the local activities of the Farm Bureau Federation. Holding a balance of power in Congress, the bloc was able to extract some reluctant concessions for agriculture at the same time that it checked somewhat the grandiose program of Eastern business interests. It irked Joseph R. Grundy, president of the Pennsylvania Manufacturers Association, not yet a Senator, to have his clients' legislative desires interfered with by Senators and Representatives from what he called "backward" — meaning "agricultural" — states. Looking upon their fraternizing with Democrats, of all things from the old "rebel" South, as a kind of party "treason," Simeon D. Fess, majority floor leader of the Senate, called these Western Farm Bloc Senators "pseudo-Republicans," while the less restrained President pro tem of the Senate, George H. Moses, damned them with the epithet of "Sons of the Wild Jackass." Thus did Republican Party leadership demonstrate its bankruptcy through factional bickering instead of making a diligent search for common grounds of party unity.

The Farm Bloc could not found a new party, as LaFollette's venture in 1924 demonstrated. His candidacy served rather to strengthen Coolidge and demoralize the Democratic Party. Though concessions could be wrung from Congress now and then, the Farm Bloc learned how hard it is to succeed with a President in the White House equipped with a rigidly business ideology. When passage was obtained for a farm measure affording agrarians some such advantage as industry almost habitually enjoyed, a presidential veto would find it uneconomic, unconstitutional, and in violation of the cherished formulas of free enterprise.

The most profoundly significant event in the history of the

Republican Party since the Civil War has been the Great Depression. It was the party's misfortune that it had posed for a generation as the infallible guarantor of national prosperity. Ill equipped as the party was ideologically to deal with the titanic social dislocation, the fact still stands that no matter how belatedly or inadequately it may have been done, Herbert Hoover was the first President of the United States to assume Federal leadership in a depression. It befitted a Republican administration to establish the Reconstruction Finance Corporation in order to afford credit to solvent enterprises and so to keep a faltering capitalistic system providing the services for which it functioned. It is no mean tribute to President Hoover that this Corporation was continued by the Roosevelt administration and that amid the bewildering maze of New Deal agencies that formed and dissolved, the Reconstruction Finance Corporation proved to be almost, if not altogether, the most stable of them all. At any rate it lasted more than twenty years, in contrast with unnumbered other Depression agencies.

As the Great Depression deepened, the time arrived for the presidential election of 1932. Four years earlier the rank and file of the Republican Party had practically forced the nomination of Herbert Hoover upon the experienced politicians whose intuitive doubts concerning the "novice in politics" were to be emphatically vindicated. Since he was utterly inexperienced in party leadership, he could exercise none of the group diplomacy of the great masters of that art in which American party history is so rich. His availability in 1928 had consisted almost solely of his superb reputation as a humanitarian and as the "Great Engineer" — a social engineer, as many hoped. He was then, to the multitude, a symbol. Unfortunately he was handicapped from the start by being over-advertised as a veritable worker of miracles. When the depression, whose magnitude no one could foresee, did not yield readily to his social engineering, when he insisted too long that relief was not a Federal but a local and private responsibility and as unemployment and distress reached the proportion of a tidal wave, the title of the "Great Humanitarian" gathered an ironic connotation among the suffering masses. It availed little that no President ever felt more keenly the responsibilities of his office in the crisis or strove more diligently within the finite limits of his unyielding ideology to deal with problems for which social wisdom has not yet developed the solution. Under the circumstances Hoover's renomination and his courageous campaigning in 1932 were not much more than formalities to keep the party in the field.

During Franklin Roosevelt's administrations the Republican Party began to manifest a marked change in its nature by the new if not strange types of candidates nominated. Since the birth of the original Republican Party in the 1850's the delegates had never nominated a presidential candidate who had not filled some Federal office, exercised some Federal power, and viewed the political scene from the vantage point of the national capital. With the exception of Grant, who was in command of the regular army at the time of his nomination, every Republican candidate for President from Frémont in 1856 to McKinley in 1900 had served in one or the other or both houses of Congress. After the turn of the century Harding had been a Senator, Theodore Roosevelt and Calvin Coolidge had presided over the Senate, and Taft and Hoover had been cabinet members at the time of their nominations.

In 1936 the Republicans, now decisively the party of the "outs," broke their uniform past practice by nominating Gov‑ ernor Alfred M. Landon, who had never occupied a Federal office. It was hoped that this unmagnetic, common-sense, business-like state administrator might serve as a symbol and so appeal powerfully to an electorate suspected of being surfeited with the charm and "theatricals" of the consummate actor Franklin Roosevelt had shown himself to be. It proved to be a vain hope; Landon carried only two small states and obtained but 36.4 per cent of the total popular vote – the most disastrous defeat the Republicans had ever suffered in a presidential election.

Having had no success with a prosaic candidate, the Republican Convention in 1940 ranged far afield for a standard-bearer and nominated Wendell L. Willkie, who for a while was expected to vie with President Roosevelt as a colorful campaigner. To what a pass had the party of Lincoln, McKinley, and Roosevelt come at last when its delegates could nominate a candidate who had never filled either a state or a national office! It can be imagined how those Republicans felt who could scarcely accept Herbert Hoover as a regular Republican, despite his eight years' service in the cabinets of Republican Presidents, to have as a candidate Wendell Willkie, whose political experience had been confined almost exclusively to Democratic organizations. This certainly did not improve the morale of a party organization already shaken by the ten years of unbroken defeat in national elections since the Democrats had captured Congress in 1930. Though Willkie tried his hand at group diplomacy with some show of skill, he did not prove adept at the new technique of radio campaigning which President Roosevelt had long since mastered. It is significant that some Republicans even took comfort from the fact that somewhat more than forty-five per cent of the major-party vote was cast for the Republican nominee.

CHAPTER XV

PRESENT–DAY DEMOCRACY

"THE 1932 election represented a major realignment of party leadership. Only 1856 and 1896 can be regarded as approximating it in intensity, but the numbers involved in 1932 were far greater. The new administration took its mandate for intervention [in business] seriously, equalling, if not surpassing the record of Woodrow Wilson's first two years in the White House. The country approved. More fortunate than Wilson's administration, Roosevelt's government was not dissuaded by outside factors from the task of finding solutions." CORTEZ A. M. EWING.*

THE TWO successive defeats of Williams Jennings Bryan in 1896 and 1900 showed that the electorate was not yet ready to abandon *laissez faire* for the populistic program of governmental regulation. Moreover, as the new century opened, Theodore Roosevelt, after the manner of an astute political leader, was taking considerable of the wind out of Bryan's sails by cavalierly appropriating plank after plank from the platform of the Peerless Leader. With Roosevelt thus turned "radical," it looked like a golden opportunity for the Cleveland Democrats to call the party back to its historic mission of the maintenance of economic freedom. This ill-fated purpose was consummated in the old-fashioned *laissez faire* platform of 1904, on which they ran a perfectly colorless candidate, Judge Alton B. Parker of New York.

The Democratic candidate even more than the platform seemed to symbolize Wall Street in the eyes of Western Democrats, who either stayed away from the polls in flocks or

---

* From *Presidential Elections*. By permission of the University of Oklahoma Press, publishers.

went the whole way of voting for Theodore Roosevelt, whose plurality mounted to the unprecedented height of nearly two and a half million votes over Parker. In seventeen states Parker did not carry a single county, and for a quarter of a century the Democratic Party was to remain a negligible factor in Michigan, Wisconsin, and Minnesota. In the South only did ultra-conservative Parker hold intact the Democratic vote, indicating incidentally the satisfaction of the Bourbon Democrats who had long before crushed poor white populism and cancelled it out by disfranchising it through poll taxes. One matter was settled once and for all in 1904; never again would Democracy be the party of governmental non-intervention. Only once before, when the party had accepted the nominees of the liberal Republicans, had the Democrats suffered such a defeat.

In 1908 there seemed nothing left to do but give Bryan a third nomination. Though defeated again, he remained unquestionably the authentic voice of the party speaking for governmental regulation of industry and finance in order to protect agriculture and common labor. The party program of 1908 was, as Ogg expressed it, "the platform . . . of a party, long out of power, ready to denounce freely, and to promise lavishly because it had lost the habit of accountability." [1] Its dominant note was expressed in the question it raised: "Shall the people rule?"

Unperceived at the time was a distinct new trend in the affiliation of native labor to the party, a trend, moreover, that, with some recessions, was to continue until it was to give the Democratic Party its invincible strength in the thirties. It will be recalled that the Republican Party in its earliest years had absorbed the northern Know-Nothing Party, which had its chief economic basis in native labor's resentment against the influx of alien competitors. Under Lincoln's leadership the Republican Party had become so largely a labor movement that, as we have seen, his first election has been attributed to the labor group.[2] Following the Civil War the native laborers

---

[1] *National Progress*, p. 1.
[2] See *supra*, pp. 230, 231.

thought of themselves rather as potential enterprisers in a land of free opportunity. About the turn of the century labor as a group began to receive distinct consideration from such Republican leaders as McKinley, Hanna, and Theodore Roosevelt. The consuming passion and hobby of Hanna's last years had been the National Civic Federation,[3] in which even such a labor leader as Samuel Gompers could sit and work with big employers. With the passing of Hanna and the retirement of Roosevelt, however, labor was left with no outstanding national champion in the Republican Party, and, moreover, the National Association of Manufacturers was just becoming a dominant force in that party's councils.

In the congressional campaign of 1906 the hitherto nonpartisan American Federation of Labor undertook a new departure by moving its forces into the Second Congressional District of Maine in an effort to prevent the re-election of Charles E. Littlefield, an anti-labor Republican Representative. During the campaign the Federation chartered twenty-nine new locals in the district and, despite the Republican importation of "big guns," including Secretary of War William Howard Taft, as campaign speakers, Littlefield's former majority of 5,000 was reduced to 1,000, and two years later he was defeated.

Unquestionably Republican leadership, if such it can be called in this case, was making what was eventually to prove a fateful shift of party policy in abandoning the cordial McKinley-Hanna-Roosevelt attitude toward labor and even ignoring Elihu Root's warning in 1904: "Never forget that men who labor cast the votes, set up and pull down governments. . . ."[4] Speaker Cannon had sworn that he would not recognize anyone to speak for the Eight-Hour Act.[5] Gompers reported that the Speaker relentlessly fought labor at the Republican Convention of 1908. The platform committee there would not give Gompers's group a hearing, but referred them to a subcommittee, where they obtained no satisfaction. Re-

[3] *Supra*, p. 331.
[4] *Miscellaneous Addresses*, p. 222.
[5] M. Josephson: *President Makers*, p. 398.

actionary delegates jeeringly advised labor to "Go to Denver," where the Democrats were convening.[6]

What labor wanted in the Republican platform in 1908 was an anti-injunction plank. This is what they got instead: "The Republican party will uphold at all times the authority and integrity of the courts, state and federal, and will ever insist that their powers to enforce their process and to protect life, liberty and property shall be preserved inviolate." It seemed to Labor that the convention underscored this anti-labor plank by nominating for President William Howard Taft, long known to them specifically as the "injunction judge" because of an order he had once issued when a Federal District Judge. In striking contrast with Hanna, Taft had written his wife concerning the Pullman strikers: "It will be necessary for the military to kill some of the mob before the trouble can be stayed. They have only killed six . . . as yet. This is hardly enough to make an impression." [7] Yet it is but one more instance of the persistent ill fortune he experienced that Taft scarcely deserved his anti-labor reputation since, even while the Pullman strike was in progress, he had given the opinion that the laborer had the right to join a union, conspire to strike, and conduct a strike. "They have labor to sell," he said. "If they stand together they are often able . . . to command better prices than when dealing separately with rich employers." [8] Labor, however, stressed his injunction in the campaign of 1908.

Whatever Taft's personal views may have been, his election coincided closely with a reversal of the attitude taken by Republican leadership toward native industrial labor, which had, from the birth of the Republican Party, been an important element of that group combination. Gompers, who had been on cordial terms with Republican Presidents since Grant, was after 1909 *persona non grata* at the White House whenever that party was in power. Henceforth as long as

---

[6] *Seventy Years,* pp. 255 ff.

[7] Quoted by H. F. Pringle: "W. H. Taft," *Dictionary of American Biography.*

[8] 62 *Fed. Rep.,* p. 817.

Gompers headed the American Federation of Labor that organization opposed Republican presidential nominees. In the tidal wave that overwhelmed the Republicans in the midterm elections of Taft's administration, the American Federation of Labor elected fifteen members of trade unions to Congress, among them W. B. Wilson, former secretary of the United Mine Workers, who became chairman of the House Labor Committee. It was considerable satisfaction to labor to feel that they had already played a part in the "insurgent" revolt that had dethroned the old labor-baiter Speaker Joseph G. Cannon in 1910. It remains to be seen how organized labor, spurned by the Republicans under the influence of the National Association of Manufacturers and compelled to look elsewhere, found in a former outspoken anti-labor-unionist Democrat the first President openly to champion the cause of organized labor as such.

Woodrow Wilson as president of Princeton would scarcely have been human had he not had his conservative economic dogmas fortified as he fraternized with the wealthy trustees and alumni of that institution. So he became accustomed in his public addresses to strike out vigorously against the trust-busters and in defense of the magnates of capital and finance. For such a purpose he became an apt user of the familiar formulas of "individual liberty" and quite naturally blamed the "hostile" legislation and policies of the "radical" Theodore Roosevelt for the panic of 1907. In 1908 he wanted to see Bryan's ideas "knocked once for all into a cocked hat" — his money inflation, government ownership of railroads, and popular election of Senators — and the Democratic Party return to "the conservative principles which it once represented." [9] No wonder, then, that Wilson caught the fancy of the very same coterie of "robber barons" who had captivated, converted, and utilized Grover Cleveland in the nineties. Catechized in person at Delmonico's Restaurant by a group of Wall Street capitalists in 1910, Wilson "made the grade," particularly since he "expressed vigorously his opposition to the

---

[9] R. S. Baker: *Wilson*, III, 185.

tendency of the times to regulate business by governmental commissions." [10] Indeed, Woodrow Wilson might just as well have applied to himself at that time what he had once attributed to another when he said: "You may think Cleveland's administration was Democratic. It was not. Cleveland was a conservative Republican." [11] To the high and mighty of the metropolis, Wilson looked like their man and so Colonel George Harvey, "Morgan's errand boy," made the necessary contacts with the new prophet, obtained what he assumed to be a gentleman's understanding, and launched the campaign that was to place Wilson in the office of Governor of New Jersey in 1911 as a stepping-stone to the presidency of the United States in 1913.

It was not the first time in history that sophisticated wise-acres had bet on the wrong horse. For Woodrow Wilson, the conspicuous persecutor of progressives, was destined to travel a Damascus road, experience an astounding social conversion, and emerge clear-visioned, the scales fallen from his eyes, to preach the gospel of the "New Freedom." Naïve though he had been amidst the ferment of progressive ideas, he was to develop an unprecedented clairvoyance as to emerging popular opinion. "He seemed to catch public opinion as by wireless." [12] Abandoned now were the reactionary conceptions of finance, politics, and labor, partly imbibed from Princeton trustees and alumni. Presently he was completely out of the hands of the financiers and politicians who had been coaching him for the role of a second Cleveland. On a Western tour this erstwhile conservative was eulogizing, in their respective homes, both Bryan and LaFollette. In December 1910 he brusquely let his Wall Street promoter, Colonel Harvey, know that his sponsorship was embarrassing the candidate for the presidency.

At almost the moment that Colonel Harvey was "dismissed" there came into the life of Woodrow Wilson Colonel Edward M. House to promote his presidential aspirations. In

[10] Ibid., p. 35.
[11] Quoted by M. Josephson: *The Politicos*, p. 518.
[12] C. E. Merriam: *Four Political Leaders*, p. 48.

due time the self-willed Wilson was to make the almost incomprehensible confession: "Mr. House is my second personality. He is my independent self. His thoughts and mine are one. If I were in his place I would do just as he suggested. . . . If anyone thinks he is reflecting my opinion by whatever action he takes they are welcome to the conclusion." [13] House was indeed a foxy Texas politician, motivated by a strong urge to ameliorate the lot of the underprivileged. He was just about to publish anonymously his strange novel *Philip Dru, Administrator,* in which he was to publicize his social philosophy. The program therein proposed proved peculiarly acceptable to the now socially awakened Woodrow Wilson, who absorbed its plan from the author's conversations rather than from the crude novel. Its bold outline proved unbelievably prophetic. For example, the work of fiction proposed a tariff looking toward ending the era of protection, a graduated income tax based on ability to pay, a "new banking law affording a flexible currency, bottomed largely upon commercial assets, the real wealth of the nation," and eliminating the money trust, the control of industrial life, with monopolies curbed, and labor protected by social laws instead of being left as "an inert commodity to be bought and sold by the law of supply and demand." Even today one must look a second time at the date of publication to be convinced that this book reached the public some twenty months before the beginning of its detailed fulfillment in the Underwood Tariff Act, the first Income Tax Law, the Federal Reserve Act, and the Clayton and Federal Trade Acts.[14] "All that book has said should be comes about . . ." wrote Secretary Franklin K. Lane in amazement as the legislation unfolded.[15]

The "New Freedom," as Wilson's campaign program was denominated, was to be the formula of his group diplomacy whereby he would integrate a party following. The old freedom had been the do-nothingness of *laissez faire,* but the new

---

[13] Lincoln Steffens: *Letters,* I, 114.
[14] *Philip Dru, Administrator,* Chapters xxxi, xxxii, xxxiii.
[15] *Letters,* I, 297.

was to be positive governmental regulation in order "to make men in a small way of business as free to succeed as men in a big way . . . to destroy monopoly and maintain competition as the only effectual instrument of business liberty." [16] Since big business generally held aloof from such a program, Wilson never managed to reach the near universality of Theodore Roosevelt's group appeal, so that Wilson was compelled to rely mainly upon labor and the middle class, including small business and the agrarians of the South and the West.

Never have the pressures of a group combination been more efficiently translated into public policies, however, than in the great statutes that ultimately gave expression to the "New Freedom." Wilson's somewhat romantic conviction that he was a premier in a parliamentary system [17] gave him, as President, a new but efficient technique for pushing his program through Congress. Such practical politicians as his two cabinet members William J. Bryan and Albert S. Burleson proved to be invaluable coadjutors. Two factors rendered the Congressmen unusually tractable: they were largely first-termers, and after twelve years of fasting there would be patronage to dispense to "deserving Democrats," as Secretary Bryan once put it, provided of course that Congressmen voted in a manner considered "deserving." Under a presidential leadership of Congress unsurpassed since McKinley's, upward of a dozen monumental statutes were enacted.

The Underwood-Simmons Act effected, for the first time since 1857, a genuine reduction of the tariff which had been making "the rich richer and the poor poorer," according to the 1912 Democratic platform. With wool, paper, wood pulp, steel rails, lumber, and sugar on the free list, the consumer got another break. Moreover, in order further to mitigate economic inequalities, there was laid the first graduated income tax shifting onto wealth some of the burden of Federal revenues hitherto confined almost exclusively to consumption taxes. The money monster was to be mastered through the newly established Federal Reserve Banking System, which

---

[16] R. S. Baker, op. cit., IV, 374.
[17] See W. E. Binkley: *Powers of the President*, pp. 225 ff.

was to distribute the reserves hitherto accumulating on Wall Street among a dozen great regional reserve banks. Incidentally a flexible currency in Federal Reserve notes would presently permit a war-time inflation such as the agrarians could never have even hoped for with Bryan's "fifty-cent," free silver dollar. The Clayton and Federal Trade Acts put monopoly on the defensive by outlawing specifically an imposing list of unfair practices. By declaring that the "labor of human beings is not a commodity or article of commerce," the new legislation so distinctly recognized a hitherto neglected economic group as to lead the too enthusiastic Gompers prematurely to pronounce the Clayton Act a "Magna Charta of Labor." Acts providing for employees' compensation, boards of mediation, the protection of seamen, and the basic eight-hour day for railway trainmen all betokened a new dawn for labor. The Federal Farm Loan Act, the Rural Credits and the Cotton Futures Acts recognized the agrarians who backed Wilson. All in all it was clear enough that a new Pharaoh who knew not Joseph had ascended the throne.

The imposing list of labor laws demonstrated that the decisive influence of the National Association of Manufacturers in the Federal government had been broken and for the first time in American history labor as such had an administration openly, officially, and effectively friendly to it. Labor, in fact, regarded Wilson's election as its victory. "I have never known a man either within or without the White House with whom it was so satisfactory to cooperate upon big matters as with President Wilson," wrote Samuel Gompers in a tone somewhat suggestive of his cordial relations with McKinley and Roosevelt but not Taft,[18] and he continued: "Any communication from me received personal and early consideration."[19]

May it not be that the Democratic Party's adoption of a program of national labor legislation in Wilson's first term is a neglected landmark and turning-point in the history of American political parties? Statutes favorable to labor had

---

[18] *Supra*, pp. 330 ff.
[19] *Seventy Years*, I, 215.

hitherto been enacted mainly in the more progressive rural and in the industrial — that is to say, Republican — states, and consequently labor legislation had been, by and large, Republican legislation. To illustrate by a typical kind of labor legislation, the first ten states to establish workmen's compensation systems did so in 1911 and every one of them had gone steadily Republican in the three presidential elections since 1900. Of the ten most laggard states on workmen's compensation all were recognized Democratic states except North Dakota.[20] The traditional dogma of *laissez faire* had to be abandoned by Democracy before it could support such legislation. The anomaly of Southern Democratic Congressmen voting for Wilson's labor program was due, perhaps, to their conviction that it would not perceptibly affect the then nonindustrial South. In any case the American Federation of Labor was entitled to the belief that the Democratic Party had become the genuine friend of labor, and accordingly it generally supported Wilson for re-election in 1916. The Republican candidate, former Associate Justice of the Supreme Court Charles Evans Hughes, was unpopular with labor. He had voted to impose the treble-damage penalty on the Danbury hatters for their boycott of a dozen years before, when the case was reheard in 1914. These luckless workers had their homes sold over their heads to pay the $240,000 including interest added in 1914 to the $60,000 they had already paid. Labor was thus made acutely aware that the Republican Party of McKinley, Hanna, and Roosevelt had deserted them. In his campaign addresses Hughes attacked the basic eight-hour day of the Adamson Act, which even the old laborbaiter Congressman Joseph G. Cannon had voted for. Believing that Hughes meant to effect the repeal of the act, the Brotherhood of Railway Trainmen almost unanimously supported Wilson. Divided though the traditionally Republican industrial labor vote undoubtedly was, Hughes, by unnecessarily appearing to threaten a repeal of the Adamson Act, apparently threw to Wilson the electoral votes of Ohio and

---

[20] See C. O. Paullin, op. cit., Plate 132a.

California and thereby lost the election. In 1917 Woodrow Wilson appeared at the annual session of the American Federation of Labor, and for the first time in American history a President addressed that organization. Thus was the Democratic Party building for the future while the Republican Party was mortgaging it.

During his first term Woodrow Wilson was a minority President confronted by a divided opposition. It became his strategy then to build a broad majority combination, which purpose he consummated by 1916, thereby achieving a place among the great Democratic leaders of American history. It is not the ecstatics of a convention orator but the sober judgment of a distinguished political scientist that pronounced Woodrow Wilson "as stout hearted as Grover Cleveland and as quick-witted as Samuel J. Tilden; he was as shrewd in partisan strategy as Van Buren, and as sensitive to popular feeling as the elder Clinton. . . . He possessed the inflexible determination and masterful will of Andrew Jackson, and joined with it the trained intelligence and broad culture of Thomas Jefferson." [21] Such was Wilson in his prime before war weariness induced the ineptitude of management that lost him the ratification of the Covenant of the League of Nations.

Like Stephen A. Douglas, Woodrow Wilson sought to combine the Western agrarians with Eastern labor and business, and as the standpat and the Progressive factions of the Republican Party recombined he endeavored to attract the dissatisfied in both elements. Analysis of the 1916 vote raises the suspicion that he succeeded in accomplishing this purpose. Yet, on the whole, the election statistics, when examined with care, bore an ominous portent for the future of the Democratic Party. In 1916 it had been a personal victory for the President and a defeat for Democracy as a party. Though Wilson's margin over Hughes had been 582,000, the Republican candidates for Congress, as a whole, had received several hundred thousand more votes than their opponents. Thus hundreds of thousands of Republicans and Progressives might

---

[21] A. N. Holcombe: *Political Parties Today,* p. 282.

vote for a Democratic candidate for President at the same time that they would not support the Democratic Party as such. So the Democrats were already on the way out and President Wilson was to learn in the ensuing four years that a personal following is a poor substitute for the backing of an organized party.

During the war years President Wilson produced an almost hypnotic effect by his felicitous phrasing of the ideological common denominators of the Great Crusade, and he obtained a hitherto unknown unity that transcended party and became national. In no other period either of peace or of war had politics become so completely "adjourned." Labor and business received unprecedented wages and profits. The middle class was inspired by the high idealism of democratic security, "and by adroit handling all groups were brought to the common purpose of winning the war." [22] For a season party opposition almost completely disappeared, and so abject was the deference to the President that "Senators of sovereign states, and leaders of parties, groveled in their marble corridors, so terrified were they of public opinion." [23] This unprecedented unanimity was suddenly broken by a revival of partisan strife precipitated by the President's maladroit appeal for the election of a Democratic Congress in the mid-term elections of 1918, despite the fact that earlier in the year he had declared: "Politics is adjourned." His charge that the Republicans had been anti-administration grew absurd in the light of the statistical facts that on fifty-one roll calls on war measures between April 1917 and May 1918 the average Republican vote in favor of them had been 72 per cent, as against the 67 per cent average support of the Democratic members of the House. [24] The rebuke of the administration on election day is most accurately measured by the aggregate majority of 1,200,000 votes for the Republican above the Democratic candidates for Congress, and this even before hostilities had been ended by the Armistice.

[22] C. E. Merriam, op. cit., p. 53.
[23] G. R. Brown: *The Leadership of Congress*, p. 187.
[24] See D. S. Muzzey: *The United States of America*, II, 706n.

From the day of the President's request for the election of a partisan Congress the unstable Democratic Party aggregation rapidly disintegrated. The incomparable leader of the first administration had become fatigued beyond measure by war responsibilities. No longer did he "catch public opinion as by wireless," but instead mistook his inner personal convictions for popular mandates. Thus ten months after the rebuke of the congressional elections of 1918 the President was appealing to his countrymen for support of the Covenant with such incomprehensible statements as: "I had gone over there with, so to say, explicit instructions. Don't you remember that we [!] laid down fourteen points which should contain the principles of a settlement? They were not my points [!]. In every one of them I was conscientiously trying to read the thoughts of the people of the United States, and after I had uttered these points I had every assurance given me that could be given me that they did speak the moral judgment of the United States and not my single judgment." [25] Under such circumstances the Democrats were worse than leaderless.

The treaty proved to be an utterly impossible formula for cementing the Democratic group combination and, in fact, it turned out to be positively disruptive, for it ran counter to one of the most persistent and deep-seated of American traditions, that of isolationism, which had been sanctified from the beginning by Washington's solemn warning against "permanent alliances." Moreover, the specific terms of the treaty alienated some of the most dependable ethnic elements of the Jacksonian party and tradition, such, for example, as the Italian-Americans who held Wilson responsible for the failure of Italy to be allotted Fiume; the German-Americans who regarded the Versailles Treaty as savagely severe, an opinion shared even by innumerable American liberals who had once joyously followed Wilson in his crusade for the "New Freedom"; and the Irish-Americans who could not be reconciled to the five votes the British Commonwealth of Nations was

[25] Ibid., II, 707n.

allotted in the Assembly of the League of Nations.

It is one of the curious anomalies of American party history that Jacksonian Democracy, whether in or out of power during a war, has always been punished with the restoration of peace, while their opponents have in every case reaped rewards at the ballot box. The Republicans exploited to the limit the reputation of having saved the Union during the Civil War, and swept the country in presidential elections following the war. McKinley's overwhelming reelection followed the Spanish War. The Democratic Party, on the contrary, suffered signal defeats in the presidential elections following the Mexican and the World Wars, both fought to victorious conclusions under Democratic Commanders-in-Chief. So far as the party experience with American wars is concerned, Democrats might well say: "In power, we lose; out of power, we don't win." The demoralized condition of the Democratic Party in 1920 can be most accurately measured by the fact that their presidential candidate, James M. Cox, received only 34.2 per cent of the popular vote, a severer defeat than was to be administered to Alfred M. Landon, who received 36.4 per cent of the popular vote in 1936.

The Democratic Party has always had a more perplexing problem in integrating its elements into the semblance of a disciplined party than the Republicans have, since it includes not only an Eastern and Western but also a Southern branch. It was the intransigence of this third element that particularly demoralized the party in the middle twenties. Al Smith was being repeatedly elected Democratic Governor of New York. To rare political leadership he added exceptional skill as an administrator, while his achieved program of social legislation gave promise of a rising champion of the masses. Such strength in the greatest of the pivotal states entitled Smith to aspire to the Presidency. But because he was a faithful Roman Catholic, of recent immigrant stock, and came out of a fish market on the sidewalks of our great American Babylon, his bid for the nomination in the Madison Square Garden convention of 1924 alarmed the old Southern rural Scotch-Irish element among the delegates. A new Ku Klux

Klan had institutionalized the post World War nativist, white, anti-Catholic prejudice everywhere, but especially in the South. The delegates became so agitated during the hectic debate on a convention resolution denouncing the Klan that extra police were present in anticipation of a free-for-all fight. The resolution lost by a vote of $542\frac{3}{20}$ to $541\frac{3}{20}$ and might have carried had not someone got the band to strike up a few bars of *Marching through Georgia,* whereupon Southern delegates froze against any suasion in support of the resolution. Unfortunately for the party, it was the first time the public had an opportunity to listen to convention broadcasts over the radio. The Democrats literally broadcast their boisterous washing of dirty linen in spectacular contrast with the decorous Republican delegates who nominated Calvin Coolidge at Cleveland and discreetly left unpublicized their own dirty linen — the oil scandals recently exposed. Since the deadlock between Smith and McAdoo could not be broken even after a hundred ballots, the Democratic Convention nominated John W. Davis, a conservative, erudite lawyer, the very antithesis of the dynamic Al Smith.

For nearly a century the strength of Jacksonian Democracy had depended primarily upon the maintenance of an entente between Southern and Western agrarians on the one hand and Northern metropolitan masses on the other. To the latter element it now seemed as if the agrarians were playing the role of a dog in the manger in the stubborn rejection of their champion, Smith. The insignificant popular vote given Davis at the polls and the surprising showing of the third-party candidate, LaFollette, revived the dread specter of populism among the Southern Bourbon Democrats. What if the party of the Solid South should be broken and its place taken by a genuine two-party system? What if one of these two were to turn out to be a party of the masses comparable to the Populists who had swept the South and threatened a social revolution in the nineties,[26] or even the Reconstruction Republicans who had temporarily effected such a revolution

---

[26] *Supra,* p. 317.

in the seventies through liberal state constitutions and statutes? [27] Here was a threat portentous indeed to the dominant economic interests of the South and to be avoided at any cost. So in 1928 the Southern delegates decided to pay the price of undisturbed local control by consenting to the nomination of the urban Tammany, wet, Catholic candidate, Al Smith. Here was indeed an anomalous standard-bearer for the party of the Jeffersonian and Jacksonian agrarian tradition.

Though Smith's Republican opponent, Herbert Hoover, unqualifiedly condemned religious bigotry, the opportunity to use the religious issue in order to drive a wedge between Catholic urban and Protestant agrarian Democrats was too much for some politicians to forgo. Some Republican campaign managers used "hot stuff" in the South, and that section was deluged with crude propaganda. "Opposition to Catholics flared throughout the section," writes Cortez A. M. Ewing. "Hundreds of thousands . . . were waiting to strike a blow for God. Those proponents of the modern jehad were fired by the subconscious memory of the threat of Wallenstein's legions of the seventeenth century. Smith's advocacy of prohibition repeal was offered as evidence of moral depravity. As the South had not, in the past, fostered minor parties as mechanics for letting off steam, the anti-Smith elector was forced to vote for the Republican Hoover or to remain at home on election day. The latter was futile protest; the former, untraditional. More than a million Southerners smashed tradition, but the number who boycotted the election will never be known." [28]

Outside the South, Republican tactics among agrarians and villagers consisted in a unique kind of social coercion. The impression was assiduously disseminated that voting for such a Babylonian as Smith was the sort of thing that respectable people simply would not stoop to do. This proved so remarkably effective that many a regular Democrat shamefacedly sneaked into the polling-place on election day glad

---

[27] Supra, pp. 289 ff.
[28] C. A. M. Ewing: Presidential Elections, p. 70, by permission of the University of Oklahoma Press, publishers.

that the ballot was secret. Other Democrats, succumbing to social pressure, openly supported Hoover.

Scientific analyses have upset some of the superficial explanations of Hoover's plurality of 6,424,000. Two American scholars examined a cross-section of the vote outside the South as revealed in the returns of 173 counties distributed from ocean to ocean. Employing an ingenious statistical technique for isolating one by one the effect upon the individual voter's decision of his being of foreign-born parentage, urban, Democratic, Catholic, or wet, they concluded that foreign parentage as such had almost no influence on the voter's choice between Smith and Hoover and being an urbanite or a farmer not much more. Catholic church membership looked like a powerful determinant, but three times more influential was the matter of whether the voter was "wet" or "dry." It was not, then, because the voter was of recent immigrant stock that he supported Smith but apparently because he was "wet" or a Catholic, or the voter was influenced by some other cause.[29]

With "wetness," then, as apparently the dominant factor in the election of 1928 and recent immigration and Catholicism as concomitant rather than decisive influences, it can be understood why Smith carried with remarkable uniformity such cities as New York, Jersey City, Boston, Chicago, Detroit, St. Paul, and San Francisco. That religion was not the chief determinant in the South is evident from the fact that it was not the strongholds of Protestant fundamentalism that voted down Smith, but "the least backward and least evangelical southern states," North Carolina, Texas, Florida, and Virginia, where the cities carried the electoral vote for Hoover.[30] Also indicative of the secondary nature of religious feeling is the conclusion from the study of returns made by Irving Fisher. Of the thirty-two states classified as Protestant, only two swung to Smith, but six out of the fourteen Catholic

---

[29] William F. Ogburn and Nell Snow Talbot: "A Measurement of the Factors in the Presidential Election of 1928," *Social Forces,* VIII (December 1929).

[30] See D. W. Brogan: *Government of the People,* p. 68.

states swung toward Hoover. A majority of the women voted for Hoover,[31] perhaps suggesting again the dominance of the liquor issue as a determinant, Hoover having called the eighteenth amendment "a noble experiment," while Smith was emphatically for its repeal.

Despite his defeat, Smith's radiant personality, aggressive campaign methods, and heavy vote revitalized the despondent party and convinced him he was entitled to the nomination in 1932. The apparent hopelessness of Hoover's re-election after three years of depression seemed to assure the Democrats of success and Smith never became reconciled to the ensuing nomination of Franklin D. Roosevelt. Governor Roosevelt had indeed exercised an astute political management in the convention of 1932 in effecting an alliance of the West and South against an opposition to him in the East led by Smith. His nomination signified that at last the party had a popular leader who united every section of his party as Cleveland, Bryan, and Wilson had never quite done. Not until late in the campaign did the Republicans become cognizant of the consummate skill of their strangely underestimated opponent, for he was not over-advertised as Hoover had been four years earlier.

While no notable political leader ever came to or passed through the presidential office with an inflexible political philosophy, it is no disparagement to say that Franklin D. Roosevelt may be the most inveterate opportunist of them all. The thumbnail platform he wrote for the 1932 convention was "synthesized overnight out of opportunism." [32] After all, it is the politician-statesman's function to ascertain, express, and translate into public policies the current balance of social forces. In the light of electoral verdicts, what political leader has been more successful in performing that particular function than the second President Roosevelt?

It was a distinct advantage that Franklin D. Roosevelt grew up economically loose-footed — that is, not definitely

---

[31] *New York Times,* November 25, 1928.
[32] Editorial, *New Republic,* July 13, 1932, p. 219.

affiliated with any major economic group. Neither agriculture, business, nor labor had tagged him. If he had any pronounced outlook it was that of the country squire with a traditional contempt for millionaires, "money-changers," or "economic royalists." Perhaps the relative seclusion of Hyde Park provided a somewhat judicial objectiveness with which to deal with the temporarily paralyzed and thoroughly bewildered economic interests of the early thirties.

A clairvoyant opportunism prompted Roosevelt's appropriation of the phrase, the "Forgotten Man." The indignation it aroused among the interests that had been dominant in the prosperous twenties emphasized the challenge it flung at the Republican formula of nurturing business as the sovereign specific for the disease of poverty. Here Roosevelt utilized an ideological common denominator with which to attract the votes of the worker, the small farmer, and the consumer. A conscious and evidently successful effort was made to win the Republican progressives as well as the estimated two million "Hoovercrats" of 1928 who had never been Republicans. Fairly specific benefits were offered in Roosevelt's addresses for each element in the new group combination he was building up. Agrarians, not yet recovered from thirty-five-cent wheat, learned of a "Domestic Allotment Plan" for striking a balance between the supply and demand of farm produce; the unemployed were to have relief from the Federal Treasury when local resources were insufficient; labor exchanges — which Hoover had vetoed — would be established and public works expanded; business would benefit from more liberal lending by the Reconstruction Finance Corporation; conservationists recalled the first Roosevelt as they heard the plans for reforestation and erosion- and flood-control; consumers saw the possibility of breaking the rigid and excessive electric-power rates in the proposed conversion of Muscle Shoals into a "yardstick," while "forgotten men" were cheered by the promised conversion of the Tennessee Valley into a medium for a model way of life; victims of the stock market did not object to the proposal of its rigid regulation. To despairing millions who voted that fall, it must have seemed as if a new messiah had appeared at long last to make the American Dream come true.

There could be no doubt about it that the old days of party regularity were gone when the balloting revealed the most notable reversal in any four years of our party history. Hoover's total of 58.12 per cent of the popular vote in 1928 fell to only 39.66 per cent four years later when he carried only 372 counties. Franklin D. Roosevelt's vote represented 57.41 per cent of the total and he carried 2,721 counties, 282 of which had never before gone Democratic.[33] West of New York the old hitherto faithful New England stock had at last deserted the Republican Party. From election maps showing returns by counties one gets the impression that the Republican Party had practically disappeared in the states where it had first come into being as the result of a spontaneous Midwestern movement three quarters of a century earlier.

It is doubtful whether a more spectacular feat of political leadership can be found in American history than that by which the newly inaugurated President rallied a despairing people in the midst of what looked to many like the disintegration of organized society. Nor is it sufficient to say that the President merely had an unprecedented opportunity to perform a miracle in mass psychology. The ball could have been muffed on that critical occasion. But Roosevelt's flair for the dramatic, his appeal to the feelings rather than the intellect, his long experience with party organizations and as a legislator, administrator, and executive, all equipped him for exploiting the unparalleled opportunity thrust at him by the crisis of 1933.

The response to the appeal made in his brief inaugural address was from a practically all-interest combination of groups, a feat unprecedented in peace-time history and seldom equalled in the midst of war. Even when the administration was four months old a nationally known business man is reported to have said "that he had voted for Hoover but he hoped God would forgive him and that he believed Franklin

---

[33] E. E. Robinson: *The Presidential Vote, 1896–1932*, pp. 29, 31.

D. Roosevelt was the greatest leader since Jesus Christ." [34] There are reasons to suspect that President Roosevelt was a disciple of his former chief, Woodrow Wilson, in considering himself a premier-President, not only the head of the government but also the party chieftain of the majority in control of it. At any rate, during the historic "Hundred Days" he carried Congress in the hollow of his hand, with his ostensibly casual fireside chats to the public practically forestalling congressional opposition. A mere glance at the microphone by the President is said to have brought visiting groups of Congressmen promptly around to his plans. Nor did this practical-politician President disdain to employ patronage as an instrument of leadership. While legislation still pended, importunate Congressmen were put off with the whispered explanation: "We haven't got to patronage yet." [35] When the time eventually came to dispense patronage, Congressmen encountered such questions as "What was your pre-convention position on Roosevelt?" and "How did you stand on the Economy Bill?" to be answered before the distribution of the "loaves and fishes." [36] In the more difficult days that followed the "honeymoon" the President's proficiency in the art of compromise sometimes dismayed New Dealers, but now and then a resurgence of his inherent Dutch stubbornness asserted itself in "must" legislation and broke the monotony.

The now familiar definition of politics as the question of "Who gets what, when, how?" was exemplified neither more nor less in the 1930's than in any other decade of our party history. Whether Hamiltonian Federalists, Jeffersonian Republicans, Jacksonian Democrats, Clay Whigs, or Lincoln or McKinley Republicans are in power, the principle runs true to form, no matter how it may be modified by high idealism or patriotic purpose. The century and a half that separates Federalists from Roosevelt Democrats reveal no essential dif-

---

[34] J. T. Flynn: "Other People's Money," *New Republic*, December 11, 1932.

[35] Earl Looker: *The American Way*, p. 67.

[36] E. P. Herring: "The First Session of the Seventy-third Congress," *American Political Science Review*, XXVIII, p. 82.

ference in the political dynamics through which a party in power enacts the desires of its articulate component groups into the statutes they deem desirable. We saw in the beginning with what thoroughness the interests that had coalesced into the Federalist Party realized their several specific desires in the Hamiltonian program.[37] No less were the policies of the New Deal an accurate expression of the hopes and aspirations of the composite Roosevelt following as the new science of statistical sampling demonstrated almost from day to day.

When the Institute of Public Opinion, better known as the Gallup Poll, revealed that after three years of the New Deal 59 per cent of the farmers favored Roosevelt, it was reasonable to assume that they appreciated the benefits of the Agricultural Adjustment Act, the Farm Credit Administration, and the Farm Mortgage Corporation. As befitted perennial inflationists these agrarians must have rejoiced at the currency legislation authorizing the devaluation of the gold dollar, liberal purchases of silver, and the issue of billions of dollars in paper currency. If Roosevelt had captured the loyalty of 61 per cent of the white-collar workers, constituting largely the middle-income group, it probably represented gratitude for such matters as bank-regulation, especially guarantee of bank deposits, and control of the stock market through the Securities and Exchange Commission. Many of them had the Home Owners Loan Corporation to thank that mortgages had not been foreclosed. Why should not 67 per cent of the skilled and 74 per cent of the semi-skilled laborers, with even 80 per cent of all those that were organized, stand by Roosevelt? Labor had received something more than polite gestures, in Section 7a of the NRA, later embodied in the Wagner Act, implemented by the National Labor Relations Board, and reinforced by the unequivocal stand of a resolute President. With 60 per cent of the middle- and 76 per cent of the lower-income group for the President, there is reason to suspect that the Social Security Program, with

---

[37] *Supra*, pp. 42 ff.

insurance or pensions for the aged and compensation for the unemployed, no less than Franklin Roosevelt's amiability, carried conviction. The 80 per cent on relief had not forgotten the FERA, the CWA, the PWA, the Employment Exchanges, and the direct relief, including the supplies made available by the Federal Surplus Relief Corporation. No age group gave Roosevelt stronger support than the voters under twenty-five, 68 per cent of whom thus expressed their gratitude for the substantial aid provided by the NYA and the CCC. The President could not have asked for anything more advantageous than the constant sniping of Republicans at the alphabetical agencies. It cemented securely the loyalty of the middle- and lower-income groups.[38]

The distribution of social groups just detailed, consisting of the supporters of Roosevelt in his contest with Landon, seemed to indicate an almost revolutionary change in the group structure of our major parties. There had always been some correlation between income and the affiliation of Democrats and Republicans in parties. The fatal experience of the *Literary Digest*, however, indicated a new development. For twenty years that periodical had forecast satisfactorily presidential elections on the basis of the mass polling of such lists as those of telephone- and automobile-users. Until 1936 one could apparently get a reasonably accurate poll of the opinion of the entire electorate without including the lower-third income group, which would largely be excluded from the lists used by the *Digest*. When, however, the *Digest* poll forecast Landon's election on the very eve of his overwhelming defeat, it became apparent that the lower- and upper-income groups had lined up respectively as Democrats and Republicans to an extent hitherto unknown. The shift of Negroes almost *in toto* from the Republican to the Democratic ranks was an important factor in this new development, as was also the fact that the poor turned out *en masse*, in many precincts,

---

[38] The percentages are from a report made by a representative of the Institute of Public Opinion to a round table on the subject: "Political Parties and Elections," at the thirty-sixth annual meeting of the American Political Science Association at Chicago, December 27–30, 1940.

exhausting a supply of ballots that had hitherto proved adequate. Nor can it be dismissed as a blind faith in a fascinating political leader. Roosevelt's total of 60.7 per cent of the popular vote represented the high-water mark of victories in the long history of the Democratic Party. Only the eight electoral votes of Maine and Vermont went to Landon.

In the second Roosevelt administration the New Deal was amplified by a number of notable new statutes enacted in response to the President's recommendations. In 1938 Beard expressed the opinion that Roosevelt "has discussed in his messages and addresses more fundamental problems of American life and society than all the other Presidents combined. He has pointed out evils, distresses, and tensions that men in high places had hitherto blandly ignored. He has done this with vigor, consistency and a rare power of expression that promises to place some of his addresses among the very greatest state papers of this country and of all time. . . . Whatever else may happen, it seems safe to say that President Roosevelt has made a more profound impression upon the political, social, and economic thought of America than any or all of his predecessors. . . ." [39]

The campaign for a third term coincided with a critical stage of the Second World War. The collapse of France and the deadly peril in which it threw Britain apparently reversed a current trend in Roosevelt's declining strength. During the summer the Gallup Poll had indicated a strong probability of the election of Willkie. As late as August 4 the President's strength was only 51 per cent, but following the furious bombings of London it rose by August 25 to 55 per cent, from which it deviated but slightly, and the balloting in the November election gave the President 54.9 per cent of the popular vote. Since Willkie had accepted in principle the major items of the New Deal, the President had the advantage of pointing to achievements as contrasted with promises. It did not help Willkie when a presidential campaign parade routed through the New York financial district was

---

[39] "Roosevelt's Place in History," *Events,* III. February 1938.

greeted by the prolonged boos of its denizens and the hinterland promptly learned how Wall Street and "economic royalists" could treat a popular idol. Speaking to the workingmen of Brooklyn the same day, Roosevelt quoted one of Willkie's rash proponents as saying that the President's supporters were "paupers, those who earn less than $1,200 a year and aren't worth that, and the Roosevelt family." "Can the Republican leaders," inquired Roosevelt, "deny that this all too prevailing Republican sentiment is a direct, vicious, unpatriotic appeal to class hatred, to class contempt?" [40] No comparable blunder had been made since a slaveholding Senator had called laborers the "mudsills of society," a term of contempt of which Lincoln kept reminding his audiences.

Never before have returns been subjected to a more searching analysis than were those of the presidential election of 1940. Considering the social composition of the Roosevelt following, it is not astonishing that he carried every city of more than 400,000, excepting only Cincinnati. It was the great cities, indeed, that wiped out Willkie's lead in the rural precincts, the villages, towns, and smaller cities, and gave Roosevelt the electoral votes of New York, Missouri, Ohio, Wisconsin, and Illinois. Illuminating the conclusions of the statistical analyses are the comments of William J. Galvin, Democratic leader in a Charlestown ward of metropolitan Boston. The ward is inhabited by longshoremen, packers, waitresses, and minor city employees, who supported Roosevelt four to one. "Probably no section in the country gained more under the New Deal," said Galvin, and he then proceeded to enumerate specific benefits received: "Hundreds got pay raises under the wage-hour law; more hundreds of seasonal workers are having slack months cushioned by unemployment-insurance benefits. The NYA is helping from 300 to 500 youths; at the worst of the depression thousands held WPA jobs; of 1500 persons past sixty-five in the ward, more than 600 receive old-age assistance; another 600 cases are on direct relief and get aid for dependent children.

---

[40] V. O. Key, Jr.: "Roosevelt Wins Again," *Events*, December 1940, pp. 409 ff.

Charlestown is a food-stamp area; the WPA improved its bathing beach; a new low-cost housing project will relieve some of the ward's congestion." For the first time in anybody's memory the Boston Irish are being appointed to Federal district judgeships. Indicative of this ethnic group's loyalty elsewhere is the comment of a Detroit Catholic priest: "If I ever attacked Roosevelt from the pulpit it would be the end of me here." [41]

The birth rate handicapped the Republican Party in that era of slowing population growth, as the analysis of the returns of 1940 plainly show. In the thirties Republican families may have outnumbered the Democratic, but the latter families were larger. The older stocks inhabiting the poorer soils of the back country and traditionally inclined to Democracy, as Turner pointed out, are scarcely less prolific than the newer stocks of the great cities. The New England Irish long ago overwhelmed the native Yankees by big families rather than by continuous immigration. "Out of Ritzy Humboldt Park they get two voters to a family," said a Polish tavern-keeper and politician of Buffalo. "I get six out of my house. I got neighbors who give me eight." Buffalo Poles supported Roosevelt on an average ratio of nine to one, with individual precincts going twenty-five to one, and a Detroit Polish precinct breaking the record with a vote of thirty to one.[42]

The Republicans have now decisively lost their own most prolific ethnic group, the Negroes, whose loyalty was too long taken for granted. Senator Guffey began luring Pennsylvania Negroes away from Republican ranks as early as 1932. That year Robert L. Vann, editor of the largest Negro paper in the state, came out for Roosevelt. "My friends," said he in a speech, "go turn Lincoln's picture to the wall. That debt has been paid in full." [43] The ethereal tradition of the Great Emancipator lost its potency as President Roosevelt

---

[41] Samuel Lubell: "Post Mortem: Who Elected Roosevelt?" *Saturday Evening Post*, January 25, 1941.

[42] Ibid., pp. 91–2.

[43] Joseph Alsop and Robert Kintner: *Saturday Evening Post*, March 26, 1938.

made one Negro appointment after another to $5,000 posi-
tions, with every one of them making the Harlem newspaper
headlines in 72-point type. Old Negroes may have muttered,
"Our people are selling their birthrights for a mess of pot-
tage," but that mattered little to the fifty per cent of Harlem
that were on relief.[44] This Negro vote helped to overwhelm
the up-state Republican precincts and give the Democrats
the greatest single bloc of votes in the electoral college.

Samuel Lubell, whom the *Saturday Evening Post* sent forth
among the great cities to discover at first hand how it happened, found a close correlation between the prevailing rent
of a precinct and the President's strength in it. Roosevelt ran
better than two and a half to one in seven Minneapolis wards
where rents were less than $30. In four wards where they
ranged between $30 and $40 he had not much better than an
even break. Three wards with the average rents exceeding
$40 voted for Willkie five to three, and where they were
highest he defeated the President three to one. This dividing
line between Roosevelt and Willkie wards varied from city
to city as prevailing rents might be higher or lower in one
city or another. In Minneapolis, for example, the break between the two was in the ward with $44 rents and in Pitts-
burgh between wards where rents averaged somewhere
between $45 and $60. In every city Lubell investigated, however, income as indicated by rents determined by and large
the Roosevelt versus Willkie alignments.

Despite the one-sidedness of the 1940 presidential election it was evident that, for the first time since World War I,
the balloting revealed a decisive shift toward the restoration
of a balance between the major parties. There had been a
difference of 26.1 between the percentages of the popular vote
cast in 1920 for Harding on the one side and Cox on the
other. The corresponding margins in succeeding elections
were 25.3 in 1924, 18.3 in 1928, 17.7 in 1932, 24.3 in 1936;
but Roosevelt's margin over Willkie had narrowed down to
9.9. Moreover, a glance at an election map showing results

---

44 S. Lubell, op. cit., p. 96.

by counties in 1940 makes it clear that Willkie had recaptured substantially Greater New England, the zone of dominant Yankee stock and culture, which, for two generations before the thirties, had been the stronghold of the Republican Party. The great cities were, of course, excluded and, in any case, neither the New England stock nor culture prevailed in these centers of more recent immigration.

The Republicans were strong in the dairy regions, the corn belt, and the wheat-land prairies. In no other classification of social groups did Willkie achieve anything so striking as his capture of 57 per cent of the Midwestern farmers, only 44 per cent of whom had voted for Landon. In brief, the counties carried by Willkie produced a configuration on the election map strikingly suggestive of the better-income rural areas east of the Great Plains as they show up on maps shaded to indicate local variations in standards of living in the United States.[45]

With ever dwindling command Willkie held the titular leadership of the Republican party in the quadrennium following his defeat. Avowedly he coveted the role of the leader of "his majesty's loyal opposition." Never whole-heartedly welcomed by the Republican leadership, he became increasingly unacceptable to the isolationist element within the party, particularly after his tour of Russia, the Middle East, and China, and his consequent emerging international ideology, epitomized in the title of his book, One World. Nor did he capture the applause of the directorate of the Republican party by championing the rights of such minority groups as Negroes, sharecroppers, and Communists, one of whom he is credited with having saved from deportation by arguing a case before the Supreme Court of the United States.

As an announced candidate for the Republican nomination in 1944 Willkie staked everything on a primary campaign for the Wisconsin delegates, waged in the very heart of isolationism. Here the telltale pronouns betrayed his not-quite-certain Republicanism when, in his Green Bay speech, he declared:

---

[45] Such a map can be found in W. F. Ogburn and M. F. Nimkoff's *Sociology*, p. 462.

"Unless *you* Republicans uphold *my* hands *your* party will be on the road to certain defeat and possible dissolution." Nor could this confessed disciple of Woodrow Wilson ever conjure before Republican audiences with the great names — John Hay, Elihu Root, William Howard Taft, and Charles Evans Hughes — that exemplify the Republican tradition in the promotion of world organization. When he failed to capture a single Wisconsin delegate Willkie withdrew his candidacy and was ignored by the Republican National Convention with a thoroughness unprecedented in the history of the party.

Freed from the responsibilities of a candidacy, Willkie became the nation's outstanding free lance in politics. In this capacity he grew in stature month by month. As the delegates to the Republican National Convention were gathering in Chicago he published a series of articles that represent a high-water mark in the discussion of national issues. Thus he became to the Republicans what a columnist denominated "the party's embarrassing conscience." Not all the ostentatious air of indifference displayed by the delegates could quite conceal the ever haunting question, "What will Willkie and his following do on election day?" Let those who assume that he achieved nothing turn again to the series of articles, compare them with Dewey's campaign speeches, and note how week by week the candidate drew closer and closer to the program proposed by the rejected leader.

Republicans had been cheered by the congressional elections of 1942 when they elected almost a majority to the lower House. But the vote had been light, especially because of considerable non-voting on the part of two of the strongest elements of the Democratic group combination: laborers who had recently migrated to new communities and were consequently disqualified by length-of-residence requirements for voting or by failure to register; and youth, absent with the armed forces. Nevertheless expectations mounted as one special election after another put a Republican in a seat just left vacant by the death of a Democratic incumbent. Partisan Republicans generally chose to ignore statistical analyses revealing that these victories were evidently due to light voting.[46]

Overshadowing every domestic issue in 1944 were the engrossing problems of winning a global war and ensuring a permanent peace. Consequently and despite recent congressional gains the delegates to the 1944 Republican National Convention gathered in an atmosphere heavy with defeatism. Unless the European War should end before November it was feared that the prestige of the Commander-in-Chief would insure his re-election. In contrast with early Republican conventions this one represented age rather than youth. For two generations after the Civil War the brains of the nation had rather gravitated to the Republican party. When, however, the Roosevelt program recognized youth in the CCC, the NYA, and remunerative positions in the agencies of the administration, the Republicans lost their traditional title as "the party of the young man," a fact steadily revealed by the various opinion polls.

After the sound and fury of convention oratory damning the New Deal had died out, John A. Lapp "counted thirty planks in this [Republican] platform taken directly from achievements of the Roosevelt Administration."[47] The Republican peace plank proved to be so enigmatic and the postwar employment plank so inadequate that both had to be clarified and amplified later by the presidential candidate.

Governor John W. Bricker of Ohio was the personal choice of the Republican delegates for the presidential nomination, but he had to be content with second place after the convention had reluctantly bowed to the sentiment of the party's rank and file for Governor Thomas E. Dewey of New York. Dewey had first won national attention after his appointment in 1935 as Special Prosecutor for the Investigation of Organized Crime in New York City. Quick and spectacular indictments were followed by prompt convictions of racketeers, bootleggers, loan sharks, and practitioners of the policy game.

---

[46] See Louis H. Bean, "What Republican Trend?" *New Republic*, May 1, 1944.

[47] Northwestern University *Reviewing Stand*, July 2, 1944, p. 7.

In 1937 he was elected District Attorney of New York County and in this office exposed police graft, removed dishonest and dictatorial trade-union officials, prosecuted the financial giants Charles E. Mitchell and Richard Whitney for fraudulent practices, had City Judge Harold Kunstler disbarred, helped expose Circuit Judge Martin Manton, and sent to prison the notorious Lucky Luciano and Jimmy Hines. Such a record provided a stepping-stone to the governorship of New York, where he soon won a reputation as an efficient administrator. The failure of his deliberate efforts to capture the Republican nomination for the presidency in 1940 was followed by four years of simulated indifference as to the nomination, during which opinion polls registered his growing strength as the Republican favorite for 1944.

Dewey's nomination marked his party's return to conventional practice in recognizing the claims of a candidate to political preferment based on outstanding public service as a party member. The candidacy of this grandson of a founder of the Republican party contrasted sharply with that of the only half-converted Willkie, who sought in the presidency his first public office. Dewey would commit no such self-revealing Freudian slip as Willkie's peculiar use of the pronouns in addressing the convention that had just nominated him in 1940 when he said: "So *you* Republicans, I call upon *you* to join *me*," and so on. Dewey flew to the Chicago convention and signified his acceptance of the nomination in a notable address to the delegates. "It was a masterpiece," wrote Dorothy Thompson. "The shortest speech by any speaker, a statement totally devoid of slogans, wisecracks or pathetic oratory, it opened a totally new type of campaign oratory." Not in a generation had anyone but an excited fellow partisan paid such a glowing tribute to a Republican candidate. Dewey's campaign addresses were all carefully prepared from material gathered by a "research" organization and directed toward definite objectives. No Republican since the leadership of Mark Hanna had conducted such a well-planned campaign. At last the party had found a competent radio voice, and Dewey delivered his addresses with a vigor so portentous to the Democrats that President Roosevelt reversed his decision not to campaign and began stumping the country.

Since Theodore Roosevelt no Republican candidate had made such a calculated essay at group diplomacy in party politics. Aware that Republican strength lay with business, the professions, and the more prosperous farmers outside the solid South, Dewey sought to reinforce this admitted minority and convert it into a majority by luring recruits from industrial labor and the lower-income groups generally. He accordingly labored diligently to commit the Republican party to the maintenance of the great labor statutes, the expansion of social security to groups not yet included, and the achievement of full post-war employment even if it required federal spending. "If there be those among you who would turn back the course of collective bargaining, they are doomed to a bitter disappointment," declared Dewey in his Seattle address. "We are not going back to anything, not to bread lines, not to leaf raking, not to settling labor disputes with gunfire and gas bombs. . . ."

In what turned out to be a futile effort Dewey sought to recover to the Republican ranks the northern Negro vote, which held the balance of power in enough states to swing the election either way. In this he was fortified by planks in the Republican platform against poll taxes, lynching, unfair employment practices, and racial discrimination in the armed forces, on all of which the Democratic platform was silent. Moreover it was with extraordinary earnestness and persistency that Dewey endeavored to free the party from its reputation for isolationism by pledging it to the building of a world organization invested with the power necessary to enforce permanent peace. In this too he evidently did not quite succeed, since Arthur Krock found it generally accepted in Washington after the election that "the Republican party's Congressional record, even after Pearl Harbor, was an unsurmountable [sic] burden for Mr. Dewey." [48]

In striking contrast with the lethargy of the Republican

---

[48] Quoted by *The World Through Washington*, Vol. II, No. 2 (November), The American University, p. 2.

Convention was the hilarity of the Democratic gathering, which verged at times on a factional mass hysteria portentous of party dissolution. Some southern delegations, raising the old cry of "white supremacy," coerced the convention into refusing any platform recognition of Negro rights by threatening to nominate state electoral Democratic tickets pledged not to vote for President Roosevelt if the convention renominated him. Yet the Democratic voting strength lay so largely in the personal following of Franklin Roosevelt that he was indubitably the party's indispensable man, and his nomination for a fourth term was consequently inevitable. Yet a dread specter haunted the delegates: the knowledge that the party's future hung on the slender thread of the life of the war-weary and rapidly aging Chief Executive. For the first time in American party history a convention recognized the enormous significance of the vice-presidency. Consequently when the nomination of a candidate for that office was reached a savage war of convention factions set in. The move to renominate Vice President Henry Wallace, the idol of industrial labor, the little agrarians, and the underprivileged generally, and moreover the favorite of the delegates, was crushed by a combination of conservative southern Democrats with northern metropolitan party bosses, functioning through the unashamed manipulation of state delegations by Robert E. Hannegan, the Democratic National Chairman. Raymond Moley, looking down on the resulting frustrations, thought "it may well be asserted that what has been shown here indicates the party may restore its unity after a defeat in November. But it can hardly survive a victory."

It was a fellow Missourian, Senator Harry S. Truman, that Democratic Chairman Hannegan had strong-armed into candidacy for the vice-presidency. Wallace had been far ahead of his competitors in all the opinion polls, and every element in the convention reminiscent of the Jacksonian tradition — the interest of the common man — had shouted for Wallace. Moreover, Roosevelt had given Wallace's candidacy his endorsement — equivocal though it was — in the first of a succession of confusing letters that almost turned the Democratic

Convention into a madhouse. Only a few days before his nomination Truman had confided to a fellow Senator that the thought of his possible nomination terrified him. This extraordinarily modest-appearing man was written off by many during the campaign as merely a typical vice presidential candidate, a comparative nonentity. In due time this public undervaluation was to work to Truman's distinct advantage, since he was to enter the presidency under no such heavy handicap as the over-advertisement of such presidents as Ulysses S. Grant and Herbert Hoover.

In sharp contrast with the Republican platform equivocation on the issue of permanent peace the Democratic Convention pledged that party "to make all necessary and effective agreements and arrangements through which the nations would maintain adequate forces to meet the needs of preventing war and making impossible the preparations for war and which would have such forces available for joint action when necessary." Nor did President Roosevelt let the matter rest there, but in his acceptance speech said: "The American people now know that all nations of the world — large and small — will have to play their appropriate part in keeping the peace by force. . . ." In the midst of the campaign he reinforced this position in an address before the Foreign Policy Association, where he supported the idea of establishing a world security organization before the end of the war and of having Congress authorize American participation in the use of force against an aggressor without specific approval of Congress in each case.

In general the Democratic platform "pointed with pride" to the party's record of achievement. In view of the strategic importance of the pivotal northern Negro vote the platform's most glaring defect was its failure to pledge the party's support to a single specific measure for racial justice. Nevertheless Dewey was unable on election day to lure the Negroes from their loyalty to Roosevelt. On October fifth the President had reassured them with the declaration: ". . . The right to vote must be open to our citizens irrespective of race, color, or creed, without tax or artificial restriction of any kind. The sooner we get that basis of political equality, the better it will be for this state of affairs. . . ."

When the Seventy-eighth Congress, under the conviction that the electorate in 1942 had given it a mandate to "get tough" with labor, passed, over the President's veto, the drastic Smith-Connally Anti-Strike Act it aroused labor from its apathy and set in motion a new force in American politics. This took the form of the Political Action Committee of the Congress of Industrial Organizations, which went to work to convince workers that their signal gains under the Roosevelt Administration might be swept away unless they registered and voted in the 1944 presidential election. Thus the anti-Roosevelt forces in Congress may have unwittingly ensured the fourth term.

The astonishing activity and efficiency of the C. I. O. Political Action Committee in support of President Roosevelt was a major sensation of the 1944 campaign. The electorate resolutely refused to be stampeded against it by the persistent and vociferous Republican charge that it was dominated by Communists. Better organized than either of the major parties, it showed veteran politicians new devices in effective canvassing and in the use of printed propaganda vivid with cartoon, pictograph, and appeals to the vital interests of the masses. It has been said that for the first time in American history a nation-wide organization rang doorbells and systematically canvassed for a cause rather than for candidates.

"Jobs," the most persistent single issue in American party history, was kept constantly before the workers by the Political Action Committee and the Democratic ward heelers. "What were you doing in 1932?" became almost a campaign refrain. Hoover and apple-selling were made symbols of unemployment, and Dewey was presented as merely another Hoover. It seemed to some Republicans as if the Democrats were making Hoover rather than Dewey the candidate. The labor-union halls of Detroit would not permit the ghosts of job lines, welfare lines, hunger marches, and eviction riots to be laid.

For some reason or other labor turned out *en masse* on election day, and while it cannot be demonstrated mathematically that the Political Action Committee induced it to do so, the preponderance of evidence points to it. It was certainly no accident that the President's majority of 770,000 in New York City overcame Dewey's up-state lead of 512,000 and gave Roosevelt New York's 47 electoral votes. In a similar manner Philadelphia's majority of 131,000 for the President wiped out Dewey's lead in the rest of Pennsylvania; Chicago's 293,-000 majority for the President made futile Dewey's downstate lead in Illinois. In Michigan the Detroit majority for Roosevelt overcame Dewey's lead elsewhere, as did St. Louis's vote in Missouri and Boston's vote in Massachusetts. The electoral votes thrown to the President by these cities alone were enough, when added to those of the Solid South, to assure his re-election. It is significant that in April 1945 Ohio's Congressman-at-Large George H. Bender, a Republican recently re-elected with the blessing of the Political Action Committee, asked Republican National Chairman Herbert Brownell to call a meeting of all the Republican county chairmen of the big industrial counties, where, Bender pointed out, the Republicans lost the election. Here at last was a significant indication of Republicans coming to grips with industrial realities in the United States.

No precise estimate can be made of the weight to be given to the personality of the late President in accounting for his sweeping victory in 1944. Certainly Dewey's contention that the administration was "old and tired and quarrelsome" and that "It's time for a change" was wasted on the idolizing crowds that cheered the indomitable Chief Executive campaigning in the chill October rain. It was, indeed, a postelection comment that the Republicans ran down their competitor instead of building up their own product. Then there was the studied air about everything that Dewey said — an almost obtrusive mathematical calculation of issues — producing merely a "synthetic liberalism" instead of the heart-warming message of a crusader for a living cause. If "the highest art is to conceal art," then Dewey's logic, enunciation, and delivery were too painfully perfect.

It was one of the misfortunes of this humorless Republican candidate to have been pitted against an American mass leader whose repeated electoral triumphs place him indubitably in the great succession of Jefferson, Jackson, and Lincoln. He was "en rapport with the American people," summarized a veteran Washington correspondent who had studied crowd reactions as he followed the President through his 1944 campaigning. Even Roosevelt's simulated indignation over Republican remarks about his dog Fala may have irked the well fed, well clothed, and well housed, but it brought the human touch to the common man.

While the campaign was in progress victories of the armed forces gave increased cogency to the pithy injunction of Quentin Reynolds to the Democratic Convention: "Never remove a pitcher when he is pitching a winning game." The women voters required no urging on this matter. On the eve of the election the Gallup poll revealed that, while the civilian men had decided to support Dewey 51 per cent, the women intended to vote for Roosevelt 52 per cent. Their belief that the President's re-election would bring the son, the husband, or the sweetheart home sooner was a mighty factor in the balloting and may have decided the election. The 2,691,160 ballots cast by soldiers apparently did not change a single electoral vote, despite pre-election speculation that they might be decisive. This was doubtless due to the fact that the soldier vote represented the same general trend as the civilian, although the percentage of soldier support of the President was, as expected, exceptionally high. Thus the soldier vote served only to emphasize the popular verdict known before midnight following the election. At any rate Dewey received only 99 of the 532 electoral votes.

What is to be the place of Franklin Roosevelt among the great party leaders of American history? Surely this President did something with the Democratic party that no other leader since Andrew Jackson had quite managed to do. In two and a half generations the Democratic party had not yet fully recovered its pre-Civil War prestige. Publicists had long been accustomed to observe that the United States was normally a

Republican nation. Before the 1930's most American voters evidently regarded themselves as Republicans. The only two Democratic presidencies since the Civil War had often been dismissed as mere aberrations or departures from normality. Significantly enough, the butt of the typical comedian's joke on the theater stage was seldom a Republican.

Franklin Roosevelt's election in 1932 was at first disposed of as just a lucky break due to the depression. Any Democrat could have won under the circumstances. Walter Lippmann merely expressed a prevalent consensus of 1932 in his statement that Roosevelt was "a pleasant man, who without any important qualifications for office, would very much like to be President." But the magisterial confidence with which Roosevelt took charge of the nation in March 1933, when it looked as if society itself might be ready to disintegrate, was the beginning of a party leadership without parallel in American history.

Whatever President Roosevelt's shortcomings may have been during his twelve years, certain facts are indisputable. He was elected four times as President. The electoral votes of his four opponents — Hoover, Landon, Willkie, and Dewey — when added do not even total the majority required for electing a president. Every political leader who has commanded the confidence of the American masses has aroused bitter antipathies. The charge that Roosevelt incited class conflict would have had a familiar ring in the ears of Jefferson, Jackson, and Lincoln. As a party leader, then, this is Franklin Roosevelt's paramount achievement. When he entered the presidency most Americans considered themselves Republicans. At the end of twelve years a majority of Americans had formed the habit of voting the Democratic ticket and doubtless considered themselves Democrats.

How did the personality of President Truman alter the political situation at the time of his accession to the presidency? A dozen years before that event Irving Brant, then editor of the St. Louis *Star Times*, had found Truman to be the only Missouri official at a better-government conference "who could discuss administrative problems on a level with the visiting experts." His official position then was merely the presidency of a Missouri county court, a non-judicial board corresponding to the county commissioners or supervisors in other states. The Pendergast machine that had been responsible for his election never dominated him in office, and in 1935 the exigencies of Democratic politics in Missouri elevated Harry Truman to the United States Senate. After the nation had become involved in World War II Senator Truman was responsible for the creation of the Senate Special Committee Investigating the National Defense Program. So efficiently were its purposes carried out under his very able chairmanship that "the Truman Committee" became a familiar household expression. Competent authority expressed the opinion at the time that, excepting only President Roosevelt, Truman through this Committee contributed more to the winning of the war than any other civilian.[49] No industrial corporation or cartel could presume immunity from scrutiny of or exposure by the Truman Committee if it fell down on war production. Big industrialists who came to Washington to exert pressure were handled courteously, but without fear or favor. There was nothing equivocal about the Truman Committee reports — the use of dollar-a-year men was not good for the defense program; Jesse Jones's aluminum expansion contract with Alcoa violated sound principle; denying raw material for production of passenger cars was the way to convince the motor industry it could produce war planes.

Truman's record in the Senate indicated what could be expected of him as President — his votes for a federal anti-lynching law, the outlawing of poll taxes, and for a Fair Employment Practices Committee gave him the Negro vote whenever he needed it. He had long been a favorite of the Railway Brotherhoods and the American Federation of Labor and his voting record commanded the confidence of the Congress of Industrial Organizations. For some unaccountable reason President Roosevelt had not kept Vice President

---

[49] Irving Brant: "Harry S. Truman," *New Republic*, April 30, 1945.

Truman in touch with what the executive department was doing. The responsibilities of the presidency were thrust upon Truman when the nation was in a two-hemisphere war; the problems of a permanent world organization were pressing and another Big Three meeting was due to be held. Yet Truman demonstrated that, by being his very own self, he too could play the presidential role. At his first presidential press conference he answered the alert newspapermen's barrage of searching questions with such promptness, simplicity, and confidence that these keen men and women rushed tingling from the conference room to tell the American people, as one ecstatic radio news commentator expressed it over and over again, "you have a President, you have a President." Such was the honeymoon that in July 1945 the opinion polls indicated Truman to be more popular than Roosevelt had been at any time except in the early months of his first term.

President Truman reveled in the game of presidential politics and played it with consummate skill. He was expert in the use of the veto power to fortify his standing with the presidential constituency and indeed with his party itself. The veto of the Taft-Hartley Act illustrates the point precisely. Even though the bill had passed the Senate by more than three to one and the House by four to one, the President was urged to veto by his national party chairman, by the Executive Committee of the A. F. of L., and by the C. I. O., which was holding rallies to that end in a dozen cities. He had received 157,000 letters, 460,000 cards, and 23,000 telegrams, most of them urging veto. A poll of the Democratic National Committee showed party officers favoring veto two to one. President Truman vetoed the act and was not dismayed when it passed over his veto. A year later he made the act a campaign issue with such telling effect that it contributed greatly to his re-election and was disastrous to many Congressmen who had voted to over-ride his veto.

The capture of the Eightieth Congress by the Republicans at the mid-term elections of 1946 proved to be utterly deceptive. At long last, they thought, the old Roosevelt magic had been broken permanently. According to precedents it was reasonable to assume that, when the Democrats lost this mid-term congressional election, they would inevitably lose the presidency in 1948. So the Eightieth Congress proceeded on its somewhat reckless legislative way confident that the Republicans would soon be in complete control of the national government. Under the circumstances the presidential nomination for 1948 became an exceedingly desirable prize for Republican aspirants to the great office.

It was Governor Thomas E. Dewey's third try in 1948, and his three successive attempts, as viewed in retrospect, demonstrate the utter impossibility of reducing to a formula the technique of capturing a presidential nomination. In 1940 he made an extraordinary pre-convention campaign to win the nomination and failed. In 1944 he pursued a course of relative indifference to the matter and won the nomination. Since this successful way seemed to be the right one he would naturally follow it again in 1948. So he simply acted as if his nomination were inevitable — he was "the" candidate. And what gave this an air of plausibility was that month after month the opinion polls showed him running ahead of every other Republican hopeful except General Eisenhower, who insisted he was not a candidate. Dewey's pose of indifference finally became so transparent as to induce him to jest about "the depth of hypocrisy to which political life will send a man."

Early in 1948 it became necessary for Dewey to admit, through a statement of his executive secretary, James C. Hagerty, that his hat was in the ring: "As the Governor has frequently said, he is fully engaged with the legislative session and cannot actively seek the nomination . . . but, if nominated, he would accept." It was soon apparent that this would not be enough, and so Dewey entered the Wisconsin primary only to see Harold E. Stassen capture nineteen delegates, Douglas MacArthur eight, and himself none. Dewey had also made a last-minute campaign in the Nebraska primary, but there he obtained only 35 per cent of the vote to 43 per cent for Stassen, who was now running ahead of him in the Gallup Poll.

Soon Stassen was barnstorming through Oregon getting vociferous cheers from immense crowds as he demanded the outlawing of the Communist Party. Precise, dignified Thomas E. Dewey had no relish for rough-and-tumble stump speaking, but he decided to go to Oregon at once, and of all things, take issue with Stassen on the very proposition that was bringing him so much applause — the outlawing of the Communist Party. Confronted with a personal crisis in his political career, Governor Dewey underwent a startling transformation. No Oregon crossroad was too insignificant for the new Dewey, no trick too corny. Not a trace remained of the old reserve and aloofness as he shook hands all around. He signed his passport to Coos County in blood drawn from his arm by the local Pirates and at Grants Pass ate raw beef with the Cave Men. One commentator said that Dewey would have climbed a telephone pole to talk with a lineman if it had been necessary.

When Stassen saw the inroads Dewey was making he returned to Oregon and then made perhaps the biggest miscalculation of his career — he challenged Dewey to a radio debate. The challenge was promptly accepted, and the listening nation then had the opportunity to hear and take the measure of the two men speaking face to face. In his opening speech Stassen urged the passage of the pending Mundt Bill, which he declared would outlaw the Communist Party. Dewey, quoting from Senator Mundt and the House Un-American Activities Committee itself, showed that both had disavowed that purpose. Stassen was so utterly outclassed that the debate worked to the overwhelming advantage of Dewey. After the debate Dewey stumped Oregon by bus, making from six to ten speeches a day. With more than 200,000 votes cast on Election Day, Dewey won the Oregon primary by 9,000.

When the Republican National Convention opened on June 21, it was Dewey against a field consisting of Taft, Stassen, Vandenberg, and Warren. After his defeat in Oregon, Stassen seemed out of the running, although he held several state delegations totaling 157 delegates. He flew to

Topeka a month before the convention to get the advice of Alfred M. Landon, the Republican presidential candidate of 1936, who advised Stassen: "Harold, you can put over Dewey, or Taft, or Joe Martin, but you can't make it yourself." Stassen was inclined to throw his delegates to Taft rather than to Dewey, but he could not yet believe that his own chances were all gone. When Vandenberg's hat was thrown into the ring only two days before the convention opened, Stassen became convinced that a deadlock was likely with Vandenberg's delegates holding the line and so, still hopeful, he declined an alliance with Taft.

Dewey's organization at the convention represented the epitome of efficiency. A legman was assigned to watch each delegation, and special effort was expended on the Pennsylvania delegation despite Governor James Duff's unalterable opposition to Dewey. The strategy developed into a conference of Dewey and Pennsylvania's favorite son, Senator Edward Martin. After this parley the delegates were electrified by the news that Martin had withdrawn and would place Dewey's name in nomination. An attempt by Taft to get the field to agree on a single candidate against Dewey failed. Governor Alfred E. Driscoll, New Jersey's favorite son, announced that he would release his 35 delegates after the first ballot and would support Dewey. House Majority Leader Charles Halleck of Indiana, having been assured by Dewey that he would be acceptable if the convention nominated him for Vice President, jumped to the erroneous conclusion that this signified he was Dewey's choice for his running mate and promptly pledged Indiana's 29 delegates to Dewey.

By this time such intense intraparty bitterness had been generated among the delegates that when Senator Martin rose to place Dewey's name in nomination he had scarcely begun to speak before booing spread throughout the hall, forcing Chairman Joe Martin to remonstrate against the extraordinary discourtesy. At 5 p.m. on Thursday, on the second ballot, Dewey had received 515 votes, so near victory that the stop-Dewey coalition in desperation moved a recess until 7:30 p.m., hoping thereby to gain time for uniting on a rival candidate. When, however, the New York delegation informed the convention that it did not object to the recess it was promptly recognized that the Dewey organization had in reserve the delegates necessary to nominate their man. When the delegates reconvened in the evening the vote on the third ballot was 1,094 to 0 for Dewey. Governor Earl Warren of California was chosen as the Republican vice-presidential candidate.

In his brief speech to the convention accepting the nomination Dewey said: "I come to you unfettered by a single obligation or promise to any living person. . . . We [Republicans] have declared our goal to be a strong and free America in a free world of free men — free to speak their own minds . . . free to publish what they believe, free to move from place to place, free to choose occupations . . . free to worship God. . . . When these rights are secure in the world, the permanent ideals of the Republican Party shall have been realized."

Especially significant was the foreign-policy plank of the Republican platform, which had been shaped largely by the influence of Arthur Vandenberg, the leader of the bipartisan foreign-policy combination in the Senate. It tended to counteract the taint of isolationism attaching to the Republican Party. The plank promised foreign aid within "prudent limits." It pledged support of the United Nations and favored freeing it of any veto in the peaceful settlement of international disputes. It even held that the United Nations should be provided with an armed force. Support of the "system of reciprocal trade" was promised. It was indicative of the almost universal conviction that the Democrats were doomed that such a responsible commentator as Ernest K. Lindley, at the close of the convention, could write: "The Dewey-Warren ticket, with the Vandenberg planks in the Republican platform, withers the last hope the Democrats may have had of drafting General Eisenhower. Only a miracle or a series of political blunders not to be expected of a man of Dewey's astuteness can save Truman, or probably any other

Democrat, from overwhelming defeat when the ballots are counted in November. The entire country, and the whole free world, as well as the Republican Party, can be thankful that history is not repeating itself: That 1948 is not another 1920." [50]

By the summer of 1948 President Truman's prestige, as measured by the opinion polls, had fallen so far down from the extraordinarily high mark of the early months of his presidency that he looked to many Democratic leaders like a hopeless candidate. Crusaders for the New Deal, even including three of the sons of Franklin Roosevelt, and left-wing Democratic leaders [51] generally were combining with such state-rights partisans as Senator Harry F. Byrd of Virginia and Governor J. Strom Thurmond of South Carolina to dump the President and draft General Dwight D. Eisenhower as the Democratic candidate for President, or if that failed, to back Associate Justice William O. Douglas of the United States Supreme Court. When the idea was unequivocally rejected by both of these men the stop-Truman revolt collapsed and Democratic National Chairman J. Howard McGrath confidently predicted President Truman's renomination on the first ballot.

The Democratic Convention opened in an atmosphere of deep despair and with appalling absenteeism evident in the vacant seats of the delegates and in the galleries. Mention of President Truman in the opening speeches brought scarcely any applause and the once magic name of Franklin Roosevelt brought not much more. On the first night, however, the wizardry of Senator Alben Barkley's old-fashioned keynote speech brought the convention to life with a wild and tumultuous demonstration. For twenty-four hours it looked as if Barkley instead of the President might be nominated for first place on the ticket. It had been the plan of the Truman

---

[50] *Newsweek,* July 5, 1948, p. 20.

[51] These even included Mayor Hubert Humphrey, Chester Bowles, Leon Henderson, Mayor O'Dwyer of New York City and such Democratic metropolitan bosses as Jake Arvey of Chicago and Frank Hague of Newark, vice chairman of the Democratic National Committee.

men merely to rewrite the mild civil-rights plank of the 1944 convention which had not proved unacceptable to the Southern delegates. But, under the leadership of Mayor Hubert Humphrey of Minneapolis, the Americans for Democratic Action were demanding an all-out civil-rights plank specifying support of anti-poll tax, anti-lynching, and fair-employment laws, opposition to race segregation in the armed services, and, to the astonishment of the Truman men, A.D.A. got their plank by a vote of 651½ to 582½. The fat was in the fire. Thirty-five Mississippi and Alabama delegates promptly walked out.

Near 2 a.m. of the last day of the convention President Truman became the Democratic nominee for President by a vote of 947½ to 263 for Senator Russell, the choice of the Southern delegates. The President had been waiting since 9:15 p.m. to deliver his speech of acceptance. Measured by its effect, this speech, delivered in the middle of the night, was one of the outstanding speeches of our party history. For the second time something like a resurrection occurred in the almost lifeless convention. The Republican Party "still helps the rich and sticks a knife in the back of the poor," he declared. "The Republican platform comes out for slum clearance and low-rental housing. I have been trying to get them to pass this housing bill ever since they met the first time and it is still resting in the Rules Committee. . . . The Republican platform urges expanding and increasing Social Security benefits . . . and yet when they had the opportunity they took 750,000 people off the social security rolls." Then the President fairly took away the breath of the convention with this startling statement: "My duty as President requires that I use every means within my power to get the laws the people need in such important matters and I am therefore calling this Congress back into session on the 26th of July." He stated he would ask Congress to enact the laws the Republicans advocated in their platform. From beginning to end it was a fighting speech and when he closed with a ringing appeal — "I need your help. You must get in and push" — the convention had been lifted from the depths of despair to an unbounded enthusiasm.

When the Eightieth Congress met, pursuant to the President's call, Dewey's campaign manager, Herbert Brownell, brushed off Truman's call for action on platform promises with the statement: "The Republican platform calls for the enactment of a program by a Republican Congress under the leadership of a Republican President. Obviously this cannot be done at a rump session called at a political convention for political effect in the heat of a political campaign." Congress adjourned without action on a single one of the President's fourteen recommendations included in his call for the special session. Since Congress had done nothing Truman promptly dubbed it the "do-nothing Congress" and the "worst Congress" in our history. His audacious coup had given him the initiative and he held it throughout the campaign.

Another factor that had made Truman's prospects for election appear to be hopeless was the initiation of two minor parties, each a splinter of the Democratic Party. Immediately after the Democratic Convention, 6,000 Southern Democrats, infuriated by the civil-rights plank of the Philadelphia convention, met at Birmingham, Alabama. With cries of "To hell with Truman" and the waving of Confederate flags this States Rights or Dixiecrat Party nominated Governor J. Strom Thurmond of South Carolina for President and Governor Fielding L. Wright of Mississippi for Vice President. Their hope was to elect enough presidential electors to prevent either Dewey or Truman receiving a majority in the Electoral College, thereby requiring the election of the President by the House of Representatives. The next week followers of Henry A. Wallace, Vice President under Franklin Roosevelt and a member of Truman's cabinet until asked to resign, convened in Philadelphia with nearly 3,200 delegates. Although Wallace was no Communist, this Progressive Party, as it was designated, turned out to be a rallying point of American Communists who practically took charge, dominated the convention, and determined what was to go into the platform. This turned out to be to the immense advantage of Truman, who could not plausibly be charged with being pro-Communist when that element was organized to fight his election.

As a campaigner President Truman proved adept at shaping his whistle-stop remarks very aptly to the special interests of each community; sometimes he got the necessary information only a few minutes before the stop. At Lima, Ohio, for example, when the train stopped and he had been introduced, he said: "I understand you manufacture locomotives here in Lima. Well, I've worn out several locomotives already in this campaign and before I am through I'll wear out a couple more and that will mean good business for Lima. Would you like to see my family?" Mrs. Truman and Margaret appeared on the rear platform with him and he introduced them. Then he made, in two sentences, an appeal for the election of the local Democratic candidate for Congress and just before the train started he said: "Tonight I am speaking over the radio at Akron. I am going to take the hide off the Republicans from head to heel. I hope you all listen." [52] It had all happened in a little more than five minutes. It was an absolutely new and effective technique that proved difficult for the Republicans to counter effectively.

The most remarkable thing about Truman's campaigning was his absolute conviction, in the face of all the evidence to the contrary, that he was going to win. Throughout the last two weeks of campaigning, in the face of the most overwhelming adverse opinion polls, Truman was confidently saying at various times and places: "The people's crusade is rolling along to victory, and it is going to leave the Republican poll-takers flat on their faces on November 3. . . . We have the Republicans on the run. . . . I'm going to be in the White House working for the people for four more years. . . . My opponent is running behind me, and that is where he belongs. . . .

"I'm going to give them hell," said Truman in Washington

---

[52] The author was present at this campaign stop.

on September 17, setting the pattern of his utterly unconventional campaigning. The Eightieth Congress had put a clause in the charter of the Commodity Credit Corporation prohibiting government construction of storage for farm crops in order to leave that to private industry. The consequent shortage of storage for crops left many farmers unable to store their grain for government loans, and, instead, they had to dump it on a falling market. This enabled Truman to tell 80,000 farmers attending the Dexter, Iowa, National Plowing Contest: "That notorious 'do-nothing' Republican Congress . . . has already stuck a pitchfork in the farmer's back." At St. Paul on October 13 he said: "The Republican Party either corrupts its liberals or expels them." At Boston on October 27 he said: "Now the Republicans tell me they stand for unity. In the old days, Al Smith would have said, 'That's baloney.' Today the Happy Warrior would say, 'That's a lot of hooey.' And if that rhymes with anything, it's not my fault."

To the very week of election the opinion polls indicated Dewey to be much stronger than Truman, and the Republicans, assuming Dewey's election to be "in the bag," conducted only a perfunctory campaign. Their disillusionment on election night was the greatest of our party history. Truman carried 28 states with 303 electoral votes to 16 states with 189 electoral votes for Dewey. Thurmond got 38 electoral votes. Truman's victory was all the more astonishing because of the two splinter parties each representing a secession from the Democratic party.

After Truman had been re-elected, the late Grove Patterson, then editor of the *Toledo Blade*, revealed that the day before Truman was nominated, he had telephoned the President and got permission to see him at the White House. "I'll give these Republicans the toughest fight they were ever up against," he said. "I'll go into every town of over ten thousand people in America. I'll do so-and-so, and so-and-so, and so-and-so," which turned out to be precisely what he did. Patterson left amazed at the President's absolute self-confidence, "his faith and his belief in his own capacity to beat

Tom Dewey. And the thing that made the situation fantastic was that apparently not a man, woman, or child in the United States believed he could do it. His cabinet and party leaders had washed him up and checked him off.

"Then came his speeches," continued Patterson. "Every time a Republican head showed up he slam banged it. Every G.O.P. policy was worse than wrong. It was vicious, dishonest, and dastardly. Republicans? They should be boiled in oil. . . . Old Doc Truman was Roosevelt without the kid gloves and the golden voice. It was barehanded Harry calling a spade a steam shovel. . . . The guy was just too busy to attend his own funeral." [53]

Truman's blistering criticism damning the Eightieth Congress was apparently fully as effective as his campaign for his own election. Private power interests had pressured the Eightieth Congress into voting down a steam plant the TVA required to take care of peak loads. All but five of the defeated Republican Congressmen had voted against the steam plant. The same interests had induced Congress to slaughter budget provisions for flood control and reclamation. All but two defeated Republican House members had voted for this cut. The government grain-storage-capacity cut was estimated to have been as much as 83 per cent. All but three of the defeated Republican Congressmen had voted for this cut. Truman had vetoed the tax cut of the Eightieth Congress on the ground that it was framed to relieve the rich. Every defeated Congressman had voted to over-ride that veto. And of the House members who were defeated for reelection all but four had voted to over-ride Truman's veto of the Taft-Hartley Act.[54] Truman had hammered away at every one of these issues. It is to be doubted whether, for effectiveness as measured by specific results, Truman's campaigning in 1948 can be matched anywhere else in the history of American political parties.

Nothing could have been more ironic in mid-century party politics than the fact that, while the opinion polls persist-

53 "The Way of the World," *Toledo Blade*, November 3, 1952.
54 See *U. S. News and World Report*, November 26, 1948, pp. 11–14.

ently indicated an overwhelming preponderance of professed Democrats, the Republicans nevertheless won presidential elections and, at times, even elected a majority of the state governors. In the 1950's the Survey Center of the University of Michigan was discovering in test after test that there were "three self-styled Democrats to every two Republicans." With such a handicap, 50 per cent more professed Democrats than Republicans, why did the Republicans nevertheless win national elections?

For one thing, the Democratic Party had a high percentage of the lower income groups, which meant fewer college and even high-school graduates among them. It is an established fact that those with less formal education are notoriously addicted to non-voting. Historically the Republicans constituted the party of social prestige, and while this status had declined during the 1930's, the party had generally recovered it by mid-century. Pollsters noted that, as lower income Democrats grew prosperous and moved from crowded city-tenements out into their own homes in the suburbs, they tended to take on the political coloration of their new neighbors and began voting Republican. It is a curious fact that as poverty throughout the nation declined the Democratic Party was losing its traditional appeal to the underdog, which since the days of Andrew Jackson it had exploited as the champion of the "common man." It should be noted that the group composition of the Republican Party, its higher percentage of the business and professional class, of college and high-school graduates, to mention but a few of its component elements, made it then a party of more faithful and habitual voters. Here were some of the factors that enabled a minority party to win elections and capture control of the government.

Republicans also enjoyed an intangible advantage because of a curious and inexplicable difference from Democrats discovered by the polling of the Survey Research Center of the University of Michigan. Their investigation into the election of 1952 revealed that, in every classification of voters — whether as to income, education, or vocation — Republicans were "very much interested" in the election while a larger percentage of Democrats of all social levels were less willing than Republicans to say they "cared a good deal which party won." Moreover, Republicans had an immense advantage in their control of the media of mass communication — the press, radio, television, and billboards — through ownership as well as ample funds with which to purchase these services. This also tended to compensate for the Republican Party's minority status. Under all these handicaps, then, the Democratic Party suffered from the difficulties of getting out the vote and mobilizing its full potential voting strength.[55]

Nineteen fifty-seven was a critical year for the Democratic Party. President Eisenhower had asked for civil-rights legislation to protect the Negroes' voting rights as prescribed by state laws. Both major parties were deeply concerned over this legislation because the Negro vote held the balances of power in populous pivotal states, and since it could determine the outcome of presidential elections, both major parties were bidding for the Negro vote. The Republicans seemed to hold the advantage because they could support the proposal solidly, but the Democrats found their Southern members, in both houses, resolutely opposed to civil-rights legislation. Under the leadership of Senator Richard B. Russell of Georgia the original bill had been whittled down and confined to the Negroes' voting rights, and Senator Russell had even succeeded in getting the bill amended so as to require a jury trial in criminal injunctions against state officials attempting to interfere with Negroes' voting rights.

It was the astute diplomacy of Majority Leader Senator Lyndon Johnson of Texas that persuaded the Southern Democrats to forego filibustering and to permit the watered-down Civil Rights Bill to pass. He convinced them that proponents of the bill were prepared to clamp down closure on a filibuster. Moreover, he argued that if this bill were defeated, a stronger one was likely to be enacted at the next session of

---

[55] See "The Case of the Missing Democrats," by Angus Campbell, Director of the Survey Research Center of the University of Michigan, in the *New Republic*, July 2, 1956, pp. 12–15.

Congress. Senator Johnson had thus prevented a split in the Democratic Party, and no sooner had he consummated his design of party harmony than he was widely hailed as a statesman of presidential caliber and a potential Democratic candidate in 1960. Senator Johnson did indeed travel extensively in the West getting pledges of delegates to supplement those from the South that fell to him quite naturally. So adroit was he at the game that, ten days before the 1960 Democratic National Convention was called to order, he had pledged to him an estimated total of 502½ delegates as compared to Kennedy's estimated total of 602½.

Ever since John F. Kennedy had been elected to Congress in 1946, Harvard professors had been providing him with ideas, information, and analyses of national issues. By January 1960 he had mobilized his Harvard brain trust to feed appropriate material to him and his speech writers. When Kennedy began his primary campaign for the presidential nomination in Wisconsin, he had already accumulated a nucleus of 114 pledged New England delegates. Of the sixteen states with presidential primaries, Kennedy entered seven while his rival, Senator Hubert Humphrey, entered five. These two met head-on in Wisconsin. Kennedy won with 56 per cent of the state-wide primary vote of Wisconsin, but he had lost in all four of the Protestant districts. At once he recognized that this victory was not spectacular enough to impress the city bosses who would control the delegations of the great pivotal states. In competition with Humphrey again, he entered the West Virginia primary, where he played to the limit the game of politics in which he had been born and nurtured. Adequately financed, he assiduously cultivated the county courthouse bosses, the key to West Virginia politics, and by primary election day an estimated 9,000 volunteer Kennedy workers were busy at some task or other. Senator Humphrey, operating on a financial shoestring, withdrew on election night with the public statement: "I am no longer a candidate for the Democratic presidential nomination." [56]

[56] Theodore H. White: *The Making of the President, 1960,* p. 108.

Hunger was a poignant problem of this depressed coal-mining state where children were bringing their school lunches home to feed their hungry parents. Kennedy, who had never known privation, was appalled at being in the midst of human beings who had to eat and live on cans of dried relief rations. One night he remarked to one of his assistants: "Just imagine kids who never drink milk." He won friends right and left as he expressed burning indignation at the human misery in the mining fields.[57] As he campaigned, it is said, "the hill folks would gather, heirs to generations of bitter anti-Catholic feeling, and they would look at Kennedy and say, 'I don't know about voting against that young man. He reminds me of F.D.R.'"[58] In one precinct with only 25 Catholic voters registered, Kennedy got 96 votes to Humphrey's 36. Kennedy's signal victory in Protestant West Virginia was sensational and Kennedy was now on his way. He won the primaries in every state he entered.

At the Democratic Convention Senator Johnson refused to be brushed aside and made it clear that he was indeed in earnest as an aspirant for the nomination. He endorsed the strong civil rights plank adopted by the convention and promised to "campaign all over the United States on the platform" as "I have always done."[59] On the second day of the Convention, in a television debate with Kennedy, Johnson highlighted the latter's uncertain position on civil rights. Thus Johnson said: "There are two things to consider about civil rights. One is to talk about it in a political platform. The other is to do something about it. Under my leadership, after 80 years of futility, two civil rights bills have been passed in three years. And let me say if we protect a man's right to vote he will protect himself better than you can.

"There were 45 roll calls on civil rights in recent months. Lyndon Johnson answered every one of them. I know sena-

[57] Ibid., p. 106.
[58] Martin Agronsky, Eric F. Goldman, Sidney Hyman, Barbara Ward, Wallace Westfield, and Ira Wolfert: *The First Hundred Days of the Kennedy Administration*, p. 12.
[59] John D. Morris: *New York Times*, July 13, 1960.

tors who missed as many as 34 of those roll calls. You may ask why I did not get into this campaign earlier. I was not paid to neglect my duty." No one could miss whom Johnson referred to as missing 34 roll calls on civil rights while collecting his salary as Senator. But Johnson's vigorous drive was all in vain. The real threat to Kennedy's nomination turned out to be Adlai E. Stevenson, supported by scarcely any pledged delegates but by emotionally impelled enthusiasts. This time Stevenson had not run in the primaries. With a vivid memory of it all, he shrank from the grueling brutality of such pre-convention politics as he had endured in order to defeat Kefauver in the 1956 primaries and win his second nomination. But now Stevenson seemed to be insisting on a draft.

Kennedy was assured of somewhat more than 600 delegates before the Convention opened, with 761 required to win the nomination. The city bosses were quite naturally somewhat concerned over Kennedy's apparent independence, while the ordinary delegates were doubtful about this youthful aspirant to the presidency in an epoch of persisting world crises. If Kennedy could manage to get 700 votes on the first ballot, there would be no contest.

The strategy of Kennedy's managers was to hold his delegates firm while whittling down the big delegations not pledged to him. The Stevenson men hoped to keep the five big delegations from breaking until there was a chance for their favorite. But Stevenson had remained undecided too long. Tuesday afternoon he took his seat among the Illinois delegates, whereupon he received a thunderous ovation. Wednesday, as the nominating speeches dragged on, an immense throng of Stevenson enthusiasts gathered outside the Convention Hall and seemed so threatening that extra police were called to prevent them from crashing into the Convention. They were hoping to perpetrate a "Willkie blitz" and thereby make Stevenson the Democratic candidate for President. A big well-rehearsed claque in the galleries created the noisiest demonstration of the Convention. But what finally determined Stevenson's fate was the answer he got on his telephone call to Boss Daley of Chicago, head of the Illinois delegation. He was told that he was without support in his own state delegation. The upshot of it all was Kennedy's nomination on the first ballot.

Only rather recently had it become customary for a presidential nominee to designate his choice of a running mate. So bitter had been the clash between John Kennedy and Lyndon Johnson for the nomination that, when Kennedy turned to Johnson as his choice for the vice-presidency, it occasioned breath-taking astonishment. Kennedy had accepted as settled Johnson's declaration that he would never, never, *never* trade his senatorial vote for the Vice President's gavel. But the morning after Kennedy had won his nomination for the presidency, a hurried conference of his closest advisers calculated that, in order to be elected President, he would need electoral votes not only from the South but also some from the Midwest which Johnson might help win for the party ticket.

Curiously enough, Johnson let it slyly leak out that he actually wanted the vice-presidential nomination. He had conferred with his friends, one of whom observed that his power would be far less as Vice President than as Majority Leader, whereupon the extraordinarily self-confident Lyndon Johnson casually remarked: "Power is where power goes." When the rumor that Johnson wanted the vice-presidential nomination reached Kennedy, he paid Johnson a visit, got confirmation of the rumor, and offered him the place on the ticket which was promptly accepted. One of Kennedy's staff commented: "It was always anticipated that we'd offer Lyndon the nomination. What we never anticipated was that he'd accept." [60]

Kennedy calculated that Johnson's name on the ticket would counter-balance anticipated inroads of Nixon in the South on account of the Democratic platform's unqualified advocacy of civil rights. Northern Democratic liberals and especially Kennedy's family grumbled, recalling the recent acid comments of Johnson on Kennedy's equivocal record on

[60] Theodore H. White: op. cit., p. 174.

civil rights. Johnson's nomination for the vice-presidency however went through the Convention by acclamation. The Democratic Convention wound up with Kennedy's acceptance speech, in the midst of which he said: "We stand today on the edge of a new frontier — the frontier of the 1960's. . . . Are we up to the task? Are we equal to the challenge? Are we willing to match the Russian sacrifice of the present for the future? . . . That is the choice our nation must make . . . between the public interest and private comfort — between national greatness and national decline."

Before Kennedy could begin his full-fledged campaign for the presidency, he had to resume his Senate seat in the post-Convention rump session of Congress, where he expected to get enacted legislation to "implement his program for the campaign and thereby reinforce his drive to win the presidency." With nearly a two-thirds Democratic majority in both House and Senate, this looked possible, especially with that wizard of legislative management, his running-mate Lyndon Johnson, still functioning as Majority Floor Leader of the Senate. But it turned out that not even Johnson's name on the ticket could assuage the bitterness of Southern Senators and Representatives in Congress over the all-out civil-rights plank in the Democratic platform. These Southern legislators, in a coalition with Conservative Republicans, mutilated Senator Kennedy's bill for raising minimum wages from $1.00 to $1.25 an hour and extending the law's coverage to an additional 5,000,000 workers. The bill squeezed through the Senate only after sacrificing coverage of nearly a million of the poorest-paid workers, after which the bill was pigeonholed by the Rules Committee of the House. Kennedy's plan for medical care for the aged was countered by Vice President Nixon's opposition to compulsory medical care, and such a bill would have run the risk of a veto by President Eisenhower if it had been passed. By the third week of the rump session and after the Senate's rejection of the medical bill by a vote of 62 to 28, Kennedy expressed his exasperation by commenting that if Congress couldn't pass "decent bills" on medical care and minimum wages, it "might as well go home." The school-aid bill also failed to be enacted. President Eisenhower, at a news conference, remarked that "the Democrats have a 2 to 1 majority in Congress" and "can do anything they want if they can get together." The Republicans, apparently taking their cue from Truman's deadly phrase in the 1948 campaign, "the do-nothing Congress," phrased one of their own for 1960, "the do-little Congress." The sabotaging of Kennedy's legislative program, due to the defection of Southern Democrats, was now complete, and managers of the Democratic campaign decided that, since the Republican candidate was already busy campaigning, the best way to compensate for their legislative disaster would be to adjourn Congress and get their candidate out campaigning instead of being tied down to his Senate seat on a hopeless legislative program. By the end of the session of Congress where all of Kennedy's legislative program had been rejected, the Gallup Poll showed Nixon ahead 53 to 47 per cent. The odds were decidedly against Kennedy when he began campaigning, worn out and discouraged, "his voice rapid and rushed as if trying to make up for lost time." His early campaign speeches contained such conventional phrases as "the importance of the Presidency"; "the world cannot exist half slave and half free"; "only the President can lead"; "we must move"; "I ask your help"; "If you are tired and don't want to move stay with the Republicans." The first ten days were discouraging. However, before the end of August, Kennedy had become aggressive. "Mr. Nixon has presided over . . . the decline of our national security," he said, and in Detroit Kennedy declared that "our security and leadership are both slipping away from us." The central issue of the campaign soon boiled down to the question as to which of the two candidates was better prepared to deal with the problems posed by Russia.

Early in September, Kennedy was confronted with the issue raised by his religion. A group, presided over by Reverend Norman Vincent Peale, had emerged bearing the name, The National Conference of Religious Freedom. It issued a statement that the Catholic Church "is a political as well as a religious organization and has in the United States repeatedly attempted to break down the wall between church and state." Kennedy chose to meet the religious issue thus raised. In a speech before the Greater Houston Ministerial Association he said: "I believe in an America where the separation of church and state is absolute . . . where no public official either requests or accepts instructions on public policy from . . . any ecclesiastical source." His forthright manner won him heavy applause from the Protestant group he addressed, which, however, did not signify that he had, to any extent, captured the Protestant vote.

In the last week of September a report came from the South indicating that the civil-rights plank had not alienated the Democratic Party in that section quite as much as had been suggested by the attitude of Southern Democratic Senators and Representatives toward the Kennedy legislative program in the post-Convention session of Congress. Ten of the eleven Governors attending a conference of Southern Governors abandoned a previously lukewarm stand toward Mr. Kennedy and announced their support of him.

But Senator Kennedy's failure to clarify his position as to McCarthyism was to plague him during as it had before the 1960 campaign. In 1956, when he was aspiring to the vice-presidency, Mrs. Eleanor Roosevelt had put the matter up to him with the statement: "I am concerned about your failure to have taken a position on McCarthy." To this Kennedy replied: "It was a political necessity in my Senate race not to speak out against him." That this did not satisfy Mrs. Roosevelt was indicated promptly by her acid comment: "It's been some time since you were elected." Later, concerning the same criticism, he is alleged to have asked: "What was I supposed to do — commit hari kari?" [61]

In a CBS televised interview with Walter Cronkite, September 20, 1960, two questions, designed to discover Kennedy's position on McCarthyism, elicited only obscure responses. Few Republicans on the stump could have given a much harsher judgment as to Kennedy's qualifications for

[61] An interview with Irwin Ross in the *New York Post*, July 31, 1956.

the presidency than what Mrs. Roosevelt had published in 1958 — that White House decisions ought not to depend on "someone who understands what courage is and admires it but has not quite the independence to have it." [62] When in Appleton, McCarthy's home town, during the Wisconsin primary campaign, Kennedy was asked by a questioner in the audience to comment on Mrs. Roosevelt's judgment of him, he replied testily: "I am not ready to accept any indictment from you or Mrs. Roosevelt on that score." [63]

Kennedy continued a hard-hitting campaign to the end. During the Eisenhower years, the nation is "moving from crisis to crisis" and showing "a tendency to react instead of act," he said. He hammered hard for weeks on the theme that "Cuba is a Communist outpost the Administration has allowed to rise only ninety miles from the United States mainland." Only a week before election, Kennedy said that one of the things he would do as President would be to create "a peace corps" of young Americans to work abroad, giving technical and other aid to underdeveloped nations. While in his first television debate with Nixon he had created an almost astounding impression, in the final one he made a proposal concerning aid to anti-Castro forces that came near foreshadowing the ill-fated Cuban fiasco of 1961. Nixon promptly scored by pointing out that this would violate our treaty obligations not to interfere in the internal affairs of other nations.

By the end of the campaign Kennedy had traveled 75,000 miles and campaigned in 44 states. But far more significant than the campaigning had been the televised debates which had enabled Kennedy to become as well known as Vice President Nixon. He was thereby enabled to publicize his policies and counteract the impression that he was too immature for the presidency. His Catholicism alienated rather fewer Protestants than had been expected and the 80 per cent support of Catholics, concentrated as they are so largely in the great cities of the pivotal states, assured him the electoral votes

---

[62] Eleanor Roosevelt: On My Own, pp. 163–4.
[63] James MacGregor Burns: John Kennedy: A Political Profile, p. 154.

to win. Negroes, Jews, and labor, likewise concentrated in the same cities, also supported him overwhelmingly. Kennedy was fortunate in having as his running mate Lyndon Johnson, who, as expected, employed his magic among Southern politicians to save most of the electoral votes of the South for the Democratic ticket.

Democratic National Chairman Henry M. Jackson declared that "the biggest single factor in Mr. Nixon's defeat was Mr. Nixon getting into . . . the debates." And when Kennedy was asked, after the election, if he would have won without the debates he replied: "I don't think so."

CHAPTER XVI

MODERN REPUBLICANISM

AFTER the loss of five successive presidential elections it looked as if the most deceptive experience the Republican Party ever had was during the decade of its apparent invincibility — the 1920's. Unfortunately it had recovered control of the national government in 1921 with no more precise purpose than a restoration of "normalcy," as hapless President Warren G. Harding expressed it. So in an era when economic society was experiencing a change unprecedented in the history of capitalism, no party ideology appropriate for dealing with the crisis of 1929 had emerged. For two long generations the Republican Party had attracted ambitious men seeking careers, and by the 1920's habits of conformity had become deeply ingrained in its dominant leadership. Far more than in the days of McKinley and Hanna serene satisfaction with the *status quo* colored party ideology and conduct as the vogue of the businessman attained its apogee. By this time natural selection had evolved a type of Republican leadership prepared to govern in a presumably static society, but bewildered in the 1930's by one suddenly become intensely dynamic. Not a trace was visible of that exhilarating crusading spirit that had marked the birth of the Republican Party in the stirring days of the 1850's. It was now even threatened with the palsying conservatism that had doomed the Whig Party to death. It was indicative of a veritable abdication of competent Republican leadership when President Truman in 1948 was permitted to maneuver the party into a corner where it was made to appear anti-labor, anti-farmer, anti-consumer, anti-conservation, and indeed almost anti-everything required to command the support of a winning group combination such as the Republican Party unquestionably had constituted in its great days. It remains to be seen how it was extricated from that corner.

Republican leadership was slow to perceive that the time had come to shift from the strategy of sections to the strategy of interest-group diplomacy. No longer was it the question of carrying the East, the West or the prairies; it had become fundamentally a matter of winning youth and labor and the urban vote. The reverse of the party trend of the city vote in the 1920's had been unperceived by Republican politicians. The cities were overwhelmingly for Harding in 1920. By 1924, however, the urban anti-Republican trend had set in and by 1928 it had attained flood tide despite the Hoover landslide.[1] Republican leadership had once been realistic enough to know that party politics functions on the basis of *quid pro quo,* no matter how much sentiment might be spilled over saving the nation and freeing the slave. Thus in the post-Civil War decades the Republican Party had built up an almost invincible group combination by giving away the public domain to farmers, laborers, railroad builders, and the lumber, cattle, and mining interests, all of which prevailing public opinion sanctioned as a matter of course. This may not have been a whit more idealistic than Franklin Roosevelt's still more effective program of capturing the support of the middle and lower income families by ministering to their dire needs in the decade of the Great Depression. Now that the public domain was practically gone, nothing remained but to play the game of party politics in accordance with mid-twentieth-century circumstance. This meant entering into a competitive game for recruits among the groups that constitute the electorate. This is precisely what President Eisenhower's programs were designed to do.

It is one of the tragedies of the Republican Party that, despite its origin as a champion of free labor, despite the fact that Republican legislators in Republican states were pioneers in enacting early labor legislation, despite the party's

---

[1] See Samuel J. Eldersveld: "The Influence of Metropolitan Pluralities in Presidential Elections since 1920: a Study of Twelve Key Cities," *Am. Pol. Sci. Rev.*, Vol. XLIII, No. 6, pp. 1189–1206.

command of the loyalty of industrial and especially union labor under McKinley's, Hanna's, and Theodore Roosevelt's party leadership, the party permitted itself by mid-century to be maneuvered into an apparently anti-labor position by elements within the party which provided relatively few votes. This defect was intensified by the "unholy alliance," as some one called it, between the Republican Old Guard and the intensely anti-labor Bourbon Democracy of the South. Whatever the merits of the Taft-Hartley Act when the Eightieth (Republican) Congress enacted it, the legislation became a loaded symbol that enabled President Truman to emphasize the Republican Party's anti-labor reputation.

For the first time in its history the Republican Party was without the advantage of party leadership in the White House for an interval of twenty years. Its titular party chieftains in the persons of former presidential candidates — Landon, Willkie, and Dewey — were one after another disavowed by the dominant Republican Senators and Representatives in Congress as too "New Dealish," as one of them expressed it. In the consequent absence of an authentic party spokesman and national leader the voting record of Republicans in Senate and House became nearly the only evidence of party purposes and this, under analysis, became almost anything else than an appeal to a cross section of the nation. The recognized Republican leadership in Congress came necessarily from the one-party, safe Republican constituencies representing the dominant conservative local interests. These Congressmen were inevitably committed to the support of narrow, local instead of broad, national policies. Never before in its history had the Republican Party been so long reduced to this unfortunate extremity. When the party, in 1946, captured a majority in Congress its experience of sixteen years as "the opposition" handicapped it, and its legislative product apparently enabled President Truman to convince a majority of the voters in 1948 that it was the "worst Congress in our history."

When the Republicans captured Congress in 1946 they naturally assumed that the grand prize of the presidency would be easily theirs in 1948. Not in decades had an administration lost the mid-term elections without losing the ensuing presidential election. Truman's prestige had declined from its initial high point to a low level as corruption appeared here and there among the administrative personnel. The conviction of Alger Hiss and the communist activities of others were utilized by Republican campaigners to discredit the administration. So certain of victory were Republicans in 1948 that scarcely more than a pretense of a campaign was conducted by Republican candidate Dewey. Meanwhile, one of the outstanding leaders of the Republican Party was rising to eminence in the person of Senator Robert A. Taft. Although he was conservative in his political and social philosophy and emphatically anti-New Deal, his mind was not closed to evidence on current issues, as is shown by his switch to support of aid for public housing and education by the federal government. By 1950 he was unquestionably the outstanding Senator of either party and, by common consent, had been dubbed "Mr. Republican." Although he had been re-elected Senator in 1944 by a margin of only a few thousand votes his re-election in 1950 by a majority of 437,000 instantly made him look like the logical Republican candidate for President in 1952.

The Taft men's hope of a clear field or easy victory was dashed by a public statement of Governor Dewey in October 1951, in which he declined to seek a third nomination, but recommended Dwight D. Eisenhower, then president of Columbia University, for the Republican nomination. Exactly a year later Senator Taft announced his decision to enter the presidential primaries. In January 1952 General Eisenhower's name was filed in the New Hampshire preference primaries. Stassen was again an active aspirant. By the time the delegates convened for the 1952 Republican National Convention Taft had 458 and Eisenhower 408 uncontested delegates.

Never was there a better opportunity for a case study of the dynamics of nominating a presidential candidate than the Taft-Eisenhower competition in the 1952 Republican

Convention. From beginning to end the Taft organization played the game of professional party politics according to the standard Republican book of rules. Taft arrived at the convention with an aggregate of pledged delegates so imposing as to make plausible his prediction of nomination on the first ballot. His organization had control of the National Committee. The Republican national chairman, Taft's own man, called the convention to order and presided during the long controversy over the rules. A Taft man was temporary chairman and instead of following the precedent of having him also deliver the keynote speech, still another avowed Taft man, General Douglas MacArthur, made that speech. The program was packed with Taft speakers. The committees were loaded with Taft men and this was especially significant with respect to the credentials committee. Herbert Brownell, a former Republican national chairman and an Eisenhower supporter, was even denied a seat on the platform. To the routine politician of a passing generation the set-up looked like a cinch — Taft's nomination was surely in the bag. But the Taft organization, the Old Guard of the Republican Party, might well have recalled that ancient proverb: Whom the gods would destroy they first make mad — with power.

The serenity of the Old Guard was suddenly shaken as by a bomb. It consisted of a challenge in the form of a statement and a demand signed by 23 of the 25 Republican governors, all of those, in fact, who were in attendance at the Governors' Conference at Houston, Texas. Here was a countermove issuing from the grass roots of the Republican Party, for a majority of the states had Republican governors, each carrying the prestige of one who had defeated a Democratic competitor. The average age of these twenty-five Republican governors was only 50; two of them were barely 40 and only four were older than 53. Warren at 61 was, in fact, the oldest of the lot. Significantly enough, ten or eleven of them were young enough never to have had the opportunity to cast a ballot for a winning Republican presidential candidate. So the group was appropriately enough denominated the New

Guard. Observers at the Republican Convention noted that, in contrast with the Old Guard, they quite naturally looked young. Moreover they represented an emerging new Republican Party mood.

The twenty-three Republican governors meeting at Houston all signed the historic statement urging that no delegate whose credentials were in question be permitted to vote on the disputed credentials of any delegate. But the Old Guard, in order to maintain its grip on the convention, absolutely needed to retain the votes of the 68 delegates who would be barred by such a change of the rule. The vote pro and con on this issue was recognized at once as an Eisenhower-Taft vote, and the adoption of the governors' "fair play" amendment to the rules by a margin of 110 staggered the Old Guard, and as the event proved, ensured the nomination of General Eisenhower. As the Old Guard's power was based so largely on delegates from the South, the border states, and the territories and possessions, which as a whole contributed almost no Republican electoral votes, the governors' triumph meant the recapture of the Republican organization by the Republican states — at any rate, by those that had elected Republican governors.

The breaking of the grip of the Old Guard by the Eisenhower forces was by no means something that just happened. It was not at all enough that — as the opinion polls revealed — Eisenhower was popular with the rank and file of Republican voters. The art of persuasion by sheer reasoning was so futile as to have been scarcely relied on at all. As in every hotly contested convention battle it was politics — and power politics, at that — which counted. Party politics inevitably involves patronage, and in the Taft-Eisenhower tug-of-war, patronage was not only a dynamic element. It was by all means the decisive one. Practiced politicians, the pro-Eisenhower governors knew well the art of utilizing patronage as a fulcrum of power, and in holding their delegations in line "they spared neither the carrot nor the goad," as Doris Fleeson put it. The only patronage available to the governors, of course, was state patronage, as Republicans had enjoyed no federal patronage for most of a generation. However, we shall see that potential federal patronage, dependent on the election of a Republican President, was no mean factor in convention dynamics. Senator Taft recognized the threat of state patronage when he stated that one of his greatest handicaps was the opposition of the Republican governors fortified by their control of state jobs. It is no exaggeration to say that state patronage eventually broke the impasse between Taft and Eisenhower and determined the nomination of the latter.

The coyness of Governor John S. Fine of Pennsylvania during the first days of the convention, his pretense that he had not yet made up his mind, made the desperate competition of Taft and Eisenhower leaders for his delegation a conspicuous example of the political dynamics of a national convention. In bidding for Fine's support both camps sought to dazzle him with prospects of a place in the cabinet, an ambassadorship, or even the vice-presidency. The Eisenhower leaders offered him the role of kingmaker in giving him the opportunity to make the speech nominating General Eisenhower. But most astounding of all was the alleged offer to Fine of the federal patronage that would be due Pennsylvania if Eisenhower became President. Now, this particular patronage is one of the most cherished perquisites of a Senator and as such would belong by immemorial precedent to the Republican Senators of Pennsylvania. Senator Duff of Pennsylvania was an ardent Eisenhower man, and though no longer a friend of Governor Fine, he was urged to relinquish his right to this potential patronage in order to ensure Fine's delivery of Pennsylvania delegates to Eisenhower. To this arrangement Senator Duff was said to have consented. At any rate, Governor Fine delivered the delegates he controlled, both on the "fair play" amendment to the rules and in the ballot on the nominees, where they may be considered as having been practically decisive for Eisenhower's nomination.

Since a Democratic politician need not mince words in commenting on Republican practices, Mayor David Lawrence of Pittsburgh declared that Governors Dewey of New York, Fine of Pennsylvania, and Driscoll of New Jersey "whipped and threatened their delegates into nominating Eisenhower." Scarcely anything in the convention was more impressive than Dewey's almost 100-per-cent command of the New York delegation despite the Taft hope and expectation of getting about twenty votes among the New York City delegates. It was no delicate hint when Dewey at the very start of the convention reminded his delegation that he would still be Governor for two and one half years and that he had "a long memory." He is said to have called to the New York delegates' attention the jobs that had been allocated to each delegate's district and asserted that there could be new appointees two days after his return to Albany. Thus the state jobs of each delegate's neighbors and even relatives hung on his following faithfully Dewey's signals during the balloting.

The time came when Governor Dewey held a press conference in order to announce that two New York delegates who had strayed to Taft had been brought back into the Eisenhower camp. One television close-up of the convention revealed Governor Dewey announcing New York's 95 to 1 vote for the Eisenhower "fair play" amendment to the rules. Nor need Governor Dewey's tactics be regarded as too far from the typical practice with respect to patronage, although there may have been more finesse and less of the battle-ax among other governors in the management of their delegations. The exasperated Taft leaders let loose a torrent of abuse against Governor Dewey. Frustrated Senator Taft can even be pardoned for denouncing his tactics as "gutter politics." But this only left wide open the door of opportunity for Dewey's comment on Taft's remark. The Governor merely said: "I never abuse a fellow Republican." The Convention nominated General Dwight D. Eisenhower as its candidate for President on the first ballot and then made his personal choice for running mate, Senator Richard M. Nixon, the Republican candidate for Vice President.

The battles of the 1952 Republican Convention had been

between the partisans of two gigantic personalities. By contrast the conflicts of the Democratic Convention consisted of the competing power drives of three or four resolute factions. The "liberal" Northern city wing included the partisans of the New Deal-Fair Deal policies. Leaders of this group were Senator Herbert Lehman and Congressman Franklin D. Roosevelt, both of New York, whose favorite for the presidency was W. Averell Harriman. Affiliated with this group were the supporters of another presidential aspirant, Senator Estes Kefauver, and such aggressive New Dealers as Senator Hubert Humphrey of Minnesota, and Senator Blair Moody and Governor G. Mennen Williams of Michigan. The right-wing faction of the convention consisted of the legatees of the old Bourbon Democracy of the South, the unreconstructed Dixiecrats, chief among whom were Governor James F. Byrnes of South Carolina, and Governor John S. Battle and Senator Harry E. Byrd of Virginia. Also representing the South was a "progressive" faction led by Senators Richard B. Russell of Georgia, John Sparkman of Alabama, and Russell Long of Louisiana, all of whom had been supporters of the New Deal domestic policies. Their presidential favorite was Senator Russell. Besides these three quite distinct groups there was a large number of delegates who might be designated the moderates. They were committed to no avowed candidate, but were eager to retain the patronage and power inherent in the presidency and were consequently in passionate search of a candidate who might be able to defeat Eisenhower. Governor Adlai Stevenson of Illinois would be acceptable to them.

The Harriman forces promptly devised a plan to prevent any state delegation from repeating the Dixiecrat strategy of 1948, by which four states had used the Democratic label in such a way as to prevent any voter in those states from having any opportunity to vote for the nominee of the Democratic Convention. To this end the Harriman delegates prepared for introduction a resolution that would require all the state delegations to pledge in advance to support the nominee of the convention. It was assumed that such a move would make so secure the hold of the Democratic Party on the Northern elements of the Roosevelt-Truman group combination that a Democratic candidate could be elected without the support of a single Southern electoral vote. "Let the South go" became the war cry of the Harriman faction. If this resolution could be sprung suddenly and rushed through while the convention was in the process of getting organized, it might set the seal of the New Deal securely on the Democratic Party, check the Stevenson movement, give a boost to Harriman's candidacy, and ensure a New Deal platform.

It was past midnight of the first day of the convention — which had been confined to preliminaries — and adjournment seemed imminent when Senator Blair Moody sprang the resolution requiring the pledge and supported it with an eloquent speech. The Southern delegates demanded a roll call, which was denied by the temporary chairman, who put the resolution to a voice vote and declared it carried. The Harriman delegates were jubilant over the setback to the Stevenson move, but the politicians were alarmed over a threatened split of the party.

On the second day of the convention the Harriman faction was becoming worried enough to propose watering down the pledge with a proviso that no delegate need sign it in contravention of the laws of his state or the instructions of his state committee. This compromise pledge was overwhelmingly approved by the delegates to the joy of the Stevenson forces and the dismay of the Harriman and Kefauver delegates. By Wednesday morning, however, the Virginia, South Carolina, and Louisiana delegates were refusing to take even the watered-down pledge. The chair ruled that consequently they might not vote, but were permitted to sit. When Governor Battle of Virginia assured the convention that the nominees of the convention would be on the ballot in Virginia a roll-call vote on a motion to permit the Virginia delegates to vote failed to receive a majority, the Illinois delegation voting in the negative. But before the very deliberate chairman had announced the result the Illinois delegation switched its vote. This ensured passage of the motion and the cry at once arose that "Stevenson wants them in." The effect was electric and portentous of a decisive Stevenson trend. Presently the Louisiana and South Carolina delegates were also granted the voting privilege.

The balloting began Friday morning with Kefauver, Russell, Harriman, and Stevenson as the principal candidates. It was slowed down almost to a standstill at times by the almost interminable polling of state delegations, a tactic of the Kefauver managers, who hoped for time to win over uncommitted delegates. Harriman, the outstanding New Dealer, dropped out and threw his votes to Stevenson. As Stevenson's stock rose the vice-presidency became the key to the outcome, but Stevenson resolutely refused to make any deals. The factions were now seeking the precise moment when switching their delegates to Stevenson would ensure his nomination and give them a place of power behind the throne if he should be elected. On the third ballot Stevenson obtained a majority and his nomination was presently made "unanimous." Senator Sparkman, a Southern liberal, became the vice-presidential nominee. Thus an almost incredible semblance of Democratic Party harmony was obtained after paroxysms of belligerency.

The nomination of Governor Stevenson was a genuine draft. Four years before he had led a forlorn hope as a candidate for Governor of Illinois and won an astonishing victory, running far ahead of Truman. He had made an exceptional record as Governor, and, a candidate for re-election at the time of the convention, he insisted that he needed to finish his job by serving another term. He had absolutely refused to participate in the competition for delegates in the state primaries, and only in response to the most persistent pressures after the delegates gathered and the logic of events unfolded did he consent to be considered by the convention. He had a reputation as a moderate, and it was hoped that he might unite the right and left wings and the other elements of the Democratic Party.

By mid-August the assumption that Stevenson's nomination had reconciled the elements of the Democratic Party was accepted by both major parties and the South was being written off as solidly Democratic. The Eisenhower managers consequently planned a strong drive for the Negro vote. This was based on the prevailing opinion that the Negro vote could throw the election to either candidate through the balances of power it held in a number of states with large electoral votes.[2] The Eisenhower organization issued a statement that a vote for Eisenhower would speed an FEPC with "adequate" enforcement power. Senator Lehman promptly denounced the Republican claim as a fraud and Stevenson could "hardly see how the Negro vote would find a refuge in the Republican party."[3] Most Negroes, however, seemed unhappy over the civil-rights plank of the Democratic platform and were threatening to boycott the election of 1952. Stevenson was being counseled to go strong on civil rights so that the ethnic, religious, and economic groups might be held securely in the Democratic group coalition. Meanwhile, Eisenhower was being urged to condemn racial and religious prejudice, but was cautioned never again to liken social security to life in a prison, as he had once done, and instead to promise increased payments to the aged. Nevertheless, Eisenhower had been confining his speeches so largely to generalities that just when the campaign was formally opening a Republican newspaper published the dismal observation "Ike is running like a dry creek."

The campaign opened formally on Labor Day, as usual, and the intense activities of both presidential candidates during the first week set the tempo of the entire campaign of 1952. After a Labor Day speech to 2,000 New York mail carriers Eisenhower hurried South for two days of campaigning in Dixie. Skipping up to Philadelphia, he was greeted on Thursday by 350,000 people in the streets on his way to a formal speech in Independence Hall. On Friday he conferred with eighty Republican leaders in Chicago, where he said he would very much like to appoint a qualified Negro to

---

[2] See Henry Lee Moon: *Balance of Power: the Negro Vote* (Garden City, New York, 1949), Appendix IV.

[3] *New York Times*, August 10, 1952.

his cabinet. No more was heard of this as soon as the Democratic Solid South appeared to be cracking. On Saturday the General spoke at the National Plowing Contest at Kasson, Minnesota, where he took away the breath of the Republicans by apparently promising the farmers 100 per cent of parity instead of the legally prevailing 90 per cent. The Eisenhower who had admitted at a press conference in Denver a few weeks earlier that he had been advised to be very careful of what he said and how he said it had now found his stride as he blazed away at the "mess in Washington." Stevenson was pronounced the "hand picked candidate of the administration and the captive of its record."

Stevenson delivered Labor Day speeches in four Michigan cities. On Friday he delivered a televised address in Denver to the Volunteers for Stevenson, and on Saturday he spoke at the Kasson Plowing Contest. Meanwhile, President Truman, after a Labor Day speech in Milwaukee, delivered "give 'em hell," whistle-stop speeches on the way back to Washington. Stevenson was so impressed by them that he asked Truman to go whistle-stopping throughout the Far West and in industrial New England.

General Eisenhower proved to be an inept reader of prepared speeches and appeared at a disadvantage on television. Soon he was throwing aside the manuscript of the ghost writers and striking out extemporaneously. He was at ease in rear-car platform speeches where his language was plain, direct, and folksy. Before long he was declaring that the "wasters, the bunglers, the incompetent, the boss politicians must go. . . . If today the driver of the school bus runs into a truck and if tomorrow he hits a lamp post and if the next day he drives into a ditch you don't say, 'I like the bus driver; his intentions are good.' You get a new bus driver." In the South the crowds shouted "Ya hoo" and "Pour it on" when he said that Washington is full of men "too small for their jobs, too big for their breeches, and too long in power." But only stony silence greeted his mention of the equality of men regardless of color.

Sophisticated Adlai Stevenson contrasted sharply with

General Eisenhower as a campaigner. He expressed at the outset what proved to be a vain hope that the campaign would not degenerate into a free-for-all. His lucid expository speeches left some observers suspecting that he might be speaking over the heads of his audiences, but now and then there would crop out a flash of wit that set them laughing — not roaring. In reply to the Republican demand for a change he asked: "Change to what? Which party best understands the meaning of change in the modern world? Which party has anticipated the need for change and done something about it? Which party has resisted about every change in the past 25 years?" There were even Democrats who thought this line more appropriate for a class-room lecture than a stump speech.

On Wednesday of the week before the campaign opened Stevenson, addressing the annual gathering of the American Legion, gave a breath-taking demonstration of his forthrightness. He expressed his frank disapproval of groups "who seek to identify their special interests with the general welfare." When the legionnaires applauded he added: "I intend to resist pressures from veterans also." Time and again in this address he made thrusts fully as audacious. But observers noted that this speech was punctuated with applause very much more often than the one Eisenhower delivered the day before, despite the latter's absolute avoidance of anything that might ruffle the legionnaires.

Just before the formal campaign opened Stevenson, by his forthrightness, had already given the Republicans the opportunity by which they eventually broke the Solid South. He unequivocally asserted the paramount right of the federal government to the submerged coastal lands, advocated a compulsory FEPC for states that failed to outlaw racial discrimination, and supported modification of Senate Rule 22, which permitted filibustering against civil rights and other measures. Thus the door of opportunity opened wide early for Eisenhower's invasion of the South to make the most of the offshore oil issue.

In the light of later developments the opinion prevailing just after the conventions, that the character of the candidates ensured a high-level discussion of issues, looked strange. At the pre-convention gathering of Republican delegates in the Devers Brown Palace Hotel in Denver, Eisenhower had spoken out against the use of half-truths and slogans in the campaign. Stevenson had expressed similar high ideals about campaigning. But before the high-level campaign was a week old it was beginning to presage the bitterness that was to accelerate into downright recrimination. The stakes were too high and the interest groups involved too eager to win to permit a sober discussion of the issues. The campaign was reverting to type as party organizations proved more powerful than the ideals of the candidates, who were both to learn that a presidential campaign is not an educational program, but a stern struggle for power in which methods are shaped by the urge to win.

In the second week of the campaign the all-important concordat of Eisenhower with Taft was consummated. Immediately after the Republican Convention the vanquished candidate had repaired to the seclusion of his Canadian summer house. There he remained during seven weeks of silence while his partisans, embittered by memories of the charges of "steal" and "fraud" hurled at them during the convention fight over contested delegates, withheld full-hearted support of Eisenhower's candidacy. Meanwhile, the General's overtures — including a letter informing Taft he would like to talk over the campaign with him — were producing no results. Finally, at 7:30 a.m. on Friday, September 12, Taft called at Eisenhower's Columbia University home. He produced a written statement he had brought with him. Eisenhower did some penciling and additions were made. The two leaders agreed that the issue between the parties was "liberty against creeping socialism." They agreed on "drastic" reduction of federal spending and retention of the fundamental principles of the Taft-Hartley Law. Both were determined "to battle communism throughout the World and in the United States." Taft promptly urged all who had confidence in his principles to work for Eisenhower's election.

The pipe of peace had been smoked and in the event it proved highly significant. But the immediate consequences were not pleasant for the General. The public was in the dark as to just what had happened and the publicity had been so mismanaged by the Eisenhower organization as to leave the impression that the General as a supplicant had signed on the dotted line conditions dictated by Taft. The Democrats made the most of the opportunity. "I am beginning to wonder," said Stevenson, "who my opponent is. It looks as if Taft lost the nomination but won the nominee."

By the middle of September Southern Democracy was in open revolt against Stevenson. This was because of his stand in favor of FEPC, his stand against the Senate rule permitting filibustering, and especially his unequivocal statement to Governor Shivers of Texas against conveying the offshore oil rights to the states. A Texas Democratic convention first fulfilled its pledge to put Stevenson and Sparkman on the ticket and then voted to endorse Eisenhower and Nixon. Governor Earl K. Long of Louisiana repudiated Stevenson in favor of Eisenhower and 53,000 persons signed a petition that put Eisenhower on the ballot of that state. Governor James F. Byrnes of South Carolina delivered a 2,500-word blast against Stevenson for not repudiating President Truman, and Senator Byrd of Virginia maintained an ominous silence.

Scarcely had the partisans of Senator Taft been rallied around the Eisenhower standard than the revelation of an existing secret fund provided by friends for Senator Nixon before he had become a vice-presidential candidate temporarily demoralized the Republican high command. Reporters got the facts from Dana C. Smith, a California attorney who was chiefly responsible for raising the $18,235 fund and who said it was raised "because Dick Nixon is the best salesman against socialism . . . and government control of everything." It had been intended that Nixon, in campaigning, would concentrate on denunciation of corruption in the Truman administration — shady government loans to businessmen, tax-fraud cases "fixed," the "right" doors opened, influence "peddled," mink coats, and free vacation trips. Only a candidate with clean hands could conduct such a campaign. So damaging did the secret fund appear that New York's leading Republican paper, the *Herald Tribune*, declared that Nixon should make "a formal offer of withdrawal." It was recalled that Nixon only six months earlier had called for the resignation of both national party chairmen Guy Gabrielson and William Boyle when it was disclosed that they had both represented claimants before the Reconstruction Finance Corporation.

The revelation of the Nixon fund created consternation in the Republican organization and for two days the question was debated as to whether the Republican vice-presidential candidate should be dropped from the ticket. Eisenhower met the problem with the inevitable confusion of an inexperienced political leader. First he expressed confidence in Nixon's honesty. Then he followed with a statement to reporters that Nixon must come out of the affair "clean as a hound's tooth." He told the newsmen he would judge the affair solely on an ethical basis; that he would not be influenced by public clamor and would not decide on terms that would make the most votes. He declared he would make his decision after a conference with Nixon and then made it less than half an hour after meeting him. Under the circumstances it is difficult to dispel the impression that Eisenhower made his decision on the basis of expediency, which after all is a cardinal principle of practical politics.

The Democrats, exultant over the Republican predicament, had the tables suddenly turned on them by one of the most audacious coups in the history of American party campaigns. At 9:30 p.m. on Tuesday, September 23, Richard Nixon was seated with his wife at a table in a Hollywood radio and television studio to deliver from fragmentary scribbled notes a thirty-minute explanation of the "fund." It would have been wrong, he admitted, to have spent the money for personal use, but it was expended "to defray political expenses, I did not feel should be charged to the taxpayer." He followed with an apparently frank statement of his modest personal finances. Then in a bold counterstroke he demanded that the opposing candidates make a similar public accounting of their finances. Growing stern, he said: "This is not the last of the smears. . . . I intend to continue the fight." The decision was up to the Republican National Committee, and he asked his listening audience to write and help the committee make up its mind. This led to a deluge of more than 150,000 telegrams in two days. Indeed, it was possible in some localities to send such telegrams at the expense of the local party organization, which undoubtedly increased considerably the volume of telegrams.

Nixon's radio and television performance, embellished as it had been by touches of sentiment concerning his wife and even a pet dog, was judged all the way from "a masterpiece" to "soap opera." In the Cleveland auditorium where the television broadcast was watched by an audience waiting for Eisenhower's address, women were weeping as Nixon finished. The veteran political commentator Arthur Krock observed that the revelation of the fund had "put Nixon in a spotlight where his combative nature and a theatrical technique reminiscent of 'East Lynne' [the sobbiest of the old-fashioned melodramas] enabled him to put on a performance that drenched the soil of the United States with tears." [4] Nixon delayed flying to Eisenhower until the public response to the speech had poured in. When he reached the General thirty hours after the television address, Eisenhower put his arm around Nixon and said: "Why, you're my boy." Meanwhile, of 138 Republican national committeemen who could be reached, 107 had voted to retain Nixon on the ticket. The Republican campaign, which just then had been bogging down, received a shot in the arm. A strong emotional appeal had been provided.

The revelation of the Nixon fund had boomeranged on the hapless Democrats. To make matters worse, the Republicans

[4] *New York Times*, September 29, 1952.

turned up a hitherto unpublicized fund of Governor Stevenson. Unlike the Nixon fund, this was used to supplement the low salaries of some state officials who were not elective, who had no knowledge as to who were their benefactors and consequently were not subject to their influence. Now it was Governor Stevenson's turn to become confused. At first he refused to make public the names of contributors on the ground that it would be a "breach of faith." Some were even supporters of Eisenhower. But in his broadcast address Nixon had said, "Mr. Stevenson should . . . come before the American people as I have. . . . If [he doesn't] it will be an admission that [he has] something to hide." Meanwhile, rumors were building up Governor Stevenson's fund to fantastic figures. Eisenhower's chief adviser, Governor Sherman Adams, declared that Stevenson was "trying to brazen it out" and that "the American people would not let him get away with it and neither will we." Under the developing pressures Stevenson gave in and published a 1,000-word statement including an audit of the fund and the names of all the contributors and of the beneficiaries.

In a challenging counterstroke Stevenson next went beyond Nixon and published an accounting of his personal finances for the preceding ten years; the Democratic vice-presidential candidate did likewise. Confronted by these revelations of the personal finances of the Democratic candidates, Eisenhower's press secretary said that the General would also report. Presently Eisenhower was saying: "I don't think I am going to do anything about it. . . . I don't see why I should dance to the other fellow's tune." But he made the mistake of asking the newsmen "not to say anything about it." When the news of Eisenhower's refusal to report his finances leaked out it dawned upon the General that he had no choice about it and he, too, reported his income for the preceding ten years. Nixon alone refused to make a similar report, and since he had accumulated such an enormous surplus of personal prestige through his television act, the Democrats refrained from pressing the matter.

From the day of Stevenson's nomination a paramount

problem of his managers had been that while Eisenhower's face was familiar to every citizen, the Governor's was so relatively unknown that whenever a crowd awaited his appearance at a whistle stop the first person to come out on the platform was likely to be applauded as Stevenson. The problem was to make his name and face known to every voter in the land. Because of this the whistle-stop campaign, which had not been too successful, was used less. Instead, use was made of coast-to-coast television addresses enabling Stevenson to be seen and heard. Stevenson here proved more adept than Eisenhower because of his exceptional facility in presenting issues lucidly and directly.

As a campaigner Stevenson may have puzzled the common man, but he fascinated the intellectuals. Samuel Lubell even found some Eisenhower Republicans wishing their party had a candidate like Stevenson. The Governor's organization was said to be dominated by the universities. Professor A. M. Schlesinger, Jr., of the Harvard faculty, was his principal speech-writer. The Governor took great pains with his speeches, which were lively, imaginative, and at times audacious. At a Cincinnati luncheon, for example, amid Democratic notables, Stevenson was seen working furiously over his speech with pen in one hand and a glass of milk in the other. He was often engrossed in sharpening his thrusts of wit — such as his remark that the Republican Old Guard "had to be dragged kicking and screaming into the twentieth century" — while seated in a speeding airplane. "No presidential candidate in our time actually wrote so many speeches or so many good speeches as Governor Stevenson." [5] He was said to be counting on the quality of his speeches, and James Reston thought that if the electorate decided on that basis he should win by a landslide.[6] Stevenson was still referring to his "distinguished and honored opponent," but now in the middle of the campaign this courtesy was more likely to be merely the prelude to some such

---

[5] James Reston: "Our Campaign Techniques Re-examined," *New York Times Magazine*, November 9, 1952, p. 8.

[6] *New York Times*, October 8, 1952.

harsh judgment as that the Republicans in charge of Eisenhower's campaign could destroy "the last vestige of the New Deal," and "if elected, Eisenhower would be as powerless as President Harding." In his acceptance speech Stevenson had promised not to "run against Herbert Hoover," but long before the campaign closed one would have concluded that he believed a Republican victory would set us back to 1929.

It did not take the Republicans long to discover that Eisenhower was most effective speaking extemporaneously. He proved adept at the personal touch and appealed to the heart instead of the head. While Stevenson was polishing his phrases Eisenhower was mingling with the local politicians, who would carry to the end of their days poignant memories of his warm handshake and his sunny smile. Somehow the General conveyed to the crowds at the whistle stops a conviction of intense sincerity. They liked Ike even before they had seen him and one newsman noted the curious fact that he got more applause before he spoke than at the close. "When he utters the most obvious platitude," observed James Reston, "they look at that serious face as if they had heard something that ought to be graven on stone and passed on to the third and fourth generation." [7] Someone said he had lost the Shakespeare vote and it was no secret that the newsmen were simply appalled. "Where are we now?" inquired one as he looked out the window of a train speeding between whistle stops. "Crossing the thirty-eighth platitude," replied a sarcastic newsman. Eisenhower, however, was making headlines in the local papers no matter what he said.

Midway in the campaign the party organizations were impelled to accelerated activity by an opinion poll that reported half the electorate still undecided. Arthur Krock thought this deep silence may have induced the premature detonations of such bombs as the Nixon and Stevenson secret funds which are usually reserved for the last weeks of the campaign, when the injured party lacks time to repair

---

[7] *New York Times*, September 21, 1952.

the damage.[8] Responding to Stevenson's invitation, President Truman was busy whistle-stopping, but opinion was divided as to whether he was helping or harming the ticket. Stevenson needed to maintain a sufficient appearance of aloofness from the President to avoid the full odium of the "mess in Washington." But at a White House press conference President Truman insisted under prodding that he was the key to the campaign; that the Democratic Party had to run on the record of the Roosevelt and Truman administrations and that this was all it could run on. Out on the road the President was making sure there would be no back tracking and that Stevenson and Sparkman would not repudiate the President's record.

The consensus in the press car was that Truman was fighting much harder than he had in 1948. He was expounding the issues in greater detail and was fortified with more research material. He was apt at quoting the *Congressional Record* as it applied to the interests of the community where he was speaking. For example, in Iowa he countered Eisenhower's statement that the farm program originated on a "non-partisan basis" with a damaging recapitulation of Republican votes on farm legislation. At Devils Lake, North Dakota, he warned the farmers: "If you vote these fellows in, you probably won't have any R.E.A. [Rural Electrification Administration] cooperatives. These votes are just typical [a reference to Republican Congressional votes against rural projects]. Of course, the Republicans want you to forget that. Don't you let them mislead you. You keep your eye on your own interests, and let that pocketbook nerve of yours tell you what to do." [9]

No one suggested that Truman was talking over anyone's head. His speeches were well prepared, he was speaking better than in 1948, and he was in deadly earnest determined to knock the halo off the five-star general who, he said, had been away a long time and did not know much about gov-

---

[8] Arthur Krock: "Both Parties Exploding Their Bombs," *New York Times*, October 12, 1952.

[9] *New York Times*, October 5, 1952.

ernment. Eisenhower, said Truman, had become the unwitting tool of lobbyists representing interests ranging from electric power to China. The press noted that Truman's reception at the whistle stops and elsewhere was good and he did not look unattractive to his listeners. He showed his expertness at adapting his addresses to specific localities. Thus in Harlem he answered Eisenhower's promise made there to eliminate the remaining racial segregation in the army by calling to their attention the General's testimony before the Senate Committee recommending segregation at the lower organizational levels. Reporters accompanying the presidential candidates noted that many of the listeners left soon after Eisenhower or Stevenson began speaking, but that the President's audiences stayed for the duration of his speeches, possibly because of the way he "poured it on." Long before Election Day it was evident that Truman was dominating the Democratic campaign and influencing the positions taken by Stevenson.

On Thursday, October 2, something occurred that, for the time being, embarrassed Eisenhower almost as much as the Nixon affair. The General had arrived with his train at Peoria, Illinois, when Senator Joseph R. McCarthy, then probably the most controversial figure in American public life, turned up unannounced, and, it was widely suspected, uninvited. The Senator dined with the General and had what he pronounced a "very, very pleasant" talk with him. The following day McCarthy stayed on the train with everyone wondering what would happen next. The General's aid said the Senator would not introduce him in McCarthy's home town. Then that he would and finally that he would not. As it turned out McCarthy resolved the confusion by rushing out on the platform and introducing Eisenhower. At Green Bay Eisenhower had already said: "The differences between me and Senator McCarthy . . . have nothing to do with the end result that we are seeking. The differences apply to methods."

General Eisenhower's Milwaukee speech of October 3 created a sensation because of his omission of a passage found in copies previously distributed to the press. The deleted passage praised General George Marshall, whom Eisenhower admired and whose beneficiary he had so largely been. It was assumed, at the time, that the deletion had been made at the request of Senator McCarthy, who in a Senate speech had denounced General Marshall as "a front to traitors." Reading that passage would have constituted a striking repudiation of the Senator in his own state. Though it was not known at the time, the deletion was made at the request of Governor Kohler of Wisconsin, who desired merely to prevent a party crisis. But five days later, President Truman, speaking "with a solemn reasonableness that silenced an audience of several thousand people around his train at Colorado Springs denounced the deletion in the most emphatic terms." [10]

The uncertainty of the outcome up to the very counting of the ballots led the candidates to extremities certainly not contemplated at the beginning of the campaign. As the accusations grew sharper the crowds waxed larger. So far as the interests backing Eisenhower were concerned the stakes were so high that he was persuaded to go far indeed in exploiting his opportunities. It looked as if he would have to break the Solid South in order to win. Consequently in Texas and Louisiana he went the limit on the offshore oil issue. In his excitement he was calling President Truman's veto of the bills quitclaiming federal title to the offshore oil lands a "shoddy deal" and a "grab," terms difficult to reconcile with Supreme Court decisions. It was effective campaigning, however, and the big-city press of Texas came out overwhelmingly for Eisenhower. Correspondents reported that oil men, ranchers, and real-estate men were contributing heavily to his campaign. Governor Allan Shivers had obtained an opinion of his Attorney General that Texans could scratch out Stevenson's name on their ballots and write in Eisenhower's.

As Election Day drew near the extreme concern of the Republican organization as to the outcome was manifested in

[10] See Alistair Cooke: "Truman's Attack on Eisenhower," *The Manchester Guardian Weekly,* October 16, 1952, p. 3.

the intensive exploitation of the Korean issue. A month before
his nomination Eisenhower had said at Abilene: "I do not
have any prescription for bringing the thing to a decisive
end. . . . I believe we have to stand firm . . . to stand
right there." But early in the campaign he was accusing the
administration of "bungling" the nation into the war and he
spoke of the "tragic toll" of casualties. He urged that South
Koreans be trained quickly to replace the United States units
in front lines. "If it must be a war, let it be Asians against
Asians." In New Jersey in the middle of October he was asserting that "it seems almost ridiculous that . . . we should
have to continue to send our men and women overseas . . .
to protect American interests, even on the battlefield." President Truman was stirred to indignation by Eisenhower's
persistent allusions to casualties in Korea and his criticizing
the administration for entering the truce negotiations. At
Hartford the President spoke out angrily: "Now he's been
my military adviser ever since I appointed him Chief of
Staff. If he knows a remedy it's his duty to come and tell me
what it is and save lives right now."

In the closing days the campaign shifted as it always does
at that period to the populous Northeast. It was at Detroit
on October 24 that Eisenhower made the grand coup of his
campaign. He had just said that Korea, "the burial ground
of 20,000 American dead," was "a damning measure of the
quality of leadership we have been given." Then, rising to his
climax, he asked: "Where do we go from here?" and answered with his breath-taking pledge to "forego the diver-
sion of politics and . . . concentrate on the job of ending
the Korean War. . . . That job requires a personal trip to
Korea. I shall make that trip . . . I shall go to Korea." [11]
The Democratic National Chairman at once pronounced it
a "grandstand play to win votes." It was undoubtedly the
most telling single stroke of the whole campaign. It is be-

---

[11] Presently it was disclosed that the idea of this earth-rocking promise
to go to Korea did not originate with Eisenhower, but with a speech-
writer. (See James Reston: "Korea Is Now Eisenhower's Most Telling Issue,"
New York Times, November 2, 1952.)

lieved to have been particularly effective with the women voters, especially mothers with teen-aged sons approaching draft age. A more experienced candidate, however, might not have adopted so casually the ghost writer's paragraph. Before Eisenhower's administration was a fortnight old Senators were being showered with letters from women asking why nothing was being done to end the Korean War.

Besides countering Eisenhower's Korean coup and his other tactics Stevenson and Truman closed the campaign by stressing the prevailing prosperity, an issue given an emotional impulse with the campaign slogan "You never had it so good" and the adopted campaign song "Don't Take It Away." Thus Stevenson said: "Most of what the Republicans are for is what most of the people of America are against. . . . They offer no evidence that they have departed from their 1930 formula of boom and bust." Truman repeated his favorite theme of the Republicans' "long established policy of running the government in the interest of big business." Almost never had an administration suffered defeat in a presidential election falling in a period of practically full employment. Eisenhower was concerned enough about the prosperity issue to go far in pledging that depression "must not return" and that "we are not going to turn the clock back — ever." He also tried to counteract Democratic prosperity claims by emphasizing high prices.

It had been the most gruelling presidential campaign in American history. General Eisenhower had made 228 speeches and traveled almost 50,000 miles. Governor Stevenson had made 203 speeches in a tour of 32,500 miles. The extraordinary pressures on the candidates prevented the holding of any news conferences and newsmen deplored the consequent impossibility of challenging wild statements. The press conference and possibly even some audience heckling would have restored a time-honored restraint on the all too frequent irresponsible outbursts. It was felt that the public had been reduced to complacent acceptance of whatever was said in the campaign.

The 1952 map showing the states carried by the presi-

dential candidates marked the completion of a cycle, for it
reproduced the pattern of 1928, when Hoover had broken
the Solid South. The only difference was that Eisenhower
failed to capture two states carried by Hoover — Kentucky
and West Virginia. It was generally recognized that it had
been an Eisenhower landslide — not a Republican victory.
But at long last the Roosevelt-Truman magic formula had
failed, however temporary that failure might turn out to be.
The Republicans had captured both houses of Congress by
narrow majorities — the Senate without a single vote to
spare. Exceptionally significant was the fact that, although
the Republicans won by 221 to 213 seats in the House of
Representatives, the Democratic candidates for Congress
had received 239,271 more votes than the Republicans.
Eisenhower's coat tails had borne to victory many a lucky
Republican candidate.

Twenty years of unbroken Democratic control of the national government had meant an accumulation of handicaps
for that party. President Truman, personally incorruptible,
had failed to deal promptly and decisively with corruption
among his subordinates. The charge of the administration's
lack of vigilance as to communist infiltration in the public
service had proved to be loaded with electoral power against
the Democratic Party. The military stalemate in Korea was
probably the greatest single handicap of the Democratic
presidential candidate. Up to the very week of the election,
however, opinion polls were showing that a large majority of
those voters who admitted party affiliation were Democrats.
Most voters then were unenthusiastic about the Republican
Party, and many of them feared that the social gains of the
Roosevelt and Truman administrations and the collective
security of the free nations might be imperiled by a Republican victory. Because of these known fears the Republicans
had turned to Eisenhower as the party candidate. At last the
well worn Republican slogan "time for a change" had proved
effective.

Eisenhower had smashed the group structure of the Roosevelt-Truman combination. For the first time since the advent

of Franklin Roosevelt young voters (under 34) had rallied in support of a Republican presidential candidate. Eisenhower captured 55 per cent of them, 12 percentage points more than had voted for Dewey in 1948. At the height of the New Deal two out of three Catholics had voted for Roosevelt, but Eisenhower barely missed getting half their votes. Two out of every three farmers voted for him while Dewey in 1948 had got only 41 per cent of their votes. The General received 59 per cent of the big-city vote, 15 percentage points more than Dewey in 1948. Eisenhower gained 20 points over Dewey's share of the skilled-labor vote, but received only 33 per cent of the unskilled laborers' support — exactly what Dewey had received. The lower income groups gave Eisenhower 21 percentage points more than they gave Dewey, but the higher income voters gave the General 2 points less. Voters with only a grade-school education supported Eisenhower 52 per cent, 15 points more than they had given Dewey, but the 74 per cent of college-educated supporters of Eisenhower was 4 points less than Dewey's percentage of their vote.[12]

A veritable novice in politics, Dwight D. Eisenhower as President was compelled at first to proceed cautiously and lean heavily upon the advice of his staff. Long before the end of his first term, however, he manifested a flair for party politics and set to work resolved to rebuild the Republican Party into what he was to call Modern Republicanism. The remolded party would frankly accept the social and economic reforms of the New Deal as *faits accomplis*, and far from repealing a single part of them, would even expand some of them. Private enterprise was to be relied on as the driving force of the American economy. It was assumed that the federal government was under obligation deliberately to maintain a stable expanding economy to be safeguarded against inflation and recession. Racial and religious discriminations were to be eliminated. No Republican president

---

[12] See summary of the analysis of major-party vote in 1952 by the Survey Research Center, University of Michigan, in *United States News and World Report*, March 29, 1957, pp. 62–7.

since Theodore Roosevelt had assumed responsibility for such a shrewd attempt at group diplomacy and it proved baffling to the Democrats, who had difficulty discovering any issues for their party.

Nevertheless as the time drew near for the 1954 mid-term election the opinion polls portended Republican defeat. The Gallup Poll of October 30, 1954, published a few days before the election, revealed that of twenty-five population groups just polled, all but one indicated a shift to the Democrats from the percentage of support of Eisenhower in 1952 — the Catholic voters' shift amounting to 12 percentage points. The Gallup Poll of October 23 gave the results of a survey to ascertain party affiliation, and on the basis of an estimated population of 97,000,000 eligible voters, it was calculated that there were then 44,600,000 Democrats, 33,-000,000 Republicans, and 19,400,000 Independents. Under such circumstances it occasioned no surprise when the Democrats in 1954 captured 232 seats in the House of Representatives to the Republicans' 203 and obtained a majority of only one in the Senate. Under pressure President Eisenhower had been induced to campaign vigorously for a Republican Congress, but his efforts were apparently exerted in vain.

Adlai Stevenson spent the four years between the 1952 and 1956 campaigns practicing law and essaying to play the role of titular chief of the Democratic Party. As the time drew near for the 1956 Democratic National Convention it looked as if his renomination was in the bag. He had broad support among factions even in the South, where he was considered a moderate on school desegregation. Some Democratic bosses of great cities in pivotal states were for Stevenson. Then, more than a week before the delegates convened in Chicago, Ex-President Truman, who had been so largely responsible for Stevenson's nomination in 1952, chose to complicate the situation by declaring that Governor Averell Harriman of New York was "the best qualified man" and that Stevenson could not win the election. Thus what had looked like a walkaway was converted into a horse race — and if the eight favorite sons only held out long enough a dark horse might be nominated. It was Stevenson who touched off a Southern reaction nearly a week before the convention by declaring in a televised statement that the platform should express unqualified approval of the Supreme Court's desegregation decision.

Truman's declaration for Harriman had stalled the Stevenson band wagon and Southern dark horses began to put in an appearance in preparation for negotiations and deals. Senator Lyndon Johnson of Texas declared himself to be a serious candidate and Senator Stuart Symington of Missouri said he would accept if nominated. Southern strategy was to force Stevenson to water down his stand on civil rights in return for Southern delegates, whereby he would be mortgaged when nominated and if elected. The Stevenson leaders kept putting pressure on Northern dark horses to withdraw. In order to bolster Harriman's sagging cause Truman charged that Stevenson's moderation on civil rights "was a surrender of the basic principles of the Democratic party" and that he was so "defeatist" he could not carry more than the nine states he did in 1952. But a *New York Times* reporter perceived that by this time Truman "had thrown himself in front of the band wagon but it just kept rolling along." [13]

With the field of dark horses weakening, leaders of seven Southern delegations suddenly found themselves on the defensive with no choice but to accept the moderate civil-rights plank that the convention adopted. Consequently Stevenson won the nomination overwhelmingly on the first ballot. He owed much to the "Grand Old Lady" of the Democratic Party, Mrs. Franklin Roosevelt, who had come to the convention to help him and had spent three busy days in shrewdly effective work among the delegates. Estes Kefauver had campaigned tirelessly in the primaries for the nomination and his decision to withdraw and persuade his fundamentally anti-Stevenson delegates to make an about-face was decisive. Moreover, Stevenson profited from the expert

[13] *New York Times*, August 19, 1956.

management of James Finnegan, who was in charge of Stevenson strategy. So extraordinarily efficient was Finnegan's card index of the delegates and alternates — not neglecting even their personal idiosyncrasies — that when he had uncannily predicted that Truman would announce for Harriman he also calculated that it would cost Stevenson only 23 delegates, which turned out to be one too low. So confident was Finnegan of his calculation that he held out resolutely against any deals for delegates with the consequence that Stevenson was nominated free of pledges to any faction.[14]

Once the nomination had been won Stevenson refused absolutely to indicate a preference for his running mate. Five candidates contended in an open field. Kefauver took a wide lead on the first ballot, although he was still 203 votes short of the required majority. On the second ballot Southern delegates began switching to Senator John Kennedy of Massachusetts, who by the close of the ballot had nearly 100 more votes than Kefauver and only 40 short of the majority. The hectic third ballot found the two running neck and neck as delegation after delegation announced its vote. This ballot ended with a photo finish in which Kefauver was nominated. Speaker Rayburn, who was presiding, was overheard to say that "this is terrible," indicating presumably that Kefauver, though a Tennessean, was *persona non grata* in the South as an unequivocal proponent of civil rights. On Friday night the candidates delivered their acceptance speeches and the convention closed, with the recently belligerent leaders staging a spectacular love feast of a kind that can happen only in a Democratic Convention. As Cabell Phillips put it, "the Democratic Party illustrates again this week its amazing capacity for knocking itself out and then coming up off the floor with more fight than ever."[15]

The Republican Convention held at San Francisco contrasted in almost every respect with the Democratic. Its function was to ratify a foregone decision, the renomination

---

[14] See column of Joseph and Stewart Alsop: *Toledo Blade*, August 16, 1956.
[15] *New York Times*, August 19, 1956.

of President Eisenhower. Since President Arthur in 1884, no President had been denied that satisfaction. To the delegates the San Francisco convention was one long Republican love feast and a gustatory one at that. A reporter commented that a convention quorum could be assembled at Fisherman's Wharf. The only ripple was Harold Stassen's abortive attempt to dump Vice President Nixon for Governor Christian Herter of Massachusetts as Ike's running mate on the 1956 ticket. It wound up by Stassen seconding Herter's speech nominating Nixon. The only issue of consequence was the civil-rights plank of the platform, which though stronger than that of the Democrats, was toned down somewhat at the President's direction in order to placate new Southern Republicans, particularly those in Louisiana. President Eisenhower was renominated unanimously.

For Stevenson the campaign was uphill from the very start. Eisenhower had been elected to the presidency four years earlier an utter novice in party politics and was consequently dependent as no other president since Grant on his advisers, especially his presidential staff. From the very beginning an aura of prestige surrounded the war hero. Assuming a deliberate aloofness from politics he tended to avoid partisanship, to assume the pose of a people's President, and at times seemed cast for the role of a constitutional monarch. The opinion polls revealed an almost unprecedented popularity, and it came to pass that Democrats attacked him at their peril. They spared him criticism as no previous Republican president had been spared. This strange immunity from criticism was even intensified by his heart attack the year before his renomination and by his intestinal operation not long before the 1956 conventions. Formidable as it was it was not the only handicap imposed by stubborn circumstances upon hapless candidate Stevenson. "It is, at bottom, a contest between a man and a party," wrote Walter Lippmann, "between Mr. Eisenhower, who is much stronger than the Republicans, and the Democrats who, when they are united and aroused, are a majority in the nation. . . . Mr. Eisenhower finds himself carrying the Republican party on his back and running against the Democratic party." [16]

Though persistently charged with being only a constitutional monarch, President Eisenhower had, nevertheless, set up a program of public policies that left scarcely an issue for Stevenson. The President had assumed leadership of the free world in the cold war against communism and had dedicated himself to the maintenance of peace. He had succeeded in creating a widespread popular impression that the Republican Party was the party of peace, and pollsters were discovering this belief frequently expressed by the statement that "the Democrats always get us into war." Ernest K. Lindley noted the appeal of the President's "more personal qualities. His charm, good will, steadiness, high standards of ethics, dignity, ability to harmonize conflicting judgments, skill as an organizer and executive and the great prestige he had acquired before arriving at the White House." [17]

Moreover, in his fourth year as President, Dwight D. Eisenhower had executed a number of shrewd pre-convention moves that put the Democratic Party on the defensive; it never recovered the initiative during the 1956 campaign. For example, he blunted the charge of neglecting bipartisanship in foreign policy by appointing the revered Senator Walter George, Chairman of the Senate Committee on Foreign Relations, as the President's personal ambassador to NATO, thereby somewhat diverting criticism of his foreign policy. The Democratic Congress framed a farm bill designed to provoke a veto only to discover, after the veto, that in the ensuing primaries in agrarian Indiana Eisenhower was more popular than ever. Indeed, his fireside chat on the veto proved very effective. When Senator Case of South Dakota exposed an attempted bribe for his support of the pending bill to deprive the Federal Power Commission of the regulation of the price of gas at the producing wells, President Eisenhower vetoed the bill, thus preventing the expected charge of a Republican "give away" issue. At the same time

---

[16] Column of October 2, 1956.
[17] E. K. Lindley: "Ike's Blue Print," *Newsweek*, June 18, 1956.

the President expressed his willingness to sign such a bill later, which of course would depend on his re-election.

Early in the campaign the Republicans were alarmed when the traditional political barometer, the early Maine election, for the second time in the history of the Republican Party shattered its ticket in a presidential election year. Reduced to precise terms the tradition has been designated the ".65 law," according to which if the three Republican candidates for Congress fail to poll 65 per cent of the total vote of Maine the party faces defeat nationally. In September 1956 the Republican percentage fell to 51.5. The Democrats had elected the Governor and one of the three Congressmen, and had almost gained one of the two other Congressional seats.

Despite handicaps Stevenson initiated his campaign with a vigorous offensive, angering the President with the argument that his heart attack and intestinal surgery would necessarily make him a part-time President without effective control of administration. He charged that, despite the administration's air of superior righteousness, corruption existed in the administration, and promised that "when it comes to casting out crooks and cronies I can promise you we won't wait for Congressional prodding and investigation." Stevenson declared furthermore that Eisenhower's appointees were undermining New Deal legislation, as for example, putting "a declared enemy of public housing in charge of the public housing program." Stirred by Stevenson's comments on his health, the President brought a conference of Republican leaders at his Gettysburg farm roaring to its feet with his hearty remark: "I feel fine." Nevertheless, a comprehensive survey conducted by *Newsweek* revealed that early in September the President's health was considered the dominant issue in the East, the Midlands, the Southwest, and the West; only in the South was it given second place.[18] Stevenson was hitting hard and ominous reports came in from the Midwest. Among the Republicans the cry

---

[18] *Newsweek*, September 17, 1956, pp. 39–42.

arose that "only Ike can save us." Presently the President was putting ginger into his speeches, denouncing the Democratic program as "political quackery," and charging Stevenson with "distortions," "wicked nonsense," "confusion," and other shortcomings.[19]

Contrary to the President's plans Stevenson was compelling him to debate the issues of the campaign as the candidate of the Republican Party and was converting a contest between Stevenson and Eisenhower into a Republican-Democratic battle. This was shrewd Democratic strategy, as the opinion polls persistently revealed that the voters were overwhelmingly Democratic. If the campaign could only be reduced to a party battle the Republicans were lost. By the end of September Democrats were jubilantly asking: "How can we lose?" Speaker Sam Rayburn and Senate Majority Leader Lyndon Johnson were even assuring Stevenson that Texas, which had gone for Eisenhower in 1952, was so safe for the Democrats that he should not waste time campaigning there. The President was under increasing pressure to expand his campaigning.

Doubtless recalling the profound effect of Eisenhower's "I shall go to Korea" of the 1952 campaign and aware of a deep-seated prejudice against the Democrats as the alleged war party, Stevenson called for ending the draft and establishing instead a highly paid, well-trained military force and for the United States to take the initiative in ending the testing of H-bombs with their perilous radioactive fallout. The President met the issue of the bomb squarely by arguing that national security required continuous testing. As to the issue of peace itself, the President said: "The plain truth is that Americans know very well the difference between today and the day of the Korean casualty lists." Stevenson "wondered whether Republicans were going to take credit for the death of Stalin, which, of course, was what finally made the armistice in Korea possible." Both of Stevenson's ventures fell flat — the "end the draft" proposal stirred the wrath of

---

[19] Arthur Krock: "Democratic Challenge Changes the Campaign," *New York Times*, October 7, 1956.

veterans' organizations and the National Guard Association, and before the end of the campaign a survey indicated that his demand for ending H-bomb tests was opposed by the voters 2½ to 1.[20] Stevenson's strictures on our Middle East policy availed him nothing even when it was collapsing as Israel, England, and France shook the marplot Nasser by invading Egypt. A fortnight before the close of the campaign it was generally recognized that Stevenson was weaker than his party and that he could ride in, if at all, only on the coat tails of fellow candidates of his party. Campaigning in Washington, along with Senator Magnuson, he said: "I just hope Maggie's coat tails are broad enough to carry me into office." The campaign closed in gloom at Democratic headquarters. One pessimistic Stevenson backer gave his candidate a chance at no more than 137 electoral votes, which, in the event, turned out to be quite optimistic as Stevenson captured only 74 electoral votes to Eisenhower's 427. The President received 57.27 per cent of the popular vote, not much below Franklin Roosevelt's 60.7 per cent in the landslide of 1936.

Eisenhower had won an overwhelming victory, breasting a Democratic tide that had been running strong since 1952, as is indicated by the Democratic Congress elected in 1954 and the fact that a Democratic Congress had been elected even in 1956. Not for a century had a President elected with a popular majority failed to carry along a Congress of his own party. Eisenhower had set out determined to win by a larger majority than in 1952 under the conviction that otherwise his hand would be weakened in the conduct of foreign policy. Moreover, he wanted an electoral endorsement of his Modern Republicanism and his project of reconstituting the Republican Party — in short, he wanted to restore his minority party to the majority party it had been for two long generations before the 1930's. In the immediate afterglow of the election the Alsop brothers wrote: "The strategy of the 1956 campaign was most definitely an Eisenhower strategy and

---

[20] *Newsweek*, November 5, 1956, p. 24.

he is now an acknowledged master of the political art, perhaps the greatest of his generation." [21]

Exploring the voting in 1956, the Survey Research Center of the University of Michigan discovered some significant shifts. Strikingly prophetic was the shift of skilled workers, who had given Truman 73 per cent of the two-party vote in 1948, but gave Stevenson only 44 per cent in 1956. Curiously enough, Eisenhower in 1956 got only 48 per cent of the union workers' vote, but 65 per cent of the non-union vote. It seemed ironic that Stevenson, the candidate of the traditional party of the underdog, attracted only 40 per cent of the low-income voters. Paradoxically he increased his percentage of the higher income groups (above $5,000 annually) from 32 per cent in 1952 to 38 per cent in 1956, and, of course, Eisenhower suffered a corresponding decline. Between the two elections the President's strength fell 5 percentage points among the college educated, but increased 7 percentage points among those with only a grade-school education. Between his two elections Ike's support even among business and professional people declined 2 percentage points. Young voters, however, among whom only one in three had been Republicans in 1932, had changed to two Republicans out of three by 1956.[22] Only 59 per cent of them, however, voted for Eisenhower that year. The Catholics (three out of five had been Democrats in the 1930's) gave Eisenhower 55 per cent of their vote in 1956. But Ike's strength among the farmers had declined from 64 to 55 per cent between his two elections. Although the President had dropped 3 percentage points to 56 per cent of the big-city vote in 1956, this was still sufficient to ruin the old Democratic formula for electing presidents — capture the Solid South and enough of the big-city vote of pivotal states to win in the Electoral College. Eisenhower had sustained a striking decline in strength only in the Jewish vote.[23]

[21] Column of November 9, 1956.

[22] Gallup Poll, May 26, 1956.

[23] See *United States News and World Report*, March 29, 1957, for a summary of the analysis of the 1956 election by the Survey Research Center of the University of Michigan.

Eisenhower's triumphant re-election in 1956 gave him a prestige that might have been exploited in his purported rehabilitation of the Republican Party had he only been expert in the art of presidential leadership. Unfortunately for his purpose, he was the first president to be prevented by the Twenty-Second Amendment from holding his party leaders in leash by keeping them in the dark as to whether he chose to run again. Before long Eisenhower was being dubbed a "lameduck" President. His second administration had an ill-omened start. No sooner had the President's budget been submitted to Congress than Secretary of the Treasury Humphrey let out a blast against it. Instead of disciplining the mutinous subordinate President Eisenhower admitted he had asked for too much and invited Congress to cut his budget. But when Congress took him at his word and began slashing he made an about-face and started defending the budget.

The division between the "modern" Eisenhower and the conservative Republicans had reappeared soon after the death of Senator Taft in Eisenhower's first year in the presidency. In the second administration the separation accelerated. To the right-wing Republicans the President's program was too "New Dealish." Indicative of the changing climate were the resolutions of the Convention of Young Republicans in Washington on June 22, 1957. Two years earlier this organization had shouted down a proposed "right-to-work" law, but now it favored it and tore to shreds the Eisenhower program. Disheartening to Eisenhower men in Congress was the President's failure to come to their aid with the prestige and power of his office when they were battling for his policies. For example, he did not lift his hand to aid them in their fight for his own bill for federal aid for school construction, whereupon it lost by only three votes. The first session of the Eighty-Fifth Congress closed with Eisenhower Republicans despondent and the Old Guard jubilant, especially as Governor Walter J. Kohler of Wisconsin had just been badly beaten for Senator after campaigning as an Eisenhower Republican. The astonishment of our people at the unexpected launching of Russian earth satellites with the implication that we had been outstripped in the race for intercontinental weapons was promptly reflected in the Gallup Poll, which revealed a new low in President Eisenhower's prestige. The November elections of 1957 provided no significant news to cheer Republican leaders. In the mid-term congressional elections of 1958 the Democrats scored the most sweeping mid-term victory since the congressional tidal wave that coincided with the second election of Franklin Roosevelt in 1936. After the ballots had been counted it was evident that the next Congress would contain 62 Democratic to 34 Republican Senators, while in the House the Democrats would hold 282 seats to only 153 held by Republicans. Consequently the omens were not auspicious for the Republican Party in the presidential election of 1960, the opinion polls having persistently indicated since 1952 that there were three eligible Democratic to two eligible Republican voters.

Moreover the Republicans had handicapped their party ten years earlier when they initiated the twenty-second amendment to the Constitution in order to prevent any Democrat from ever repeating anything like Franklin Roosevelt's four successive elections to the presidency. This amendment now ruled out the possible candidacy of President Dwight D. Eisenhower who, by almost certain re-election in 1960, might have continued Republican supremacy in the executive branch of the national government.

In 1960 then, so far as Republican aspirations were concerned, Vice President Richard Nixon looked like the heir presumptive to the presidency. However he was confronted with the problem of a possible sturdy rival for the Republican nomination. Nelson Rockefeller had been elected Governor of New York in 1958 by a majority of more than half a million when the Republican Party, nation-wide, was sliding down grade. Suddenly Rockefeller had become a likely candidate for the presidency. Richard Nixon and his promoters were baffled by the uncertainty as to what Rockefeller might do. Would he enter and run through the state primaries?

They hoped he would, for they were confident they could finish him off there.

Nixon had risen from near poverty, to which he sometimes alluded during his campaigning. Nelson Rockefeller, on the contrary, had the serenity of one who had never known economic insecurity. Someone had denominated him a "grownup boy scout." By early 1960 he is said to have had enough of the Eisenhower administration and was becoming frustrated with its policies. Thus he had become something of a problem to the directorate of the Republican Party in New York. They had tried to steer him into running for the Senate, but he wanted to be Governor and that is what he became. At once he attracted attention as chief executive of the nation's leading state and as a potential national party leader.

Besides his official staff as Governor in Albany, Nelson Rockefeller gathered in New York City a private personal staff organized with an apparent objective of capturing the Republican nomination for President in 1960. He sensed an approaching period of major international crises which he did not consider Nixon capable of handling. As Governor Rockefeller moved about the country, big business received him courteously but that was all. Here was a maverick with a positive program of action in mind, while business wanted a negative program, one that would preserve the status quo. Nixon seemed to be their man for that purpose. The Governor's political "intelligence reports" soon informed him that the Republican Party regulars everywhere were promoting the choosing of Nixon delegates to the National Convention. Christmas week, 1959, Rockefeller issued a startling statement: "I believe that those who will control the Republican Convention stand opposed to any contest for the nomination." A contest under such circumstances, he averred, would make it impossible for him to carry out his duties as Governor and he consequently would not be a candidate for the nomination. Nixon's staff, convinced that they could have overwhelmed Rockefeller in one primary after another, were disappointed by the lost opportunity.

Governor Rockefeller continued to be dismayed by the

Eisenhower policies at home and abroad. On May first, Nixon let it be rumored that he would like Rockefeller to be his running mate. Almost simultaneously the Republican National Committee offered the Governor his choice of either chairing or keynoting the Republican Convention. His response was that he did not even plan to attend the Convention. He had served the Eisenhower administration until he had become disillusioned and frustrated. Now he was convinced that the managers of the Republican Party were leaving the people in the dark as to party policies and where they were leading the nation. He protested against Nixon's announced purpose to disclose his policies only after and not before his nomination. Governor Rockefeller seemed about to renounce not only the Eisenhower administration but the leadership of his party as well.

For months Richard Nixon had had Charles Richard Percy, a forty-year-old business man, working diligently with a forward-looking group of Republicans endeavoring to formulate a program for Modern Republicans. Percy was co-operating with the Resolutions Committee of the Republican Convention when he flew to New York to show Governor Rockefeller the emerging Republican platform. The Governor found it utterly unsatisfactory. He wanted a positive program including care for the aged, civil rights for Negroes, stimulation of capital investments with growth of the national economy, a new foreign policy, and the closing of what he considered the approaching missile gap. The Resolutions Committee was instead formulating a platform including a ringing endorsement of the Eisenhower administration — a plank utterly repugnant to Governor Rockefeller. The Rockefeller men at the Convention decided to carry the platform battle to the floor of the Convention, particularly as to national defense and civil rights. This would have been disastrous to the party in general and Nixon in particular. Nixon decided at once on a bold move to prevent the impending disaster. Flying to New York, he had an eight-hour conference with Governor Rockefeller at his Fifth Avenue home. There he invited Rockefeller to be his running mate. The result of the conference was the famous "Fourteen-Point Compact of Fifth Avenue" comprising Rockefeller's views on foreign as well as domestic policies: economic growth, medical care for the aged, civil rights, and total reorganization of the executive branch of the government. This sudden reversal of policy trend outraged the Resolutions Committee, and two days before the Convention opened, confusion mingled with indignation prevailed among the delegates. Nixon arrived, stood resolutely by the "Fifth Avenue Compact," set to work placating the indignant members of the Resolutions Committee, and gradually the tumult subsided. Never before had an outsider such as Rockefeller so dominated the policies of a Convention. Nixon was adamant on civil rights. The tour de force by which he had resolved the strife and unified the Republican Party marked him as an exceptional party leader.

In the midst of his acceptance speech, Nixon captivated the Convention with the sentence: "When Mr. Khrushchev says our grandchildren will live under communism let us say his grandchildren will live in freedom." He took occasion in this speech to declare that he would campaign in all 50 states, a promise which was to handicap him later when Kennedy was concentrating on the big pivotal states. Nixon was possibly deceived as to the significance of the extraordinary enthusiasm accorded him in Atlanta, where 150,000 turned out to greet him with ecstatic enthusiasm despite the fact that on election day he was to get only 37.4 per cent of the popular vote of Georgia. He may have then begun to doubt the prudence of his insistence on an all-out civil-rights plank in the platform. Might he not soft-pedal civil rights and possibly carry Southern states? Eventually he lost both the South and the Northern Negro vote. In the midst of the campaign Martin Luther King, the outstanding Negro leader, was sentenced to four months of hard labor in a Georgia prison. A Republican Deputy Attorney General prepared a draft statement to support an application for the release of Reverend King. A copy of this was sent to President Eisenhower and another to Vice President Nixon, then campaigning in Ohio. Neither acted on it. Kennedy, despite the warning of three

Southern Governors to desist, promptly telephoned to Mrs. King his concern for her husband and offered intervention if necessary. This may have decided the election.

Nixon's pace in campaigning exhausted the accompanying members of the press and, unlike Kennedy, he neglected to cultivate cordial relations with them. One newsman made a curious discovery by bringing in a television set and placing it where he could observe Nixon speaking and at the same time see his televised image; the TV picture caricatured Nixon's actual appearance. Those who watched the televised debates were to discover the same thing.

Kennedy came to the first debate fortified with a dozen years' experience on the House and Senate Labor Committees and was consequently familiar with salient domestic issues. He spent the day before the first debate in an around-the-clock session with a staff of three "like college men cramming for an exam," and had another skull session with them the morning of the debate. Nixon had spoken that very morning to a hostile group, the United Brotherhood of Carpenters and Joiners, and otherwise spent the day in solitude except for the presence of his wife. His television advisers were out of touch with him, and he permitted only one television adviser to accompany and hastily brief him in the ten-minute drive to the studio. He was advised to "come out swinging," which he chose not to do. Instead of presenting the Republican case, he rebutted Kennedy's "affirmative speech" point by point, as if debating before judges in a contest. In his opening statement he declared that he and Kennedy differed only as to the means of attaining the same goals. Unlike Kennedy, he scarcely seemed aware of his unseen audience, which was puzzled by his ghastly appearance. During the successive debates, Kennedy seemed to grow upon his audience as gloom enveloped the Republicans. After the last debate the Gallup Poll reported that 42 per cent held Kennedy to be the winner of the debates to 30 per cent who thought Nixon won.

On the stump Nixon was making the most of his greater experience on the executive level — his attendance at cabinet meetings, presiding over the National Security Council, and counseling with President Eisenhower. Khrushchev was in the United States in the midst of the campaign, highlighting the question of which of the two candidates as President might deal better with him. Nixon climaxed one of his claims with the statement: "I know Khrushchev." Kennedy meanwhile was saying that Cuba had become a Communist satellite "within ninety miles of the United States" and "Those who say they will stand up to Mr. Khrushchev have demonstrated no ability to stand up to Castro."

When, in the fourth televised debate, Kennedy advocated more stringent economic sanctions against Castro "such as the seizing of Cuban assets in this country . . . to strengthen anti-Castro elements inside and outside Cuba and to move against further Communist inroads in the hemisphere," Nixon pronounced these proposals "dangerously irresponsible," asserting that to give help to anti-Castro forces would violate United States treaty obligations not to interfere in another nation's internal affairs and "would be an open invitation to Khrushchev to come in." Later, concerning Kennedy's call for help to anti-Castro forces, Nixon charged that "this incident alone shows an immaturity and rashness" which raises "a serious question" whether Mr. Kennedy "has the balanced judgment to be President." The nation, Nixon then observed, "cannot sleep well with a man like that in the White House." Near the end of October President Eisenhower, now campaigning, said: "By all odds Richard Nixon is the best qualified man to be the next President."

Nixon carried out his announced purpose to campaign in every state and traveled more than 60,000 miles doing it. He proved to be difficult to his managers. He was often inaccessible to them, indecisive, and unwilling to delegate authority. The Republican National Chairman could not persuade him to set policy and leave details to his staff. His attitude and manner during the campaign dismayed President Eisenhower. It was reported that in the final days of the campaign, after Nixon had lunched with the President, Eisenhower plaintively protested to an old friend: "What's the matter with Dick? He's acting like a loser. You can't win if you feel beaten. Why, if I had a general commanding troops in Europe with that attitude, I would have relieved him of command." [24]

Although the Kennedy-Johnson ticket carried less than half the states, it won 300 presidential electoral votes to 223 for the Nixon-Lodge ticket. The popular vote, however, was razor-edge close, with the Democratic ticket receiving less than 0.2 per cent more votes than the Republican ticket — a popular majority averaging less than one vote per precinct throughout the United States. In this sense it was the closest presidential election in the history of the nation. The turnout of voters on Election Day, 1960, about 62.7 per cent of the estimated total of eligible voters, was the highest yet for a presidential election. The closeness of the election was due, among other reasons, to the fact that Republicans, outnumbered three to two by Democrats, compensated for their minority standing by much greater party loyalty than Democrats are accustomed to practice.

The election of 1960 revealed, as usual, that the Democratic Party suffers from the fact that its greatest strength is among the least politicized classes, those least concerned with politics and hardest to stimulate into political action.[25] "On balance across the nation Nixon led Republican tickets while Kennedy trailed behind other Democratic candidates especially outside of the Northeast." [26] There is no question but that Nixon often ran ahead of other Republican candidates. Thus he had majorities over Kennedy in 228 congressional districts, although only 176 Republicans won seats in the House of Representatives. Kennedy on the other hand tended to run behind and had majorities in only 208 congressional districts while 261 Democrats were elected to seats in the House. There is no question but that the 1960 vote polarized along religious lines. Thus the Catholic vote, which

[24] *Newsweek*, October 9, 1961, p. 27.

[25] Angus Campbell: op. cit.

[26] Philip E. Converse, Angus Campbell, Warren E. Miller, Donald E. Stokes: "Stability and Change in 1960," *American Political Science Review*, Vol. LV, No. 2 (June 1961), p. 270.

had divided 50–50 in the two Eisenhower contests, shifted to 80–20 in 1960. But if Nixon had retained only the Eisenhower Democrats of the two Eisenhower contests, he would have lost 54 per cent to 46 per cent. It was because Nixon drew a new stream of Democratic defections that he almost won.[27]

In the 1960 campaign the Republicans were confronted with the fact that the big cities in pivotal states were usually controlled by well-oiled political machines. Organized labor was heavily concentrated in these cities, and the labor unions were even more effective than the Democratic organization in getting Democrats registered and to the polls on Election Day. The Democratic strength tended to be concentrated in the unions. Republicans depended largely on voluntary organization workers. The unions may have swung the election.

Nixon had to stand by the Eisenhower administration, that is, the party record which, regardless of its merit, put him on the defensive, while Kennedy could blame the Eisenhower administration for whatever shortcomings he chose to attribute to it. Any unemployment at the time handicapped Nixon, especially with Negroes, who are peculiarly sensitive to unemployment since there is a tendency for them to be the first laid off and the last to be re-employed.

In 1960 the Democrats had the great advantage of controlling more statehouses, courthouses, and city halls than the Republicans. In contrast with 1952 when a majority of the state Governors were Republican (25 out of 48), in 1960 there were only 15 Republican Governors, a rather meager minority out of a total of 50. Since most of these numerous Democratic officeholders had been elected during the Eisenhower years, this constituted another measure of the decline in strength of the Republican Party. When one takes into consideration all the handicaps under which Richard Nixon campaigned, the marvel is that he missed victory so narrowly.

Nearly a year after the election of 1960, William Miller, the Republican National Chairman, set a committee to work under the extraordinarily competent Ray Bliss, the Ohio Republican State Chairman, to conduct a post-mortem on the

---

[27] Ibid., p. 280.

Republican defeat. As might have been expected, the key to Kennedy's election had been the votes that Democrats rolled up in 27 of the 41 cities of more than 300,000 population. A shift of 4,500 votes in Chicago would have given Illinois's 27 electoral votes to Nixon. A change of 5,000 votes in St. Louis would have given him Missouri's 13 electoral votes. Changes of 91,500 votes in Pittsburgh, Philadelphia, and Detroit would have swung the 52 electoral votes of Pennsylvania and Michigan. In the 41 cities mentioned above, the Democrats had outvoted the Republicans by 2,250,000, a gain of more than 2,000,000 Democratic votes in only two years. Union members and middle-income families had been moving into suburbs and keeping up their membership in the Democratic Party. Suburbs of Los Angeles, Baltimore, Denver, Detroit, New York, and Philadelphia all reflected the drift from the Republicans. Like Dewey in 1944, Nixon had rolled up impressive majorities in the hinterland of one great pivotal state after another, only to have his lead wiped out by the Democratic majority in the cities. It was heartbreaking to Nixon, in view of his near win, to learn from the Bliss Committee's eight months' research that while the highly efficient Democratic city organizations along with the labor unions had been busy getting voters to the polls on Election Day in 25 cities with a population of 25,000,000, the Republicans had only 37 full-time paid workers in those cities, and even on Election Day not all their precincts had been fully manned.[28] A visitor from Mars might have concluded that the Republican Party lacked not only the organization but even the will to win.

---

[28] "The Republicans Face the Future," *United States News and World Report,* February 5, 1962, pp. 58, 59.

Bibliography

&

Indexes

BIBLIOGRAPHY

ABBOTT, LYMAN: *Silhouettes of My Contemporaries.* New York, 1922.

ABERNETHY, T. P.: "Andrew Jackson and Southwestern Democracy," *American Historical Review,* XXXIII.

——: *From Frontier to Plantation: A Study in Frontier Democracy.* Chapel Hill, N. C., 1932.

ADAMS, C. F.: *Charles Francis Adams* (American Statesmen).

——, ed.: *The Works of John Adams.* 10 vols. Boston, 1851.

ADAMS, HENRY: *The Degradation of the Democratic Dogma.* 1919.

——: *The Education of Henry Adams* (Modern Library). New York, 1931.

——: *John Randolph* (American Statesmen).

——: *History of the United States during the Administrations of Jefferson and Madison.* 9 vols. New York, 1890, 1891.

—— (W. C. FORD, ed.): *A Cycle of Adams Letters.* 2 vols. Boston, 1920.

——: "The Session," *North American Review,* CXI.

ADAMS, JAMES T.: *The Living Jefferson.* New York, 1936.

ADAMS, JOHN QUINCY: *Memoirs of John Quincy Adams,* edited by CHARLES FRANCIS ADAMS. 12 vols. Philadelphia, 1874–7.

ADAMS, S. H.: *The Incredible Era: The Life and Times of Warren Gamaliel Harding.* Boston, 1939.

AGAR, HERBERT: *The Pursuit of Happiness.* Boston, 1938.

AGRONSKY, MARTIN, et al.: *The First Hundred Days of the Kennedy Administration.* New York, 1961.

ALEXANDER, DE A. S.: *A Political History of the State of New York.* 4 vols. New York, 1906–23.

ALSOP, JOSEPH W., and KINTNER, ROBERT E.: "The Guffey: Biography of a Boss, New Style." *Saturday Evening Post,* March 26, 1938.

AMBLER, C. H.: *Sectionalism in Virginia from 1776 to 1861.* Chicago, 1910.

ANDERSON, D. R.: "The Insurgents of 1811," American Historical Association *Reports* (1911), I, 167 ff.

Annals of the Congress of the United States. 42 vols. Washington, 1834–56.

ARBUTHNOT, C. C.: "The Economic Interpretation of Present Politics," *Popular Science Monthly*, LXXXI (1912).

ASCOLI, MAX: "Political Parties," in MAX ASCOLI and FRITZ LEHMAN (editors): *Political and Economic Democracy*. New York, 1937.

BADEAU, ADAM: *Grant in Peace: A Personal Memoir*. Hartford, 1885.

BAKER, R. S.: *Woodrow Wilson, Life and Letters*. 4 vols. Garden City, 1927.

BALDWIN, L. D.: *Whiskey Rebels; the Story of a Frontier Uprising*. Pittsburgh, 1939.

BANCROFT, GEORGE: *History of the Formation of the Constitution of the United States of America*. 2 vols. New York, 1882.

BARR, ELIZABETH N.: "The Populist Uprising," *A Standard History of Kansas and the Kansans* (Chicago, 1918), II, 1115–95.

BARTLETT, R. J.: *John C. Frémont and the Republican Party*. Columbus, 1930.

BASSETT, J. S.: *The Federalist System, 1789–1801* (*American Nation*, XI). New York, 1906.

——: "The State of Society," *Social and Economic Forces in American History* (A. B. HART, ed.). Chautauqua, 1913.

BEALE, H. K.: *The Critical Year: A Study of Andrew Johnson and Reconstruction*. New York, 1930.

BEARD, C. A.: "Some Economic Origins of Jeffersonian Democracy," *American Historical Review*, XIX.

——: *The American Party Battle*. New York, 1928.

——: *Contemporary American History*. New York, 1914.

——: *The Economic Interpretation of the Constitution of the United States*. New York, 1913.

——: *Economic Origins of Jeffersonian Democracy*. New York, 1915.

——: "Emerging Issues in America," *Current History*, November 1934.

——: *The Open Door at Home; a Trial Philosophy of National Interest*. New York, 1934.

——: "Roosevelt's Place in History," *Events*, III (February 1938).

—— and BEARD, MARY R.: *The Rise of American Civilization*. 2 vols. New York, 1927.

BEER, THOMAS: *Hanna*. New York, 1929.

BENTLEY, A. F.: *The Process of Government*. Chicago, 1908.

BENTON, E. J.: "The Movement for Peace without Victory during the Civil War" (Western Reserve Historical Society *Collections*, No. 99). Cleveland, 1918.

BEVERIDGE, A. J.: *Abraham Lincoln, 1809–1858.* 4 vols. Boston, 1928.

———: *Life of John Marshall.* 4 vols. Boston, 1916.

BILLINGTON, R. A.: *The Protestant Crusade, 1800–1860: A Study of the Origins of American Nativism.* New York, 1938.

BINKLEY, W. E.: *The Powers of the President: Problems in Democracy.* New York, 1937.

BLAINE, J. G.: *Twenty Years in Congress.* 2 vols. Norwich, Conn., 1884–6.

BLAKE, NELSON M.: "The Background of Cleveland's Venezuela Policy," *American Historical Review,* XLVII (1942), p. 272.

BOUCHER, C. S.: *Nullification Controversy in South Carolina.* Chicago, 1916.

BOWERS, CLAUDE: *Beveridge and the Progressive Era.* Boston, 1932.

———: *Jefferson and Hamilton, the Struggle for Democracy in America.* Boston, 1925.

———: *The Tragic Era; the Revolution after Lincoln.* Boston, 1929.

BOWERSOX, L. K.: *Reconstruction of the Republican Party in the West, 1865–1870.* Doctoral dissertation, Ohio State University, 1931.

BRACKENRIDGE, HENRY M.: *History of the Western Insurrection in Western Pennsylvania.* Pittsburgh, 1859.

BRETZ, J. P.: "Economic Background of the Liberty Party," *American Historical Review,* XXXIV.

BROGAN, D. W.: *Government of the People.* New York, 1933.

BROOKS, VAN WYCK: *The Flowering of New England.* New York, 1936.

BROWN, G. R.: *The Leadership of Congress.* Indianapolis, 1922.

BRYAN, W. J.: *The First Battle: A Story of the Campaign of 1896.* Chicago, 1896.

BUCK, PAUL H.: "Poor Whites in the Old South," *American Historical Review,* XXXV.

———: *The Road to Reunion, 1865–1900.* Boston, 1937.

BULEY, R. C.: "The Political Balance of the Old Northwest, 1820–1865," *Studies in American History,* inscribed to Albert J. Woodburn. Bloomington, Ind., 1926.

BURDELL, WILLIAM F.: *William McKinley:* an address before the Buz Fuz Club. Dayton, Ohio, April 19, 1902.

Burns, E. M.: *James Madison, Philosopher of the Constitution,* New Brunswick, 1938.

Burns, James MacGregor: *John Kennedy: A Political Profile.* New York, 1959.

Butler, Nicholas Murray: *Across the Busy Years: Recollections and Reflections.* New York, 1939.

Butler, W. A.: *Martin Van Buren: Lawyer, Statesman and Man.* 1862.

Byrdsall, Fitzwilliam: *The History of the Loco-Foco or Equal Rights Party.* New York, 1842.

Calhoun, John C. (R. K. Cralle, ed.): *The Works of John C. Calhoun.* 6 vols. New York, 1851–6.

Carroll, E. M.: *Origins of the Whig Party.* Durham, N. C., 1925.

Carroll, M. R.: *Labor and Politics.* Boston, 1923.

Chamberlain, John: *Farewell to Reform; the Rise, Life and Decay of the Progressive Mind in America.* New York, 1932.

Channing, Edward: *A History of the United States.* 6 vols. New York, 1905–25.

Chase Correspondence, American Historical Association *Reports* (1902).

Clay, Henry (Daniel Mallory, ed.): *The Life and Speeches of the Honorable Henry Clay.* 2 vols. New York, 1843.

—— (C. Colton, ed.): *Works of Henry Clay.* 6 vols. 1856.

Colcord, Lincoln: "Review of G. R. Albion's *Rise of the Port of New York, 1815–1860,*" *New York Herald Tribune Books,* March 12, 1939.

Cole, A. C.: "Daniel Webster," *Dictionary of American Biography,* XIX, pp. 586 ff.

——: *Era of the Civil War, 1848–1870.* Springfield, Ill., 1919.

——: *The Irrepressible Conflict, 1850–1865.* New York, 1938.

——: "Lincoln's Election an Immediate Menace to Slavery in the States?" *American Historical Review,* XXXVI.

——: *Lincoln's "House Divided" Speech. Did it reflect a doctrine of class struggle?* Chicago, 1923.

——: "Nativism in the Lower Mississippi Valley," Mississippi Valley Historical Association *Reports,* VI.

——: *The Whig Party in the South.* Washington, 1913.

Commager, H. S.: *Documents of American History.* 2 vols. New York, 1934.

——: "Lincoln Belongs to the People," *Yale Review,* Winter 1940, p. 377.

——: *Theodore Parker*. Boston, 1936.

——: "The Whiskey Rebels," *New York Herald Tribune Books*, May 7, 1939, p. 19.

COMMONS, J. R.: "Horace Greeley and the Working Class Origins of the Republican Party," *Political Science Quarterly*, XXIV.

CONKLING, A. R.: *Life and Letters of Roscoe Conkling, Orator, Statesman and Advocate*. New York, 1889.

COOLIDGE, L. A.: *The Life of U. S. Grant*. Boston, 1917.

COREY, LEWIS: "The Crisis of the Middle Class," *Nation*, August 4, 1935, p. 176.

COULTER, E. M.: "Henry Clay," *Dictionary of American Biography*, IV.

CRANDALL, W. C.: *Early History of the Republican Party*. Boston, 1930.

CRAVEN, AVERY: *Democracy in American Life*. Chicago, 1941.

——: *The Repressible Conflict, 1830–1861*. Baton Rouge, 1939.

CROLY, HERBERT: *Marcus Alonzo Hanna*. New York, 1913.

CUBBERLY, E. P.: *Public Education in the United States*. Boston, 1920.

CUSHMAN, ROBERT E.: *Leading Constitutional Decisions*. New York, 1941.

DARLING, A. B.: "Jacksonian Democracy in Massachusetts," *American Historical Review*, XXIX.

DEBS, EUGENE V.: *Debs: His Life, Writings and Speeches*. Girard, Kansas, 1910.

DENNETT, TYLER: *John Hay* (American Political Leaders). New York, 1933.

DESMOND, H. J.: *The Know Nothing Party*. Washington, 1905.

DEWEY, D. R.: *Financial History of the United States*. New York, 1931.

DODD, W. E.: "Andrew Jackson and His Enemies," *Century Magazine*, CXI.

——: *Expansion and Conflict* (*Riverside History*, III). Boston, 1915.

——: "The Federal Constitution and Its Application," *Bulletin of College of William and Mary in Virginia*, XXVIII, No. 5 (August 1933).

——: "The Fight for the Northwest," *American Historical Review*, XVI.

——: "The Making of Andrew Jackson," *Century Magazine*, CXI.

——: "The Place of Nathaniel Macon in Southern History," *American Historical Review*, VII.

——: "Patrick Henry," *Dictionary of American Biography*, VIII.

——: *Statesmen of the Old South*. Boston, 1911.

DONAVAN, H. D. A.: *The Barnburners*. New York, 1926.

DU BOIS, W. E. B.: *Black Reconstruction in the South, 1860–1880*. New York, 1935.

——: "Reconstruction and Its Benefits," *American Historical Review*, XV.

DUNN, A. W.: *From Harrison to Harding*. 2 vols. New York, 1922.

DUNNING, W. A.: "The Constitution in the Civil War," *Political Science Quarterly*, I.

——: *A History of Political Theories from Rousseau to Spencer*. New York, 1922.

——: "The Second Birth of the Republican Party," *American Historical Review*, XVI.

DWIGHT, TIMOTHY: *An Oration*. Hartford, 1801.

EASLEY, R. M.: "Senator Hanna and the Labor Problem," *Independent*, March 3, 1904.

EASUM, C. V.: *The Americanization of Carl Schurz*. Chicago, 1929.

EGGLESTON, EDWARD: "Nathaniel Bacon, the Patriot of 1676," *Century Magazine*, XL (1890), pp. 418–35.

EMERSON, RALPH WALDO: *Journals*. 6 vols. Boston, 1909–11.

EWING, C. A. M.: *Presidential Elections*. Norman, Okla., 1940.

FARRAND, MAX: "Compromises of the Constitution," *Annual Report of the American Historical Association* (1903), I, 73 ff.

——, ed.: *Records of the Federal Convention of 1787*. 3 vols. New Haven, 1911.

FERGUSON, RUSSELL J.: *Early Western Pennsylvania Politics*. Pittsburgh, 1938.

FESSENDEN, FRANCIS: *Life and Public Services of William Pitt Fessenden*. 2 vols. Boston, 1907.

FISH, C. R.: "The Decision of the Ohio Valley," American Historical Association *Report* (1910).

——: *The Rise of the Common Man, 1830–1850* (*History of American Life*, VI).

FITE, E. D.: *The Presidential Campaign of 1860*. New York, 1911.

FITZHUGH, GEORGE: *Sociology for the South*. Richmond, Va., 1854.

FLYNN, J. T.: "Mark Hanna," *Scribner's Magazine*, XCIV (1933).

——: "Other People's Money," *New Republic*, December 11, 1932.

Ford, H. J.: *The Cleveland Era* (*Chronicles of America*). New Haven, 1919.

——: *The Rise and Growth of American Politics*. New York, 1898.

——: *The Scotch-Irish in America*. Princeton, 1915.

Fox, D. R.: *The Decline of Aristocracy in the Politics of New York*. New York, 1910.

——: "The Negro Vote in Old New York," *Political Science Quarterly*, XXX (June 1917), pp. 225 ff.

Gammon, S. R.: "The Presidential Campaign of 1832," Johns Hopkins University *Studies*, XL, No. 1. Baltimore, 1922.

Garrison, Curtis W. (ed.): "Conversations with Hayes, A Biographer's Notes," *Mississippi Valley Historical Review*, XXV.

Gauss, Christian (ed.): *Democracy Today: An Interpretation*. New York, 1919.

Gettell, R. G.: *History of American Political Thought*. New York, 1928.

Gibbs, George: *Memoirs of the Administrations of George Washington and John Adams*. 2 vols. New York, 1846.

Giddings, F. H.: "Conduct of Political Majorities," *American Political Science Quarterly*, VII.

——: *Democracy and Empire*. New York, 1900.

Gompers, Samuel: *Seventy Years of Life and Labor*. 2 vols. New York, 1925.

Gordy, J. P.: *Political History of the United States with Special Reference to the Growth of Political Parties*. 2 vols. New York, 1902.

Greeley, Horace: *The American Conflict*. Chicago, 1866.

Grosvenor, Charles H.: *Marcus A. Hanna, A Memorial Address Delivered in the Senate and House of Representatives*. Washington, 1904.

Hacker, L. M.: *The Triumph of American Capitalism*. New York, 1940.

——: *The United States; a Graphic History*. New York, 1937.

Hadley, A, T.: *Undercurrents of American Politics*. New Haven, 1915.

Hall, C. R.: *Andrew Johnson, Military Governor of Tennessee*. Princeton, 1916.

Halstead, Murat: *A History of the National Political Conventions of the Current Presidential Campaign* (1860). Cincinnati, 1860.

HAMILTON, ALEXANDER (H. C. LODGE, ed.): *The Works of Alexander Hamilton.* 9 vols. 1885.

HAMILTON, J. G. DE R.: "Hinton Rowan Helper," *Dictionary of American Biography.*

HAMMOND, J. D.: *History of Political Parties in the State of New York from the Ratification of the Federal Constitution to December, 1842.* Buffalo, 1850.

HARLOW, R. V.: *The History of Legislative Methods in the Period before 1825.* New Haven, 1917.

Harper's Encyclopedia of United States History. 10 vols. New York, 1905.

HART, A. B.: *Slavery and Abolition* (*American Nation,* XVI).

——, ed.: *Social and Economic Forces in American History.* Chautauqua, 1913.

HAWORTH, P. L.: *The Hayes-Tilden Disputed Presidential Election of 1876.* Cleveland, 1906.

——: *The United States in Our Times, 1865–1935.* New York, 1935.

HAY, JOHN: *Letters and Diaries.* (Privately printed) 1908.

HENDERSON, JOHN B.: "Emancipation and Impeachment," *Century Magazine,* LXXXV (December 1912).

HERRING, E. P.: "The First Session of the Seventy-third Congress," *American Political Science Review,* XXVIII.

——: *The Politics of Democracy: American Parties in Action.* New York, 1940.

——: *Public Administration and the Public Interest.* New York, 1935.

HERTZ, E.: *The Hidden Lincoln.* New York, 1940.

HIBBEN, PAXTON: *The Peerless Leader, William Jennings Bryan.* New York, 1929.

HICKS, J. D.: *The Federal Union; A History of the United States to 1865.* Boston, 1937.

——: *The Populist Revolt.* Minneapolis, 1931.

——: "The Third Party Tradition in American Politics," *Mississippi Valley Historical Review,* XX.

HILDRETH, RICHARD: *History of the United States.* 6 vols. New York, 1849–52.

HOAR, GEORGE F.: *Autobiography of Seventy Years.* 2 vols. New York, 1903.

HOCKETT, H. C.: *Constitutional History of the United States, 1776–1826.* New York, 1939.

——: *Constitutional History of the United States, 1826–1876.* New York, 1939.

——: "Federalism and the West," *Essays in American History,* dedicated to Frederick J. Turner. New York, 1910.

——: "Influence of the West on the Rise and Fall of Political Parties," *Mississippi Valley Historical Review,* IV, 455.

——: *Political and Social Growth of the American People, 1492–1865.* New York, 1941.

——: *Western Influences on Political Parties to 1825* (Ohio State University *Contributions in History and Political Science,* No. 4). 1917.

HOFSTADER, RICHARD: "The Tariff Issue and the Civil War," *American Historical Review,* XLIV, 50 ff.

HOLCOMBE, A. N.: *The Middle Classes in American Politics.* Cambridge, 1940.

——: *The New Party Politics.* New York, 1933.

——: *The Political Parties of Today.* New York, 1924.

HOLMES, OLIVER WENDELL: *Collected Legal Papers.* New York, 1921.

HOLT, EDGAR ALLAN: "Party Politics in Ohio, 1840–1850," *Ohio Archæological and Historical Society Publications,* XXXVIII.

HOUSE, E. M.: *Philip Dru, Administrator.* New York, 1912.

HOWE, DANIEL WAITE: "The Mississippi Valley in the Movement for Fifty-four Forty or Fight," Mississippi Valley Historical Association *Report,* V.

HUBBERT, H. C.: "Pro Southern Influences in the Free West," *Mississippi Valley Historical Review,* XX.

HURST, LAWRENCE: "National Party Politics, 1837–1840," Indiana University *Studies in American History,* dedicated to James Albert Woodburn. XII. Bloomington, 1925.

JAMES, MARQUIS: *The Life of Andrew Jackson.* New York, 1938.

JAMESON, J. F.: *The American Revolution as a Social Movement.* Princeton, 1926.

——, ed.: Calhoun Correspondence, American Historical Association *Report* (1899), II.

JEFFERSON, THOMAS: *Notes on the State of Virginia.* 1782.

—— (P. L. FORD, ed.): *The Writings of Thomas Jefferson.* 10 vols. New York, 1892–9.

JOHNSON, ALEXANDER: *History of American Politics.* New York, 1910.

JOHNSON, ALLEN: "The Nationalizing Influence of the Party," *Yale Review*, XV.

——: *Stephen A. Douglas*. New York, 1908.

——: *Union and Democracy (Riverside History, II)*. Boston, 1915.

JONES, J. B.: *A Rebel Clerk's Diary*. 2 vols. Philadelphia, 1866.

JOSEPHSON, MATTHEW: *The Politicos, 1865–1900*. New York, 1938.

——: *The President Makers*. New York, 1940.

JULIAN, G. W.: "The First Republican National Convention," *American Historical Review*, IV, 313.

——: *Political Recollections, 1840–1872*. Chicago, 1874.

KEIR, R. MALCOLM: *Labor's Search for More*. New York, 1937.

KENDRICKS, B. B.: "Agrarian Movements," *Encyclopedia of the Social Sciences*, I, 504.

KENT, F. R.: *The Democratic Party*. New York, 1928.

KING, CHARLES R., ed.: *Life and Correspondence of Rufus King*. 6 vols. New York, 1894–1900.

KITSON, A.: "William Jennings Bryan," *Fortnightly Review*, October 1914.

KROUT, JOHN A.: "Philip Schuyler," *Dictionary of American Biography*, XVI.

LAFOLLETTE, R. M.: *Autobiography*. Madison, Wisconsin, 1913.

LANE, FRANKLIN K.: *Letters of Franklin K. Lane, Personal and Political*. 2 vols. Boston, 1922.

LEECH, MARGARET: *Reveille in Washington*. New York, 1941.

LIBBY, O. G.: *Geographical Distribution of the Vote of the Thirteen States on the Federal Constitution, 1787–8*, University of Wisconsin Publications in Economics, History and Political Science, I, No. 1.

LODGE, HENRY CABOT, ed.: *The Federalist*. New York, 1898.

LOOKER, EARL: *The American Way*. New York, 1933.

LOWELL, JAMES RUSSELL (C. E. NORTON, ed.): *Letters*. 2 vols. New York, 1894.

LUBELL, SAMUEL: "Post Mortem: Who Elected Roosevelt?" *Saturday Evening Post*, January 25, 1941.

LYNCH, W. O.: "Anti-Slavery Tendencies of the Democratic Party in the Northwest, 1848–1850," *Mississippi Valley Historical Review*, XI, 319 ff.

——: *Fifty Years of Party Warfare*. Indianapolis, 1931.

MACDONALD, WILLIAM: *Documentary Source Book of American History*. New York, 1926.

MacMahon, A. W.: "Political Parties in the United States," *Encyclopedia of the Social Sciences,* XI.

Macy, Jesse: *Political Parties in the United States, 1846–1861.* New York, 1900.

Madison, James: *Letters and Other Writings* (Congress edition). 4 vols. Philadelphia, 1865.

—— (Gaillard Hunt, ed.): *Works: Writings.* 9 vols. New York, 1900–10.

Malone, Dumas (ed.): *Dictionary of American Biography.* 20 vols. New York, 1928–36.

Martineau, Harriett: *Society in America.* 3 vols. London, 1837.

McCarthy, Charles: "The Anti-Masonic Party," American Historical Association *Reports* (1902), I.

McClure, A. K.: *Our Presidents and How We Make Them.* New York, 1900.

——: *McClure's Recollections of Half a Century.* Salem, 1902.

McCulloch, Hugh: *Men and Measures of Half a Century.* New York, 1888.

McLaughlin, A. C.: *History of the American Nation.* New York, 1919.

——: "The Significance of Political Parties," *Atlantic Monthly,* CI (February 1908).

——: "Western Posts and British Debts," American Historical Association *Reports* (1894).

McMaster, J. B.: *The Acquisition of Political, Social and Industrial Rights of Man in America.* Cleveland, 1903.

——: *A History of the People of the United States from the Revolution to the Civil War.* 8 vols. New York, 1883–1913.

——: *With the Fathers.* New York, 1896.

Merriam, C. E.: *Four American Party Leaders.* New York, 1926.

Miller, Francis P., and Hill, Helen: *The Giant of the Western World.* New York, 1930.

Miller, M. M.: *American Debate.* 2 vols. New York, 1916.

Milton, George Fort: *The Eve of Conflict: Stephen A. Douglas and the Needless War.* Boston, 1934.

Minor, Henry: *The Story of the Democratic Party.* New York, 1928.

Montgomery, Horace: "The Crisis of 1850 and Its Effect on the Political Parties of Georgia," *Georgia Historical Quarterly,* XXIV, No. 4 (December 1940).

Moon, T. P.: *Imperialism and World Politics.* New York, 1926.

MOORE, C. H.: "Ohio in National Politics, 1865–1896," Ohio Archæological and Historical Society *Publications,* XXXVII.

MORISON, S. E.: "The First National Nominating Convention," *American Historical Review,* XVIII, 735 ff.

——: *The Life and Letters of Harrison Gray Otis.* 2 vols. Boston, 1913.

——: *Oxford History of the United States.* 2 vols. Oxford, 1917.

—— and COMMAGER, H. S.: *The Growth of the American Republic.* 2 vols. New York, 1937.

MORSE, A. D.: "Causes and Consequences of the Party Revolution of 1800," Annual *Report* of the American Historical Association, 1894, pp. 531–9.

——: "Our Great Political Parties," *Political Science Quarterly,* VI (December 1891) and VII (September 1892).

——: "Whig Party," *Encyclopædia Britannica,"* eleventh edition, XXVIII, 589.

MORSE, A. E.: *The Federalist Party in Massachusetts to the Year 1800.* Princeton, 1909.

MUZZEY, D. S.: *The United States of America.* 2 vols. Boston, 1933.

MYERS, W. S.: *The Republican Party, a History.* New York, 1928.

NEVINS, ALLAN: "Richard Olney," *Encyclopedia of the Social Sciences,* XI, 466.

NICHOLS, THOMAS L.: *Forty Years of American Life, 1821–1861.* Reprint, New York, 1937.

NICOLAY, JOHN G., and HAY, JOHN: *Abraham Lincoln: A History.* 10 vols. New York, 1890.

—— (editors): *The Complete Works of Abraham Lincoln.* 10 vols. New York, 1894.

NORTON, THOMAS J.: *The Constitution of the United States: Its Sources and its Application.* New York, 1922.

OBERHOLTZER, E. P.: *History of the United States since the Civil War.* 5 vols. New York, 1917–37.

——: *Jay Cooke, Financier of the Civil War.* 2 vols. Philadelphia, 1907.

ODEGARD, P. H., and HELMS, E. A.: *American Politics.* New York, 1938.

OGBURN, W. F., and NIMKOFF, M. F.: *Sociology.* Boston, 1940.

—— and TALBOT, NELL S.: "A Measurement of Factors in the Presidential Election of 1928," *Social Forces,* VIII (December 1929).

OGG, F. A.: "Jay's Treaty and the Slavery Interests of the United States," American Historical Association *Reports*, 1901, pp. 275 ff.

——: *National Progress (American Nation, XXVII)*. New York, 1918.

—— and RAY, P. O.: *Introduction to American Government*. New York, 1928.

O'HIGGINS, H. J. (with E. H. REEDE): *The American Mind in Action*. New York, 1924.

OLCOTT, C. S.: *The Life of William McKinley*. 2 vols. Boston, 1916.

OLMSTEAD, F. L.: *Journeys and Explorations in the Cotton Kingdom*. 2 vols. London, 1861.

ORTH, S. P.: *Our Foreigners (Chronicles of America, XXV)*. New Haven, 1920.

OSTROGORSKI, M.: *Democracy and the Party System in the United States*. New York, 1910.

PARRINGTON, V. L.: *Main Currents of American Thought*. 3 vols. New York, 1927–30.

PARTON, JAMES: *Life of Andrew Jackson*. 3 vols. New York, 1860.

PAULLIN, CHARLES O.: *Atlas of the Historical Geography of the United States*. Washington, 1932.

PAXSON, F. L.: "U. S. Grant," *Dictionary of American Biography*, VII.

——: *A History of the American Frontier, 1763–1893*. Boston, 1924.

PEARSON, DREW, and ALLEN, R. S.: *More Merry-go-round*. New York, 1932.

PECK, H. T.: *Twenty Years of the Republic, 1885–1905*. New York, 1906.

PEEL, ROY V.: "James G. Blaine: A Study in Political Leadership," *Abstracts of Doctoral Dissertations*, University of Chicago, Humanistic Studies, V, 215.

PERLMAN, SELIG, and TAFT, PHILIP: *A History of Labor in the United States, 1896–1932*. New York, 1935.

PHILLIPS, U. B.: "The Central Theme of Southern History," *American Historical Review*, XXIV.

——: *The Course of the South to Secession*. New York, 1939.

——: "Georgia and State Rights," American Historical Association *Report*, 1901, II, 3–224.

——: *Life and Labor in the Old South*. Boston, 1929.

——: "The Southern Whigs," *Essays in American History*, dedicated to F. J. Turner. New York, 1910.

——: "William H. Crawford," *Dictionary of American Biography,* IV.

PIKE, JAMES S.: *The Prostrate State: South Carolina under Negro Government.* New York, 1876.

POMPHRET, J. E.: "John Witherspoon," *Dictionary of American Biography,* XX, 437.

PORTER, G. H.: *Ohio Politics during the Civil War.* Columbia University Studies in History, Economics and Public Law, XL, No. 2.

PRICHARD, WALTER: "The Presidential Campaign and Election of 1840," *Studies in American History,* dedicated to James A. Woodburn. Bloomington, Indiana, 1926.

PRINGLE, H. F.: *Theodore Roosevelt.* New York, 1931.

——: "W. H. Taft," *Dictionary of American Biography,* XVIII.

PUTNAM, G. H., and LAPSBY, A.B. (editors): *The Complete Works of Abraham Lincoln.* New York, 1888–96.

RANDALL, J. G.: "Abraham Lincoln," *Dictionary of American Biography,* XI.

——: *Constitutional Problems under Lincoln.* New York, 1926.

——: *The Civil War and Reconstruction.* Boston, 1937.

RAY, V. O.: "Roosevelt Wins Again," *Events,* December 1940, pp. 409 ff.

RHODES, J. F.: *A History of the United States from the Compromise of 1850.* 9 vols. New York, 1893–1922.

RICHARDSON, J. D.: *Messages and Papers of the Presidents, 1789–1877.* 10 vols. Washington, 1897.

ROBINSON, E. E.: *The Evolution of American Political Parties.* New York, 1924.

——: *The Presidential Vote, 1896–1932.* Stanford University, 1934.

ROBINSON, W. A.: *Jeffersonian Democracy in New England.* New Haven, 1916.

ROOSEVELT, ELEANOR: *On My Own.* New York, 1958.

ROOT, ELIHU: *Miscellaneous Addresses.* Cambridge, Mass., 1917.

ROSEBOOM, E. H.: "Ohio and the Presidential Election of 1824," Ohio Archæological and Historical Society *Publications,* XXVI, 153 ff.

——: "Salmon P. Chase and the Know Nothings," *Mississippi Valley Historical Review,* XXV, 335 ff.

—— and WEISENBURGER, F. P.: *A History of Ohio.* New York, 1934.

Ross, E. D.: "The Civil War's Agricultural New Deal," *Social Forces*, XV, 97.

——: "Horace Greeley and the West," *Mississippi Valley Historical Review*, XX.

——: *The Liberal Republican Movement*. New York, 1919.

Royce, Josiah: "Frémont." *Atlantic Monthly*, LXVI (1890).

Sandburg, Carl: *Lincoln: The Prairie Years*. 2 vols. New York, 1926.

——: *Lincoln: The War Years*. 4 vols. New York, 1939.

Savage, John: *The Life and Public Services of Andrew Johnson*. New York, 1866.

Schafer, Joseph: *Social History of American Agriculture*. New York, 1936.

——: "Who Elected Lincoln?" *American Historical Review*, XLVIII, 51 ff.

Schlesinger, A. M.: *Political and Social Growth of the United States, 1865–1940*. New York, 1941.

——: "Significance of Jacksonian Democracy," *New Viewpoints in American History*. New York, 1922.

Schlüter, Herman: *Lincoln, Labor and Slavery*. New York, 1913.

Schrader, F. F.: *The Germans in the Making of America*. Boston, 1924.

Schurz, Carl: *Henry Clay*. 2 vols. Boston, 1887.

Sedgwick, Henry D.: *Francis Parkman*. Boston, 1904.

Shilling, D. C.: "Relation of Southern Ohio to the South during the Decade Preceding the Civil War," *Quarterly Publication of the Historical and Philosophical Society of Ohio*, VIII (1913), No. 1.

Shippee, L. B.: *Recent American History*. New York, 1913.

Simkins, F. B.: "New Views of Southern Reconstruction," *Journal of Southern History*, V.

Simon, A. M.: *Class Struggles in America*. Chicago, 1916.

——: *Social Forces in American History*. New York, 1911.

Smith, E. C.: "Fernando Wood," *Dictionary of American Biography*, XX.

Smith, T. V.: "The Compromise Principle in Politics," *Edmund J. James Lectures in Government*, Second Series, Urbana, Ill., 1941.

Smith, W. E.: *The Francis Preston Blair Family in Politics*. 2 vols. New York, 1933.

STANWOOD, EDWARD: *A History of the Presidency from 1788 to 1897.* Boston, 1898.

Statistical Abstract of the United States, 1931.

STEFFENS, LINCOLN: *Letters.* 2 vols. New York, 1938.

STEPHENSON, W. H.: "Helper's Impending Crisis in the South," *Dictionary of American History,* III, 25.

STEVENSON, MARIETTA: *William Jennings Bryan.* Doctoral Dissertation, University of Chicago.

STOKES, H. W.: "The Paradox of Representative Government," *Essays in Political Science,* in honor of W. W. Willoughby.

STRYKER, L. P.: *Andrew Johnson, A Study in Courage.* New York, 1929.

SULLIVAN, MARK: *Our Times; the United States, 1900–1925.* 7 vols. New York, 1926–35.

SUMNER, CHARLES: *Works.* 15 vols. Boston, 1870–83.

SUMNER, W. G.: *Andrew Jackson.* Boston, 1924.

——: *History of Banking in the United States.* New York, 1896.

——: "Politics in America, 1776–1876," *North American Review,* CXXII.

TAFT, W. H.: *The Anti-Trust Act and the Supreme Court.* New York, 1914.

TAUSSIG, F. W.: *The Tariff History of the United States.* New York, 1910.

—— (ed.): *State Papers and Speeches on the Tariff.* Cambridge, Massachusetts, 1892.

TAYLOR, GEORGE R.: "American Discontent in the Mississippi Valley Preceding the War of 1812," *Journal of Political Economy,* August 1931.

TAYLOR, JOHN: *A Definition of Parties, or the Political Effect of the Paper System Considered.* Philadelphia, 1794.

——: *An Inquiry into the Principles and Tendencies of Certain Public Measures.* Fredericksburg, Va., 1914.

TOCQUEVILLE, ALEXIS DE: *Democracy in America.* 2 vols. New York, 1928 edition.

TRACY, GILBERT A. (ed.): *Uncollected Letters of Abraham Lincoln.* Boston, 1914.

T. R. B.: "Washington Notes," *New Republic,* February 18, 1931, p. 18.

TURNER, FREDERICK J.: *The Significance of Sections in American History.* New York, 1932.

——: *The United States, 1830–1850.* New York, 1935.

TYLER, M. C.: "Declaration of Independence in the Light of Modern Criticism," *Harper's Encyclopedia of United States History*, III.

USHER, R. G.: *The Rise of the American People.* New York, 1915.

VAN BUREN, MARTIN: *Autobiography* (JOHN C. FITZPATRICK, ed.), American Historical Association *Report*, 1918, II.

VAN METRE, T. W.: *Economic History of the United States.* New York, 1921.

WAKEFIELD, SHERMAN D.: *How Lincoln Became President.* New York, 1936.

WALKER, FRANCIS A.: "Immigration and Degradation," *Discussions in Economics and Statistics*, II, 426. New York, 1899.

WALLING, W. E.: *American Labor and American Democracy.* New York, 1926.

WASHINGTON, GEORGE (W. C. FORD, ed.): *Writings.* 14 vols. New York, 1889.

WEBSTER, DANIEL (J. W. MCINTIRE, ed.): *Writings and Speeches of Daniel Webster.* 18 vols. Boston, 1903.

WEBSTER, H. J.: "History of the Democratic Party Organization in the Northwest, 1824–1840," *Ohio Archæological and Historical Society Publications*, XXIV.

WEED, HARRIET A.: *Life of Thurlow Weed.* Boston, 1884.

WEEKS, O. D.: "The Democratic Victory of 1932," *Arnold Foundation Studies in Public Affairs*, I, No. 3, Southern Methodist University.

WEISENBURGER, F. P.: "The Time of Mark Hanna's First Acquaintance with McKinley," *Mississippi Valley Historical Review*, XXL.

——: *History of the State of Ohio: The Pioneer State*, Columbus, 1941.

WEST, W. M.: *History of the American People.* Boston, 1918.

WHITE, HORACE: *Money and Banking.* Boston, 1911.

WHITE, THEODORE H.: *The Making of the President, 1960.* New York, 1961.

WHITE, WILLIAM ALLEN: *Masks in a Pageant.* New York, 1928.

——: *A Puritan in Babylon: The Story of Calvin Coolidge.* New York, 1938.

WHITNEY, H. C.: *Life of Lincoln.* New York, 1908.

WILLIAMS, C. R.: *The Life of Rutherford Birchard Hayes.* 2 vols. Boston, 1914.

WILSON, WOODROW: *Division and Reunion.* New York, 1893.

WITHERSPOON, JOHN: *Works.* 4 vols. New York, 1800–1.
——: *A History of the American People.* 5 vols. New York, 1902.
WITTKE, CARL: *We Who Built America, the Saga of the Immigrant.* New York, 1940.
WOOD, F. S.: *Roosevelt As We Knew Him.* New York, 1927.
WOODBINE, GEORGE, E.: "Joseph Story," *Dictionary of American Biography,* XVIII.
WOODBURN, J. A.: *Political Parties and Party Problems in the United States.* New York, 1914.
——: *The Life of Thaddeus Stevens.* Indianapolis, 1913.
WOODBURY, LEVI: *Writings, Political, Judicial and Literary.* 3 vols. Boston, 1852.
WOODWARD, W. E.: *Meet General Grant.* Garden City, 1928.
——: *The New American History.* New York, 1937.
WRIGHT, B. F.: *Source Book of American Political Theory.* New York, 1929.

PERIODICALS

American Federationist.
Boston Herald.
Chicago Daily Democratic Press.
Cincinnati Commercial.
Cleveland Plain Dealer.
Congressional Globe.
Congressional Record.
Crisis.
De Bow's Review.
Harper's Weekly.
Literary Digest.
National Economist.
National Magazine.
New England Magazine.
New York Times.
New York Tribune.
New York World.
Ohio Statesman.
Reports of the American Anti-Slavery Society.

INDEX

Abolitionists, 182; condemn Lincoln, 241

Adams, Henry: on Thurlow Weed, 164; quoted, 329, 336

Adams, John: Ambassador to England, 9; frames Massachusetts Constitution, 17; on political parties, 19, 49; President, 48; quoted, 67; makes peace with France, 82; on defeat for re-election, 83, 84

Adams, J. Q.: qualifications for presidency, 109; election by House, 111; non-partisan President, 112; "corrupt bargain" charge, 112; nationalist program, 112, 113; victim of "smear" campaign, 113; quoted, 133

Adams, S., 7

Adet, Pierre A., 79

Agar, Herbert, quoted, 73

Agrarian distress: in 1780's, 10, 12, 13; in 1890's, 316

Alien and Sedition Acts: enacted, 79, 80; attacked by Jeffersonians, 81

Aliens: spurned by Federalists, 80; courted by Jeffersonians, 80

Allen, William, Ohio expansionist, 148

American Federation of Labor, 361

American System, Clay's, 101

Ames, Fisher: on Jeffersonians, 85; on Federalist demoralization, 89

Annapolis Convention, 14

Anti-Federalists, 52 ff.; anti-nationalists, 61, 62; debtors, 62; oppose Hamilton's policies, 62

Anti-Masonic Party: origin, 158; cultivated by Whigs, 158; in Pennsylvania, 159; in New England, 159; anti-aristocratic, 159; absorbed by Whigs, 159

Anti-Monopoly Party, 309

Anti-Nebraska Men, 193

Arbuthnot, C. C., quoted, 281

Articles of Confederation, 7; satisfied yeomanry, 25

Artisans, Federalists, 43

Assumption of state debts, 37; log-rolling, 38; opposed by agrarians, 45

Backwoodsmen, colonial, grievances, 4, 5

Bacon, Nathaniel, 6; Rebellion, 5, 6; "Bacon's Laws," 6

Ballinger, R. A., 342

Ballinger-Pinchot controversy, 341 ff.

Bank of the United States: First, 39; Hamilton's argument for, 40; Jefferson's opposition, 40; sale of stock, 40; constitutionality argued, 65, 66. Second, chartered, 98; Jackson's veto, 136, 137

Banks, N. P., Speaker of the House, 207

Barkley, Alben, delivers keynote speech at 1948 Democratic Convention, 403

Barnburners: overthrow New York Regency, 145; anti-canal party, 145, 146; anti-slavery, 146

Beard, C. A., quoted, 7, 327, 382; on Jay's Treaty, 48; on Jefferson, 87

Beard, C. A. and Mary, quoted, 306, 307

Bender, George H., opinion, 394

Berkeley, Sir William, 5

Beveridge, A. J., quoted, 52, 206, 225

Bingham, J. A., quoted, 156

Birney, J. A., presidential candidate, 183

Blaine, J. G., quoted, 250; presidential candidate, 322

Blair, F. B., vice-presidential candidate, 276

"Blue Lights," 95

Border Ruffians, 216

Bourbon Democracy, 291

Brisbane, Albert, 212

Brown, John, raid, 228

Brownell, Herbert, quoted on special session of 80th Congress, 405

Bryan, W. J.: background, 318; anti-capitalistic, 318, 319; group coordinator, 319; Cross of Gold speech, 319; Republicans adopt

WILFRED E. BINKLEY

Professor of History and Political Science at Ohio Northern University, was born in Ohio in 1883. He was educated at Ohio Northern University, Antioch College, Harvard University, and at The Ohio State University, from which he received his doctorate. In 1953, Bowling Green State University conferred on him the degree of Doctor of Public Administration and in 1960 Ohio Northern University conferred on him the degree of Doctor of Laws. He has served as visiting professor at Ohio State, Bowling Green, Biarritz American University (France), and Columbia University, and he lectured for a year at Oxford University.

In 1954 President Eisenhower appointed Dr. Binkley to a four-year term on the National Historical Publications Commission, a post to which he was reappointed in 1957. He was president of the Midwest Political Science Association and vice president of the American Political Science Association in 1957 and president of the Ohio Academy of History in 1961.

Dr. Binkley's absorption in party history is a heritage from his father. As a boy he haunted party caucuses and participated in political rallies, and he began serving as a delegate to local and state party conventions as soon as he became a voter. Dr. Binkley has been a stump speaker, and he has lost only one election in nine tries for municipal office. In 1952–3 he was mayor of Ada, Ohio, where he still lives.

A NOTE ON THE TYPE USED IN THIS BOOK

The text of this book is set in Caledonia, a Linotype face which belongs to the family of printing types called "modern face" by printers — a term used to mark the change in style of type-letters that occurred about 1800. Caledonia borders on the general design of Scotch Modern, but is more freely drawn than that letter.

The book was composed by the Plimpton Press, Norwood, Massachusetts, and printed and bound by The Book Press, Brattleboro, Vermont. The typography and binding design are by W. A. Dwiggins.